The Companion to
Latin American
Studies

The Companion to Latin American Studies

Edited by Philip Swanson

Professor of Hispanic Studies,
University of Aberdeen, UK

A member of the Hodder Headline Group
LONDON
Distributed in the United States of America by
Oxford University Press Inc., New York

First published in Great Britain in 2003 by
Arnold, a member of the Hodder Headline Group,
338 Euston Road, London NW1 3BH

http://www.arnoldpublishers.com

Distributed in the United States of America by
Oxford University Press Inc.,
198 Madison Avenue, New York, NY10016

The advice and information in this book are believed to be true and
accurate at the date of going to press, but neither the authors nor the publisher
can accept any legal responsibility or liability for any errors or omissions.

British Library Cataloguing in Publication Data
A catalogue record for this book is available from the British Library

Library of Congress Cataloging-in-Publication Data
A catalog record for this book is available from the Library of Congress

ISBN 0 340 80681 8 (hb)
ISBN 0 340 80682 6 (pb)

2 3 4 5 6 7 8 9 10

Typeset in 10 on 12½ Sabon by Phoenix Photosetting, Chatham, Kent
Printed and bound in Malta.

What do you think about this book? Or any other Arnold title?
Please send your comments to feedback.arnold@hodder.co.uk

For Nev Mars and all those teachers who first inspired us
and
in memoriam Tony Higgins

Contents

List of contributors

Arturo Arias is Director of Latin American Studies at the University of Redlands, California. He is co-writer of the screenplay for the film *El Norte*, author of five novels (*After the Bombs*, *Itzam Na*, *Jaguar en Llamas*, *Los caminos de Paxil* and *Cascabel*), and winner of the Casa de las Américas Award and the Anna Seghers Scholarship for two of his novels. In 1998 he published two books of criticism, one on twentieth-century Guatemalan fiction, *La identidad de la palabra*, and another on contemporary Central American fiction, *Gestos Ceremoniales*. Recently, he has finished a new novel in Spanish, *Sopa de caracol*. Also recently published are two edited books by him, the critical edition of Miguel Angel Asturias's *Mulata*, and *The Rigoberta Menchú Controversy*. He is President of the Latin American Studies Association (LASA).

Jon Beasley-Murray is Co-Director of the University of Manchester's MA in Latin American Cultural Studies. He has published widely in Latin American Studies and is co-editor (with Alberto Moreiras) of the collections *Subaltern Affect* and *Culture and State in Latin America*.

Silvia Bermúdez is Associate Professor of Peninsular and Latin American Literature and Director of the Latin American and Iberian Studies Program at the University of California, Santa Barbara. Her forthcoming book *La esfinge de la escritura: Blanca Varela y el canon poético peruano contemporáneo* deals with the role of gender and the aesthetics of modernism in Varela's writing. Her current work focuses on the issues of immigration and border-crossing in the musical production of Latin America and Spain, with particular reference to *rock en español* and pop music.

Nikki Craske is Director of the Institute of Latin American Studies, University of Liverpool, where she is Senior Lecturer in Latin American Politics. She has written extensively on Mexican politics and is the author of *Women and Politics in Latin America*, associate author (with Sylvia Chant) of *Gender in Latin America*, and co-editor (with Maxine Molyneux) of *Gender and the Politics of Rights and Democracy in Latin America*. She is currently preparing a manuscript entitled *The Feminisation of Politics in Mexico*.

Brian Gollnick teaches in the Department of Spanish and Portuguese at the University of Iowa. His research focuses on modern Mexican literature and Latin American cultural theory.

Gareth A. Jones is Senior Lecturer in Development Geography at the London School of Economics and Political Science. He is Associate Fellow at the Lincoln Institute of Land Policy, Massachusetts, and the Institute of Latin American Studies, London. His recent research has been on access to land for low-income groups in Mexico, the sociology of land law reform and resistance, the policy discourses of international urban agencies, and the urban and cultural geographies of historic centre conservation in Latin America. His future research will explore how young women and men negotiate the work–life balance between employment, training and leisure in the context of poverty and changing labour markets and 'family' expectations (with Sylvia Chant). Dr Jones is a trustee of two non-governmental organizations, the International Consortium for Street Children and the International Children's Trust.

William Luis is Professor of Spanish and English at Vanderbilt University. He is the author of several works, including *Literary Bondage: Slavery in Cuban Narrative, Dance Between Two Cultures: Latino Caribbean Literature Written in the United States* and *Culture and Customs of Cuba*. Born and raised in New York City, he is widely regarded as a leading authority on Latin American, Caribbean, Afro-Hispanic and Latino US literatures.

Andrea Noble is Lecturer at the University of Durham with teaching and research interests in Latin American visual culture. She is author of *Tina Modotti: Image, Texture, Photography* and co-editor of *Phototextualities: Intersections of Photography and Narrative*. She has published articles on Mexican film and photography in *Screen, Women: A Cultural Review, Tesserae* and *Framework*, and is currently completing a book on Mexican cinema.

Luis Fernando Restrepo is Associate Professor of Spanish and Latin American Studies at the University of Arkansas, Fayetteville. His area of specialization is colonial literature and culture. He has published *Un nuevo reino imaginado: Las elegías de varones ilustres de Indias de Juan de Castellanos*. His work has also appeared in several journals, including *MLN, Thesaurus, Cuadernos de Literatura, Revista de la Universidad Pontificia Bolivariana* and *Pensamiento y Acción*. In 2000 he was a Fulbright visiting scholar at the Pontificia Universidad Javeriana in Bogotá, Colombia. He is currently preparing a critical anthology of Castellanos's epic history and researching post-conquest Muisca culture.

Elzbieta Sklodowska is Professor of Spanish American Literature at Washington University in Saint Louis and general editor for Latin American literature of *Revista de Estudios Hispánicos*. She is the author of *La parodia en la nueva novela hispanoamericana, Testimonio hispanoamericano: historia, teoría, poética, Todo ojos, todo oídos: control e insubordinación en la novela hispanoamericana* and numerous articles on testimonial literature, Spanish American narrative and Cuban literature. She is the co-editor (with Ben Heller) of *Roberto Fernández Retamar y los estudios latinoamericanos*.

Philip Swanson is Professor of Hispanic Studies at the University of Aberdeen. He has published widely in the field of modern Latin American literature and Spanish film, including books on José Donoso, Gabriel García Márquez and Spanish American fiction. His most recent book is *The New Novel in Latin America: Politics and Popular Culture after the Boom*. He is currently working on books on Hispanic American fiction and on borders and crime in film and fiction. Professor Swanson has held posts in Ireland, the UK and the USA.

Peter Wade did a PhD in Social Anthropology at Cambridge University, focusing on the black population of Colombia. He was a Research Fellow at Queen's College, Cambridge, before becoming a Lecturer in Geography and Latin American Studies at the University of Liverpool. He is currently Professor of Social Anthropology at the University of Manchester. His publications include *Blackness and Race Mixture*, *Race and Ethnicity in Latin America* and *Music, Race and Nation: Música Tropical in Colombia*. He has a forthcoming book called *Race, Nature and Culture: An Anthropological Perspective*. His current research focuses on issues of racial identity and embodiment.

Map of Latin America

Introduction

Philip Swanson

Every schoolboy or girl knows that a European mariner, Christopher Columbus, discovered America, the New World, in 1492. Yet behind this apparently simple 'fact', there lies a weight of problematic cultural assumption. Columbus did not really 'discover' anything: he simply stumbled across something that was already there. Indeed he did not really know what it was he had found, since he thought he had reached the Indian subcontinent via a western route (hence the region was originally referred to as the Indies and the natives as Indians). Moreover the 'New World' was not 'new' at all. The indigenous inhabitants of the area had been there since about 7000 BC, fairly developed societies flourished in the first thousand years or so AD, and large empires with much of the organizational apparatus of a state (the Toltecs, the Chimú, the Mayas and, most famously, the Aztecs and the Incas) had begun to appear from about AD 900 onwards – all long before the arrival of Columbus. The very term 'Latin America' refers to the transformed space that grew out of European (essentially Spanish and Portuguese, i.e. 'Latin') conquest and colonization, with the name America coming from that of the fifteenth- and sixteenth-century Florentine explorer Amerigo Vespucci who is sometimes credited with first formulating the notion of a 'new world'.

In other words, from the moment of its inception as a concept, Latin American history has been perceived through an alien, basically European, mindset. The argument is that the development of Latin American identity subsequently involved an internalization of a fundamentally foreign sense of self that in many ways persists to the present day. Even political independence was the result of the drive of a Latin American-born elite who nonetheless prided themselves on the purity of their inherited European blood which was untainted by the indigenous. Paradoxically, post-independence 'progress' was also fuelled by European or, increasingly, North American values and practices, leading to, for example, the overwhelming economic influence of Britain in the nineteenth century and the USA in the twentieth century. The ideas which have dominated Latin American development up to the twenty-first century (independence, civilization, progress, democracy, capitalism, neo-liberalism and so forth) are all basically imported concepts. In many ways, it was not until 1992 that there was large-scale public debate and revisionism of this slanted perspective on Latin America, as – amidst something of an outcry – the quincentennary celebrations of 'discovery' were hastily transformed into a celebration of 'encounter' between two cultures. And, of course, Latin American intellectuals have long been vexed by the question of national and continental identity, while outside commentators have come to focus more and more on the redressing of the imbalance in our understanding of 'Latin America'. The thrust, then, of much of Latin American studies, and the thrust of much of this volume, is to question and problematize the very idea of Latin America and to present it as a complex and varied phenomenon that has to be understood on its own terms as well as on European or North American ones, even if the nature of those terms is itself highly mobile and irreducible.

This book is edited by a specialist in Latin American literature. In a sense, it is thinking about the ways in which Latin American literature has been traditionally presented via Eurocentric models that has prompted the production of this book. The term 'Eurocentric' alludes to the ways in which Latin American and other cultures have tended to be examined by means of paradigms that were inherited from European criticism and that are now seen to underpin much thinking not only in Europe but also in North America and what has come to be known at various times as the First World, the West or the North. To be sure, the precipitous rejection of so-called European models is itself a problem: the European inheritance is very much part of Latin American cultural identity and Latin America today is part of and a contributor to an increasingly global consciousness. So, when talking of, say, Latin American literature, the book will use the conventional periodizations of accepted models of literary history as applied to Latin America, while exploring alternative ways of approaching that literature. It will also extend the notion of 'culture' so as to separate it from its traditional association with literary high culture in order to explore other cultural manifestations such as film, painting, muralism, photography, music and even forms of 'popular' culture such as dance, soap opera, football and religion.

A basic underlying principle of the book is the idea that literature and culture do not exist in a vacuum, but very much grow and operate in a specific socio-political environment. Hence, the book will also explore Latin American politics and society, as well as issues such as race, gender and sexuality. In a way, the book is aimed at students who might have traditionally approached Latin America via literature, and the hope is that students will be helped to contextualize that literature in a more informed sense of a Latin American context while simultaneously garnering a wider and fuller sense of Latin American culture and society. At the same time, it is anticipated that the book will be of interest and value to those whose interests are not primarily literary or cultural, and it will hopefully demonstrate how literary and other cultural artefacts and practices are just as essential to an understanding of Latin American society as, say, the study of geography, history, sociology or politics

– indeed the hope is that the book will establish intimate connections between these fields and cultural activity, and show that the two are not separate.

The book opens and closes with chapters that deal with the fundamental questions of 'What is Latin America?' and 'Where is it situated?'. Even a concept as seemingly obvious as 'place' will be questioned, and a consideration of Latin American geographies will point up just how constructed and mobile our sense of place in relation to Latin America is. The chapter on politics and society will give a broad overview of Latin America, sketching its history and how its contemporary institutions and characteristics have been shaped. A detailed history of the subcontinent is not the main concern here, nor is a consideration of the indigenous pre-Colombian civilizations. *Latin* America is the starting point, and hence another early chapter will concentrate on the culture of the colonial period when the region was still ruled by the Spanish and Portuguese crowns. The Independence movement and the process of emancipation will not be considered in historical detail as such, but these nevertheless form the background to the chapter on 'civilization and barbarism', a key notion and tension to emerge in the post-independence period of consolidation and nation-building that would not only mark cultural production in the nineteenth century but affect it throughout the twentieth century too.

Having considered this cultural framework, the book will then offer an authoritative survey of Latin American literature itself, while following that up with a consideration of the various debates about how best to approach that literature in the light of new awareness about the potential limitations of Eurocentric and related perceptions. Moreover, it is acknowledged that Latin American culture has spread far beyond its physical geographical boundaries and is now a highly important feature of the cultural life of the USA: a lengthy chapter on Latino US literature will cover this relatively under-studied area. Notions of culture will then be expanded with a consideration of visual cultures (including film and art) and so-called popular culture (ranging from unofficial religions to soccer, from tango to rock music, from salsa to soap opera).

Fleshing out the social and political context will be the concern of the next two chapters, which deal in depth with issues of race, gender and sexuality in the subcontinent. Finally, and returning to the idea of unstable and imaginative geographies, the book will close with a chapter that looks outwards to Latin America's position in and in relation to not only the global system but also global consciousness: rather than simply being 'elsewhere', Latin America will be seen to inhabit all of us in certain ways.

Obviously, a book like this, which covers a considerable amount of terrain and diverse disciplines, is a tricky undertaking. Inevitably, there will be omissions, overlaps and differences of opinion, but also continuities and consistencies. The enthusiasm and commitment of all the contributors are warmly acknowledged. In particular, I would like to thank Luis Fernando

Restrepo, who, like me, put together a chapter at a late stage due to unforeseen circumstances. The advice and technical suggestions of a range of friends and colleagues are also much appreciated, amongst them Daniel Balderston, Jon Beasley-Murray, Silvia Bermúdez, Julia Biggane, Alvaro Félix Bolaños, Sara Castro-Klarén, Sylvia Chant, Paul Garner, Tony Higgins, Kaarina Hollo, John King, Cathy Shrank and Gustavo Verdesio. Any limitations of the book are, of course, entirely my own responsibility. Finally, I would like to thank Elena Seymenliyska, who first encouraged me to do the book, and Eva Martínez at Arnold for all her support.

1

Latin American geographies

Gareth A. Jones

The principal question posed in this chapter is 'where is Latin America?'. At one level this is a simple geographical question that should not vex anybody who has ever opened an atlas. Indeed, compared to the frenzy of cartographic updates necessary for Africa in the wake of decolonization or for Eastern Europe after the Cold War, the maps of Latin America appear to be fairly stable. A closer inspection would reveal some contested borders, between Ecuador and Peru for example, and some contested sovereignty, such as Las Malvinas/the Falklands. At a different level, however, the cartographic stability of Latin America is misleading. As Harley has observed:

> all maps, like all other historically constructed images, do not provide a transparent window on the world. Rather they are signs that present 'a deceptive appearance of naturalness and transparence concealing an opaque, distorting, arbitrary mechanism of representation, a process of ideological mystification'. (Harley 1992: 523, citing Mitchell 1986)

Maps, then, are imagined representations of space just as subjective as other 'texts' such as travel accounts, films, paintings, surveys and exhibitions (Driver 1992). So, while in the process of becoming objects these texts appear to convert imagined geographies of Latin America into 'real' geographies, in this chapter I want to consider how all such texts must still be understood as subjective. In order to do so I want to suggest that Latin America needs to be understood as geographically displaced through complex connections of commodities, people and images (Tomlinson 1996). Latin America is not contained in a collection of nation-states 'over there' but is, increasingly, also 'over here'. Latin America might be a distinct place on a map, but its geography is everywhere. Latin America has become de-territorialized.

IMAGINATIVE GEOGRAPHIES

Appadurai (1990) has usefully categorized these connections of global cultural flows as ethnoscapes, mediascapes, technoscapes, finanscapes and ideoscapes. Ethnoscapes describe the persons who constitute the shifting world in which we live: tourists, refugees, guestworkers and students (1990: 297). In my classes at the London School of Economics I have students from Argentina, Brazil, Chile, Colombia, Mexico and Puerto Rico. I am implicated in an intellectual globalization in which I am either 'adding value', for an elite that can afford it, or encouraging a vicious 'brain drain' of young talent from the region. On my journey home across London, however, I encounter a different ethnoscape. On the bus, generally on the upper floor, is a transnational community of mostly Ecuadorians and Colombians. This is also a brain drain, quite well educated and entrepreneurial people now working as cleaners, porters and shop assistants in central London. And at the weekend, the ethnoscape is represented by a Latin American football league in a nearby park and by salsa classes in a community hall.

A displaced Latin America is also encountered through a technoscape of technology and information moving around the world. This is baffling to my father, who emails to tell me that his new up-and-over garage door is made in Hermosillo, Mexico, although he seems unaware that his car was probably made in Toluca and his computer in Tijuana. The technoscape, however, is also delivering news about Latin America's engagement with the ideoscapes of world-views such as democracy and rights. My email account in mid-2002 has recently been full of messages about the economic collapse of Argentina, the attempted coup in Venezuela, and environmental activist concerns about the Mexican government's decision to allow multinationals to grow genetically modified grain.

Latin America is part of the finanscape in which a small part of my mortgage depends upon the performance of 'emerging' stock markets. In this respect the technoscape of how those branch plants on the US–Mexico border produce circuit boards for my father's computer and whether Venezuela's ambiguity towards democracy is affecting the price of oil takes on a direct importance. To get away from it all, I encounter Latin America in the mediascape, the image-based narratives of what Appadurai calls 'strips of reality'. For a moment, I indulge myself with the Sunday newspapers offering insights into snow boarding in the Andes and coral reef diving off Belize, an interview with a 'black' Peruvian singer about to tour Britain, a review of Argentine wines and the latest Mario Vargas Llosa novel. Meanwhile, my newsagent conveys to me his fears about the Latin Americanization of crime as a local 'drugs war' to distribute cocaine is fought by Jamaican Yardies and 'Colombians'.

These are some of my connections to Latin America and they instil in me a 'map' of what Latin America 'must be' like which is not objectively arrived at but reflects my cultural and political situatedness (Appadurai 1990: 296). My set of imaginative geographies, my multiple ways of building a relationship to Latin America, are different from those of a multinational corporation or an environmental non-governmental organization (NGO), and differ according to whether I am a cinema-goer, a drug-taker, a football fan or a coffee-drinker. All imaginative geographies, however, are constructed upon the reception, interpretation and retention of discourses and images that represent Latin America as real.

To illustrate, I take two media that construct imaginative geographies of Latin America. The first is the flow of images and ideas about Latin America contained in nineteenth- and early twentieth-century travel accounts, and which have become established forms of knowledge through reproduction in books, exhibitions, contemporary travel writing, as well as a part of the 'British' cultural landscape, for example at the Royal Botanical Gardens at Kew in London. A great deal about what we think we know about Latin America today derives from travel writers who nevertheless gave preference to certain places and overlaid meanings onto landscapes according to the ideological and philosophical conventions of the day.

The second medium is the process of consumption, specifically of bananas and coffee, the two principal commodities from 'tropical' Latin America (Llambi 1994). The inscription of imaginative geographies onto commodities is by no means new. Sugar, spices, chocolate, even Fray Bentos tinned beef have all been associated with representations of Latin America and the Caribbean, and have become domestic cultural icons at home (Naylor 2000; Roseberry 1996). The construction of contemporary imaginative geographies of Latin America through consumption builds an image of Britain as cosmopolitan and multicultural. But, while globalization is bringing Latin America in one sense ever nearer, the imaginative geographies represent Latin America in a series of stereotypical ways so as to create distance and mark the difference between the places of origin and the place of consumption (Cook and Crang 1996; Smart 1994). Good taste and chic may depend, briefly, on the consumption of an image of Latin America as exotic, although to somebody else the 'gourmet' coffee will be agribusiness.

TRAVEL WRITING AND IMAGINATIVE GEOGRAPHIES

The shelves of any large bookshop reveal the importance of the travel writing genre to the geographical imagination. Today's collection, however, pales compared to the outpouring of travel accounts and works of natural history during the nineteenth century that constituted perhaps as much as 10 per cent of titles in libraries in England, Germany and the USA (Cicerchia 1998). This enormous output was written by 'imperial citizens' who were often directly implicated in the scientific and political projects of empire. The clearest examples are the accounts emanating from official expeditions, such as Charles Darwin's *The Voyage of the Beagle*, Robert Schomburgk's survey of the Orinoco river and Guyana borders, and La Condamine's attempt to map the Amazon (Burnett 2000; Dunbar 1988; Stepan 2001).[1] Travel accounts also emerged from involvement in surveying the routes for rail companies, land colonization schemes and diplomatic missions (Dickenson 1997; Naylor and Jones 1997; Pratt 1992; Walker 1992).

Many of these travel accounts are the precursors and occasionally the more conscious guides to contemporary travel writers.[2] A good example is Toby Green's *Saddled with Darwin*, which recounts his attempt to follow the routes taken by Darwin across South America to reveal how the landscapes that were important to the study of evolution had changed by the late 1990s. In places, Green's attempts to mimic Darwin's journey on horseback prove impossible, cut across by freeways or industrial zones, provoking Green to wonder whether, had Darwin been travelling today, he would have been able to make the kind of observations to generate a theory of evolution. Darwin's ghost serves as an accomplice for Green's critique of modern science, relating contemporary landscapes to ideas of global warming and genetic theory.

Contemporary travel writing borrows from earlier accounts in more subtle ways. Here I am interested in the appropriation of representations established in the nineteenth-century writers' narrative as a system of 'truths' (Cicerchia 1998).[3] These representations derive their (lasting) power from the construction of objectivity by writers, who mostly lacked a formal academic position, but whose class, race and gender gave them the mandate to imagine themselves as ethnographers, to pursue knowledge as a right and a symbol of their status (Salvatore 1996).[4] This kind of privilege provided travellers with a detachment from the landscape that allowed them to represent their subjective observations as objective accounts.[5] The opening to Reginald Koettlitz's paper in the *Scottish Geographical Magazine* is fairly typical:

> Having a wish to see this famous stream [the Amazon!] . . . I took an opportunity offered me last April . . . Though the opportunities for studying the people, especially the Indians, as well as the natural history of north-eastern Brazil and the lower Amazon were very few, I propose to give a short account of facts observed, together with information gathered during the South American portion of this voyage, in the hope that some of the matter may be of interest to the members of the Scottish Geographical Society, and some possibly even new. (Koettlitz 1901: 12)

Koettlitz does not mention the purpose of his trip to Brazil or his legitimacy for disseminating his geographical understanding, but he is sure that the 'facts' will be useful.

Koettlitz and others add to their credibility by giving the impression of being 'alone'. This device positions the travel writer in a wilderness or against a frontier of the unknown, and is particularly vital in Latin America where there was little *terra incognita* and many preferred to follow established routes linking a European presence (Dickenson 1997). Seeming 'alone', however, enhances the power of the traveller to 'see' Latin America from a particular vantage point. Koettlitz, for example, gazes upon the shore from a boat, but for more drama travellers would look 'down' upon the landscape, dominating the scene as the 'master' or 'monarch' of all they survey (Burnett 2000; Pratt 1992).[6] Today, Latin America is viewed from trains or light aircraft, or even from space using satellite imagery to 'show' global warming.

Representations of Latin America

Detachment from and dominance over the landscape set up the most important representation of Latin America, namely the enormity of nature. According to Cicerchia, ever since Humboldt's thirty-volume travel accounts appeared in the early nineteenth century, 'part of the European imagery of the "new continent" has been framed by nature' (1998: 4). In his *Personal Narrative of Travels to the Equinoctial Regions of the Americas* (1814–25), von Humboldt fused aesthetic appreciation with his tentative scientific understanding of nature, raving about the 'abundant fertility' and 'organic richness' (Arnold 2000). Writing to his brother, von Humboldt commented in 1799:

> What a fabulous and extravagant country we're in! Fantastic plants, electric eels, armadillos, monkeys, parrots, and many, many, real half-savage Indians.

And Henry Bates wrote:

> To the westward we could see a long line of forest rising apparently out of the water; a densely packed mass of tall trees, broken into groups, and finally into single trees, as it dwindles away in the distance. This was the frontier, in this direction, of the great primeval forest characteristic of this region, which contains so many wonders in its recesses, and clothes the whole surface of the country for two thousand miles from this point to the foot of the Andes. (Dickenson 1997: 112)

Unlike the pastoral or increasingly industrialized landscapes of Europe, Latin American nature was physically over-powering and abundantly fertile, a possible paradise or Eden, adding a sexualized desire to the representation (Stepan 2001).

To the nineteenth-century traveller size did matter. It added to the sublime, the awe that served to make the visualization of the scene important, and captured an audience back home (Martins 2000).[7] Latin America was a region of giants – usefully so in the case of Robert Schomburgk, whose expedition to Guyana was saved by the discovery of a huge water lily that he named after Queen Victoria, and which became a centrepiece of the Great Exhibition of 1851 (Burnett 2000). More or less everyone makes some reference to the apparently endless sky-lines or the open landscape (Naylor 2001). Lady Florence Dixie was able to gallop and:

> penetrate into vast wilds, virgin as yet to the foot of man. Scenes of infinite beauty and grandeur might be lying hidden in the silent solitude of the mountains which bound the barren plains of the Pampas, into whose mysterious recesses no one as yet had ever ventured. And I was to be the first to behold them! (*Across Patagonia*, 1880, cited in Robinson 1995)

Alone against the power of nature is a geographical imagination that resonates with a contemporary distress at environmental destruction (note Toby Green) and the discourse of 'eco-warriors'.

The representation of Latin America as a landscape dominated by nature is frequently contrasted with observations of poverty and disease to legitimate calls to order nature. Dr David Christison, for example, writing of his journey to the River Plate in 1866, describes how the immense open grasslands gave Uruguay the potential to be 'a second Australia'. The point is illustrated by a drawing of an unusual cloud formation rather like the trail of a jet plane going from horizon to horizon underneath which the 'wild and picturesque' *gauchos* drive cattle. The paper concludes with a lament about the cornucopia going to waste such that mutton that should be brought to 'our use in these overcrowded and pauper-stricken islands' is just rotting (Christison 1909: 481). As Pratt (1992) has argued, such representations of Latin America as 'nature' were far from innocent. In accounts that indicated the possibilities or practice for improvement through rail or the introduction of new crops, nature was converted into a resource – a representation often supported by paintings and, later, photographs showing rural and forest scenes cut into by railways, roads, bridges (Matless 1992; Stepan 2001).

Travellers and scientists did not represent all forms of nature as suitable to man-power. In the 'tropics' the dominance of nature over man was portrayed as beyond the capacity of science to tame (Arnold 2000). Albert Hale, for example, is careful to point out that the region of the River Plate is 'by no means a tropical country', noting how Buenos Aires and Montevideo are on similar parallels and share the same climate as Los Angeles and Cape Town, but he then notes that 'only the extreme northern tip of the whole area is actually between the Tropic of Capricorn and the Equator, and therefore nearly every mile is susceptible of just such productive activities as we, in the United States, understand and have within broad limits put into practice' (1909: 428–9). By implication the area within the tropics was likely to be less productive and unsuitable for improvement.

More broadly, however, the term tropical became a synonym to denote a conceptual space where nature was magnificent, Eden-like, dominant, but man was indolent and, in the absence of science and civilization, vulnerable to flood, hurricane, disease, and even rebellion. According to Arnold:

> Although describing the tropics as 'nature's garden' might seem to suggest unqualified approval, in an age obsessed with improvement and progress, with racial origins and competitive evolution, there were definite disadvantages to being the denizens of an earthly paradise. (2000: 10)

Travellers such as Henry Bates clearly preferred nature to the population of Belém, whom he described in 1848 as idle soldiers, slovenly dressed women, naked children and:

> people of all shade of colour of skin, European, Negro, and Indian, but chiefly of an uncertain mixture of the three . . . So striking, in the view, was the mixture of natural riches and human poverty . . . but amidst all, and compensating every defect, rose the overpowering beauty of the vegetation. (Naylor and Jones 1997: 103)

Over a half century later, Koettlitz describes travelling from Para to Manaus on a steamboat dirty from the 'filthy habits of the people', and he devotes more column inches to insects and flora than to people, whom he rarely mentions other than in relation to their race, conditions of disease/mortality and laziness. Noting the uncared-for cocoa plantations, Koettlitz writes that 'the ordinary Brazilian loves laziness, and is so indolent that he will rarely do a stroke more work than he is compelled' (1901: 23). And thirty years later again, Huxley describes the villages of southern Mexico as stagnant places:

> The spectacle, I confess, always made my blood run pretty cold. Not so cold as the spectacle of an industrial town in Lancashire, say, or the Ruhr (*that* has power to chill the heart of man to its absolute zero); but cold, heaven knows, enough. The industrial town is intensely and positively, whereas these Mexican places are only negatively, appalling. They are appalling not so much because of what is there as because of what isn't there. A Black Country town is a fearful sin of commission; Miahuatlan and its kind are sins of omission. Omission of the mental and the spiritual, of all that is not day-to-day animal living. 'Lilies that fester smell far worse than weeds'; the Black Country is more horrible than Miahuatlan because it embodies the corruption of a higher good than has ever been aimed at, at any rate since the fall of the indigenous empires, by the Indians. (1934: 146–7)

These representations of people in the tropics as backward, lazy, as well as temperamental and prone to sexual ill-discipline, found an echo in 'science' which mapped them onto race/climate (Livingstone 1999). This same literature, however, also showed how climate and disease served against the ability of a 'white' population to work in the tropics. Better, therefore, to manage the locals or, as was observed during the construction of the Panama Canal, encourage labour migration from Spain (but also Italy, Ireland and Eastern Europe), as these workers were more productive than either the North Americans doing lighter work or the 'Negroes' (Matless 1992). The paradox serves to the present day. Left to its own devices tropical Latin America is incapable of development, necessitating external assistance, while those from outside consider themselves unsuited to work under the same conditions.

Representations of 'man-power' in the tropics stand in counterpoint to the depictions of indigenous peoples. First, as already illustrated by Lady Florence Dixie's gallop across Patagonia, indigenous peoples were often absented entirely. Second, they served as additions to a picturesque landscape by encroaching onto riverbanks or a village nestled against foothills. Third, indigenous peoples were represented within a framework of human improvement. Had indigenous societies degenerated from a more advanced civilization? Had they 'become' savages and primitives? It is a representation contemplated by Huxley:

> Indian men are often handsome; but I hardly ever saw a woman or young girl who was not extremely ugly. Endemic goitre does not improve their native homeliness; and without exaggeration, I should guess that at least a third of the women of Chichicastenango [Guatemala] have bulging necks. One would expect to find cretins in a population so much afflicted with goitre. But I never saw a single one. Doubtless they are born, but fail, in the unmerciful environment of an Indian *rancho*, to survive. (1934: 103)

Fourth, indigenous people were seen as the objects of science. While some travellers, such as Henry Bates, Alfred Wallace and Richard Spruce, sought to map the diversity of language and indigenous uses of nature to pose a dynamic understanding of their existence, the dominant representation was established by von Humboldt, who often treated vegetation and indigenous artefacts in the same taxonomical framework (Barreto and Machado 2001). This framework placed indigenous people and objects in the same form as natural specimens, showing similar objects next to one another even when originating from different ethnic groups thousands of miles apart. This Linnaean model, as it is technically called, is still used in museum display but it is being challenged by exhibitions such as the *Unknown Amazon* at the British Museum, which shows the complexity of indigenous societies and how they use the environment productively (see www.thebritishmuseum.ac.uk).

While nature was represented as a sublime populated by 'innocents', most cities in Latin America were represented rather differently. Marianne North's paintings of Rio de Janeiro show the Corcovado mountain as a scenic backdrop but one could be forgiven for thinking that a city was not remotely near. Charles Fox-Banbury described settlements in Brazil as monotonous, except for the occasional church, and inhabited by 'ugly and scantily clad negresses' and 'an abundance of layabouts' (Dickenson 1997). When cities had to be entered, Salvatore (1996) argues that travellers sought out the marks of civilization, checking the quality of the museums, libraries, hospitals and prisons. In this vein Koettlitz describes parts of Para as having some 'handsome and imposing edifices' built with stone from Europe and 'several small public gardens and fine plazas', although George Fracker deplored 1820s' Buenos Aires, commenting that 'the theatre is a low and miserable building ... and the performances are in keeping with it' (Cicerchia 1998: 15). According to Salvatore (1996), some writers gave impressionistic accounts of the social landscape of cities, describing the bustle of the streets and shortcomings in local manners. The main features of the urban landscape therefore were often described in relation to the standards of Europe, while the slums or more mundane parts of the city were ignored.

Comparison is a powerful form of representation. Through evoking landscapes, institutions and peoples back home, writers could make the diverse and strange intelligible to their audience (Naylor and Jones 1997; Salvatore 1996), while also making little attempt to hide their preference. Thus, Saussure compared tropical nature in Mexico unfavourably to that of his native Switzerland (Dunbar 1988), Charles Fox-Banbury compared the better parts of Minas Gerais to Caernarvonshire, and Marianne North compared the Rio de Velhas to the River Tweed except that the former was 'a bit more tropical' (Dickenson 1997). The urban landscape too was compared to home. Luther Schaeffer compared the Emperor's chapel in Rio de Janeiro to the Boston Exchange, and Nathaniel Bishop compared the Buenos Aires jail to reformatories in the USA (Salvatore 1996: 105). More abstractly, Aldous Huxley compared the church at San Felipe in Guatemala to Keble chapel, Oxford, and the Preparatoria in Mexico City as 'most refreshingly' unlike Rugby or Roedean public schools. Sometimes comparison represented a joint distaste. Huxley again:

> We lunched at Quezaltenango in a most forbidding German hotel. Pretentious, dirt, expense – one was painfully reminded of inedible lunches in South Shields, of a weekend in Middlesbrough, with a dark tide-mark of grit and the pubic hairs of commercial travellers running round the bath. (1934: 116)

Comparison also extended to ideologies, folklore and political condition. Travellers from the USA compared the life of blacks in South America to those in the American South (Salvatore 1996). Others, more esoterically, compared the religious idolatry of the Maya to that of the Romans, political populism to Stalin, Hitler and Mussolini, and social and philosophical contexts to the civilizations of Egypt, India, Greece and Babylonia (Huxley 1934; Naylor and Jones 1997).

Travel writing on Latin America created a series of stereotypes that represented both the human and the physical landscape as different from those of Europe or North America. While Latin America was not seen as the antithesis of Europe – compared to Africa for example, the people could not be easily grouped as 'natives' or 'barbarians' – it was imagined to be less productive, less civilized or more natural, more dangerous. This imagined geography of other places was useful to the constitution of economic, political and cultural imaginations about how Europeans and North Americans saw themselves. The 'others' were regarded as inferior and therefore in need of authority and science.

Representations of Latin America as 'British' culture

I suspect that few people have read Darwin's *The Voyage of the Beagle*, Burton's *Explorations of the Highlands of Brazil*, Wallace's *A Narrative of Travels on the Amazon and Rio Negro*, or any of the hundreds more narratives like them. Yet, we may be familiar with the imagined geographies of Latin America, in part because representations of 'other places' are a staple part of the Western cultural landscape. In Britain, for example, London is littered with sites that display Latin America, from the Victoria and Albert Museum, to the Natural History and British Museums, London Zoo, even Harrods. Outside, some of the 'great' country houses that serve as settings for novels-to-film and are managed by English Heritage were built with proceeds from the slave trade or sugar plantations (Seymour *et al.* 1998).

Through re-representation these sites celebrate and confirm a particular geographical imagination of Latin America. They operate as a form of 'information technology' by organizing, deleting and interpreting scattered objects brought back from travel and (scientific) exploration (Richards 1993). Today's exhibitions might not include 'real' Indians in this exercise (Anthropology Day at the 1904 Louisiana Purchase Exposition displayed 'Patagonians' to demonstrate the virtues of health and exercise on the body of 'primitives'), but most exhibitions remain based on Euro/US-centric ideas of 'universal values' in which the curators decide what is worth collecting, thereby dividing the world into the 'curating cultures' and the 'curated cultures' (Mosquera 1994: 135).

We can appreciate this power of re-representation of Latin America by thinking about the botanical gardens. As Martins (2000) observes, the botanical garden was already an established part of the landscape of Europe by the early nineteenth century and many travellers' first experience of 'tropical nature', including Charles Darwin's, was an encounter in these tamed surroundings. Botanical gardens are marvels of order in which plants that exist in nature in seemingly chaotic display – the 'abundant fertility' of von Humboldt – are placed inside hothouses, set out in taxonomical clusters in which orchids from Brazil could sit among palms from Sri Lanka, and are given Latin names and scientific explanation (Stepan 2001).

The botanical garden, therefore, domesticates other places by putting their plants into our framework of reference. At the Royal Botanical Gardens at Kew, Latin America becomes part of Western, or more specifically British, culture, and not only because of the tropical plants within the famous glasshouses. If one walks along the eastern edge of the gardens one passes a Victorian villa complete with wrought iron balcony and a slightly incongruous pediment. This is the Marianne North Gallery, opened in 1882 to house the 500 or so paintings of flora and fauna from over a dozen countries including Jamaica, Brazil and Chile. The gallery is a marvel of travel, science and imperial power. Inside, overhead in gold letters, are the names of the countries or regions that are the subject of the paintings beneath. The gallery is testament to how a single middle-aged Victorian woman could travel across the world, aided by private wealth and the support of company agents, virtually without hindrance in the scientific endeavour of painting and botany (then, usually no more than a lady's hobby) (Losano 1997).[8]

The gallery and the paintings exhibit some of the representations of Latin America that dominate the contemporary geographical imagination. Within the gallery hardly an inch of wall is blank, giving the feeling of nature's power. Furthermore, in the paintings themselves North positioned the plants as the foreground, again reinforcing the dominance of nature and accentuating what Stepan (2001) notes is the flowers' exotic presence. While the subject is presented as the foreground, it is also displaced. Through the order of the gallery and the incredible attention to detail (some paintings show little more than the fine points of a single plant stem), North gives the impression that these 'exact' representations are already in a European botanical garden. Certainly, they are not touched by the dirty hands of imperialism, a representation reinforced by North's minimal use of background, sometimes no more than a misty mountain or lake, that conveys almost no human presence whatsoever. Throughout, human scale is dwarfed by nature, the 'enormous vivid flowers, itty bitty grey people' (Losano 1997: 433). Indeed, in her memoirs North provides thick descriptions of nature but the few people get short shrift, including herself – against the solitude of nature, North is working alone (Losano 1997; North 1993). Just like the gardens outside, the scene at the gallery is quintessentially British, the landscape style European, their content Latin America, Africa or India.[9]

CONSUMPTION AND IMAGINATIVE GEOGRAPHIES

My second illustration of imaginative geographies of Latin America seems far removed from travel writing and paintings at Kew Gardens. However, just as books, paintings and botanical specimens brought images of Latin America into many homes during the nineteenth century, so the globalization of agro-food is drawing Latin America into our daily world. A tour of my local supermarket revealed asparagus, avocados and strawberries from Mexico, mangoes from Peru, honey from Guatemala, melons from Panama, paw paw from Costa Rica, flowers from Colombia, grapes from Chile, plus processed products such as tortillas and sauces, wines from Argentina and Chile, and beers from Mexico.

We can understand the presence of these commodities on our shelves in a number of ways. One argument is that they form part of a new international food space economy supported by global institutions and enabled by dramatic changes to the division of labour and technology (Andreatta 1998; Friedland 1994; Gwynne 1999; Murray 1998; but see Goodman and Watts 1994). Consumers in the North are presented with an increasingly wide selection of commodities regardless of season and presented as 'fresh' despite long transport distances from their place of origin (Friedland 1994; Gwynne 1999). Behind these scenes this economy has adopted industrial techniques of 'just in time' production and aggressive social policies such as anti-unionization, and encouraged the feminization of labour at both the point of production (fruit packing in Chile) and consumption (supermarket shelf filling in Britain) (Barrientos and Perrons 1999; Murray 1998; Raynolds 1998).

A second argument understands the international food space economy through the representation of commodities rather than purely economic relations between producers and consumers. As Cook (1994) argues, supermarket trading managers have been active in constructing meanings for particular new fruits and especially 'exotics' (what they used to call 'queer gear') through advertising campaigns and placement on cookery programmes that associate them with particular social classes, 'healthy' lifestyles, and sexuality. To some extent these representations are a response to economic and political change. In 2000, the Banana Protocol that gave preferential treatment to bananas imported into the European Union from former colonies in the Caribbean collapsed after a challenge at the World Trade Organization by Ecuador, Guatemala, Honduras and Mexico. Their argument was that the Protocol contravened the principles of free trade and was obliging European consumers to pay an additional $US 2 billion per annum (only $US 150 million of which reached the farmer, most being retained by shippers and distributors) (*The Economist*, 10 April 1999). Yet, bananas from the Caribbean are still available in my supermarket and they still cost more than the larger varieties from Ecuador. But they are now explicitly labelled as from the Windward Islands, and are advertised as smaller, sweeter and more environmentally friendly. Managers are now representing these as specifically 'Caribbean' bananas.

Am I making better-informed consumption decisions when I purchase my 'Caribbean' as opposed to 'Latin American' bananas or am I buying into an imaginative geography? This imaginative geography presents me with a fairly remunerated smallholder in the Caribbean compared to large plantations in South and Central America using temporary, possibly child, labour and stuck in an unfair contract with a multinational company (Human Rights Watch 2002). Of course, really, I have no idea how much of the extra price paid for 'Caribbean' bananas makes its way back to the smallholder, and whether it is paying for better labour standards or a mismanagement of local eco-systems that make larger-scale production difficult (Andreatta 1998). To what extent am I being duped by an imaginative geography into thinking that I am exerting my agency as a consumer?

Representations of Latin America in a coffee cup

The conventional understanding of consumer–product relations has stressed what Marx called commodity fetishism. This illustrated how consumers are kept ignorant of the exploitation or violations of human rights that take place in the process of getting an item to the store (Harvey 1990). Commodity fetishism allows consumers to think of their purchases as moral actions. Yet, commodity fetishism is constantly being exposed. Aldous Huxley, visiting a coffee estate in highland Guatemala during the 1930s, noted how '"the cups that cheer but not inebriate" require the use of children to raise the productivity of the only paid worker and that to pay such "sweated coloured" labour European wages would raise costs to the consumer by eight or ten times' (1934: 140).

Appadurai (1990), however, suggests that Marx's commodity fetishism has been replaced by what he calls production fetishism and the fetishism of the consumer. According to Appadurai, production fetishism is the illusion that transnational production is not about placeless capital, global management and faraway workers, but a spectacle of idyllic local industries and of national sovereignty. Rather than hide links back to production, therefore, some retailers represent their 'direct' link to the grower in the field into a corporate boast, claiming that this way they can ensure the quality of the product, which is good news for the company, the grower and the consumer. Describing the image of Guatemalan plantations contained in a Starbucks' brochure, Michael Smith (1996) notes how these are depicted as peaceful places of honest toil, operated as small family farms, in which the buyer and the grower are 'friends'. It is a representation extended by Starbucks' glossy *Corporate Responsibility Annual Report*, which gives details of support for NGOs to undertake social projects related to health and literacy in coffee-producing areas and of encouragement to producers to adopt environmentally sustainable practices overseen by organizations such as Conservation International (Starbucks 2002).

Of course, a harder look at the international coffee market does not fully support this benevolent representation. According to Fitter and Kaplinsky (2001), only about 40 per cent of the pre-consumption price of coffee (i.e. the price before it reaches the coffee shop) accrues to the country of origin and, at best, only about 10 per cent is received by the farmer (also Renard 1999). Moreover, world coffee prices have declined from over $US 3 per pound in the early 1970s to below 50 cents in 2001 due to both the substitution of supply from countries such as Vietnam where labour costs and environmental regulations are low and the collapse of the International Coffee Agreement in 1989 which had attempted to sustain price agreements among major producer nations (Llambi 1994; Roseberry 1996). Despite a modest increase in the size of the global coffee market (which grew by between 1 and 2.6 per cent per annum during the 1990s), the small family-run farms have been badly hit.

How do these conditions tally with the explosion of coffee bars on the high street as well as the range of coffees that they sell? A recent article in the *Guardian Weekend* reported that in a ten-minute walk from Charing Cross station along The Strand in London, one would pass two Starbucks, three Coffee Republic, two Caffe Nero and two Costa coffee shops (14 August 2001). Given that, in 2002, Starbucks is opening six new shops per month in Britain, Costa is opening four and McDonald's is planning to follow up its control of Aroma with the introduction of a McCafé chain, these figures are likely to be significantly out of date by the time this chapter goes to press. This rapid growth in places selling 'gourmet' coffee in Britain follows a trend in the USA where coffee consumption rose from $US 13.5 billion in 1993, of which less than $US 1 billion was in gourmet coffees, to $US 18 billion in 1999, of which $US 7.5 billion was in gourmet (Roseberry 1996; Starbucks 2002). Although Starbucks does pay over the global market rate for coffee, and especially for organic and shade-grown varieties, it has also benefited from the decline in prices generally, new technology and deregulation in producer companies. All of this suggests that my 'tall' cappuccino should become cheaper over time. One reason why the price seems resilient to the market is that only about 4 per cent of the price of a 'gourmet' coffee is actually coffee (Fitter and Kaplinsky 2001). So what am I paying for?

Part of the explanation might lie with Appadurai's second concept, the fetishism of the consumer, in which an image is created for consumers to believe that they are agents in the flow of commodities rather than just 'choosers'. Appadurai, however, is rather vague as to how images that pretend to empower the consumer are constructed. One insight into the relationship between consumers, commodities, and the construction of knowledge is through work on the notion of 'taste' (May 1996; Smart 1994). For consumers, and perhaps especially those from the 'new cultural class' of young professionals, it is increasingly important to invest symbolic meanings into commodities and the surroundings in which they are consumed in order to signify their social distinction from others. One particular symbolic meaning is 'exotic', which projects the consumer as cosmopolitan, travelled, multicultural, upwardly mobile. 'Exotic' draws the consumer directly into an imaginative geography that consciously plays on a relationship with the Third World.

A good example is provided by Paul Smith (1989), who shows how the clothing chain Banana Republic Travel and Safari Clothing Company is comfortable appropriating images that play on the exotic. Indeed, the company consciously conveys cliché images of political instability in Central America (in which no one is killed), the racist language of colonialism and the re-representation of travel narratives in catalogues, likening shopping to a safari. Smith quotes the founders explaining the origin of the Banana Republic name:

> because our merchandise came from countries where one regime had
> deposed another and declared all the old uniforms surplus. The new general
> could never be seen in the old general's uniform ... and [it was] part of a
> whimsy of creating an imaginary republic where I was Minister of
> Propaganda and Finance and Patricia was Minister of Culture. (Smith 1989:
> 130)

Rather than deny the relationship between the company and the Third World,
Banana Republic is building imaginative geographies of what the place of
origin for their goods might be like.

The extent to which consumers are implicated in the construction of the
'exotic' through particular geographical imaginations needs further
understanding. According to Cook and Crang (1996), we can consider three
ways in which geographical imaginations interact with consumption. First, the
'setting' or where one eats is important to the signals of status and taste. The
'setting' for the consumption of gourmet coffee is modern stylized
surroundings that offer a West Coast USA-meets-European coffee house
environment, open-plan design with sofas and small tables to encourage social
interaction, and floor-to-ceiling glass frontages and outward facing stools to
see the street, and be seen from it (M. D. Smith 1996). These restaurants and
bars are also associated with sites of gentrification. Indeed, Starbucks makes a
virtue of this relationship, claiming that 'a new Starbucks is evidence the area
is ripe for redevelopment. It's yet another step in the right direction' (Starbucks
2002: 14).[10]

There is also, however, a less tangible notion of 'setting'. At a Starbucks in
Washington DC I picked up the 'mission statement' that claimed the 'guiding
principle' of the company was to 'contribute positively to our communities and
our environment'. In practice this contribution seemed to mean 'putting in
many hours of volunteer time for our local neighborhoods and non-profit
groups', the donation of old pastries and past-date coffee, the formation of
'Green Teams' to organize litter pickups, and support for community projects.
All of these are worthwhile acts, but they also create the belief that consumers
are not buying coffee from a faceless multinational but from a locally in-touch
retailer.

The second interaction of geographical imagination and consumption
works by creating 'biographies' of how a commodity arrived in the store or
dinner table. The biography may involve a play on distance, on how the
materials were brought from afar for just this drink or meal. Again, I can
illustrate with a leaflet picked up at a Starbucks in central London called *The
Story of Good Coffee: Whole Bean Coffee*. This describes the process by which
the bean is bought, roasted and served. In addition to the obvious attention to
the flavour and freshness, the leaflet tells a story involving only two principal
actors: the buyer for Starbucks and the *baristas* who are 'trained professionals
dedicated to helping you find your perfect cup'. Working together, this team is

willing to go to 'extreme' lengths. In the biography, however, nobody seems to grow the coffee bean which is purchased on the unlikely assertion of 'taste alone, regardless of price'.

The third interaction is the identification of 'origins'. This geographical imagination has been fundamental to wine consumption for a long time, where consumers (are asked to) associate drinking with a particular valley in Chile. In the case of coffee, retailers have trained the consumer to appreciate origins by, for example, the use of 'maps'. One map is on Starbucks' website, which offers consumers the opportunity to 'Taste the Sights' through 'World Coffee Tours' by receiving every eight weeks a selection of 'exotic' coffees from around the world. A narrative style map is Starbucks' leaflet *The World of Coffee: In Search of the Best Beans*, which guides the consumer to coffee-producing areas, noting how climate, altitude and soil affect the quality of the bean. This map works by conflating places into 'coffee regions' such as Arabia or Central America, while presenting others, such as Costa Rica, as outside these regions in order to accentuate the distinction of their coffees (M. D. Smith 1996: 515). Even greater imagination is at work when Yukon Blend, symbolized by a grizzly bear, is described as made from the 'brisk qualities of Latin American coffees [and] the heaviness of a select Indonesian coffee'. Harmless fun? Or does the 'exotic' rely upon imaginative geographies of race (May 1996)? It is notable that coffee, place and people become interchangeable through terms such as 'wild', 'mysterious', 'sun-blasted', 'chocolatey', 'spicy', or sexualized as 'inviting', 'satisfying', and with 'enough full-bodied muscle to stand up to cream' (also M. D. Smith 1996).

CONCLUSION

In this chapter I have tried to show through the concept of imaginative geographies how Latin America is both a real site and a sight, a representation of a place that is displaced beyond physical space through discourses and images. We can expect that with globalization Latin America will appear an ever greater part of everyone's landscape and material culture. But in so doing the geographical imagination may also place Latin America as further away, as different, more 'exotic'. In earlier travel writing this was achieved by representing Latin America as nature, pastoral productivity or a space of disease, laziness, immorality, violence, compared to which Europe was perceived as superior. Many of these representations are invoked today in the marketing of gourmet coffee and on our television screens. While writing this chapter news broke of an episode of *The Simpsons* that was set in Rio de Janeiro and depicted men as bisexuals, a samba school teaching a fictitious dance called the *penetrada*, Copacabana beach being roamed by vicious monkeys, and tourists being kidnapped by taxi drivers and mugged by street children (*The Guardian*, 9 April 2002).

Should we be concerned by these imaginative geographies? The simple answer is 'yes'. The Brazil government is arguing that the episode will cost Rio millions of dollars in lost tourist revenue. Furthermore, imagining Latin America to be full of lazy, emotional, violent people is not going to help the employment prospects of those on my bus home from work. But the answer is 'yes' for another reason. By imagining other peoples and places through stereotypical representations we are simultaneously imagining the 'West' in ways that are superior – we work harder, hold to 'universal' moral values and so forth – and builds false assumptions about our skill at decoding geographical imaginations. As Banck (1994) describes, the poorly educated *favela* (slum or shanty-town) youth of Rio de Janeiro consciously appropriate and manipulate 'Western' commodities as signs of distinction. I wonder whether the cultural class in Britain can deconstruct the meanings of their cappuccino with equal skill.

NOTES

1   The will to produce travel accounts was not always appreciated by expedition patrons. The Royal Geographical Society had to remind Robert Schomburgk on numerous occasions to keep his mind on the job and not become distracted by adventures (Burnett 2000: 84).

2   This is not new. The surveyor Robert Schomburgk followed the routes of Alexander von Humboldt and Walter Raleigh through Guyana. Moreover, imperial nostalgia becomes an ever more prominent part of the 'unpackaged' travel experience for 'ego' tourists to 'follow Darwin' on trips to the Galapagos and Alfred Wallace up the Amazon (Munt 1994).

3   Not all imaginative geographies were predetermined. Darwin records being constantly challenged by Latin America, and his reworking of that experience into formal science changed traditional 'ways of seeing' (Martins 2000).

4   Travellers claimed to be competent amateurs in the human and physical sciences, as well as occasionally proficient in landscape and technical drawing, as indicated by the copious use of illustration in texts (see Barreto and Machado 2001; Burnett 2000; Stepan 2001).

5   Objectivity through detachment was enhanced by the inability of many travellers to speak Spanish, Portuguese or indigenous languages. This did not hinder their confidence in their ability to understand beliefs in idolatry and moral standards. Of course, some travellers, such as Henry Bates, Carl von Martius and Robert Cunnnighame Graham, took a more interactive approach to local cultures (Barreto and Machado 2001; Walker 1992).

6   Scaling peaks was often undertaken to the consternation of locals, as Dunbar (1988) describes for von Humboldt and de Saussure in Mexico. There is also perhaps an implicit masculinity involved. Annie Peck, leading

a party to scale Mount Huascaran in Peru, was 'robbed' by a male colleague of putting first footfall on the summit as she engaged in taking altitude readings (Robinson 1995: 433).

7 The enormity of nature implied danger, as is clear in Lady Richmond Brown's account of travel through the Panamanian jungle of the 1920s, although she reduced that danger considerably by appearing to shoot every animal in sight.

8 Unlike many women travellers of the day, North's travel writing displays little sense of escaping a repressive Victorian Britain (Naylor 2001; Robinson 1995).

9 Cultural representation can also be displaced. It has been announced that Kew has been nominated as a UNESCO World Heritage Site in acknowledgement of Britain's global influence and contribution to the management of biodiversity (Department of Culture, Media and Sport press release, 18 January 2002).

10 Starbucks operates a joint venture with the Johnson Development Corporation to site stores in 'underserved urban communities', a euphemism for poor and (as the Johnson Corporation is run by the black basketball player 'Magic' Johnson and has an explicit mission of developing pro black American business) a synonym for race too.

REFERENCES AND SELECTED FURTHER READING

Andreatta, S. 1998: Transformation of the agro-food sector. *Human Organization* 57, 414–29.

Appadurai, A. 1990: Disjuncture and difference in the global cultural economy. *Theory, Culture and Society* 7, 295–310.

Arnold, D. 2000: 'Illusory riches': representations of the tropical world, 1840–1950. *Singapore Journal of Tropical Geography* 21, 1, 6–18.

Banck, G. 1994: Mass consumption and urban contest in Brazil: some reflections on lifestyle and class. *Bulletin of Latin American Research* 13, 1, 45–60.

Barreto, C. and Machado, J. 2001: Exploring the Amazon, explaining the unknown: views from the past. In C. McEwan, C. Barreto and E. Neves (eds), *Unknown Amazon*. London: British Museum Press, 232–51.

Barrientos, S. and Perrons, D. 1999: Gender and the global food chain: a comparative study of Chile and the UK. In H. Afshar and S. Barrientos (eds), *Women, Globalisation and Fragmentation in the Developing World*. Basingstoke: Macmillan, 150–73.

Burnett, D. G. 2000: *Masters Of All They Surveyed: Exploration, Geography, and a British El Dorado*. Chicago: University of Chicago.

Christison, D. 1909: The River Plate region forty-three years ago. *Scottish Geographical Magazine* 25, 9, 469–81.

Cicerchia, R. 1998: *Journey, Rediscovery, Narrative: British Travel Accounts of Argetina (1800–1850)*, ILAS Research Paper No. 50. London: Institute of Latin American Studies.

Cook, I. 1994: New fruits and vanity: symbolic production in the global political food economy. In A. Bonanno, L. Busch, W. Friedland, L. Gouveia and E. Mingione (eds), *From Columbus to ConAgra: The Globalization of Agriculture and Food*. Lawrence: University Press of Kansas, 232–48.

Cook, I. and Crang, P. 1996: The world on a plate: culinary culture, displacement and geographical knowledges. *Journal of Material Culture* 1, 2, 131–53.

Dickenson, J. 1997: Britons in Brazil: nineteenth-century travellers' tales as a source for earth and social scientists. In W. L. Bernecker and G. Kromer (eds), *Die Wiederentdeckung Lateinamerikas: Die Erfahrung des Subkontinents in Reiseberichten des 19. Jahrhunderts*, Frankfurt am Main: Vervuert Verlag, 107–21.

Driver, F. 1992: Geography's empire: histories of geographical knowledge. *Environment and Planning D: Society and Space* 10, 23–40.

Dunbar, G. S. 1988: 'The compass follows the flag': the French scientific mission to Mexico, 1864–7. *Annals of the Association of American Geographers* 78, 229–40.

Fitter, R. and Kaplinsky, R. 2001: Who gains from product rents as the coffee market becomes more differentiated? *IDS Bulletin* 32, 3, 69–82.

Friedland, W. H. 1994: The new globalization: the case of fresh produce. In A. Bonanno, L. Busch, W. Friedland, L. Gouveia and E. Mingione (eds), *From Columbus to ConAgra: The Globalization of Agriculture and Food*. Lawrence: University Press of Kansas, 210–31.

Goodman, M. and Watts, M. 1994: Reconfiguring the rural or fording the divide? Capitalist restructuring and the global agro-ford system. *Journal of Peasant Studies* 22, 1, 1–49.

Green, T. 2000: *Saddled with Darwin: A Journey through South America on Horseback*. London: Phoenix Books.

Gwynne, R. 1999: Globalisation, commodity chains and fruit exporting regions in Chile. *Tijdschrift voor Economische en Sociale Geografie* 90, 2, 211–25.

Hale, A. 1909: The River Plate region and its possibilities. *Scottish Geographical Magazine* 25, 8, 426–31.

Harley, J. B. 1992: Rereading the maps of the Columbian encounter. *Annals of the Association of American Geographers* 82, 3, 522–42.

Harvey, D. 1990: Between space and time: reflections on the geographical imagination. *Annals of the Association of American Geographers* 80, 418–34.

Human Rights Watch, 2002: *Tainted Harvest: Child Labour and Obstacles to Organizing on Ecuador's Banana Plantations*. New York: Human Rights Watch.

Huxley, A. 1934: *Beyond the Mexique Bay*. London: Chatto and Windus.

Koettlitz, R. 1901: From Para to Manaos: a trip up the Lower Amazon. *Scottish Geographical Magazine* 17, 1, 11–30.

Livingstone, D. N. 1999: Tropical climate and moral hygiene: the anatomy of a Victorian debate. *British Journal for the History of Science* 32, 93–110.

Llambi, L. 1994: Opening economies and closing markets: Latin American agriculture's difficult search for a place in the emerging global order. In A. Bonanno, L. Busch, W. Friedland, L. Gouveia and E. Mingione (eds), *From Columbus to ConAgra: The Globalization of Agriculture and Food*. Lawrence: University Press of Kansas, 184–209.

Long, N. and Villarreal, M. 1998: Small product, big issues: value contestations and cultural identities in cross-border commodity networks. *Development and Change* 29, 725–50.

Losano, A. 1997: A preference for vegetables: the travel writings and botanical art of Marianne North. *Women's Studies* 26, 5, 423–48.

Martins, L. 2000: A naturalist's vision of the tropics: Charles Darwin and the Brazilian landscape. *Singapore Journal of Tropical Geography* 21, 1, 19–33.

Matless, D. 1992: A modern stream: water, landscape, modernism and geography. *Environment and Planning D: Society and Space* 10, 569–88.

May, J. 1996: A little taste of something more exotic. *Geography* 81, 1, 57–64.

Mitchell, W. J. T. 1986: *Iconology: Image, Text, Ideology*, Chicago: Chicago University Press.

Mosquera, G. 1994: Some problems in transcultural curating. In J. Fisher (ed.), *Global Visions: Towards a New Internationalism in the Visual Arts*. London: Kala Press, 133–9.

Munt, I. 1994: The 'other' postmodern tourism: culture, travel and the new middle classes. *Theory, Culture and Society* 11, 101–23.

Murray, W. E. 1998: The globalisation of fruit, neoliberalism and the question of sustainability: lessons from Chile. *European Journal of Development Research* 10, 1, 201–27.

Naylor, S. 2000: Spacing the can: empire, modernity, and the globalisation of food. *Environment and Planning A* 32, 9, 1625–40.

Naylor, S. 2001: Discovering nature, rediscovering the self: natural historians and the landscapes of Argentina. *Environment and Planning D* 19, 2, 227–48.

Naylor, S. and Jones, G. A. 1997: Writing orderly geographies of distant places: the regional survey movement and Latin America. *Ecumene* 4, 3, 273–99.

North, M. 1993: *Recollections of a Happy Life*. Charlottesville: University Press of Virginia.

Pratt, M. L. 1992: *Imperial Eyes: Travel Writing and Transculturation*. London: Routledge.

Raynolds, L. 1998: Harnessing women's work: restructuring agricultural and industrial labour forces in the Dominican Republic. *Economic Geography* 74, 2, 149–69.

Renard, M-C. 1999: The interstices of globalization: the example of fair coffee. *Sociologia Ruralis* 39, 4, 484–500.

Richards, T. 1993: *The Imperial Archive: Knowledge and the Fantasy of Empire*. London: Verso.

Robinson, J. 1995: *Unsuitable for Ladies: An Anthology of Women Travellers*. Oxford: Oxford University Press.

Roseberry, W. 1996: The rise of yuppie coffees and the reimagination of class in the United States. *American Anthropologist* 98, 4, 762–75.

Salvatore, R. D. 1996: North American travel narratives and the ordering/othering of South America (c. 1810–1860). *Journal of Historical Sociology* 9, 1, 85–110.

Seymour, S., Daniels, S. and Watkins, C. 1998: Estate and empire: Sir George Cornewall's management of Moccas, Herefordshire and La Taste, Grenada 1771–1819. *Journal of Historical Geography* 24, 3, 313–51.

Smart, B. 1994: Digesting the modern diet: gastro-porn, fast food and panic eating. In K. Tester (ed.), *The Flâneur*. London: Routledge, 158–80.

Smith, M. D. 1996: The empire filters back: consumption, production, and the politics of Starbucks' coffee. *Urban Geography* 17, 6, 502–24.

Smith, P. 1989: Visiting the Banana Republic. In A. Ross (ed.), *Universal Abandon? The Politics of Postmodernism*. Edinburgh: Edinburgh University Press, 128–48.

Starbucks 2002: *Corporate Responsibility Annual Report*, www.starbucks.com.

Stepan, N. L. 2001: *Picturing Tropical Nature*. London: Reaktion Press.

Tomlinson, B. 1996: Cultural globalisation: placing and displacing the West. *European Journal of Development Research* 8, 2, 22–35.

Walker, J. 1992: British travel writing and Argentina. In W. Hennessey and J. King (eds), *The Land that England Lost: Argentina and Britain, A Special Relationship*. London: British Academic Press, 183–200.

2

Politics and society

Arturo Arias

Politics in general tend to be about dividing the scarce resources of a nation among its population. In all countries of the world there are never enough resources to benefit all of the people that live in each nation, even under the best of circumstances: that is, if all benefits were actually to be divided in equal parts among all citizens of a given country, instead of the more common practice of having a small minority claim most of them, while a large majority basically survives on extremely limited means.

In Latin America, this disparity has always been especially eschewed. The 'haves' have always owned much more than their share, and the 'have nots' have seldom had the minimum necessary elements for eking out even a barely decent existence. As a result, Latin American people have spent most of their history living in a never-ending political turmoil, as the 'haves' perpetually struggle to preserve their uncommonly high benefits, while the 'have nots' forever struggle to improve their lot or at least to guarantee their own survival.

The roots of this problem lie in the peculiar form of Spanish colonization endured by the native peoples of the Americas. Indigenous peoples (mistakenly called 'Indians' by Columbus upon landing in 1492 because he thought he was in India), who had in the early sixteenth century some of the most developed civilizations on Earth – the Aztec in the central valley of present-day Mexico, the Maya in the present-day Mexican state of Chiapas and in Guatemala, and the Inca in present-day Ecuador, Peru and Bolivia – were conquered militarily by the Spaniards, and had to endure the destruction of all their cities and their culture, the rape of their women and the enslavement of their men, as well as the loss of approximately six-sevenths of their total population, in what is considered the world's first modern Holocaust. Despite ambitious plans at Catholic conversion and humane treatment of the natives on the part of the Spanish king and his court, most ordinary conquistadors, themselves coming from the lower strata of Spanish society, were only interested in their self-enrichment and in gaining titles of nobility. They did not care to save either the souls or the bodies of their conquered victims, but did feel obliged to pretend hypocritically that they were doing their misdeeds in the name of a Catholic God. Thus, from the very first moment when present-day Latin American nations came into contact with the Western world, they were placed in a subordinate position and in an asymmetrical relationship of power to the West, politically, economically and culturally. Given this antagonistic relationship, colonial rule had to be enforced primarily through military means. Conquistadors obviously favoured the use of arms, the means by which they achieved their own ends. As such, they imposed an unhealthy respect for wielding arms in the new world. Indeed, the *fuero militar*, a colonial ruling which established that bearers of arms were not subject to civilian common laws and were not the equal of ordinary citizens, was the basis for future military dictatorships that came to power in the nineteenth and twentieth centuries through innumerable *coups d'état*.

Once the colonial enterprise was in place, Catholic priests and Church authorities, themselves formed in the wave of Counter-Reformation measures imposed in Spain by the Holy Inquisition, acted more as cultural censors and as dogmatic enforcers of regulatory social practices than as true missionaries. Spanish functionaries, in their turn, did not much care for those vast, exotic and often inaccessible lands where they were sent to govern. They had only disdain for the growing *mestizo* (mixed Spanish and indigenous) population. Their tour of duty in the colonies was to them simply a stepping stone for returning to Spain at a higher rank than when they originally left their mother country for 'the Indies'. While in the colonies, they were suspicious not only of indigenous and *mestizo* peoples, but even of Spaniards born in the Americas, who were often older and wealthier than 'peninsular' (native Spaniard) functionaries, and more attached to the land where they were born, made their fortunes, and which they planned to bequeath to their children and grandchildren.

These precedents created the basis for Latin America's future political chaos. At the top of the social echelon, Latin American colonies had 'peninsular' government bureaucrats sent by the king to administer the colonies. With few exceptions, these bureaucrats never fully understood the people they governed and were more interested in the goings-on of court politics back home in Madrid, yearning for the moment when their 'exile' would end, and they would be able to return. Seething right under them were *nouveau-riche* Spaniards, direct descendants of the original conquistadors who settled in these lands. They were now named *criollos*, implying that they were 'locals', instead of 'real' Spaniards born in the Iberian peninsula. They always felt misunderstood by the court bureaucrats who mechanically tried to apply Spanish laws to a very different environment from the one for which they were originally conceived, and made no allowance for the ethnic tension and frontier conditions of the New World. *Criollos* resented having to pay taxes to a distant government located on the other side of the ocean, and lived off the nostalgia of their glory days of conquest and adventure. They were also responsible for the creation of a *mestizo* middle-sector, the product of the continual rape of indigenous women by common Spanish soldiers and parvenus. Given these origins, *mestizos* were always looked down upon as sub-human. Indeed, the constant abuse of indigenous females created the basis for much '*machista*' (male-centred, woman-demeaning) behaviour in the twentieth century. At the bottom of the ladder were indigenous peoples, greatly reduced in number and treated as virtual slaves despite the fact that the New Laws of the Indies expressly forbade this behaviour in 1541. Also at the bottom were African slaves, imported as forced labour to tend to low-altitude plantation work, which explains their abundance in both Brazil and the Caribbean, where sugar cane plantations became the major economic *modus vivendi* from very early on. All tending of sugar cane and production of sugar in the mills (the principal source of wealth during colonial times) was done by African slave work. Indigenous peoples, traditionally rooted in the mountains (the Mexican Sierra Madre or the South American Andes) were more adept at high-altitude work. Thus, their labour was reserved for mining – which generated great wealth in Bolivia and Mexico during the seventeenth century but became virtually exhausted by the beginning of the eighteenth, when diamonds boomed in Brazil – and house chores, as well as for agriculture at higher latitudes, a practice mostly used for feeding the colonies themselves. Most indigenous peoples were forbidden from learning Spanish. As a result, they were at the mercy of their translators, often priests or legal advisors, whenever they had a matter to settle with the Spanish authorities; these authorities often sided against them anyway, out of an innate racial prejudice.

A legacy of the Counter-Reformation was also the fact that cultural endeavours were discouraged in the Americas, when they were not directly affiliated to specific Church celebrations. Laicized cultural activities of any kind were forbidden and suspected of being subversive. As a result, illiteracy and general ignorance of the world's advances during the seventeenth and eighteenth centuries became the heritage of nearly three hundred years of Spanish colonialism when most countries of the Americas gained their independence in the early nineteenth century. Virtually the only exception was the individual effort of Sor Juana Inés de la Cruz (d. 1695). She reinvented neo-Platonism on her own, studied mathematics, composed and performed music, and wrote the best poetry in Spanish during the seventeenth century. However, her feminist writings ran foul of the Church. Her religious superiors believed that what she was doing was 'unnatural' in a woman, and she was pressured to renounce her scientific and cultural interests. She died soon after, while taking care of fellow nuns during a plague.

The entire legacy of the Enlightenment was virtually unknown in the Americas, and considered subversive by the Spanish authorities. Only a tiny elite of *criollos* had access to smuggled books from England or France. However, even if Enlightenment theories were only known by a few, often wealthy, radical organizers, they exercised a great deal of influence over society as a whole. Radicalized pro-independence *criollos* took pains to spread them in liberal newspapers, despite the threat of incarceration. In this way, much of the thinking of the French Revolution became the intellectual basis for Latin

American independence movements. Ultimately, however, the major factor aiding independence was the French occupation of Spain. With Spain itself militarily occupied and Joseph Bonaparte reigning (1804–15), the country had little to say or do while Latin American independence movements, aligning themselves with the liberal French constitution (written in Cádiz, Spain, in 1813), began to fight 'peninsular' supporters of captured King Ferdinand VII.

In many places of the Americas (most of the Southern Cone and Andean South America, Mexico), independence was won only after a long and bitter struggle that unravelled what little progress or stability had been achieved under colonial rule. Mexico was under continuous civil war from 1810 until 1821; most Hispanic countries of South America suffered the same fate from 1810 until 1825. Thus, the new countries began their independent life in severe financial ruin, and soon became indebted to either England or France, who then took it upon themselves to try to control their debtors' destinies by pulling the purse strings. Whatever agriculture had existed previously was destroyed by marching armies from both sides going back and forth over the span of many years. The mines were already exhausted by the time the Spaniards left the continent, so little benefit was to be reaped from them. Because Spain made a point of not manufacturing products in the colonies but exporting them from the mainland, most newly independent countries did not have even a rudimentary industry on which to build an economic base. Besides, societies themselves had become fractured. The Spaniards were gone, but the *criollos* were now the rulers, and, contented with power, they often disdained *mestizos*, who did the bulk of the fighting and the dying in most independence armies in the vain hope of becoming equal citizens under the law. Ever more ruthless and racist because of the insecurity generated by their own ambiguous identity, *criollos* spent a good many of the ensuing decades fighting among themselves as well. Liberal *criollos*, most of them urban-dwellers with liberal professions, believed in the principles of both the French and the US Revolutions, and wanted to implement a similar model in Latin America (as well as creating a United States of Latin America, an idea espoused by the greatest independence hero, Simón Bolívar, who named it 'Greater Colombia'), not because they wanted to abolish class or caste differences, but because private initiative had few outlets in the 'corporatist' state inherited from colonial times, in which groups rather than individuals were recognized in a rather strict hierarchy that left little room for individual will or self-reliance. In this light, liberals espoused faith in progress and a belief that modernity could only happen if one allowed the free play of market forces, and in politics they sought a government that maximized individual liberties. Whereas these ideas captured the imagination of large sectors in many urban centres, they were contrary to the economic reality of most countries at this early stage of their development. In most of them, *haciendas* were the only forms of economic production. To run these large holdings efficiently, conservative *criollos* preferred the semi-feudal model inherited from Spanish colonialism, based on the caste system, the union of

Church and state to keep the masses productive and under tight control, and a lack of individual liberties to prevent any challenges to their own power. The Church also benefited from this as an institution, since just as military *fueros* were created in colonial times, religious *fueros* existed as well. Not only were the religious the largest landholders in many countries, but most citizens had to pay a tithe of 10 per cent of their earnings to the Church. Obviously, the Church as an institution thus supported conservative landholders and, with them, also took advantage of the disappearance of the court's administrators to try to impose laws that benefited their large holdings. Most rural *criollos* became 'oligarchs': that is, a small elite of landowners who converted their holdings into autonomous, self-sufficient entities, rather than producing goods for domestic or foreign markets.

As a result, a good part of the first decades of the nineteenth century was spent in devastating civil wars, where divided *criollos* attempted to impose their different ideas of government, while English or French interests built economic concerns on both sides so as to guarantee their *de facto* control of the new nations. In general terms, after a brief period of liberal rule during the 1820s, conservative sectors, where the most powerful families in most countries were grouped, displaced them from power and governed in dictatorial fashion until the middle of the century, when the power of their social model was finally spent. As manufacturing, mostly done by artisans in very small establishments, began to lag in competitiveness, and their countries' economies, already in ruins, turned for the worse, a series of modernizing liberal regimes (Benito Juárez in Mexico, Justo Rufino Barrios in Guatemala, Domingo Faustino Sarmiento in Argentina) began to substitute them after overthrowing previous dictators (Santa Anna in Mexico, Carrera in Guatemala, Rosas in Argentina).

Since this period coincided with the rise of white supremacy in modern Europe, racist explanations were often given as to why Latin American nations failed to evolve into modern democracies. Very few paid attention to the exceptions, such as Paraguay, a landlocked nation where Dr Gaspar Rodríguez de Francia was elected dictator for life by his mostly Guaraní population, and where after closing its borders to foreign incursions, particularly from the British, Francia ruled a nationalist authoritarian democracy that became for a while the wealthiest country in this part of the world, until his death. Another exception was tiny Costa Rica, where a sparse, relatively homogeneous population, a lack of significant indigenous presence and an abundance of land in relation to its population created a more egalitarian society, not unlike what happened in the New England states of the USA.

The rise of liberal regimes in the second half of the nineteenth century was, to some degree, precipitated by the Industrial Revolution in Europe. The larger countries, such as Argentina, became major producers of agricultural and pastoral goods. The development of these exports was accompanied by the importation of manufactured goods. Despite the unevenness of the economic trade, modernity gradually took hold, although it did not always succeed in implanting democracy, either because of the great dependence on only one agricultural product for export and for obtaining foreign exchange (wool in Argentina, coffee in Central America), or else because of a heavy debt and a dependence on a European country (France, Great Britain) for the acquisition of industrial goods, thus granting a foreign power too much say, and too much power to meddle, in the internal affairs of nations. However, improvements did happen. Between 1851 and 1854, slavery was abolished in Venezuela, Colombia, Ecuador, Peru, Argentina and Uruguay. Other countries preceded or followed within a few years, with the exceptions of Cuba and Brazil. Oligarchs realized that they could no longer remain isolated in their *haciendas* under the new conditions, and began to vie for national power as a way of preserving their privileges. As a result, rather than a truly democratic system, what came out of the nineteenth-century liberal model was either an 'oligarchic democracy' such as those of Argentina or Chile where landowners sought to build strong regimes with military support, or else liberal dictatorships, such as those of Mexico, Guatemala, Venezuela or Peru, where elites carried out their rule through the means of a ruthless dictator (Porfirio Díaz in Mexico, Manuel Estrada Cabrera in Guatemala) who was not a member of their own class. In all cases, however, the goal was to establish stability and social control, so as to stimulate 'order and progress', a positivist saying that became engraved on the Brazilian flag. In consequence, political dissidents were persecuted, tortured or exiled, and power was centralized in capital cities. The erstwhile power of local *caudillos* (chieftains, regional power-brokers) was severely curtailed as this new model consolidated itself.

Despite the inherent weaknesses built into these new models, Latin American societies stabilized for the most part during this period as investment flowed into Latin America, agricultural exports boomed, and the area enjoyed for the very first time a wave of prosperity. National economies became integrated into the global system centred on European markets, and later on the USA. New professional groups emerged as power-brokers as the economies became more complex. However, because industrial goods were all imported, manufacturing remained extremely weak, and so did local merchant sectors. The cherished notion of political stability to generate greater foreign investments created a climate of political oppression, keeping nascent middle sectors (professionals, merchants, shop-keepers, small businessmen) from playing any leading political role or benefiting from export profits. Also, the legacy of both slavery and indigenous oppression had left too many people disenfranchised, too many marked traces of racism that went largely unacknowledged. The great majority of the poor were primarily descendants of African or indigenous peoples, living in the most abject conditions of poverty. Finally, the liberal elites became themselves advocates of the European discourse of the racial inferiority of their own native peoples. As a result, they sponsored heavy European immigration. Believing in the superior entrepreneurial skills of white Europeans, they favoured immigrant interests in most Latin American nations, thus destabilizing further existing social sectors in favour of those newly arrived groups. All of these factors would eventually come to haunt many nations in the early twentieth century.

The twentieth century saw a long and complex process of political change, mostly concerned with the consolidation of national states, and their urge to modernize. The concept of nation-building may suggest the coexistence in the same territory of various social groups with a consciousness both of their place in society and of the mutually beneficial nature of their relationship with other social groups. However, this process was hard to implement over the rugged Latin American territories, where marginalization, exclusion, and lack of tolerance for otherness resulted in the formation of nations through social antagonism and *de facto* racism or cultural prejudice against any group different from the ruling elites.

The complexities of modernity brought about a more heterogeneous social landscape in the early twentieth century. Despite the new barriers existing between newly arrived immigrants and descendants of native peoples, most immigrants quickly became part of a nascent working class as the trappings of modernity (railroads, telegraphs, modern mining, large seaports) began to take hold. Such work began to be done in many places by the new arrivals, who also brought with them their political experience and unionizing traditions from Europe. Although industrialization had not yet fully developed, it was already emerging, in areas such as textiles, leather goods, beverages, food processing or construction materials, and its workers quickly followed the same pattern as in the service sector.

The period from the beginning of the First World War to the start of the Great Depression saw the full-fledged emergence of a working-class movement in most of Latin America. It was the high point of the anarchist, anarcho-syndicalist and labour-organizing influence, with its strikes, mass protests and heavy unionization. The early decades of this century saw much labour activity, but also tremendous acts of repression against its nascent organizations. The 1916 university reform, begun in Argentina in 1916, soon spread throughout Latin America, transforming university campuses into free territories with autonomous rule, where local law enforcement could not legally enter. These reforms empowered students, and transformed them into virtual leaders of all social protests up to the 1980s, when globalization brought about the decline of national universities in favour of private institutions.

The emerging working class lived, for the most part, in urban slums that began to grow like rings around capital cities and a few other industrial centres (São Paulo in Brazil, Monterrey in Mexico). This led to the large-scale growth of cities. Modernity had brought about the urbanization of Latin America, as well. From these slums, some of the salient traits of popular culture (tango in Buenos Aires, samba in Rio de Janeiro, son in Havana) would soon emerge and become the source of local culture industries.

The twentieth century also began for Latin America with a new nightmare: the USA began its expansion into the Caribbean basin as a result of the Spanish-American War (1898). The entrance of the USA initiated a new era of difficult North–South relations, as the USA attempted to control the politics and economies of most countries of the Caribbean basin such as Cuba, the Dominican Republic and Haiti, while it artificially created the Republic of Panama by taking it from Colombia by force (1901), and began constructing an inter-oceanic canal in this thin isthmus so as to control traffic between the Atlantic and Pacific oceans. President Theodore Roosevelt justified this intervention with the so-called 'Roosevelt Corollary' to the Monroe Doctrine, which implied that the USA could intervene in Latin America at will, supposedly in order to prevent intervention by Europe. When Nicaragua threatened to build a competing canal across its great lakes, the USA occupied the country (1909), overthrowing its liberal president José Santos Zelaya, and imposing a conservative dictatorship in his place, led by Adolfo Díaz, who then requested US military aid to protect North American economic interests from the ravages of civil war. The USA obliged by landing marines in Nicaragua (who would stay until 1933), just as it had previously done in Cuba, the Dominican Republic, Puerto Rico and Panama. These interventions initiated the era of the so-called 'big stick' or 'gunboat diplomacy', which would poison US–Latin America relations during most of the twentieth century, and would initiate a long period in which the USA's internal peace and prosperity were bought by the political catastrophes it imposed on its neighbours to the south.

In the twentieth century, the first revolution that attempted to create a modern nation-state was in Mexico (1910–20). The Mexican Revolution was led by different factions, representatives of the poor peasant sector (Emiliano Zapata), poor northern ranchers (Pancho Villa), marginalized provincial middle-class people (Alvaro Obregón) and propertied provincial ranchers (Venustiano Carranza). All these factions formed an unstable unity to overthrow the dictatorial regime (1911–14), then collaborated in writing Mexico's modern constitution (1917) before degenerating into in-fighting among themselves. In this inner struggle, Zapata and Villa were assassinated by 'Carrancistas' (1919), before Carranza himself was gunned down (1920). As the only surviving leader of the Revolution, Obregón became the country's first constitutional president (1920), and began the process of nation-building under modern nationalist principles that attempted to homogenize disparate cultures under middle-class *mestizo* ideals. Whereas this enabled Mexico to develop a new nationalist elite, the first *mestizo* elite in the continent, and allowed it to create the most independent foreign policy of any nation in Latin America, it also led to the creation of a one-party state where, instead of democratic principles, issues among different social groups (peasants, workers, industrial bosses) were negotiated at the top party levels, in secrecy, while maintaining a façade of unity, and preventing independent power groups from truly emerging on the political landscape. The Revolution also attempted to create a homogeneous national culture to reaffirm the superiority of its chosen path. This centralization enriched Mexico in many respects (such as the emergence of the Mexican school of muralism, best represented by Rivera, Orozco and Siqueiros) but was also detrimental to the cultural autonomy of most indigenous groups, which were forced to identify with *mestizo* values and abandon their own.

The Mexican Revolution was aided, as was the rest of the continent, by European demand for raw materials during and for several years after the First World War. This brought about sustained prosperity during the 1920s, which was to come down crashing along with Wall Street in 1929. The collapse of the world economy in October 1929 modified in a radical way the political landscape of Latin America. The economic consequences were catastrophic for the continent. As a result of the global economic collapse, markets shrank throughout the region, and foreign demand for Latin American products virtually disappeared. Thus, Latin American exports dropped in a significant way, and this led to unemployment, bankruptcy and political chaos. As a result, and to stem the disarray, many military *coups d'état* took place. By 1930 the only countries not to have suffered a coup were Mexico, still emerging from its own revolutionary chaos, and Cuba, which would later suffer one in 1933.

The crash of 1929 made it obvious to most Latin American countries that the export–import model of growth that had been pursued since the end of the nineteenth century was no longer viable. It also helped discredit old political elites, brought back the military to the front line of Latin American politics, and created the basis for the emergence of a new industrial working class in the larger countries (Brazil, Argentina, Mexico). Under existing circumstances, Latin American rulers had basically only two options: either to develop a local industry so as to be able to produce those industrial goods that the country could no longer afford to import, thus achieving greater independence in the long run, or else to tighten the political control of society so as to weather the storm without major chaos, sometimes by suppressing all dissent by whatever means necessary. The latter method was favoured by large companies, such as the United Fruit Company, which had implanted itself throughout Central America and the Caribbean basin, becoming the sole proprietor not just of large tracts of land for banana and fruit production, but also of their countries' basic utilities (seaports, electric companies, railroads), which were managed as an integral part of the company's assets, instead of as public services belonging to a given nation. This model was called an 'enclave' economy.

Obviously, the first approach was more welcome, but the capital and know-how it required could only be supplied by the largest nations of the continent. Also, it could not be done without risk, as it also required bending whatever power the old rural elites still had left. Because of this, the industrialization process was stimulated by the central government, which alone could provide the capital for such a costly investment, and which benefited from the process by providing employment to a large segment of the population, and creating unions loyal to the government which could then be used to break the power of the old agricultural elites. This process came to be known as 'import-substitution industrialization'.

As a result of import-substitution, the larger nations such as Brazil, Argentina and Mexico were able to build sizeable industrial plants that helped generate economic growth into the 1960s. This created both a new modern-looking industrial elite that aspired to a cosmopolitan way of life and yet needed the apparatus of state for upward mobility and capital expansion, and an urban working class that became the forefront of all popular and political movements of the day.

However, in smaller nations with 'enclave' economies, the 1930s gave way to atrocious dictatorships (Trujillo in the Dominican Republic, Ubico in Guatemala, Hernández Martínez in El Salvador, Somoza in Nicaragua or Gómez in Venezuela are salient examples) that limited themselves to protecting the interests of large American corporations operating in their territory. As a result, public opposition to dictatorship easily transformed itself into anti-American attitudes, and this laid the tragic groundwork for future insurgency movements and long-term political instability, often lasting into the 1980s. In these unstable regimes, the negative role of the US government, perpetually supporting dictatorial power and opposing popular yearning for an American-style democratic process, would also contribute to further instability, both before and after the Second World War.

The main difference between European/North American and Latin American industrialization was that whereas the former was achieved primarily by private capital while governments took a *laissez-faire* attitude, in the latter central governments were the mainstays of industrial growth, with public capital as the source of funding. This led to all sorts of measures to protect industrialization, from tariff barriers and raising the prices of imported goods, to creating near monopolies for so-called strategic industries and making sure that other branches of government purchased manufactured goods from them.

As industry grew, the working class, and the unions that represented them, grew in both power and strength. Thus, for governments from these countries (Argentina, Brazil, Mexico), not only was control of unions crucial, but also the development of a populist rhetoric that catered to this new and most powerful sector of modern society. As a result, political forms changed during the 1930s. Populist alliances became the norm in many of these nations, grouping unions, industrialists and progressive middle-class sectors with government bureaucrats in forging a governing block that challenged the traditional interests of the old landed elites. These multi-class urban-based populist coalitions governed in Argentina (Juan Perón), Brazil (Getulio Vargas), Mexico (Lázaro Cárdenas) and Chile (Pedro Aguirre Cerda), even though the latter was more of a coalition of pro-labour and pro-industrialist parties supporting a 'popular front', rather than a single party representing the convergence of these sectors, as in the case of the other countries (Party of the Mexican Revolution, or PRM, later transformed into the Institutional Revolutionary Party, or PRI, in Mexico; Justicialist Party, or PJ, in Argentina; National Liberation Alliance or ANL, later transformed into the Brazilian Labour Party, or PTB, in Brazil). The legacy of these parties would also work its way into the politics of the last quarter of the twentieth century. More often than not, the governmental rhetoric was more radical than the actual doings of these governments, as happened in Argentina or Mexico with Peronists and 'Cardenistas' (the progressive wing of the PRI which followed the nationalist model of President Lázaro Cárdenas). Nonetheless, the rhetoric succeeded in scaring both the traditional sectors and the USA, which had become the most powerful political player in the region since the end of the Spanish-American War.

In the lesser countries, however, this same period led to the emergence of guerrilla warfare. In El Salvador, the consequences of the depression led to the collapse of coffee growth. The unemployed masses, starving to death, launched into a spontaneous insurrection in January 1932, to which the Salvadoran Communist Party, led by Farabundo Martí, latched on at the last minute. However, the masses, armed only with machetes and hunger, were no match for the Salvadoran army. Repression was unleashed with full force, and it is estimated that as many as 30,000 peasants, most of them indigenous peoples, were killed during this one month alone. The tragedy reached such proportions that fleeing indigenous peoples abandoned their clothes and cultural traditions in fear of their lives, and a fertile indigenous culture virtually came to an end in this country, despite some attempts to relaunch it in the 1990s. Farabundo Martí was shot to death. He became a symbol of martyrdom, and in the 1980s a new guerrilla movement adopted his name.

In Nicaragua, liberal general Augusto César Sandino refused to put down his arms in the late 1920s until all US marines occupying his country since 1909 left Nicaraguan soil, and a government of national reconciliation could launch a truly sovereign political agenda. Sandino's war became the first true guerrilla warfare fought in the Americas. Despite the arrival of greater numbers of marines, and aerial bombardments, the USA and its proxy, the Nicaraguan National Guard, were unable to defeat the guerrilla bands operating in the Sierra of Las Segovias in northern Nicaragua. Finally, after President Franklin D. Roosevelt came to power in the USA in 1932, a peace treaty was negotiated, general elections were held, and Sandino turned in his weapons and became an ordinary citizen. Unfortunately the head of the National Guard, Anastasio Somoza García, had Sandino assassinated (1934), and six months later launched a coup that brought him to power and ended Nicaraguan democracy. Somoza ruled like a prototypical tropical tyrant until his own assassination in 1956, but he was succeeded by his two sons, Luis and Anastasio Jr, who ruled their country until 1979. In that year, a new liberation movement that took its name from Sandino, the Sandinista Front of National Liberation (FSLN), ended the Somozas' rule once and for all.

The Second World War brought relative prosperity to many Latin American nations, as it spurred economic growth. Most countries exported their agricultural production to the nations grouped around the Allied cause, but manufactured goods were also exported for the first time, as European industrial goods disappeared in the midst of the war effort and the German occupation. Since warring nations were geared for war and had nothing to sell back, Latin American countries for the first time were able to build foreign exchange reserves, and further expand and diversify their industrial production in the case of the larger countries, or else relaunch, revamp and diversify their agricultural production, as well as modernizing harvest methods, in the case of the smaller ones. Growth occurred despite the difficulty in obtaining capital machinery, almost all of which came from Western Europe and the USA. The concept of planned economies took hold as well. At the same time, Allied rhetoric, especially President Roosevelt's Four Freedoms programme for the Allies, as well as the implementation of the Good Neighbor Policy towards Latin America as a necessary wartime substitute for the 'big stick', led many reform-oriented sectors of various countries suffering either dictatorship or an authoritarian populist regime to dream of a multi-party democracy and economic modernization and espouse these ideas publicly, without fearing the worst excesses of dictatorial repression.

Thus, most of the nations of the Latin American continent began the post-war period in a more solid economic condition, with a minimum consolidation of modern and democratic advancements, but with great ambition and optimism for evolving out of 'underdevelopment', as it was then named, in the near future. Unfortunately, the Cold War would deal these dreams a major setback. By preventing meaningful reforms, it pushed most of the continent into a long and traumatic revolutionary path.

A case in point was Guatemala. Like all small nations of the continent, the country endured a long dictatorship during the depression and the war (General Jorge Ubico, 1931–44). During the 1930s, the USA supported the dictatorship to prevent another chaotic situation like the slaughter or 'matanza' in El Salvador from taking place. However, as the decade progressed, Ubico's sympathy for Nazi Germany made him an uncomfortable ally. Thus, when he was overthrown in 1944 by a broad movement representing all sectors of society and employing Roosevelt's 'Four Freedoms' as the basis for a new government, the USA tolerated his fall and at first supported change. However, as Guatemala's new government attempted to transform the nation by imitating Mexico's model of a modern, nationalist regime, it clashed with the economic power of the United Fruit Company (UFCO), the most powerful US corporation in the Caribbean basin. When the Guatemalan government tried to apply a land reform modelled on the one implemented by the USA in Japan at the end of the Second World War, UFCO denounced it in Washington as a 'communist government' according to the new Cold War rhetoric. It then began to finance a secret military intervention in the country. The Eisenhower administration gave the green light to intervention in 1954, given its close links to UFCO – Secretary of State John Foster Dulles and his brother Allen, head of the CIA, were both on its board, and General Walter Bedell Smith, who led the operation, became chairman of the board the following year.

The overthrow of Guatemalan democracy in 1954 was the beginning of a new interventionist approach in the continent on the part of the USA. Its callous and insensitive attitude angered major sectors of Latin America, who began in their turn to develop an 'anti-imperialist' discourse, and to support more radical measures to oppose the US presence in Latin America.

Struggles against dictatorships in other countries had led to decades of political instability, as dictatorships would collapse, a coalition government led by a civilian but lacking a substantive base would ensue, only to be soon toppled by yet another general, and the same vicious cycle would be repeated all over again. Because of this continuous instability, middle sectors of society remained suspicious of 'bourgeois democracy'. As a result, when the cycle reached a breaking point in the 1960s, it was much easier to turn to more radical solutions. This was a decade when guerrilla struggle flowered throughout much of the continent, and led to serious political conflict followed by turmoil and massive repression in many mid-sized nations (Colombia, Peru, Uruguay). However, the point of departure for this period was the Cuban Revolution (1959).

In Cuba, Machado had come to power in 1933 in a bloodbath, soon to be followed by still another coup led by Sergeant Fulgencio Batista, as different sectors of Cuban society organized themselves against dictatorship. Democracy flowered briefly in the late 1940s, but soon Batista made another grab for power (1952). These efforts would constitute the groundwork for the struggle led by Fidel Castro and his July 26th Movement, which took its name from the date in 1953 when he unsuccessfully assaulted the Moncada barracks in Santiago de Cuba. The Castro brothers were both arrested, but were later freed and sent to Mexico. There, they organized their return to Cuba, and were joined by a young Argentinean who was working as a doctor in Guatemala, had lived through that country's invasion in 1954 and had developed anti-American positions as a result. His name was Ernesto Guevara, but in Guatemala he was called 'Che', a common nickname for all people of Argentinean origin.

After Castro landed in the province of Oriente and disappeared in the mountains of the Sierra Maestra, Batista's repression pushed most social sectors to group themselves around him. The US invasion of Guatemala in 1954 and air support of Batista transformed Castro decidedly into a foe of America. As support for Batista dwindled and Cuban soldiers defected to Castro's side, his guerrillas succeeded in defeating Batista's army in Santa Clara, and Castro marched unimpeded into Havana (January 1959).

One of the immediate consequences of the Cuban Revolution was that some democratic successors of past dictators developed more radical strains in their own discourse to gain hold of their supporters (João Goulart, heir of Getulio Vargas's PTB in Brazil, or Arturo Frondizi in Argentina), established governments developed more radical foreign policy positions supportive of Latin American nationalism (successive PRI governments in Mexico), or else radical revolutionaries gained local and international support from invoking the Guatemala case as they called for more radical options and social models like the one being developed by Castro in Cuba. Oblivious to the real needs of Latin Americans and obsessed with its rivalry with the Soviet Union, the USA was caught entirely by surprise by the emergence of the first socialist government in the Americas, its broad support in the continent from even middle-of-the-road nationalist democrats, and its emulation by guerrilla movements throughout the continent during the 1960s.

Part of the problem, of course, was linked to the economy. The economic solutions from the 1930s began to run out of steam by the mid-1950s, when both the European and Japanese economies recovered from their respective destruction from the war. Latin America also depended too much on government-run industrial plants, and this prevented a quick manufacturing reconversion when late 1950s' industrial production began to transform the nature of industrial products and to cheapen their costs. At the same time, Latin America's traditional agricultural exports began to undergo a steady decline, thus limiting their nations' ability to obtain foreign exchange for new industrial goods and cheaper machinery needed for competitive manufacturing. The unequal distribution of income also prevented government-run industrial plants from fully developing a national market. In other words, because most citizens were too poor to buy industrial goods, the productivity of most state-run factories went to waste, and they could not compete in the international market with American, European or Japanese-made industrial goods. At the same time, with a high population growth, Latin American countries were unable to employ many of their citizens, despite bloated bureaucracies in all areas of government and industry that only lessened productivity. All of these factors led to inflation, and began to affect both the stability of the middle sectors and the earnings of the working class. Given the fervent hope that after the Cuban Revolution all Latin American nations could theoretically become free of dependency on capitalist economic markets and create true egalitarian societies, combined with the resentment still felt against the USA for its invasion of Guatemala in 1954 and its support of Batista's dictatorship in Cuba, it is not hard to imagine why heretofore stable nations in appearance, such as Chile or Argentina, would lean towards radical politics in the 1960s. The US involvement in Vietnam during these decades certainly did not aid its cause.

As pressure mounted in the early 1960s, with a middle-class leaning towards democratic rule and sympathy for nationalist rebellion, versus an enormous amount of pressure from the USA to force Latin American governments to break diplomatic relations with Cuba and align themselves with the guidelines of the Alliance for Progress and the embargo against Cuba, democratic processes collapsed in most countries and yielded to highly repressive military regimes. Coups took place in El Salvador (1962), Guatemala (1963), the Dominican Republic (1963), Brazil (1964), Argentina (1966), Panama (1968), Peru (1968), Uruguay (1973) and Chile (1973). The Dominican Republic was also invaded by US marines in 1965 to eliminate a progressive coup led by Colonel Francisco Caamaño in support of pro-Cuban president Juan Bosch, democratically elected in 1962 and overthrown in 1963. Indeed, the only countries that managed to preserve the rudiments of democratic principle during this difficult period were Mexico, whose one-party state led by the PRI would remain in power from 1929 until 2000, exercising a model of 'authoritarian democracy' in which a progressive foreign policy tried to compensate for repression at home, and Costa Rica, which underwent a social-democratic revolution in 1948 and remained the only uninterrupted functional democracy during the entire second half of the twentieth century.

As the crises of the 1960s became more intense, guerrilla movements emerged in every Latin American country with the sole exception of Costa Rica. They became the justification for repressive coups in many countries, where a new pattern emerged: military governments would raise repression to new levels while they simultaneously appealed to the USA to ignore their violations of human rights and to send in military aid and CIA personnel skilled in counter-insurgency methods to prevent Soviet expansionism in the Americas. The fact that the USA always complied and even taught repressive regimes how to torture better, among other counter-insurgency skills, brought North–South relations to a new low, radicalized students inside the USA, and created rancour against it throughout the Third World, a phenomenon that has not dissipated at the beginning of the twenty-first century, and whose roots can be traced to policies against most nationalist movements developed in the 1960s. During this critical period in Latin America, people suspected of sympathizing or else being allied with the guerrilla cause began to 'disappear'. They were kidnapped and often murdered in secret after long torture sessions, by death squads composed of military and intelligence elements, operating with the consent of their rulers but outside of the boundaries of the law. It is widely believed that these practices began in Guatemala in 1965, but became common throughout the 1970s, when the secret Condor Plan led to cooperation among the security agencies of all South American countries to pursue refugees and political exiles in their own territory, regardless of their country of origin. The total dead from this period remains unknown but must amount to tens of thousands. In Argentina alone the number of dead most likely totalled some 30,000.

The most important guerrilla movements in the 1960s were mostly urban and middle-class in composition: the Tupamaros in Uruguay, and the

Montoneros in Argentina. Chile elected a socialist president, Salvador Allende, in 1970. Through him, a broad coalition from the left exercised political power and advertised itself as a 'peaceful revolution' along the lines of Western Europe's 'Eurocommunism', presenting itself as an alternative to violent revolution, until it too was overthrown from power violently on 11 September 1973 by General Augusto Pinochet and the Chilean army, in conjunction with the CIA.

Most guerrilla movements that appeared on the landscape in the 1960s were defeated and eliminated before the end of the decade, with the exception of Colombia's, which lingered on and eventually transformed itself into a *narco-guerrilla*, a guerrilla movement living off its cocaine benefits. The Montoneros and Tupamaros were mostly stamped out by the mid-1970s, although their respective countries were still run by repressive military regimes until the mid-1980s. However, their experience would contribute to the creation of mightier guerrilla struggles in Central America in the 1970s, which would lead to a guerrilla triumph in Nicaragua in 1979, and fully-fledged civil wars in both El Salvador and Guatemala during the 1980s.

It was Central American countries' inherent weaknesses that facilitated insurrection in these countries. Unlike Mexico, Brazil or the Southern Cone countries, Central American nations did not undergo a major industrialization in the 1930s, nor did they benefit from large reserves of foreign exchange at the end of the Second World War. On the contrary, their economies remained weak, largely dependent on traditional agricultural products for export. As indicated before, Guatemala attempted a progressive democratic experiment that ended in a US invasion in 1954. This was followed by a succession of military regimes. Opposition to them generated a coup attempt led by young, nationalist military officers on 13 November 1960. When this coup failed, the US-trained officers became the leaders of a nascent guerrilla movement, and were briefly joined by Nicaraguan opponents of Somoza's long dictatorship in their country.

The particularly ruthless nature of dictatorship in Central American countries during the 1960s, the growth of peasant movements in conjunction with the 'popular church' led by priests linked to Theology of Liberation, an offshoot of the Second Vatican Council presided over by Pope John XXIII in 1963, as well as the weakness of local communist parties, and the particulars of Maya struggle against racism in Guatemala, all combined to create successful guerrilla-led peasant movements in the region during the 1970s. In most cases, peasant movements were Catholic in character and had been organized by radicalized priests and nuns from the 'popular church'. Eventually, these movements linked forces with small guerrilla units, often created by dissidents from local communist parties. Their combined strength gave them enough political clout to build a broad-based mass movement around them, which usually attracted middle-of-the road sectors as well. In Nicaragua, where the Somoza family had held power since Sandino's death in

1934, even conservative sectors joined the movement to overthrow the last survivor of the Somoza dynasty. Anastasio Somoza Debayle did nothing to enhance his cause. He had Pedro Joaquín Chamorro assassinated, the most respected conservative leader of his country and editor of *La Prensa*, the leading national paper, as well as Bill Stewart, ABC correspondent covering the 1978 insurrection for a US audience. President Carter of the USA, the first leader of his country concerned with human rights, withheld military aid to Somoza and negotiated with Sandinista leaders for a peaceful transition endorsed by the Organization of American States (OAS). The governments of Venezuela, Panama, Costa Rica and Mexico aided the Sandinistas with arms and logistical support. Feeling betrayed by the USA, Somoza fled his country, and the Sandinistas took over on 19 July 1979.

Emboldened by the Sandinista triumph, Guatemalan Maya villages rose against their own military dictatorship during the second half of 1979, and a nationalist coup in El Salvador on 15 October of the same year began the process that would ultimately lead to civil war. By 1980, the Salvadoran opposition was launching its first general offensive, and in March 1981 Archbishop Oscar Romero, the most respected Catholic leader in the region, was assassinated while saying Mass on behalf of the notorious right-wing leader Eduardo D'Aubisson.

However, the government had changed in the USA. The conservative administration of Ronald Reagan saw the Central American war as the last stand against communism, refusing to believe in the true nationalist and modernizing aspirations of the region's citizens, and in their own process of empowerment. For Reagan, there was no such thing as a Central American conflict. Everything was an East–West conflict, and to the degree that the 'Soviet empire' was brought down, insurrection would disappear in Central America.

Thus, military aid and military advisors were sent to the region, a military blockade similar to Cuba's was slowly implemented against Nicaragua, and a '*contra* war' was launched against the latter from Honduras. Whereas militarily the *contras* failed to make significant advances and the Salvadoran army never succeeded in getting past a stalemate against El Salvador's Farabundo Martí National Liberation Front (FMLN), the region was devastated economically, and as significant sectors of the population began to starve, Nicaraguans voted the Sandinistas out of power (1990). The FMLN in its turn entered peace negotiations in earnest after its 'final offensive' (1989), when, in an act of desperation, the Salvadoran army murdered leading Jesuits of the Catholic Central American University (UCA) thinking that they were the brains behind the insurrection. A peace accord was finally signed in 1992, and the FMLN became an opposition party. After the Guatemalan Maya population was massacred and over 450 villages were completely destroyed in a savage offensive led by the army, combined with strategic mistakes on the part of the country's own guerrilla forces, the Guatemalan National Revolutionary Unity (URNG), the latter began a long, protracted, negotiated peace process as well, until peace was finally signed in 1996. The collapse of the Berlin Wall in 1989, and the end of the Soviet Union in 1990, made it easier for the USA to recognize its erstwhile opposition and negotiate peace processes between opposing factions in all Central American countries. In 1998, President Clinton visited the region and apologized to its people for his country's mistake of becoming linked to terrorism.

However, while most Latin American countries returned to democratic ways after the various military dictatorships collapsed, to the point that by the early 1990s only Cuba continued to have a non-elected government, the economic landscape had become significantly brittle as a result of neo-liberal economic policies implemented in the 1980s by the Reagan administration and the World Bank. As the world began to move in the direction of globalization while undergoing a high-tech revolution, Latin American nations began to need massive economic aid to survive. The only new product generating foreign exchange became cocaine, and indeed it can be said that the cocaine trade saved most Latin American nations from bankruptcy. Nonetheless, cocaine was part of a broader underground economy that included contraband and marijuana instead of a legitimate product of export, and the 'cocaization' of Latin American economies led to the hijacking of most national economies by drug lords and drug mafias, who became fully responsible for the well-being of the population under their control, along the line of classical populist models. Cocaine afflicted most countries: coca was grown in Peru and Bolivia, transformed into cocaine in Colombian laboratories, shipped to the USA via Central America and the Caribbean, introduced and distributed inside the USA via Mexico, and its profits were laundered in both Panama and Southern Cone countries as far south as Argentina. Traditional armies, government functionaries, and even distinguished bankers and other members of the elite became involved in drug-trafficking, and most benefited from the high yield of profits that this business generated for those in its upper echelons. However, a culture of violence also became the norm as a result of drug cartels becoming more powerful than even elected governments. This process either corrupted governments such as Mexico's PRI, where many of its top cadres became involved in various drug cartels, or else split up countries such as Colombia, where society became divided into regional fiefdoms run by competing sectors that controlled different aspects of cocaine production or distribution. The violent nature of drug cartels, combined with the inherent weakness of newly instituted democratic regimes and the lack of genuine means for generating foreign exchange beyond tourism and the *maquila* industry (sweat-shops producing at low cost for globalized corporations while benefiting from tax protection and skirting industrialized nations' tough labour and ecological laws), began to spell the disintegration of protectionist elements that had enabled government-owned manufacturing to bloom in the past, as well as of all remnants of state-controlled legislation created with the intention of strengthening national states through a massive build-up of the public sector.

'Industrial reconversion' meant selling-off at a pittance national industries or companies (airlines, electric and telephone companies) to the private sector, usually under singularly corrupt arrangements, or as means of favouring global corporations. Privatization meant greater unemployment, and increasing misery for the majority of Latin Americans, who could no longer envision even the utopian dreams of a revolution overthrowing the status quo. Thus, the only alternative became massive emigration to the USA. The 1990s became, as a result, a decade when poor people from all over Latin America, and not only from Mexico, the USA's neighbour directly to its south and a traditional source of cheap labour, emigrated illegally to the USA with the hope of finding the minimal human conditions for existence, after it became apparent that those conditions would never exist in their countries of origin.

One positive sign within the emergence of global politics was the arrest of General Augusto Pinochet in Great Britain in 1998. Whereas it is still unclear whether justice will ultimately be done in Chile, the precedent-setting event has made it more difficult for unaccountable dictators to do as they will inside their own countries and then fly away scot-free, and for dictatorial power to receive the aid from the USA and European nations that it did in the past as long as it did not challenge the international status quo.

As a result, the beginning of the twenty-first century found Latin America deeply submerged in a crisis of confidence, in an identity crisis, unable to feed its appalling number of poor, and increasingly surviving from the hand-outs mailed home by families residing inside the USA, usually under difficult circumstances themselves, and yet growing in political clout within North America as an emerging 'Latino' power block within the US political landscape. Political debates featuring President George W. Bush speaking in Spanish and promising to do for Latinos what he had done as Texas governor for Mexican-Americans became emblematic of the growing power of this emerging voter block. The creation of the North American Free Trade Agreement (NAFTA) in 1994, and the promise of a continental trade agreement for 2005, are features of the integration of the Americas along globalizing patterns, and of the interdependence of the continent's economies. Economic relations in the continent have indeed become more autonomous from political controls, and, as a result, national sovereignties have declined. At the same time, these arrangements reflect the exclusion of any possibility of upward-mobility or meaningful future for impoverished masses unable or unwilling to migrate illegally to the USA. Along parallel lines, growing scandals among nascent Latin American democracies such as those that shook Peru (2000), Argentina (2000) and Venezuela (2000) reflect poorly on the ability for democracy to take root in the continent in the near future. Whereas Mexico's peaceful transition to democracy while dismantling the power of the PRI (2000) was the source of cautious optimism, the ambiguous rise to power of new-style populist Hugo Chavez in Venezuela, the virtual dissolution of small nations such as Haiti, the transformation of Paraguay into a contraband haven for the entire continent, and the potential dissolution of Colombia as *narco-guerrillas* and drug cartels keep the country in havoc, all point to a more pessimistic assessment of the viability of Latin American nations as independent entities in the immediate future, and signal our need to rethink our historical understanding of what we understand as 'Latin American politics' within the scope of the new political order of globalization and the implications of their hybrid identities and their expanding frontiers.

In the latter context, perhaps the most dramatic event to signal the collapse of neo-liberal policies imposed on all emerging democracies in Latin America by the Reagan administration, the World Bank, and the International Monetary Fund (IMF) has been the collapse of the Argentinean economy at the end of 2001. President Carlos Menem (1989–99) had become the poster-boy of effective application of neo-liberal policies in the continent. He eliminated what remained of economic nationalism in his country, and, following the recommendations of the IMF, privatized all state-run corporations, public works and state-owned assets. All of them were bought by foreign corporations, with Spanish companies becoming the major investors at this initial stage. Menem pegged the Argentine currency to the US dollar and deregulated capital flows, removing limits on profits that corporations could take out of the country. He eliminated subsidies that made basic foodstuffs and public services available to the poor and rolled over the external debt into long-term bonds in order to make the payment affordable. At first, Menem was hailed because he managed to stop hyperinflation, and foreign investors flooded Argentina, allowing its elite and middle class to become US-like in their 'yuppy' consumption habits. As millions lost their jobs – either with the collapse and downsizing of national industries, or as a result of the disappearance of trade barriers that undermined small, privately owned businesses which could not compete with transnational corporations – political instability began once again. At the same time, no mechanisms of checks and balances were implemented in the country, and, as a result, corruption ran rampant. Those close to Menem began to operate as a 'mafia', profiting from the flow of capital in and out of the country by acquiring the banks that oversaw these transactions, and getting involved in illegal deals such as arms-trafficking and the laundering of drug money. These phenomena prevented the government from both reducing government spending, which became the private treasure chest of Menem's 'mafia', and balancing the budget. When the De la Rúa government that succeeded Menem tried to implement again some subsidies and reintroduce state-run services, it ran into the opposition of Menem's *nouveau-riche* sector, which pulled all the capital out of Argentina, leaving the country literally dry. Banks closed and were forbidden to dispense cash to anyone. Argentinian citizens literally had no money on their hands, and credit cards were no longer accepted. Riots ensued, the De la Rúa government fell, and Argentina went through three governments in seventy-two hours before Eduardo Duhalde was sworn in as president. Four months into his term, however, it remains far from unclear how Argentina will extricate itself from this mess, and what the consequences of the collapse of neo-liberal policies will be both for MERCOSUR (the South American Common Market) and for the rest of the continent.

SELECTED FURTHER READING

Alvarez, S., Dagnino, E. and Escobar, A. (eds) 1998: *Cultures of Politics, Politics of Cultures*. Boulder, CO: Westview Press.

Bethell, L. (ed.) 1985, 1986, 1991: *The Cambridge History of Latin America*. Cambridge: Cambridge University Press.

Castaneda, J. 1993: *Utopia Unarmed: The Latin American Left after the Cold War*. New York: Vintage.

Craske, N. 1999: *Women and Politics in Latin America*. New Brunswick, NJ: Rutgers University Press.

Dunkerley, J. 1992: *Political Suicide in Latin America and Other Essays*. London: Verso.

Escobar, A. and Alvarez, S. (eds) 1992: *The Making of Social Movements in Latin America: Identity, Strategy, and Democracy*. Boulder, CO: Westview Press.

Foweraker, J. 1995: *Theorizing Social Movements*. London: Pluto.

Fowler, W. 2002: *Latin America 1800–2000*. London: Arnold.

Galeano, E. 1973: *Open Veins of Latin America: Five Centuries of the Pillage of a Continent*. New York: Monthly Review Press.

Green, D. 1995: *Silent Revolution: The Rise of Market Economics in Latin America*. London: Cassell/LAB.

Gunder Frank, A. 1969: *Capitalism and Underdevelopment in Latin America: Historical Studies of Chile and Brazil*. New York: Monthly Review Press.

Rosenberg, T. 1992: *Children of Cain: Violence and the Violent in Latin America*. London: Penguin.

Sarlo, B. 2001: *Scenes from Postmodern Life*. Minneapolis: University of Minnesota Press.

Wearne, P. 1996: *Return of the Indian: Conquest and Revival in Latin America*. London: Cassell/LAB.

Weschler, L. 1998: *A Miracle, A Universe: Settling Accounts with Torturers*. Chicago: University of Chicago Press.

Williamson, E. 1992: *The Penguin History of Latin America*. London: Allen Lane/Penguin.

Yúdice, G., Franco, J. and Flores, J. (eds) 1992: *On Edge: The Crisis of Contemporary Latin American Culture*. Minneapolis: University of Minnesota Press.

3

The cultures of colonialism

Luis Fernando Restrepo

Despite its geographical, cultural and social diversity, one significant unifying factor of the region we know today as Latin America has been a shared history of European colonialism. Roughly three centuries of mainly Iberian (Spanish and Portuguese) colonization have reshaped and left a marked imprint on the cultures of the region and defined, to a great extent, its relation to the rest of the world, violently and unevenly incorporating it into the European modern world system. This process, however, was far from unidirectional, since the colonial exchange had multiple repercussions on both sides of the Atlantic, contributing significantly to the Western world.

This chapter will provide a general overview of Iberian colonization from 1492 until independence: 1810 in Spanish America and 1822 in Brazil.[1] Special emphasis will be given to some of the intellectual and cultural debates that emerged in the context of colonialism, including the 'invention' of America, discussions on the legitimacy of the conquest, Amerindian responses to the colonization, and *criollo* (Americans of European descent) cultural politics.

ANTECEDENTS

The Iberian colonization of the Americas was built on hundreds of years of Mediterranean experiences in trade and intercultural exchanges. It also erected a system of dominance that strategically adopted and modified many structures of Native American cultures, including socio-political units, tribute systems, exchange networks and agricultural production. For this reason it is necessary to look back to the histories of both hemispheres to understand Iberian America better.

The earliest inhabitants of the Americas migrated from Asia across the Bering Strait between 40,000 and 25,000 BC. Small groups of hunters and food-gatherers extended throughout the continent. Several millennia later, agricultural societies emerged. By the time of the Spanish invasion, numerous complex societies had formed. In Mesoamerica, there were the Olmecs, Maya, Teotihuacans, Zapotecs, and more recently the Mexica (Aztecs). In the Andes, the Tawantinsuyo (Inca) empire was only the most recent of a long line of civilizations including the Horizon, Nazca, Moche and Tiwanaku. In other areas, middle-range societies emerged at different time periods, like the Muisca in the northern Andes (present-day Colombia), the Tupi-speaking groups of eastern Brazil, the Guaraní in South America and the Taino in the Caribbean. At the turn of the fifteenth century, the indigenous population of the area now known as Latin America may have been about 30 to 40 million.[2]

On the other side of the Atlantic, three main historical precedents would significantly determine the course of events that unravelled after Christopher Columbus's 1492 voyage: the trade with the Orient, the Portuguese colonization of Western Africa and the Atlantic Islands, and the *Reconquista*.

At the dawn of the early modern period, Florence, Venice and Genoa became powerful merchant city-states trading spices, textiles and other goods with the Orient. With the rise of the Ottoman empire, the route to the East, known as the 'silk road', was cut off. Consequently, by the mid-1400s the Mediterranean economy began shifting towards Iberia and the Atlantic.

During the fifteenth century, the Portuguese became a maritime empire, controlling the western coast of Africa, the Azores, Madeira and other islands in the Atlantic, and a trade route to India opened in 1498 by sailing around the southern tip of Africa. Several factors made possible Portugal's rise to a world power. Under the auspices of King Henry the Navigator (1395–1450), the Portuguese incorporated numerous Mediterranean (including northern African) technological and scientific developments related to navigation, such as the caravel (a light, long-range ship), cartographic charts, and instruments such as the astrolabe and the quadrant. Their maritime capabilities allowed them to establish a system of fortified slave and ivory trading-posts (*feitorias*) along the western coast of Africa, without major inland colonization – a system that was implemented later in Brazil.

In the Atlantic, the Portuguese established colonies and sugar mills (*engenhos*) in Madeira, the Azores and the Cape Verde islands. Initially developed in the Mediterranean, the sugar export agriculture was adopted by the Portuguese and turned into a large-scale enterprise with African slave labour. To a lesser extent, Spain also participated in this developing Atlantic economy with the Canary Islands.

Another historical event that greatly determined the dynamics of the Iberian colonization of the Americas was the *Reconquista*, the Christian war against the Muslims who had controlled the southern part of the Iberian peninsula since 711. The *Reconquista* provided Christian Iberians with military expertise, religious unification, and key juridical precedents for the American conquest.[3] Santiago Apostol, also known as *matamoros* (killer of moors), the patron saint of the *Reconquista*, for example, was often invoked in the military campaigns in the Americas. His image can be found in numerous churches throughout Latin America. It is also a common icon in Latin America's rich popular culture.

THE PATHS OF CONQUEST

Shortly after defeating Granada in 1492, ending Muslim rule in the peninsula, the Spanish monarchs agreed to finance the voyage of a Genoese sailor experienced in the Portuguese ventures in the Atlantic. A small exploration fleet of three ships and ninety men departed the Spanish port of Palos de Moguer on 3 August 1492. After a short stop in the Canary Islands, the fleet sailed west, reaching the Bahamas on 12 October 1492. In his log book, Christopher Columbus discussed his intention to find a trade route to the Orient. His detailed description of the natural resources of the Caribbean, on the other hand, invoked an enterprise similar to the Portuguese factories on the African coast. To a lesser extent, the preoccupation of converting the natives into Christianity is also expressed in his log book. Evidently, the project was, from the beginning, ambiguous if not contradictory. The following year (1493), a second voyage to the Indies was organized. It was clearly a fully-fledged colonial enterprise: seventeen ships and 1,200 men, including soldiers, six priests, and, according to Columbus, 'people of all sorts of trades with their instruments to build a city'. They also brought horses, cattle, seeds and plants. However, no women were included, adding other dimensions to the invasion: rape, sexual slavery, and also interracial marriages. Even though later voyages did include European women, race mixture or *mestizaje* occurred frequently and became from early on a defining element of the new colonial society.

The Caribbean was a crucial stepping stone for the Spanish colonization of the continent. It laid down the basic patterns of settlement, defining the new colonial society and the interactions between Spaniards and Amerindians. On a logistical level, La Española, where settlement began in 1492, and Cuba, conquered in 1510, provided ships, soldiers, horses, and all the necessary provisions for several expeditions into the continent. With the depletion of natives and minerals, and the conquest of densely populated areas like central Mexico and the Andes, the Caribbean colonies would lose their initial importance. The Caribbean would regain some importance later in the seventeenth and eighteenth centuries with a sugar export economy dependent on African slaves.

In a few years, Spaniards founded towns in the Caribbean and organized placer gold mines, agricultural and livestock farms, and sugar plantations, all based on Amerindian labour. The Arawak or Taino population of the Antilles may have been well over a million at the turn of the fifteenth century.[4] Enslavement, European diseases, and starvation reduced them to a few thousand in the first decades of Spanish colonization. With the rapid collapse of the native population, the Spaniards started conducting slave raids in the nearby islands and the Caribbean coasts of Central and South America.

The early stages of the colonization of Brazil were somewhat different from the Spanish experience in the Caribbean. In 1500, on his trip to South Africa, Pedro Alvares Cabral drifted westward and landed somewhere along the Brazilian coast, calling it Vera Cruz. The region, however, soon became known by the name of a local dye tree, *Pau Brasil*. In the first years, the Portuguese showed little interest in Brazil. Their main overseas interests were Africa and India. The initial settlements in Brazil were much like the African factories. But soon the presence of French and Spanish traders prompted the Portuguese crown to take more decisive steps in claiming Brazilian territory. Between 1533 and 1535 the land was divided into fifteen captaincies. The grantees (*donatarios*), mostly members of the middle nobility or second sons of the high nobility, were given ample administrative and fiscal powers over the assigned territories. Following peninsular traditions, the *donatarios* awarded tracts of land (*sesmarias*) to individuals. In Brazil, the *sesmarias'* extension was significantly much larger, creating large landholders.

The donatory system did not result in the investments and settlements that the crown expected. Some *donatarios* even refused to go to Brazil. Only later, with more direct royal involvement and the reorientation of the colonies towards the sugar export economy, would Brazil become an important Portuguese possession.

In the Spanish colonies, numerous expeditions and settlements inland were made during the course of the sixteenth century. The military expansion of the Spanish empire is a topic that has received considerable attention by traditional historiography. A common image of the colonization of the Americas is the figure of a bearded Spanish *conquistador*. However, the story of the colonization is a complex enterprise that cannot be reduced to a few biographies of certain individuals nor to the military defeat of Amerindians. Great attention has been given to the military power of Europeans and the ritual orientation of Amerindian warfare. The eventual implementation of social structures of dominance and exploitation such as the *encomienda* or the sugar mill complex were less dramatic but nonetheless more significant in the long term.

Spanish expeditions were generally large, costly enterprises. Each needed much planning and organization. First, it had to be approved by the crown. Financial support came from investors and the participants themselves. Even soldiers had to pay for their own fleet and provide their own horses and arms. Internally, the expedition was organized by military rank and social status, although in the Indies social hierarchies were less rigid than in the peninsula. Royal concessions, investment made and rank were determining factors in the distribution of loot and assignment of *encomiendas* and colonial posts such as governor.

Since the crown had to sanction the awards, the *relaciones* or expedition reports tended to emphasize the conquistadors' efforts to 'serve' the crown.

This explains in part the heroic narratives of the period. Cortés's letters to Charles V are an illustrative example. A skilful writer, Cortés accentuated his role in every aspect of the expedition, minimizing the participation of other Spaniards. Nineteenth-century Romantic historiography also contributed to the image of the *conquistador*. Individual action and the hero figure are two themes that attracted Romantic writers and historians. William Prescott's *Conquest of Mexico* (1843) is a good example.

Several determining events in Mesoamerica and the Andes preceded the Spanish military conquest of Mexico and Peru. The Mexica empire had risen to power only a couple of centuries before the Spanish arrival. Through a mixture of alliances and conquests, the Mexica had gained control over most of Mexico's central valleys. It was, however, an unstable network of power. The Mexica also had strong adversaries like the Tlaxcalans. The Spaniards cleverly used the local rivalries to build a coalition army against the capital city of the Mexica empire, Mexico-Tenochtitlán. After an unsuccessful resistance against Cortés's forces, the Tlaxcalans joined the Spanish army. In Peru, Gonzalo Pizzarro and a small group of Spaniards entered Tawantinsuyo (Inca) territory in 1532 at a critical point in the empire's history. A few years before, Inca ruler Huayna Capac had died probably of a European disease that had reached the northern Andes from Panama via trade routes. His two sons, Huascar from Cuzco and Atahualpa from Quito, violently disputed the empire's control. These events considerably favoured the Spanish, who captured Atahualpa by surprise in Cajarmarca. Pizarro executed Atahualpa on charges that he had ordered the death of his half-brother Huascar. Soon after, Manco Inca emerged as the new Andean leader. He organized a large army and unsuccessfully sought to expel the invaders from the region. After a failed siege of Cuzco, Manco Inca retreated with his troops to Vilcabamba, resisting Spanish rule for several decades.

Throughout the colonial period, Amerindian resistance took numerous forms, including armed rebellion, passive resistance, and native religious movements like the Takiy Onkoy (dancing sickness) in the 1560s in Peru.[5] Despite some rebellions, the Spanish were able to establish relative control of most central areas. However, vast frontier territories remained outside colonial rule both in Spanish America and Brazil.

From the first contacts, European colonialism brought world-wide biological and ecological changes. Numerous plants and animals crossed the Atlantic in both directions: tomatoes, potatoes and maize from America and wheat, grapes, coffee and sugar cane from Europe, Africa and Asia. Diseases too were part of the colonial exchange.[6] N. D. Cook (1998) has traced the fragmentary documentary evidence of the impact of European epidemics in the Indies. Smallpox, influenza, measles, typhus and other European illnesses spread and recurred several times during the colonial period, reducing the Amerindian population to nearly 12 per cent of the estimated 30 to 40 million in 1500 (Cook 2000: 317). Unfortunately, European diseases were an unexpected but implacable ally in the colonization of the Americas. Indigenous diseases also took their toll, according to recent research. Two major epidemics in New Spain (Mexico) in 1545 and 1576, referred to as 'cocolitzli' in Nahuatl, may have been indigenous haemorrhagic fevers (Acuña Soto 2002).

INVENTING AMERICA

'All these islands are extremely fertile . . . full of rivers . . . and trees of a thousand different kinds.' Columbus's writings about rich, exotic islands and humble natives were rapidly disseminated throughout Europe. His early 1493 letter to the Catholic monarchs announcing the 'discovery' of the 'New World' was soon translated into Latin (nine editions), Italian (three editions) and German. Like Columbus's letter, many other texts about America circulated amply in Europe. Hernán Cortés's 1520 letter to Charles V described the conquest of a rich and vast empire in central Mexico. Gonzalo Fernández de Oviedo's *Historia general y natural de las Indias* (1535–55) carefully detailed American flora, fauna and native cultures drawing from his personal experience in the Indies as well as several first-hand reports. Epic poems such as Alonso de Ercilla y Zúñiga's *La araucana* (1567–89) and Juan de Castellanos's *Elegías de varones ilustres de Indias* (1589) portrayed Amerindians as idealized, heroic warriors. Early Portuguese writings about Brazil also presented the Americas as a fertile, exotic landscape, including Pero vaz Caminhas's 1500 letter, Pero de Magalhaes Gandavo's *Tratado da terra do Brasil* (*c.*1570) and Gabriel Soares de Sousa's *Tratado descritivo do Brasil em 1587* (1587).

Texts by authors who never set foot in the Americas also proliferated. Two examples were Peter Martir's *Décadas del nuevo mundo* (1493–1525) and López de Gómara's *Historia de las Indias y la conquista de México* (1552). The engraver Theodore de Bry also produced numerous, freely composed images of America (Bucher 1981). Stories and rumours of treasures and cities of gold found fertile ground in a public avid for information about American wonders. At the same time, dreadful tales of cannibalism and savage women emerged. A vivid story of cannibalism is *The True History of his Captivity* (1557), an early account about Brazil by Hans Staden. Cannibalism is also a recurring theme in many chroniclers including André Thévet, Jean Léry and Fray Pedro Simón.

Images and discussions about America proliferated well beyond Iberia. In literature, for example, the New World generated profound reflections on humanity and European civilization in a variety of texts, including Thomas More's *Utopia* (1516), Michel de Montaigne's essay 'On cannibals' (1580), and Shakespeare's *The Tempest* (*c.*1608).

This ample corpus of writing is referred to as colonial discourse by contemporary critics.[7] Presupposing language as the producer of social reality, these texts are considered an integral part of the colonial enterprise, justifying for example the need to civilize Amerindians. This is illustrated by two figures that appear in many New World chronicles: the cannibal and the Amazon. These figures were read as signs that marked Amerindians as savages. Ritual cannibalism was practised by several indigenous cultures. Europeans interpreted these practices as sheer gluttony: an unrestrained appetite for human flesh. One engraving by Theodore de Bry, for example, portrays indigenous men, women and children feasting on human body parts and licking their fingers. The classic myth of female warriors is another colonial characterization that appears in several colonial representations, from Columbus's first-voyage letter to eighteenth-century narratives like *L'Amerique méridionale* (1745) by the French scientist Charles Marie de la Condamine. The erotic and dangerous figure of the Amazon expressed little about American realities. In contrast, it revealed a deep European fear of an inverted social order, including colonial subversion.

Europeans produced an ambivalent image of the Americas as an erotic paradise and a dangerous landscape. Amerindians, in turn, were also ambivalently portrayed either as idealized, uncorrupted beings or as savage beasts. Colonialism tested the limits of language itself. Reading these contradictory and ambivalent documents, it appears that colonialism tends to underscore language's unstable and ambivalent nature. Missionaries, for example, had great difficulties explaining the differences between ritual cannibalism and the consumption of the flesh and blood of Christ in Catholic communion.

The cultural colonization of the Americas cannot be reduced to 'negative' or 'positive' portrayals of its peoples and lands. It runs much deeper. European structures of knowledge were systematically imposed, whereas Amerindian forms of knowledge were either marginalized or suppressed in a process that extended well beyond the colonial period. Oviedo's *Historia general y natural*, for example, offered a comprehensive view of the New World based on the ordering scheme of a classical text, Pliny's *Natural History* (first century AD). At the same time, Amerindian pictograms and other non-alphabetic systems of 'writing' were being ignored, marginalized or destroyed. Numerous Maya codices were burnt by missionaries and only four have survived to the present day (Tedlock 1996: 25).

The 'invention of America' is a far-reaching process by which Western paradigms and disciplines become the hegemonic codes for understanding the history of the hemisphere. This is more than an epistemological quarrel since controlling knowledge is an essential element of colonialism (Mignolo 2000). Colonial discourse, however, did not go unchallenged, as we will see below when we discuss Amerindian and creole intellectual production.

THE COLONIAL COMPLEX

To administer the American colonies, the Spanish created a much more centralized political structure than the Portuguese. Nonetheless, there were common elements between both colonial powers, especially taking into consideration that during several time periods the two countries were politically united (1383–85, 1474–79, 1497–1500 and 1580–1640) (Oliveira Marques 2000: 35). Nonetheless, even during unification, both colonies were run separately and distinctly. From Spain, the Council of Indies oversaw the American colonies. Two main viceroyalties were created, New Spain (Mexico) and Peru, which controlled smaller administrative units, called *audiencias* (i.e. Santo Domingo, Quito, Santa Fe de Bogotá).[8] *Audiencias'* jurisdictions often included several regions divided into *gobernaciones* and Spanish towns. Although the towns or cities were at the lower level of this hierarchical structure, their impact in the colonization of the Americas was substantial. Spanish towns were strategically located adjacent to native populations, mines, trade routes, rivers or ports, composing an intricate network of colonial exploitation that integrated the hinterlands into the Atlantic economy. Town officials were in charge of land distribution. They could also relocate Amerindian populations to secure a labour pool near the town or to expropriate their lands.

Rural colonial Latin America was interconnected to the urban centres and the world economy through several institutions, including the *encomienda*, the *hacienda*, sugar mills, mines, and textile mills (*obrajes*). The *encomienda* was central in the colonial complex. Amerindian communities paid tribute in goods to their Spanish *encomendero* (trustee of tribute), who would sell the products in the local market. They would also work in his agricultural fields (*hacienda*), which supplied local cities and nearby mines. The *encomienda* communities had to work in the mines, sending work crews in a rotating system called *mita* in the Andes. As a result, the *encomienda* granted a small group of people great prestige and power.

Mining was one of the most important sectors of colonial economy. Gold was central in the Caribbean phase of the colonization and later in areas like New Granada. Silver, above all, was the main export of colonial Spanish America. The mines of Potosí and Mexico were large-scale operations that attracted a substantial number of people and created ample circuits of trade. The Potosí mines, for example, drew wheat from Cochabamba, hundreds of mules from Tucumán and Córdoba, and other services and goods from as far away as Lima, leaving at least 60 per cent of the silver in the colony (Bauer 1996: 36).

The Church was a key component of the colonial complex. Besides the evangelizing role, the Church established schools, universities, lay brotherhoods, hospitals, and other social service institutions. Its police role, exercising religious conformity through the Inquisition, cannot be ignored, although there tends to be a general misconception of this institution.[9] The different divisions of the Church were also major players in the colonial economy. They had large *haciendas*, sugar and textile mills, urban properties for rent, and money to lend. The Jesuits in particular were by far the most successful in these worldly enterprises in Spanish America as well as in Brazil.

Portugal's administration of its American colonies was based on its previous experience in Africa and the Atlantic islands. The factory system and the donatory captaincies established early in the sixteenth century only yielded a handful of loosely connected coastal towns supported mainly by the dyewood trade and some sugar mills. Unsatisfied with this situation, the crown appointed Tomé de Sousa as governor-general of Brazil in 1549. Sousa made Salvador the main administrative centre of the colony. Along with Sousa came the Jesuits, an order that shaped Brazil's colonial society more than any other division of the Catholic Church. After their arrival, the Jesuits enjoyed strong royal support, and they became an important bastion of the colonization, assisting the crown in the incorporation of Amerindian populations into the colonial circuit of production and exchange and also founding schools in the colonial cities. As in Spanish America, their intellectual and cultural contributions were substantial, writing histories, studying Amerindian cultures, and composing grammars and vocabularies of indigenous languages. These activities were accompanied by more mundane ones as in Spanish America. They owned large properties, sugar mills, and hundreds of slaves.

The early stages of colonial Brazil depended mainly on the exploitation of dyewood and a growing export agriculture. The dyewood trade was more easily established in part because, for the Tupi-speaking peoples, tree cutting was a male activity. Agriculture, in contrast, was a female activity. As a result, sugar mills, which required intensive labour, had difficulties inducting native populations except through slavery. The Jesuits opposed the planters' efforts to enslave native populations, so the planters sought a labour force elsewhere. The Portuguese African slave trade provided Brazil with the labour pool necessary to increase the sugar export industry to unprecedented dimensions. By 1600 Brazil produced some 10,000 tons of sugar a year (Lockhart and Schwartz 1991: 249). In the late seventeenth century, the French, Dutch and English set up sugar plantations in the Caribbean, significantly affecting Brazil's profits. The staggering colonial economy was alleviated by the discovery of gold in Minas Gerais early in the eighteenth century. Gold production peaked by mid-century. Its impact, however, was significant. It created new settlements inland and reoriented the colony towards Rio de Janeiro, the closest coastal city. The new mining towns had a heterogeneous population, of which well over half the population were blacks and mulattos.

So far we have discussed the colonial complex mainly in terms of its social structures and institutions. This, however, provides a limited vision of the social dynamics, excluding, for instance, the actions and viewpoints of the individuals and groups that formed colonial society. In the following passages we will explore, even if briefly, the colonial society.

Iberian preoccupation with 'racial' purity (*pureza de sangre*), which also included religious conformity (discriminating against Muslims, Jews and new

Christians), would continue in the Americas. For this reason, colonial society was divided into mainly four groups, 'whites', *castas* (*mestizos, mamelucos, mulattos, zambos*), Amerindians and Africans. Their interaction and racial consciousness are a complex story. In *Race Mixture in the History of Latin America*, Magnus Morner shows, for example, that although Amerindians had high legal status, their social status was at the bottom of the scale, except *caciques* and native elites (1967: 60). The Spanish administration tried to maintain separate Amerindian communities from Spanish towns, although in practice their intricate relationship brought them together in many ways. On the whole, even though they were a growing sector of colonial society, mixed-blood people were considered troublemakers, immoral and inferior. They were generally barred from public offices, religious orders, guilds, and other associations. Another important sector of the colonial population was the Africans. Throughout the colonial period about 1.5 million African slaves were imported to Spanish America and 2.5 million to Brazil, most of them during the eighteenth century (Burkholder and Johnson 1990: 119). (For more on race, see Chapter 10.)

For Iberian society urban life was synonymous with civilization. The apex of colonial society – bureaucrats, miners, *encomenderos*, planters or merchants – would establish their residences in the cities. The layout of the colonial city reflected the social hierarchy. Around the main square were usually the church, the municipal and administrative buildings, and the houses of the elite. Further out lived mid-income Spaniards, including local merchants, small farmers, and artisans. Amerindians, free blacks and mulattos lived in the outskirts of the city. Education was provided by the Church, which founded schools in most cities and twenty-five universities. In Brazil, the Jesuits founded schools in several places including Rio, Bahia, Olinda, Recife, São Paulo and São Luiz. The Portuguese, however, did not allow the founding of a university in Brazil, despite several petitions from New World residents.

A prominent feature of Spanish American cities was their convents. These were large enclosures where women would retreat in search of physical protection and spiritual development. One of the largest convents was La Concepción in Lima. It had 1,041 inhabitants, but only 318 were nuns, novices or lay sisters. Most convents, however, housed about 50–100 nuns (Lavrin 1986). Convents reflected their social milieu, and only white women with a dowry or other form of patronage to cover living expenses could enter the convent. Although subordinated to the ecclesiastical hierarchy, these convents were spaces where women enjoyed a certain degree of autonomy within the colonial patriarchal society. From the convents, women produced a great corpus of writing as well as considerable artistic creation. Sor Juana Inés de la Cruz from Mexico and Francisca Josefa del Castillo from New Granada (present-day Colombia) are two well-known writers, but they are not alone, as recent scholarship and editions have shown (Myers 2000; Arenal and Schlau 1989). In Brazil, no female convents were founded until 1677.

In the cities there were also large groups of artisans, silkweavers, blacksmiths, sculptors, masons, carpenters, gold and silver smiths, and others amounting altogether to about 20–40 per cent of the urban population (Socolow 1986). Through guilds and lay brotherhoods an intricate, multi-layered social fabric developed. Their prestige and organization were evident in processions, festivals and other public events. Indians were permitted in several guilds, but not *mestizos* (Socolow 1986: 237). Blacks were for the most part excluded from the guilds. Many slaves and free blacks did work under white artisans, although without ever achieving the same status as other craftsmen. Blacks and mulattos, nonetheless, formed important social groups such as the Nossa Senhora do Rosario dos Pretos and Misericordia, two of the largest black brotherhoods in Brazil.

Not far from the cities were the Amerindian towns. Natives were often resettled to European-style towns to facilitate evangelization and to teach Amerindians to live 'properly' (*en policía*). Despite royal ordinances barring non-natives from Amerindian towns, poor Spaniards, *mestizos* and *mulatos* settled there. The further away from Spanish towns, the greater was the autonomy of Amerindian towns. Some were run by the native elite throughout the colonial period. A parish was established or a rotating priest would visit a few times each year. They still had to pay tribute to their *encomendero* or *corregidor* (Amerindian tax collector). They also had to work for a period of time at the mines, *hacienda* or nearby town. These remote communities were thus integrated into the colonial system, but many aspects of their lives continued according to native customs, including the widespread use of indigenous languages. In Brazil, the areas oriented towards the export economy were more European, including Minas Gerais, despite its large slave population. In the interior and the Amazon basin, where there were less Europeans and slaves, contacts with Amerindians were more constant and *mamelucos* were more accepted. In São Paulo and other areas of the interior colonists adopted many Amerindian crafts, foods, materials and customs. Tupi was also widely spoken in these places (Schwartz 1987: 30).

DEBATING THE CONQUEST

Was the colonization of the Americas just? Could the Spaniards wage war against Amerindians? What rights were Amerindians entitled to? Although the colonization of the 'New World' was built on previous Iberian experiences with non-Christians at home and abroad, the American experience forced Europeans to pose such questions in modern terms. From the Iberian colonial experience emerged the legal tenets that defined humanity in universal terms and the juridical framework that conceived the world as a community of separate nations. This fact allows critics like Walter Mignolo and Enrique Dussel to argue that modernity was not simply handed down from Europe to

America, but rather produced in America or, at least, co-produced by it. This point of view provides a less Eurocentric perspective of world history. Let us look closer at that debate.

The colonial enterprise created a growing, intricate legal corpus which built on previous Iberian experiences. In moral terms, the monarchs of both Spain and Portugal were responsible for the well-being of the indigenous populations. This was expressly stated by the papal sanction of the Treaty of Tordesilles (1494) which divided the Atlantic between Spain and Portugal. Also in 1537, Pope Paul III issued the bull *Sublimis Deus*, which stated that 'the Indians are truly men . . . capable of understanding the Catholic faith . . . [They] are by no means to be deprived of their liberty or possession of their property, even though they be outside of the faith of Jesus Christ' (cited in Hanke 1979: 39). In this context, monarchs were compelled to give attention to Amerindian matters.

The rapid demographic collapse of the native Caribbean population, and the oppressive work in the mines and plantations, soon generated sharp criticism in the Indies and in the peninsula. Dominican missionaries, in particular, opposed the unjust social order that was unravelling. Other orders, like the Franciscans and the Jesuits, sought to protect Amerindian communities and compensate for the souls 'lost' in Europe with the emergence of Protestantism.[10]

One strong critic of the Spanish colonization and the *encomienda* system was the Dominican priest Fray Bartolomé de las Casas (1474–1566), a former *encomendero* himself. Among his writings are the *Historia de Indias* (*c.*1540), a general history of the early stages of the colonization, *De unico vocationis modo* (1537), a treaty rejecting military colonization and advocating a peaceful incorporation of Amerindians, the *Apologética historia sumaria* (1550), a defence of the rationality of Amerindians based on Aristotelian thought, and the *Brevíssima relación de la destrucción de las Indias* (1555), a vivid and somewhat inflated description of the atrocities committed by the Spaniards. Las Casas's efforts were influential in the drafting of the New Laws (1542), which regulated new conquests, outlawed slave raids, and limited the *encomienda* to only two lives, the grantee and his or her heir. These laws were widely opposed in the Indies, especially in Peru, where the *encomenderos* violently refused to accept them. Despite regulations, some families were able to hold *encomiendas* for over a century.

One strong opponent of Las Casas was Juan Ginés de Sepúlveda, a Spanish theologian, whose treatise *Democrates segundo* (*c.*1547) justified the war against Amerindians. Based on Aristotelian thought, Sepúlveda saw four reasons that justified war against Amerindians: (1) natural inferiority; (2) acts against 'nature' (cannibalism, sodomy); (3) protection of the innocent; and (4) holy war. Las Casas's texts had many ripple effects. On the one hand, his sharp criticism of *encomenderos* and local officials allowed the crown to exert greater control over the Indies. On the other hand, his text helped Spanish enemies. The *Brevíssima*, which portrayed Amerindians as innocent and defenceless sheep being devoured and massacred by power-hungry *encomenderos*, soon started circulating in several European countries with vivid illustrations by Theodore de Bry. Protestants found in the *Brevíssima* a good arsenal to defame their Catholic enemies, creating what has been called the 'Black Legend'.

Another noteworthy participant in the debate on the legitimacy of the colonization of the Americas was Fray Francisco de Victoria, a Dominican priest and chair of theology in Salamanca, the most prestigious Spanish university at the time. Victoria, who was consulted on several occasions by Charles V, wrote two lectures on the topic, *De indis* and *De jure belli*. In the first lecture he defended the rights and autonomy of Amerindians and questioned the Pope's jurisdiction over them, a cornerstone of Spanish conquest legislation. If Amerindians do not obey the Spaniards, there is no just case of war against them. The second lecture addressed the legality of war, seen only as a valid recourse in self-defence and to remedy a considerable injustice. Extension of the empire was not a just cause of war. In both cases Victoria's recourse to natural law, *jus gentium*, set important precedents for the modern, universal conception of humanity and international order (Brown Scott 1934). In Brazil, Jesuit writers also addressed these issues. Manuel da Nobrega (1517–74) wrote the *Diálogo sobra a conversão do gentio* around 1556. In this work, Nobrega saw Amerindians as equal to Jews, Greeks, Romans and Portuguese (Haberly 1996: 54).

AMERINDIAN VISIONS

Amerindian thought and intellectual practices were a specific target of colonial officials and missionaries. For policing and evangelizing purposes, Amerindian languages and cultures were persistently studied by missionaries. At the same time, in an effort to 'civilize' Amerindian societies, natives were introduced to Western forms of expression, writing, art, music and drama. As a result, the colonial context brought together native and European cultural practices, yielding a broad range of results including syncretism, hybridism and juxtaposition.[11]

Europeans saw Amerindians' lack of alphabetic writing as a clear sign of cultural inferiority. Amerindians had in fact other forms or writing and transmitting knowledge: pictographic texts and other symbolic systems like the Andean *quipus* as well as a dynamic oral culture (Lienhard 1991). Colonial native intellectuals learned alphabetic writing and combined it with local forms of expression. As a result we have numerous texts in native languages written in alphabetic forms and others with drawings that combine Western perspective with native painting styles (Gruzinski 1992). For a long time Hispanic literary studies neglected this plurilingual and multiform cultural repertoire, focusing more on European-style literature.[12] Recent attention to native forms of expression has pointed out the limits of traditional literary analysis, and the challenges of cultural and linguistic competence to begin understanding the rich archive of post-conquest intellectual production (Boone and Mignolo 1994). As a result, recent approaches to these texts tend to be quite interdisciplinary, drawing on semiotics, anthropology and ethnohistory.

Three important post-conquest native intellectual 'traditions' are the Maya, Nahuatl and Andean. The Maya book *Popol Vuh* is an illustrative example of the problematics we have just discussed. The ancient (*c.*AD 250–750) pictographic book was lost. Around 1550, however, it was transcribed into alphabetic writing by three indigenous nobles from the town of Quiché, in the Guatemala highlands. Written in Quiché-Maya, the *Popol Vuh* (Council Book) tells the story of the Maya from creation to the arrival of the Spaniards in the sixteenth century. On the first page, the Maya writers express their desire to tell their own history, and they state that they have to hide their identity. Why? They now live under Christianity. Other Maya texts are the books called *Chilam Balaam* (Secrets of the Soothsayers) found in the Yucatec towns of Chumayel, Tizimín and Maní. In the *Chilam Balaam* of Chumayel the Spaniards are condemned for destroying everything in their path. *Rabinal Achí*, a Maya drama that circulated orally, was transcribed by the French ethnologist Charles Brasseur in the nineteenth century.

The Nahuatl cultures of central Mexico produced an ample corpus of works during the colonial period, including codices, murals, histories and poems. A significant body of works developed under the auspices of the Franciscan order, which founded a school for the local elite in Tlatelolco, producing intellectual works in Nahuatl, Spanish and Latin. The *Florentine Codex* (1579), for example, is a comprehensive encyclopedia of Mexica (Aztec) history and culture composed of pictograms and Nahuatl text in alphabetic form, continuing the *tlacuilos* practice, which combined painting and writing. Among the works of Tlatelolco alumni are the *Crónica mexicana* (1598) and the Nahuatl text *Crónica mexicayotl* (1609) by Hernando Alvarado Tezozomoc (*c.*1600), grandson of Emperor Moctezuma II; the *Relación de Texcoco* written in the last decades of the sixteenth century by Juan Bautista del Pomar, a *mestizo* descendant from Texcoco rulers; and the *Historia chichimeca* by Fernando de Alva Ixtlilxóchitl (*c.*1578–1648). In addition, there is a rich collection of pre-Hispanic Nahuatl texts known as *cuicatl* – songs, hymns and poems – gathered as the *Cantares mexicanos*, including the works by Netzahualcóyotl, Axayácatl, Moctezuma, Izcoátl and others (Garibay 1954; Bierhorst 1985).

In the Andes native intellectuals also produced a variety of texts in Quechua and Spanish paralleled by a strong oral culture. An Inca vision of the conquest can be found in the *Ynstrucción del Ynga don Diego de Castro Titu Cussi Yupanqui* (1570). Joan de Santacruz Pachacuti Yamqui Salcamaygua, a *curaca* or native lord of Collahuas in the Peruvian highlands, wrote *Relación de antiguedades deste reyno del Piru* (c.1600). Felipe Guamán Poma de Ayala's *El primer nueva corónica y buen gobierno* (1615) is a richly illustrated chronicle of Andean culture and a strong critique of Spanish abuses. Born and raised in Cuzco from an Inca *colla* (princess) and a Spanish *conquistador*, El Inca Garcilaso de la Vega wrote *Comentarios reales de los Incas* (1609, 1617), a history of the Tawantinsuyo empire that stressed the achievements of Quechua culture in arts, philosophy, architecture and government. An important Quechua manuscript from the Huarochirí province in Peru written in the seventeenth century traces the genealogy of Andean deities. There is also a rich tradition of Quechua plays, including two dramas from the eighteenth century, *Ollantay* and the *Tragedia del fin de Atahualpa*.[13]

Spanish chroniclers including missionaries left a considerable record of Andean cultures and languages. Among these works are the *Descripción del Perú* (1553) by Pedro de la Gazca, *Historia natural y moral de las Indias* (1590) by the Jesuit priest José de Acosta, and *La extirpación de la idolatría en el Pirú* (1621) by Pablo Joseph de Arriaga, also a Jesuit. Several Andean grammar books were composed, including the *Grammatica o Arte de la lengua general de los indios de los Reynos* (1560) by Fray Domingo de Santo Tomás. Although we have focused on Quechua texts, there are Aymara, Chibcha and other important cultural productions in the Andean region. Additionally, there is a vast corpus of texts or *memoriales* produced by Amerindian individuals and communities in Spanish for legal, religious and other purposes which needs to be taken into consideration as an integral part of the documentation expressing the native experience of colonialism. Their competence in and use of the legal and other colonial discourses do not preclude their native perspective.

CRIOLLOS, THE ENLIGHTENMENT, AND EIGHTEENTH-CENTURY REFORMS

Early in the sixteenth century, European writers living in the Americas expressed a strong admiration for the land, the cities the *conquistadors* and their descendants had founded, and their 'heroic' deeds in the military campaigns. Far from the metropolis, colonial societies soon developed a regional sense of a shared history, a vernacular language, and local customs. Here we will discuss the consciousness developed by the white elite (*criollos*), expressing a proto-national identity, key in the nineteenth-century independence movements and national projects, although very problematic in terms of its selective process of appropriation and suppression of metropolitan, indigenous and African cultural elements.[14] It is perhaps the suppression of these other visions that has made the early histories of the Latin American nations so conflictive.

From the beginning, Europeans expressed that American realities needed a new language. For Fernández de Oviedo, no European fruit could be compared to the pineapple. Indigenous words filled daily experience, while a distant metropolitan speech changed at a different pace, leaving the Americas with a language new and archaic at the same time. Ironically, Amerindian cultures, subjugated and violently exploited, would be at the same time idealized and exalted by white intellectuals. For example, Alonso de Ercilla y Zúñiga's epic poem *La araucana* (1569–89) describes with great pride the heroic plight of the Mapuches in Chile. In the seventeenth century, in his *Teatro de virtudes políticas*, Carlos Sigüenza y Góngora (1645–1700) portrayed pre-Hispanic Mexica leaders as exemplary rulers for the incoming viceroy. His sympathy for the ancient rulers, however, did not extend to the contemporary natives, as can be seen in his 'Alboroto y motín de los indios en México', a description of the urban riot of 1692 in Mexico City.

Spanish society invested enormous wealth and energy in the new-founded cities, seeking to emulate the metropolis: cathedrals, convents, palaces, schools, universities and mansions. Artistic and literary creations were also part of this symbolic economy that validated creole society (Mazzotti 2000). Colonial cities were praised in Bernardo de Balbuena's poem *Grandeza Mexicana* (1604) and in numerous paintings including Gregorio Vázquez de Arce y Ceballos's depiction of Santa Fe de Bogotá (*c.*1680) or Cristóbal de Villalpando's panoramic description of Mexico City in the eighteenth century. Iconography and narratives related to local saints and patrons, such as Santa Rosa de Lima, the Virgin of Guadalupe in Mexico, or the Virgin of Copacabana in the Andes, can also be seen in the context of the symbolic inscription of the colonies in the early modern Catholic world order. This self-fashioning of creole society, however, cannot be seen isolated from the constant interpellations by imperial policies, such as religious conformity enforced through the Inquisition, legislative acts, fiscal and economic regulations, and the like.

During the second half of the eighteenth century, a series of reforms instituted by the new Bourbon dynasty in Spain and by the Prime Minister Marquis of Pombal in Portugal would have a long-lasting impact on both colonies, although in slightly different ways. The Bourbon and Pombaline programmes sought to make the colonies more efficient and productive. For this purpose a series of fiscal, economic and political reforms were designed and implemented. Among the measures taken was the expulsion of the Jesuits from Brazil (1759) and Spanish America (1767) whose power and independence rivalled regalist policies. From the creoles' point of view, one significant difference between these reforms was that whereas the Spanish crown gave preference to European-born Spaniards in newly established offices and city councils, the Portuguese did not exclude creoles in their new measures. The Spanish measures were greatly resented by creole intellectuals. In contrast, the unity of the Portuguese metropolis and colony was strengthened.

The administrative reorientation of the colonies was a product of the new social and political thoughts of the Enlightenment. The Spanish crown's support of Alexander von Humboldt's scientific expedition illustrates the modernizing, albeit colonial, spirit of the reforms (Pratt 1992). The ideas of the French philosophers, however, were adopted and put to use in many other ways by creole intellectuals (Higgins 2000). Scientific and literary groups formed in both Spanish America and Brazil (Soto Arango *et al.* 1995). The creole intellectuals discussed literature, botany, history and politics. In Spanish America, they produced numerous periodical publications, and they brought news from the American and French Revolutions. In Brazil similar groups also emerged in Rio, Bahia and Minas Gerais (Carvalho 1984). Although an intellectual group from Minas Gerais was charged for conspiring against the government in 1789, these groups' contributions to either the independence or modernization of Brazil were not as significant as in Spanish America. Instead it was the short exile of João VI of Portugal in Brazil (1808–21) which brought dramatic changes including the founding of schools, libraries and the first printing press (Haberly 1996: 66).

Although many enlightened ideas were appropriated by creole intellectuals to articulate an anti-colonial discourse, they also resented and disputed many prejudiced claims by European writers and scientists. Reynal, La Condamine, Buffon, de Pauw, Hegel and others wrote about the Americas as an inferior or degenerate land where fruits, animals and people lacked the vigour of the Old World. Exiled in Bologna, Jesuit Fray Francisco Clavijero, among other creoles, responded to these outrageous claims. His *Storia antica del Messico* (1770) strongly disputed the European allegations (Gerbi 1973). Unlike his creole antecedents, Clavijero's writing about the classical Mexican past did not discriminate against contemporary indigenous peoples (Pagden 1987: 76).

Altogether, colonial Latin American intellectual activity generated a considerable and varied collection of works: histories, literary and artistic works, philosophical and scientific treatises. This large creation, however varied, came mainly from the literate, dominant society, an elite from or strongly tied to the colonial civil and religious bureaucracy. Colonial society was, in a sense, a city ruled by the men of letters, as Uruguayan critic Angel Rama suggested in his seminal work *La ciudad letrada* (1984). This close relation to the bureaucratic apparatus produced a corpus of writing greatly influenced by legal discourses and rhetoric (González Echeverría 1990). Notwithstanding the historical contexts and institutions that circumscribed intellectual production in colonial Ibero-America, many works were highly critical of colonial society. It was most often expressed in veiled forms, since the political climate of Counter-Reformation Spain was hardly tolerant of open criticism. Censure was a reality (Friede 1959), and the Church kept an index of forbidden books. Open criticism could be dangerous, as in the case of Father Antônio Vieira (1608–97), an outspoken Jesuit who was pursued by the Inquisition. In Mexico, Sor Juana Inés de la Cruz was reprimanded for writing about theology, a domain restricted to men. Despite censorship, books circulated clandestinely, as Irving Leonard has documented in *Books of the Brave* (1949). Censure could also be bypassed by clever language games and ambivalences. Through satire authors like the poet Juan de Valle y Caviedes were able to denounce the hypocrisy of colonial society. There was also recourse to popular and accepted genres to camouflage forbidden matters. Juan Rodriguez Freile's seventeenth-century chronicle *El carnero* intertwines stories of witchcraft, adultery and debauchery with a historical narrative of the conquest and colonization of New Granada. A fictive indigenous narrator allows Alonso Carrió de la Bandera's *Lazarillo de ciegos caminantes* (1775) to express openly and humorously his opinions of colonial society as he travels from Montevideo to Lima.

On the whole, from the colonial context emerged an intellectual production that cannot be well understood using the conceptual frameworks of European literature (i.e. Renaissance, Baroque). There are resemblances, but they cannot be reduced to copies. Through satire, irony, parody and other means, creole intellectuals appropriated and transformed metropolitan aesthetic forms, creating what has been described as an American Baroque (Moraña 1994). It is nonetheless a cultural tradition that cannot break away completely from metropolitan aesthetics, since colonialism runs through it. There is, however, always room for contestation. In this sense, Cuban critic Roberto Fernández Retamar argues that Latin American intellectual production is like Caliban, Shakespeare's enslaved character in *The Tempest*. Caliban uses against his master the language he was forced to learn. By this virtue, Iberian tongues, languages of colonialism, became creole, Amerindian, African and *mestizos*.

NOTES

1 However, Cuba and Puerto Rico were to remain under Iberian control until 1898. In a sense, the end of Iberian rule did not eliminate colonialism, given the internal colonization campaigns after independence and the neo-colonial relations that emerged from industrial capitalism. Although not discussed in this chapter, the French, Dutch and English also took part in the colonization of the Americas in places such as Haiti, Dominique, Surinam, Guyana, Belize and other areas. I thank Bryan McCann for his useful comments with regard to this chapter.

2 Pre-Hispanic population estimates are still being debated. Estimates have ranged from 12 to 57 million inhabitants, although the lower figure is presently considered too low. See Lockhart and Schwartz (1991), Bethell (1984), and Burkholder and Johnson (1990).

3 The legal justification for the colonization was based, in part, in the legislation for Muslim communities (*aljamas*) under Spanish rule (Seed 1995: 85).

4   Estimates vary because of scant and contradictory documentation (Cook 1998: 23).

5   In the eighteenth century, for example, two major indigenous revolts took place. In 1712 in Chiapas, organized around a native cult to the Virgin, twenty-one Maya towns took control of the highland region for several months and sought to re-establish the region's autonomy. At the end of the century, another rebellion took place around Cuzco, Peru. Protesting against Spanish abuses and seeking to restore the Inca empire, the rebels gained control of a vast region in the highland Andes of Peru and Bolivia. The rebel leader, José Gabriel Condorcanqui, changed his name to Tupac Amaru, invoking the sixteenth-century Inca ruler executed by the Spaniards in 1572. Two other examples are the Comunero (1780) revolt in New Granada and the rebellion in Haiti (1791).

6   See Cosby (1972).

7   For a discussion of European visions of the Americas, see Todorov (1984), Hulme (1986), Greenblatt (1993) and Rabasa (1993).

8   In the eighteenth century two new viceroyalties were created: New Granada and Rio de la Plata.

9   Without doubt, the number of people burned and tortured by the Inquisition was exaggerated as part of the 'Black Legend' propagated by Spain's rival nations. Still, the Inquisition itself helped towards this image. Terror was a policing tactic, instilling fear as a deterrent. See Splendiani *et al.* (1997) and Kamen (1998).

10 See Baudot (1995) for the Franciscan project in the Americas.

11 Cultural mixture is a much-debated topic in Latin American studies. See for instance García Canclini (1989) and Gruzinski (2000).

12 For a recent discussion of the omissions of Hispanic literary studies see Bolaños and Verdesio (2002).

13 García Bedoya (2000) provides a comprehensive survey of Andean colonial texts.

14 We use the word *criollo* to designate the 'whites' born in the Americas. This word, however, was only used in this sense towards the end of the colonial period in Spanish America.

REFERENCES AND SELECTED FURTHER READING

Acuña Soto, R. *et al.* 2002: *Emerging Infectious Diseases*. Forthcoming.

Adorno, R. 1996: Cultures in contact. In G. González Echeverría and E. Pupo-Walker (eds), *Cambridge History of Latin American Literature* Vol. 1. Cambridge: Cambridge University Press, 33–57.

Arenal, E. and Schlau, S. 1989: *Untold Sisters: Hispanic Nuns in Their Own Works*. Albuquerque, NM: University of New Mexico Press.

Baudot, G. 1995: *Utopia and History in Mexico*. Niwot, CO: University of Colorado Press.

Bauer, A. 1996: The colonial economy. In L. Hoberman and S. Socolow (eds), *The Countryside in Colonial Latin America*. Albuquerque, NM: University of New Mexico Press, 19–48.

Bethell, L. 1984: A note on the Native American population on the eve of the European invasion. In L. Bethell (ed.), *The Cambridge History of Latin America* Vol 1. Cambridge: Cambridge University Press, 45–6.

Bierhorst, J. 1985: *Cantares mexicanos*. Stanford, CA: Stanford University Press.

Bolaños, A. and Verdesio, G. (eds) 2002: *Colonialism Past and Present*. Albany, NY: State University of New York Press.

Boone, E. and Mignolo, W. (eds) 1994: *Writing without Words*. Durham, NC: Duke University Press.

Brown Scott, J. 1934: *The Spanish Origin of International Law: Francisco de Victoria and his Law of Nations*. Oxford: Clarendon Press.

Bucher, B. 1981: *Icon and Conquest*. Chicago: University of Chicago Press.

Burkholder, M. and Johnson, L. 1990: *Colonial Latin America*. New York: Oxford University Press.

Carvalho, R. 1984: *Pequena história da literatura brasileira*. Belo Horizonte: Editora Itatiaia.

Colon, C. 1992: *Textos y documentos completos*, ed. de Consuelo Varela. Madrid: Alianza editorial.

Cook, N. D. 1998: *Born to Die: Disease and New World Conquest*. Cambridge: Cambridge University Press.

Cook, N. D. 2000: Epidemias y dinámica demográfica. In Franklin Pease (ed.), *Historia General de America Latina*, Vol. II. Paris: UNESCO, 301–18.

Cosby, A. 1972: *The Columbian Exchange*. Westport, CT: Greenwood Publishing.

Dussel, E. 1995: *The Invention of the Americas*. New York: Continuum.

Fernández Retamar, R. 1974: *Calibán: apuntes sobre la cultura en nuestra América*. México: Editorial Diogenes.

Friede, J. 1959: La censura española del siglo XVI y los libros de historia de América. *Revista historia de América* 47, 45–95.

García Bedoya, C. 2000: *La literatura peruana en el período de estabilización colonial*. Lima: Universidad Nacional Mayor de San Marcos.

García Canclini, N. 1989: *Culturas híbridas*. Mexico: Grijalbo.

Garibay, A. M. 1954: *Historia de la literatura náhuatl*, 2 vols. Mexico: Porrúa.

Gerbi, A. 1973: *The Dispute of the New World*. Pittsburgh, PA: University of Pittsburgh Press.

González Echevarría, R. 1990: *Myth and Archive*. Cambridge: Cambridge University Press.

Greenblatt, S. (ed.) 1993: *New World Encounters*. Berkeley: University of California Press.

Gruzinski, S. 1992: *Painting the Conquest*. Paris: UNESCO.

Gruzinski, S. 2000: *El pensamiento mestizo*. Barcelona: Ediciones Paidos.

Haberly, D. 1996. Colonial Brazilian literature. In G. González Echeverría and E. Pupo-Walker (eds), *Cambridge History of Latin American Literature* Vol. 3. Cambridge: Cambridge University Press, 47–68.

Hanke, L. 1979: *Selected Writings*. Tempe, AR: Center for Latin American Studies.

Higgins, A. 2000: *Constructing the Criollo Archive*. West Lafayette, IN: Purdue University Press.

Hulme, P. 1986: *Colonial Encounters*. New York: Methuen.

Kamen, H. 1998: *The Spanish Inquisition*. New Haven, CT: Yale University Press.

Lavrin, A. 1986: Female religious. In L. Hoberman and S. Socolow (eds), *Cities and Society in Colonial Latin America*. Albuquerque: University of New Mexico Press, 165–95.

Leonard, I. 1949: *Books of the Brave*. Cambridge, MA: Harvard University Press.

Lienhard, M. 1991: *La voz y su huella*. Hanover, NH: Ediciones del Norte.

Lockhart, J. and Schwartz, S. 1991: *Early Latin America*. Cambridge: Cambridge University Press.

Mazzotti, J. A. (ed.) 2000: *Agencias criollas*. Pittsburgh, PA: Instituto Internacional de Literatura Iberoamericana.

Mignolo, W. 2000: *Local Histories, Global Designs*. Princeton, NJ: Princeton University Press.

Moraña, M. 1994: *Relecturas del Barroco de Indias*. Hanover, NH: Ediciones del Norte.

Mörner, M.1967: *Race Mixture in the History of Latin America*. Boston: Little and Brown.

Myers, C. 2000: Crossing boundaries: defining the field of female religious writing in colonial Latin America. *Colonial Latin American Review* 9, 2, 151–65.

Oliveira Márques, A. 2000: El mundo ibérico. In F. Pease (ed.), *Historia general de América Latina* Vol. 2. Paris: UNESCO, 33–48.

Pagden, A. 1987: Identity formation in Spanish America. In N. Cany and A. Pagden (eds), *Colonial Identity in the Atlantic World*. Princeton, NJ: Princeton University Press, 51–93.

Pratt, M. L. 1992: *Imperial Eyes*. New York: Routledge.

Rabasa, J. 1993: *Inventing America: Spanish Historiography and the Formation of Eurocentrism*. Norman: University of Oklahoma Press.

Rama, A. 1984: *La ciudad letrada*. Hanover, NH: Ediciones del Norte.

Schwartz, S. 1987: Formation of a colonial identity in Brazil. In N. Cany and A. Pagden (eds), *Colonial Identity in the Atlantic World*. Princeton, NJ: Princeton University Press, 15–92.

Seed, P. 1995: *Ceremonies of Possession*. Cambridge: Cambridge University Press.

Socolow, S. 1986: Introduction. In L. Hoberman and S. Socolow (eds), *Cities and Society in Colonial Latin America*. Albuquerque: University of New Mexico Press, 3–18.

Soto Arango, D. *et al.* (eds) 1995: *La Ilustración en América colonial*. Madrid: Consejo Superior de Investigaciones Científicas.

Splendiani, A. M. *et al.* 1997: *Cincuenta años de inquisición en el Tribunal de Cartagena de Indias*, 4 vols. Bogotá: Instituto Colombiano de Cultura Hispánica.

Tedlock, D. 1996: *Popol Vuh*. New York: Touchstone.

Todorov, T. 1984: *The Conquest of America*. New York: Harper and Row.

4

'Civilization and barbarism'

Philip Swanson

The year 1845 was a key one in the development of Latin American thought. It was the year of publication of a seminal work by Argentina's Domingo Faustino Sarmiento, a book which came to be popularly known as *Facundo* and which bore the subtitle commonly quoted as *Civilización y barbarie*. In this phrase was crystallized one of the principal concerns affecting Latin American identities and nationhoods after independence; in it also was born a polemic that would rage throughout the rest of the nineteenth and early twentieth centuries and would indeed cast its shadow over much of the subcontinent's thinking and writing up to the present day. The term 'civilization and barbarism' essentially encapsulates an anxiety about the state and direction of the relatively newly independent Latin American nations as they sought to consolidate a precarious sense of order, progress and modernity (usually associated with the emerging urban metropolises) in the face of a perceived threat of instability from the supposedly wild, untamed, chaotic, native masses (associated largely with the undeveloped interior).

Of course, with hindsight the opposition implied in the idea of civilization-versus-barbarism can be seen as a highly problematic one, an opposition which is not necessarily 'natural' but rather a reflection of the particular interests of certain elite social groups. To be sure, the seemingly neutral concept of 'independence' already betrays, in the Latin American context, this ambivalence or inexactitude. It is not the purpose of this chapter to trace the historical background to the independence movements and battles nor to give an account of the nation-building projects and struggles that followed independence (for a brief account, see Chapter 2). What is plain, though, is that 'independence' is a selective term. Yes, independence meant the ejection of the Catholic European monarchy and the establishment of republican self-rule (except at first in Brazil, where there was a transition to a constitutional monarchy, which nonetheless, despite certain tensions, smoothed the way to relatively representative government too). But did this really mean independence for ordinary people? While it would be wrong to deny the political idealism behind the push for independence, it is nevertheless clearly the case that a key driving force behind it, and more especially behind its consolidation, was the desire for privilege on the part of the *criollo* or European-descended creole elite. In a sense, independence was about securing the authority of the creole (as opposed to European) elites in their own land, to put control of wealth and trade in the hands of an American-born ruling class. And so, societal structures did not necessarily change with independence – the break with the Spanish crown did not mean a complete break with tradition. The discourse of freedom held only limited significance in a region still characterized by extreme social hierarchy, near-feudal agrarian systems, racial division and even, in some parts, slavery. Not surprisingly, instability and conflict quickly became the offshoot of independence, and it is from this antagonistic situation that the apparent dichotomy of civilization-versus-barbarism is engendered.

The picture is a complex one, and often varied. For instance, Brazil, as has been suggested, went down a different path, and Chile, for example, managed to create a harmonious state early on. Edwin Williamson (1992) offers an excellent and accessible account of the 'quest for order' that characterized post-independence Latin America, and the reader is referred there for more detail. The main area of initial contention to be considered here is Argentina, for this would become the conceptual fulcrum for the many theories and debates that would proliferate around the notions of nation and identity in the subcontinent. Widespread arguments between liberals and conservatives in the area now known as Argentina soon coalesced into a fundamental conflict between centralism and regionalism or federalism. Basically, there was a series of wars between the 1820s and the 1870s between so-called *unitarios* or Unitarians (often liberal intellectuals who favoured a centralized state run from the great port of Buenos Aires) and Federalists (often landowners or ranchers who preferred a decentralized system of semi-autonomous provinces that would underpin their own local power). The former were pro-European and favoured progress through modernization on the model of Great Britain or France, while the latter were Catholic, traditionalist and jealous of the urban elite and their foreign allies. Unsurprisingly, in time, the former would come to be broadly associated with the forces of 'civilization' and the latter with the forces of 'barbarism'.

A major figure who rose to power in this conflict was Juan Manuel de Rosas, a big boss or *caudillo* from the provinces who eventually assumed full dictatorial powers (1829–33, 1833–52). Rosas relied at first on *gaucho* fighters from the interior, but soon developed a mass movement of support. With the aid of the organization La Mazorca, run by his wife, a huge and hysterical personality cult was developed behind Rosas, and his power was cemented via fanaticism, terror and the expulsion of opponents. Rosas did eventually fall from power (he actually fled to England and died near Southampton in 1877). Not long afterwards, the liberals managed – with some hiccups – to realize their unitarian dream with Buenos Aires becoming the capital of a united republic under President Bartolomé Mitre (who ruled from 1862 to 1868). He was succeeded by Domingo Faustino Sarmiento himself. However, many would argue that the dangerous populist personality cult of the dictator inaugurated by Rosas left its mark on much subsequent Argentine history, finding echoes in, for example, Peronism, the fascination with Evita, the nationalist fervour encouraged by the military dictatorship during Argentina's home soccer World Cup victory in 1978, and the misplaced patriotic fanaticism of the invasion of the Malvinas or Falkland Islands sponsored by General Galtieri in 1982.

Sarmiento's essay *Facundo* was basically a bitter and blistering attack on Rosas's regime, told via the story of another corrupt and violent federalist *caudillo*, Facundo Quiroga. It came to be seen as espousing the values of 'civilization' connected to the sophisticated urban centre that Buenos Aires was thought to be, a city that was a port, open to the ocean route linking Argentina with Europe and its enlightened values; and it came to be seen as attacking the ignorance and 'barbarism' of the provinces, of the vast *pampas* and its *gaucho* inhabitants. The idea grew that only by defeating barbarism and installing the values of civilization could Argentina (and Latin America as a whole) genuinely move forward and become real nations like the USA.

Even more crude was the version of Rosas's era conveyed by Sarmiento's friend Esteban Echeverría in his short piece of satirical prose *El matadero* (1838). This piece is recommended to students, as it is rather more readable than *Facundo* and, despite its extremism, gives a sense of liberal, unitarian feeling. It presents the Rosas regime via the none-too-subtle allegorical setting of a slaughterhouse (the meaning of the title), complete with gruesome butchers in traditional provincial dress (echoes of *caudillos*), a sort-of-grotesque master butcher who exercises absolute power in the '*pequeña república*' (mini-republic) of the abattoir (a clear stand-in for Rosas), and assorted vile, stinking, sweaty labourers wallowing in blood and filth and scrapping over animals' innards (Rosas's followers, even the *gauchos*?): 'simulacro en pequeño era éste del modo bárbaro con que se ventilan en nuestro país las cuestiones y los derechos individuales y sociales' (this was a microcosm of the barbaric manner in which matters concerning individual and social issues and rights are aired in our country) (Echeverría 1977: 144, 148). The masses are meanwhile clearly associated with the passivity of the cattle who plod docilely to slaughter. However, one brave bull, said to be as stubborn and aloof as a unitarian, stands out and resists – its eventual capture and castration equalling the cruel emasculation of decent liberal values. Lest the message has been missed, Echeverría has a real-life Unitarian turn up. Civilized and elegantly turned out, his language and appearance contrast with the ritualistic sloganizing and conformist sporting of pro-Rosas symbols that characterize the others. In an obvious parallel with the fate of the fiercely independent and masculine bull, this man 'with balls', who thinks for himself, dies in a fit of apopletic rage when his torturers strip him and thus metaphorically castrate his dignity and humanity. Indeed, as the mob prepare him for torture, he is 'atado en cruz' (159), like Jesus on the Cross, a moral superior and potential saviour betrayed by a savage and hypocritical society.

Echeverría's own values are summed up in his *Dogma socialista* of 1837, though his concept of *socialismo* is really closer to the idea of 'sociability', that is the idea of a fair and functioning mutually respectful and socially cohesive society. In fact, this is the sort of doctrine behind Sarmiento's thinking. *Facundo* has been unfairly caricatured as an elitist rant, when really it is simply arguing that any system of government not based on fairness and consensus is akin to barbarism. In fact, despite his seeming slating of the *gauchos*, Sarmiento's prose cannot hide an admiration for their proudly held traditions. There is, then, an element of doubt or uncertainty behind Sarmiento's grand gestures, a feature that would characterize much of the debate in literature on civilization and barbarism in the future. And the ambivalence remains. Buenos Aires today celebrates *gaucho* and working-class tango culture, yet Sarmiento's mausoleum is the only one signposted in Buenos Aires's prestigious Recoleta cemetery – but with one final irony: Facundo Quiroga is buried just across the way.

One immediate legacy of Sarmiento was, though, the unfortunate association of the *gaucho* with barbarism. This position soon came under revision. Indeed gauchesque writing, especially poetry, had been popular for some time. It was not, in fact, *gaucho* literature as such but very much poetry and other literary forms written by educated city-dwellers generally who sought to capture the customs or, in a more romantic vein, the mood of the *gaucho*'s life. Even Sarmiento was influenced by European Romanticism and Echeverría is considered the father of Romanticism in Latin America. Moreover, the *gaucho* was effectively beginning to disappear as a type: many had been wiped out in the frontier wars against the 'Indians' or indigenous peoples against whom they had been conscripted to fight; and, in any case, their traditional way of life was being erased by the modernization of the *pampa* in the name of progress. The gauchesque increasingly became seen as a means of preserving dying *gaucho* tradition. The climax to this trend was undoubtedly the publication in the later nineteenth century of the dramatic book-length adventure in poetic form, *El gaucho Martín Fierro* (1872 and 1879) by José Hernández. The classic of Argentine literature, *Martín Fierro* rescues the *gaucho* from the image of lawless barbarian and depicts him sympathetically, exposing above all his abuse at the hands of society. This seems to represent an inversion of the civilization-versus-barbarism ethic: now the peaceful rural-dweller and his own civilization have been destroyed by the capricious and chaotic policies of central government. The central contention of the poem seems to be that if the *gaucho* is seen as a lawless element, it is precisely because society has forced a good people beyond the pale:

> Y atiendan la relación
> que hace un gaucho perseguido,
> que padre y madre ha sido
> empeñoso y diligente,
> y sin embargo la gente
> lo tiene por un bandido.

(You should understand why the *gauchos* become persecuted, for even though they have been hard-working and diligent parents, people cast them as outlaws.) (lines 109–14)

This is the story of Martín, a decent man, who through no fault of his own gets into trouble with a species of small-town politician and is banished to the frontier to fight in the war against the Indians. It is precisely because he is law-abiding and trusts authority that he is undone:

> Juyeron los más matreros
> Y lograron escapar.
> Yo no quise disparar,
> Soy manso y no había por qué,
> Muy tranquilo me quedé
> Y ansí me dejé agarrar.

(Some fugitives got away and managed to escape. I didn't want to run off, I'm meek and had no reason to run, so I stayed there quite calmly – and that's how I got caught.) (lines 313–18)

Martín loses his wife and family and his home is in ruins. Eventually, he breaks his guitar – the symbol of the essence of his being as a *gaucho*, the source of his instinctive and traditional form of *gaucho* self-expression through song. Yet, if this seems a radical reversal of Sarmiento's perceived position, it is also a deeply conservative reaction against the liberal project of progress. Much of the poem is really an act of preservation of a disappearing way of life. Hernández's aim, he explained in a letter, was to 'retratar, en fin, lo más fielmente que me fuera posible, con todas sus especialidades propias, ese tipo original de nuestras pampas, ... tan erróneamente juzgado muchas veces y que, al paso que avanzan las conquistas de la civilización, va perdiéndose casi por completo' (portray, in short, as faithfully as possible, and with all his special characteristics, this originary man of our pampa lands, ... who has often been so wrongly judged and who, as the ravages of civilization advance, is almost completely disappearing).[1] Part II of the poem was published seven years after the first and underscores the lack of real radicalism. The tone is more didactic now and Martín's apparent return to civilization is held up as an example to other *gauchos* who should learn to integrate with the new society. Even though the mistreatment of the *gauchos* continues to be asserted in Part II, implicit in it is the assumption that the *gaucho*'s ills are at least in part due to his own anti-social tendencies. The era of the *gaucho* is over and adaptation is the only way forward. This is really a similar awkward ambivalence to that visible in Sarmiento, an ambivalence that was to repeat itself later in the twentieth century when the *gaucho* genre was revisited and the topic of civilization and barbarism spread more widely in Spanish American literature.

In Brazil meanwhile there was a parallel Romantic fascination with figure of the Indian. Given the differential path of independence here, the need for a national literature to reflect national identity emerged more slowly. But when it did, it came in the guise of Romanticism. Hence the Indians became emblematic of national identity because they were authentically Brazilian yet still distant and exotic, unlike the uncomfortably close non-native Africans who had been imported as slaves. Effectively *indianismo* was escapist literature with not much real social content and often no *real* social referent: the images of Indianist literature owe as much to Henry Wadsworth Longfellow, James Fenimore Cooper and François René Chateaubriand as they do to Brazilian social reality. However, the nation's greatest romantic poet, Antônio Gonçalves Dias (1823–64), probably had some contact with the indigenous people and even compiled a Tupi dictionary. When the adjective 'bárbaro' is used in his poetry, it seems to suggest innocent primitivism rather than barbarism as such. For example, a poem like 'I-Juca-Pirama', on the surface at least, is written, with its Tupi title, from an Indian perspective. It deals with cannibalistic sacrifice in a rather matter-of-fact way: there is little sense of wonderment or repulsion here. At the same time the colourful *costumbrismo* of the 'festival Timbira' does imply an outsider's gaze. But when the Indian chieftan surprisingly sets free his captive, it is not done out of a more 'advanced' society's notion of pity, but because the prisoner's pleading for his life means that the chief does not want to eat a coward, for cowards die without the recompense of the gods. Of course, the released Indian prisoner is cursed by his shamed father and goes on to live in exile and silence. Indeed exile and nostalgia (echoing the traditional Portuguese theme of '*saudades*'), both personal and in the form of longing for the homeland, are important features of Gonçalves Dias's poetry, as in his most famous poem 'Canção do exílio'. But pride in the potential of the nation is also strong, as in 'O gigante de pedra', where Brazil is portrayed as a sleeping giant which will one day awake and surprise the world. The national spirit evoked in Gonçalves Dias, then, reveals some inconsistencies not so different from those of the gauchesque, but more laced with fantasy and poetic lyricism.

The major Romantic novelist of Brazil was José de Alencar. Like Gonçalves Dias before him, he too failed to finish an Indianist epic in verse, but wrote a variety of novels often regarded as the basis for Brazilian national literature. In this sense, there is another link with Spanish America, for a number of Brazilian romantic novels were sentimental fictions similar to a series of novels in Spanish which have more recently come to be regarded as foundational in their own way. Doris Sommer's basic contention in her *Foundational Fictions* is that the mid-century vogue for novels about young lovers seeking each other across class, regional or racial divides was a projection of a desire for nation-building and national conciliation. Her concern is:

> to locate an erotics of politics, to show how a variety of novel national ideals are all ostensibly grounded in 'natural' heterosexual love and in the marriages that provided a figure for apparently nonviolent consolidation during internecine conflicts at midcentury. Romantic passion, on my reading, gave a rhetoric for the hegemonic projects in Gramsci's sense of conquering the antagonist through mutual interest, or 'love', rather than through coercion. And the amorous overtones of 'conquest' are quite appropriate, because it was civil society that had to be wooed and domesticated after the creoles had won their independence. (1991: 6)[2]

This implies a more benign interpretation of the civilization-versus-barbarism debate. However, if Alencar's *O Guaraní* (1857) projects a sort of ideal world of harmony between Indians and Portuguese, his *Iracema* (1865) offers a less promising vision. In the latter work, the Indian Princess Iracema is forced to abandon her community to pursue her love with the white man Martim. Though some commentators detect an optimistic note in the birth of their son Moacir, who may represent the future of an authentic (mixed-race) Brazil, the relationship with Martim becomes problematic and Iracema dies as a result of the birth. Is this meaningful transculturation or a process of assimiliation or loss?[3] The Argentine José Mármol's *Amalia* (1851), meanwhile, is a pretty clear standard civilization-versus-barbarism novel aimed against a despotic Rosas, while Bartolomé Mitre's *Soledad* (Solitude, 1847) reveals an ambiguous idealizing of the barbarian as in other works of the period. Disappointment is at the core of the Cuban novel *Cecilia Valdés* (1882) by Cirilo Villaverde: in this anti-slavery work, the lovers are unable to overcome the racial barrier that separates them. However, Colombian Jorge Isaacs's *María* (1867), by far the most popular of the mid-century sentimental romances, is often seen as giving a kind of utopian picture of Latin American life as manifested in the consensual community of the *hacienda* or plantation. This is the story of an orphaned girl brought up on her uncle's estate who falls in love with her more upscale cousin Efraín. But, though their marriage is sanctioned, María succumbs to disease and dies before it can take place. Thus the fantasy of national conciliation is allowed, while the reality of social division holds sway in practice.

These narratives, then, are as uncertain as the liberal political ideology behind them, struggling as it did between privilege and representation, social order and freedom, outward-looking modernization and inward-looking national identification. One important point to be made, though, is the link between literature and history. One of Sommer's starting points is Benedict Anderson's famous establishment of 'continuities between nation-building and print communities formed around newspapers and novels'.[4] And, following Pedro Henríquez Ureña, she notes the long list of Hispano-American writers who became presidents of their country[5] (those mentioned here include Mitre, Sarmiento and below Gallegos, while others like Hernández and Mármol held political office; most recently the acclaimed below-mentioned author Mario Vargas Llosa ran for the Peruvian presidency in 1990). Literature is not, then, separate from history but an important part of the project of forging history. Literature is part of the nation-building enterprise, and writers, for Sommer, were driven 'by the need to fill in a history that would help establish the legitimacy of the emerging nation and by the opportunity to direct that history toward a future ideal' (1991: 7).

This somewhat confused legitimizing aim mixed with national ideals was not easy to achieve, and, unsurprisingly, the civilization-versus-barbarism polemic strongly reasserted itself in the literature of the early twentieth century, in particular in the so-called Regionalist novel (see Chapter 5). From the later nineteenth century onwards, the modernizing project took hold in much of Latin America and its ideological justification was further reinforced by the rise of Positivism. The philosophy of the Frenchman Auguste Comte, Positivism was a kind of religion of science (sometimes called the Religion of Humanity: that is, rather than that of a deity) and its application in some parts of Latin America encouraged the view that only a small educated elite could build the path to progress. This contributed to the reinforcement of the idea of the masses (particularly the natives) as backward. And this led in turn to a trend for writers or intellectuals to regard the countryside from an experimental perspective as the laboratory of national reform. Once again, though, ambiguities would seep in: many writers and intellectuals of the early twentieth century were seduced by the raw energy and seeming national or continental authenticity of the interior. Even more than before, the relationship between city and countryside made for a heady mix of anxiety and attraction.

Oddly enough an important work which probably helped encourage movement away from positivistic thinking was also rather close in some ways to traditional forms of elitist thinking. The Uruguayan José Enrique Rodó's influential essay *Ariel* (1900) takes the form of a valedictory speech by a teacher nicknamed Prospero after the character from Shakespeare's *The Tempest*. The speaker is addressing his young pupils, who obviously represent the future of Latin America. The lesson is built around the images of two other figures from Shakespeare's play, the spirit Ariel and the monstrous Caliban. Ariel is the ideal of wisdom, beauty, spirituality, the values of civilization to be transmitted by the new generation of the elite. Caliban is the gruff materialism and utilitarianism of vulgar North American capitalism that is threatening the values of true civilization. While Rodó pays tactful lip-service to modernization and progress, he also appeals for a future civilization based on the timeless values of ancient classical European civilization. As can be imagined, the influence of *Ariel* went in all sorts of directions, both conservative and progressive. But its context of production is important – just two years earlier the Spanish had been defeated in Cuba by the USA and this was seen as the beginning of a possible new era of North American intervention and even imperialism. Williamson makes the point that one key effect of the *Ariel* phenomenon was that it 'stimulated resentment against US cultural influence' and provoked 'a new preoccupation with *americanismo*' (1992: 305). Indeed, theorist Roberto Fernández Retamar would later reverse the Caliban image into a more contestatory direction (1976: 64, 94, 233). So, as the Regionalist novel developed, it became bound up with questions of identity and essence, and the very nature of the terms 'civilization' and 'barbarism'. These novels in many ways begin the conscious or unconscious struggle to define or gravitate towards some kind of notion of what it means to be Latin American, the question of identity – the most repeated and most vexatious topic of Latin American culture and criticism in the twentieth century and beyond.

It is not the intention of this chapter to discuss Regionalist fiction as such in any detail, but to trace an important theme as it resurfaces in some representative texts. Two key works will be considered here: *Doña Bárbara* (1929) by the Venezuelan Rómulo Gallegos and *Don Segundo Sombra* (1926) by Argentina's Ricardo Güiraldes. At first sight, Gallegos's views seem close to those of Positivism or extreme readings of Sarmiento. He believes in the idea of an *alma de la raza*, a national mentality predisposed towards barbarism, particularly prominent in his country's huge plains or *llanos* which must be tamed or civilized by the importation of city values. In this novel the city-educated Santos Luzardo returns to his rural family estate called Altamira where he confronts and ultimately defeats barbarism in the shape of the evil and rural landowner Doña Bárbara whose estate is called El Miedo. Progressive values rooted in the European Enlightenment are thus rather unsubtly pitted against darkly retrograde native tradition. However, much of the novel actually centres on Santos's practical attempts to manage and modernize the environment in an effective socio-economic way. This emphasis would seem to dilute the significance of the *alma de la raza*, suggesting that social and economic reform is the real key to change. Indeed the attitude to the interior and its human personification is, once again, quite ambivalent: 'la llanura es bella y terrible a la vez' (the plains are beautiful and terrible at the same time) (Gallegos 1982: 66); Bárbara has 'algo de salvaje, bello y terrible a la vez' (something of the savage, beautiful and terrible at the same time) (36). And Santos is only ultimately able to defeat his barbaric enemies by substantively adopting their methods. Whether there is more subtlety here than initially thought or mere confusion is open to question. But a generous reading would make something of Santos's relationship with young Marisela, a girl who has been abandoned to nature and in a sense represents the *alma de la raza* in a pure uncontaminated state, untouched by either 'civilization' or 'barbarism'. Santos may at first seem like a Hispanic Henry Higgins sprucing up his tropical Eliza Doolittle, but what he really learns is not to impose an artifical notion of civilization on her but to bring out the positive qualities latent within her and the rural culture from which she hails. Marisela effectively teaches the civilizer 'su verdadera obra, porque la suya no podía ser exterminar el mal a sangre y fuego, sino descubrir, aquí y allá, las fuentes ocultas de la bondad de su tierra y de su gente' (his real task, for his could not be to wipe out evil with blood and fire, but instead to uncover the hidden sources of goodness in his people and his land) (264).

Equally (maybe more) ambivalent is the other great classic novel of civilization-versus-barbarism, *Don Segundo Sombra*. This book marks the climax of the process of rehabilitation of the *gaucho* started by Hernández and posits the figure of the *gaucho* as the essence of true Argentine national identity, an apparently complete abrogation of popular versions of Sarmiento. The eponymous hero Don Segundo is the incarnation of the noble and free spirit of the nomadic cowboy *gauchos* and the embodiment of all that is best in the *gaucho* tradition, to the extent that he is 'una sombra, algo que pasa y es más una idea que un ser' (a shadow, something which passes by and is more of an idea than a human being as such) (1939: 17): in other words, a symbol of those essential *gaucho* virtues that should form a mythical basis for Argentine identity. At the same time, Don Segundo is seen largely through the eyes of his young protégé and the story's narrator Fabio.[6] In this sense, he is the projection of the ideals or fantasies of the younger generation that Fabio represents. Most of the novel is in fact about the trials and tribulations of young Fabio as he learns the skills and values of the *gaucho* from his older mentor. But at the end of the novel, the hitherto anonymous young narrator is identified as the son of a landowner and is returned to the family estate to claim his inheritance. The idea seems to be that the new generation of leaders must base their beliefs and practices on traditional *gaucho* lore and custom, on the authentically national, rather than on some alien foreign notion of modernity. However, not only is this a rather vague model for national identity, it is only part of the story. In an extraordinary and hastily despatched episode,[7] the otherwise idealized Don Segundo intervenes in a quarrel so as to prompt a peaceful young man into a knife-fight that results in the gory death of the opponent and the ruination of the young man's life. Fabio tries to brush off his horror, but in some ways it is inevitable that Don Segundo has to be seen to ride off into the sunset at the end while the youth is left behind to carry the torch for the new generation. Behind the idealization of the *gaucho* lies a tradition that does seem here to be based on a dangerous propensity towards lawlessness and violence. And therefore the glorification of the *gaucho* as a national symbol may seem to be setting a rather dangerous precedent for the future. Indeed *Don Segundo Sombra* itself may be seen as conservative as much as it is revisionist. Güiraldes was a literary-orientated French-educated landowning aristrocrat with a thing for *gauchos* and the gauchesque. But by the time the novel was written the *gauchos* had basically disappeared as a distinct social group and the *pampa* had been transformed by agricultural modernization, transport systems and European immigration. The novel may be taken then as a nostalgic elegy for a lost age at a time of change, an expression of the anxiety of a traditional ruling class on the brink of a new era of modernization and urbanization.[8]

The problem is that this anxiety of identity is, in varying forms, an unresolved dilemma for much Latin American thought and culture up to this day, since the same tension between Latin Americanism and outside influence remains. This tension is a defining feature of the various culture wars or debates that rage in the academy over Latin American cultural studies, with regard to diverse but related areas such as transculturation, modernity, globalization, high modernism, popular culture, the mass media, postmodernism, post-colonialism, race, gender, sexuality and subalternity. The intention here is not to engage with the discourse of cultural studies, but to look at some 'modern' authors whose works seem to show the continuing relevance of the civilization-versus-barbarism dualism even well into the later twentieth century. Chapter 5 on Latin American literature will survey the literary history in more detail, but the so-called 'new narrative' from the 1940s onwards, culminating in the 'Boom' of the 1960s and a subsequent phase often now referred to as the 'Post-Boom', was generally regarded as marking a radical break with and strong reaction against Regionalism. The Regionalist novel is also usually seen as the central manifestation of the 'civilization and barbarism' ethic in the subcontinent's literature. The simple contention here is that, despite this periodization, the question of civilization and barbarism remains a central element today in much conspicuously modern (or even postmodern) fiction, as it was the central element nearly a hundred years ago. Moreover, the same ambivalence is visible, as is the same dual thrust of assertion and revisionism.

The revisionist thrust gained precedence as the new, more self-confident 'modern' writing gained ground during the twentieth century. The idea of 'lo real maravilloso' in Alejo Carpentier or the mixture of subjectivity and indigenous belief in Miguel Angel Asturias (later evolving into the broad trend referred to as Magical Realism) implicitly continued the complex and shifting discourse between Latin Americanism, sometimes even nativism, and European modernity (and Modernism). The climax to this trend and the climax to the 'Boom' was Gabriel García Márquez's masterpiece *Cien años de soledad* (One Hundred Years of Solitude, 1967). Magical Realism in this novel is, in part at least, a question of giving voice in a First World (European or North American) form (the novel) to the 'Third' (or 'Developing') World perspective of a rural and largely oral Latin American culture. Hence, famously, the accoutrements of civilization (such as trains, phonographs, ice, false teeth) are seen as bizarre, while events that would elsewhere be considered fantastic (like a girl ascending into heaven, a trail of blood making its way through the streets to find the victim's mother, a child being born with a pig's tail) are described with deadpan realism. 'Civilization' emerges as a hoax or myth here and that idea is carried into the text's recreation of the experience of Latin American history.[9] The establishment of the town of Macondo on the site where the founder had a dream of a great city of shining lights is an echo of the European dream of the

New World, but the inheritance of European civilization is shown to be a myth as isolation and vulnerability prevail, and the Spanish heritage is mocked via the image of a Spanish galleon uselessly stranded inland and the ridiculous and contextually irrelevant Spanish aristocratic pretensions of the lacklustre Fernanda del Carpio. But even the modern brand of nineteenth-century 'civilization' is shown to be false. 'Independence' leads to the cementing of the privileges of the ruling classes by pacts between landlords and local politicians (such as José Arcadio and Arcadio – the repetition of the family names hinting at an incestuous alliance), and 'progress' leads to civil war, exploitation, foreign interference and boom-and-bust economics. Moreover, there is a fairly direct repudiation of the crude version of Sarmiento's argument in the story of the intervention of central government into the affairs of the rural community in the form of Apolinar Moscote. A 'corregidor', Moscote is not needed because according to the town's founder 'aquí no hay nada que corregir' (there is nothing here that needs correcting) (1978: 56). The effect of his first decree, forcing the people to paint their houses in the colours of the Conservative Party, is actually to 'implantar el desorden' (implant disorder) (57). He further introduces 'progress' in the form of democracy and elections (another myth in this context), yet provokes a civil war with the Liberals by rigging the vote. Mutual destruction now follows in a place whose inhabitants were, before the arrival of central government, 'tan pacíficos que ni siquiera nos hemos muerto de muerte natural' (so peaceful that none of us have even died of natural causes) (57). So, it is the forces of the centre, the supposed bearers of civilized values, who actually bring chaos and discord to the regions. 'Civilization and barbarism' is one of the great falsehoods foisted on Latin America, which has always been forced, ever since 1492 and no less so with supposed independence, to perceive its own identity and history through the lens of other dominant cultures' version of it. And this internalized dependency would continue into the acquiescence to US economic imperialism (dramatized in the novel by the story of the all-powerful North American banana company) and lead to a generalized state of neo-colonial submission. Thus a variation on the reading of Magical Realism is that its function is also to encourage Latin Americans to see through obfuscatory versions of their own history and identity (another kind of myth or magic) and see the reality, to assert an authentically Latin American consciousness not based on slavish adherence to foreign models.

The most famous novel of the Post-Boom and a direct descendant (ironic or otherwise) of *Cien años de soledad*, Isabel Allende's *La casa de los espíritus* (The House of the Spirits, 1982) takes a similarly revisionist approach, though using a brand of feminism to nuance further García Márquez's master discourse. Another family saga corresponding to Latin American (particularly here Chilean) history, the story of the patriarchal landowner Esteban Trueba is also presented through his eyes as the enlightened introduction of civilization to a barbaric countryside, a 'región inhumana', in his sister's words, 'donde no funcionaban las leyes de Dios ni el progreso de la ciencia' (an inhuman region where neither the laws of God nor of scientific progress work) (1985: 104). However, Trueba's version of civilization is mocked. He heaps admiration upon Jean de Satigny, whose rationalism he compares to native barbarism (191), but the European turns out – as presented in the novel – to be a ludicrous homosexual dandy and a confidence trickster ripping off the country's natural resources. And on another occasion, Trueba – who prefers North American medicine because local doctors are no better than witch doctors (216) – has his broken bones fixed by an old peasant retainer in a way that baffles conventional science (145). Another manifestation of the fascination with European 'civilization' is the patriarch's desire to overcome nature by replacing wild local vegetation with orderly French gardens. But Trueba's eccentric yet beloved wife Clara is herself like 'una planta salvaje' (a wild plant) whose 'madness', as it is thought to be, cannot be cured by modern European medical treatments (75). Clara's 'madness' is akin to 'barbarism', thought to be threatening but nothing more than the pure natural exuberance and energy of Latin Americanness. Indeed it is a woman who brings Trueba closer to a more meaningful sense of civilization. 'Woman', like the peasantry, is that which is perceived as mysterious, 'other' and threatening to patriarchal notions of stability, yet, like barbarism, is merely an imagined threat. The peasant woman whom Trueba rapes and takes in tames him and helps him usher in 'un poco de civilización' (59), and he is further mellowed by his wife and ultimately his grand-daughter Alba. The latter's experience of torture and rape at the hands of those responsible for a military coup designed to restore order (an obvious reference to Pinochet) leads him to re-evaluate radically what might be termed the conventional categories of civilization and barbarism.

This impulse against nineteenth-century liberalism is often portrayed as the real momentum behind Latin American intellectual (and often popular) culture since the early twentieth century. That feeling has been reinforced among students of the area thanks to the essentially leftist nature of cultural criticism in the field, increasingly so in recent decades. However, that is not the complete picture. Even early liberal novels like Mariano Azuela's dealing with the Mexican Revolution, *Los de abajo* (The Underdogs, 1916) – despite sympathy with the *campesino* and disgruntlement with bourgeois opportunism and a cynical political class – presents popular revolution as a barbaric cataclysm that destroys a painfully erected civilization. One of Latin America's most successful writers and cultural commentators today, the Peruvian Mario Vargas Llosa, is often painted by his critics as embodying a reactionary neo-liberalism that is suspicious of the masses – though, from another point of view, he represents a remarkably radical stance in the generally dominant context of nationalist leftism in politicized Latin American culture, at least as largely presented via the filter of academic Latin American studies.

Fingers began to be pointed at Vargas Llosa in the 1970s after his break with the left and when his fiction began to dwell on the dangers of extremism and utopianism.[10] His (surprising for such a serious writer) comedy *Pantaleón y las visitadoras* (Captain Pantoja and the Special Service, 1973), basically a Post-Boom novel, marks the shift. Sex-starved horny soldiers in the Amazon region have been jumping the local women. To offset scandal, the central military authorities dispatch from the capital the hapless Captain Pantaleón Pantoja to set up a mobile prostitution service to minister to the men's unruly urges. The story seems at first to be a satirical take on Sarmiento's presumed notion of civilization and barbarism as in some of the texts mentioned above. The town of Iquitos and its surrounding jungle area are presented as provincial, even primitive and backward. The disorderly conduct of the soldiers is even attributed to local primitivism. The lack of priests and women is blamed, suggesting underdevelopment and a milieu beyond the reach of civilization. Moreover, the real culprit is the heat, which drives men wild: the hot steamy jungle is a metaphor for the savage barbarism of the interior. Of course, this seems to be all a joke. And an even bigger joke is the absurd scheme of the army and central authorities, which shows a complete ignorance of local conditions: not only are the military (a supposedly civilizing influence in the region) the very source of the problem, their bizarre plan actually provokes more social disorder as it inevitably leads to scandal. The hilarious parody of Pantilandia, as the troupe is known, has the same effect as the lampooning of García Márquez's Apolinar Moscote. But it is not that simple, for the novel also deals with the fanatical religious sect known as the Brotherhood of the Ark whose influence extends from the jungle even as far as the capital. Their practices of violence and ritual sacrifice are distinctly *not* funny, unlike the antics of the amiable Pantoja. Barbarism is a real and dangerous force after all, and the unthinking glorification of the interior and primitivism a perilous by-product of earlier revisionism.

The idea is taken further in Vargas Llosa's *La guerra del fin del mundo* (The War of the End of the World, 1981). This is a historical novel about the incredibly bloody suppression of a revolt of messianic royalist peasants against the Republic at Canudos in remote north-east Brazil in 1896–97. This revolt was actually the subject of one of the landmark novels of Brazilian literature, *Os sertões* (Rebellion in the Backlands, 1902) by Euclides da Cunha, another ambivalent liberal piece that defends modernization but sympathizes with the ordinary people. Vargas Llosa's version retains the sympathy but comes down much more firmly on the side of progress. Two of the principal characters are the charismatic Antonio Conselheiro, who forecasts the apocalypse and leads the poverty-stricken peasants into rebellion against the 'Anti-Christ' of the Republic, and Galileo Gall, an anarchist phrenologist who jumps on the bandwagon of the uprising to promote anarchist insurrection through the channelling of religious fanaticism. The results of their actions are devastating (though the novel does not shirk the brutality of the republican forces – their leader, General Moreira César, is just as much of a fanatic). Idealism all too easily leads to fanaticism, unleashing a terrifying barbarism that must be countered by a civilizing programme of modernization. This was to become a key theme in Vargas Llosa's work and in his political development, with an obvious relevance to Peru given the rise of the Sendero Luminoso (Shining Path) guerrilla movement in the 1980s.

In some ways, then, Vargas Llosa is not all that dissimilar to Sarmiento, and this full-circle journey not only underscores the centrality of the civilization-verus-barbarism conflict in Latin American thought but also begs the question of how effective modernity and progress have been in the subcontinent. The circle, though, is not quite complete. Competing voices do share the public space. Hence, when Vargas Llosa – following predecessors like Mitre, Sarmiento and Gallegos – ran for the Peruvian presidency in 1990 on what many saw as a Thatcherite ticket, he lost. Unfortunately, the winning candidate, Alberto Fujimori, said to have more appeal to the 'popular' masses, later sought to dissolve the constitution and eventually fled the country under a cloud of corruption. The debate about 'civilization' and 'barbarism', despite the crudity of the terms to today's ears, remains, in essence, open.

NOTES

1   Quoted in Hernández (1976: 20–1).
2   The reference is to the Italian Marxist cultural theorist Antonio Gramsci and his *Notes on Italian History*.
3   Transculturation is a favoured term in cultural studies discourses as it implies the fluid and complex process of interaction or negotiation between contact cultures in which each side of the supposed divide is influenced or affected by the other. Acculturation would, on the other hand, imply the subsuming of a culture into an opposing dominant culture.
4   Sommer (1991: 6). She refers to Anderson (1983: 30).
5   Sommer (1991: 4). She refers to Henríquez Ureña (1945: 243).
6   The narrator is actually the adult Fabio recalling his youth. The tensions within the novel are further reinforced by the educated and often poetic style of the adult as he attempts to recall and even recreate the rough-and-tumble world and language of the *gauchos*.
7   See Beardsell (1981), who offers a perceptive reading of this episode.
8   The stories (and poetry) of Argentina's and Latin America's greatest writer Jorge Luis Borges a couple of decades later often display similar tensions and anxieties. Conspicuously universal and pro-European, they are often also very Argentine. They display a somewhat snobbish disdain for the vulgar populism Borges saw as embodied in Juan and Eva Perón, yet come close to glorifying a mixture of heroic creole past, *gaucho* culture, the knife-fight and the tango. Behind the 'civilized' knowledge of the lessons of history lies an ambiguous yearning for the spirit of noble adventure

embedded in the 'barbaric' myth of the *gaucho*. See my 'The Southern Cone' in Davies (2002).

9   James Higgins gives an excellent and accessible account of the text's recreation of history in Swanson (1990: 141–60). See also Swanson (1991). Worthwhile too in this regard are the sophisticated essays by Gerald Martin and Edwin Williamson in McGuirk and Cardwell (1987).

10 Vargas Llosa's break with the left is often dated as 1971, when the poet Heberto Padilla was imprisoned in Castro's Cuba and subsequently forced to sign a denunciation of 'counter-revolutionary' activities. The Padilla affair is sometimes seen as marking the end of the Boom, which was said to be given unity and identity by the exciting example of the Cuban Revolution. Kristal (1998) gives a good account of the case of Vargas Llosa.

REFERENCES AND SELECTED FURTHER READING

Allende, I. 1985: *La casa de los espíritus*. Barcelona: Plaza y Janés.

Alonso, C. 1990: *The Spanish American Regional Novel*. Cambridge: Cambridge University Press.

Alonso, C. 1998: *The Burden of Modernity*. New York: Oxford University Press.

Anderson, B. 1983: *Imagined Communities*. London: Verso.

Beardsell, P. 1981: *Don Segundo Sombra* and *Machismo*. Forum for Modern Language Studies 17, 302–11.

Beardsell, P. 2000: *Europe and Latin America*. Manchester: Manchester University Press.

Bethell, L. (ed.) 1998: *A Cultural History of Latin America: Literature, Music and the Visual Arts in the 19th and 20th Centuries*. Cambridge: Cambridge University Press.

Crawford, W. R. 1963: *A Century of Latin American Thought*. Cambridge, MA: Harvard University Press.

Davies, C. (ed.) 2002: *The Companion to Hispanic Studies*. London: Arnold.

Echeverría, E. 1977: *La Cautiva/El matadero*. Buenos Aires: Huemul.

Fernández Retamar, R. 1976: *Algunos usos de civilización y barbarie*. Buenos Aires. Editorial Contrapunto SRL.

Fiddian, R. (ed.) 2000: *Postcolonial Perspectives on the Cultures of Latin America and Lusophone Africa*. Liverpool: Liverpool University Press.

Fowler, W. 2002: *Latin America: 1800–2000*. London: Arnold.

Franco, J. 1970: *The Modern Culture of Latin America*. Harmondsworth: Penguin.

Gallegos, R. 1982: *Doña Bárbara*. Madrid: Espasa-Calpe.

García Márquez, G. 1978: *Cien años de soledad*. Buenos Aires: Sudamericana.

González Echevarría, R. 1985: *The Voice of the Masters*. Austin: University of Texas Press.

González Echevarría, R. 1998: *Myth and Archive*. Durham, NC: Duke University Press.

Güiraldes, R. 1939: *Don Segundo Sombra*. Buenos Aires: Losada.

Henríquez Ureña, P. 1945: *Literary Currents in Hispanic America*. Cambridge, MA: Harvard University Press.

Hernández, J. 1976: *Martín Fierro*. Buenos Aires: Losada.

Kristal, E. 1998: *Temptation of the Word: The Novels of Mario Vargas Llosa*. Nashville, TN: Vanderbilt University Press.

McGuirk, B. and Cardwell, R. (eds) 1987: *Gabriel García Márquez: New Readings*. Cambridge: Cambridge University Press.

Martin, G. 1989: *Journeys through the Labyrinth*. London: Verso.

Masiello, F. 1992: *Between Civilization and Barbarism*. Lincoln, NE: University of Nebraska Press.

San Román, G. 2000: Political tact in José Enrique Rodó's *Ariel*. *Forum for Modern Language Studies* 36, 279–95.

Sommer, D. 1991: *Foundational Fictions*. Berkeley, CA: University of California Press.

Sommer, D. (ed.) 1999: *The Places of History: Regionalism Revisited in Latin America*. Durham, NC: Duke University Press.

Swanson, P. (ed.) 1990: *Landmarks in Modern Latin American Fiction*. London: Routledge.

Swanson, P. 1991: *Cómo leer a Gabriel García Márquez*. Madrid: Júcar.

Swanson, P. 1995: *The New Novel in Latin America*. Manchester: Manchester University Press.

Williamson, E. 1992: *The Penguin History of Latin America*. London: Allen Lane.

5

Latin American literatures

Elzbieta Sklodowska

The remarkably vast and diverse domain of the literatures of Latin America does not lend itself to easy overviews. Nonetheless, it is possible to identify a variety of criss-crossing movements, tropes and categories that link the literary production of the region (Mexico, Central America, Hispanic Caribbean islands, South America, including Portuguese-speaking Brazil). At the same time, the stylistic and thematic coordinates shared by national literatures – such as common language, artistic movements, colonial legacy and the nation-building experiences of the nineteenth century – should not let us de-emphasize regional differences, nor should they obliterate diverse creative expressions of indigenous people. Large portions of South and Central America (the Andean region, Mexico, Guatemala, Paraguay) continue to be influenced by the legacy of the great pre-Colombian cultures of the Inca, the Aymara, the Nahua, the Maya and the Guaraní. On the other hand, the African-based cultures of the enslaved have undergone a violent 'hybridization' or 'transculturation' with European elements in the crucible of plantation economy in Brazil and the Hispanic Caribbean. Finally, various countries of South America (Argentina, Uruguay, Chile) have been most significantly shaped by European immigration of the late nineteenth and early twentieth centuries. To provide a meaningful picture of Latin American literatures means to recognize all facets of its richness and diversity, including the works of women writers and the growing literary output of Latino/a authors in the USA. This task also requires a reassessment of the traditional notion of the 'literary' by bringing into focus forms of writing previously excluded from the canon (travel accounts; confessions and other autobiographical forms; journalism; testimonial narrative).

The process of gaining independence from Spanish and Portuguese rule that began in the early nineteenth century followed different patterns – Mexico, for example, gained independence in 1821, while Cuba had to wait until 1902 – but most of the newly formed states failed to build the stable democracies envisioned by the liberators. Consequently, literary production became further diversified as it strived to embody, both ideologically and aesthetically, the nation-building projects of local elites and to confront the anarchical times dominated by despotic regimes and punctuated by violent political strife between competing ideological groups.

While it is impossible to decide on an emblematic date that represents a watershed between the writings of the colonial period and national literatures, the entry of Latin America into the new era is associated with the publication of the first Latin American novel, *El periquillo sarniento* (1816; tr. 1942 *The Itching Parrot*) by the Mexican José Joaquín Fernández de Lizardi (1776–1827). The novel's pedigree can be traced to the Spanish picaresque, on the one hand, and to the ideas of the French Enlightenment, on the other. Unlike some of his contemporaries whose imagination was captivated by the euphoria of national liberation movements, Fernández de Lizardi did not extol the heroic spirit of his fellow citizens. Instead, through an intermixture of oral traditions, moralizing anecdotes and satire he engaged in a critique of corruption and hypocrisy among the emerging Mexican bourgeoisie. Fernández de Lizardi's overly didactic lead was followed by Ignacio Manuel Altamirano (1834–93), whose sentimental novel *Clemencia* (Clemency, 1896) depicted Mexican society divided by the civil war at the time of the French invasion (1864–67) and proposed an agenda for national reconciliation. In keeping with the emerging tenets of Realism, his later novel *El Zarco* (1901; tr. 1957 *El Zarco: The Bandit*) enriched the portrayal of national reality by blending local patterns of speech with 'true-to-life' characters.

The revolutionary events of the early nineteenth century did not inspire many novelists, but they did trigger an outpouring of heroic verse, which often combined neo-classical style with Romantic imagery. Best exemplified by José Joaquín Olmedo (Ecuador, 1780–1847) and his ode *La victoria de Junín, canto a Bolívar* (The Victory of Junín, Song to Bolívar, 1825), the heroic poetry of the liberation era soon gave way to celebrations of autochthonous nature and the pre-Colombian past. In such widely acclaimed works as the epic 'Silva a la agricultura de la zona tórrida' (Silva to the Agriculture of the Torrid Zone, 1826) by the prominent Venezuelan poet and thinker Andrés Bello (1781–1865) or 'En el teocalli de Cholula' (In the Temple-Pyramid of Cholula, 1820) by the Cuban exiled poet José María Heredia (1803–39), Romanticism emerged as a more clearly defined style asserting its own Latin American identity. Unified by recurring themes of native landscapes, nostalgic evocations of indigenous legacies, political exile and struggle against tyranny, romantic poetry resonated with equal force throughout the continent.

Prominent Brazilian writer Antônio Gonçalves Dias (1823–64) contributed to the solidification of Romanticism in his country with three volumes of songs, *cantos* (1846–51), which included a perennial favorite, 'Canção do exílio' (The Song of Exile, 1846). The author of *Poemas americanos* (American Poems, 1840) and of an unfinished epic *Os Timbiras* (The Timbira Indians, 1857) grew into prominence as the founder of Brazilian Indianism, a widespread movement steeped in the autochthonous past, for which Romanticism provided the basic mould. In Brazil this trend reached its height with José Martinano de Alencar (1829–77), whose masterpiece *Iracema* (1865; tr. 1886 *Iracema, the Honey-Lips, a Legend of Brazil*) – a melodramatic novel of tragic love between the indigenous woman whose name is an anagram of 'America' and a Portuguese soldier – has enjoyed lasting popularity. Similar attempts to forge models of a more inclusive post-independence identity by rebuilding the connection with the indigenous past were cultivated by numerous Indianist texts from Spanish America: *Tabaré* (1886; tr. 1956 *Tabaré: An Indian Legend of Uruguay*) by the Uruguayan Juan Zorrilla de San Martín (1855–1931), *Cumandá, o un drama entre salvajes* (Cumandá, or a Drama Among Savages, 1871) by the Ecuadorean Juan León Mera (1832–94), *Enriquillo: leyenda histórico dominicana* (1879–82, tr. 1954 *The Cross and the Sword*) by the Dominican writer Manuel de Jesús Galván (1834–1910).

According to some scholars, the publication in Peru of *Aves sin nido* (1889; tr. 1904, *Birds without a Nest*) by the distinguished writer and journalist Clorinda Matto de Turner (1852–1909) marked the birth of literary Indigenism, which turned away from the melodramatic models of Indianism by incorporating native vocabulary in order to render more 'objective' descriptions of social and cultural practices. Whereas the first novels in this vein, such as *Raza de bronce* (Race of Bronze, 1919) by the Bolivian Alcides Arguedas (1879–1946) and *Huasipungo* (1934; tr. 1964 *The Villagers*) by the Ecuadorian Jorge Icaza (1906–78) were based on realist or naturalist conventions, mature Indigenism produced a notable body of remarkably original and experimental narratives, including César Vallejo's (Peru, 1895–1935) sombre novel *Tungsteno* (1931), Miguel Angel Asturias's (Guatemala, 1899–1974) *Hombres de maíz* (1949; tr. 1974 *Men of Maize*) and Rosario Castellanos's (Mexico, 1925–74) *Balún Canán* (1957; tr. 1958 *The Nine Guardians*). It was, however, the Peruvian José María Arguedas (1911–69) who was justly hailed as the most original and innovative *indigenista* writer. His *Yawar fiesta* (1941; tr. 1985) and *Los ríos profundos* (1958; tr. 1978 *Deep Rivers*) captured a genuine and complex image of Peruvian ethnicity by means of striking formal experimentation, which included interweaving of Spanish and the native language Quechua, structural fragmentation and the mythical concept of time. In a different vein, the concept of 'transculturation' – borrowed by the Uruguayan critic Angel Rama (1926–83) from Fernando Ortiz's (Cuba, 1881–1969) essay *Contrapunteo cubano de tabaco y azúcar* (1940; tr. 1995 *Cuban Counterpoint: Tobacco and Sugar*) – proved critically productive when approaching the hybrid complexity of Arguedas's masterpiece. Finally, in a unique ideological development, José Carlos Mariátegui's (Peru, 1895–1930) landmark essay *Siete ensayos de interpretación de la realidad peruana* (1927; tr. 1971 *Seven Interpretative Essays on Peruvian Reality*) infused Indigenist principles with Marxist ideology.

Early treatment of indigenous cultures was firmly rooted in romantic nativism, which informs also the iconic text of Latin American Romanticism, *María* (1867; tr. 1890) by the Colombian writer Jorge Isaacs (1837–95). No Latin American novel captures the romantic spirit better than this tale of star-crossed lovers set against the idyllic landscapes of the Cauca Valley. Acting upon local sources of inspiration, Isaacs created a narrative unparalleled for the subtlety of psychological portrayal, structural complexity and stylistic achievement. *María* has been re-read for generations, but it was not until the 1990s that the critics reconsidered its significance – alongside other Latin American romances – in light of the nation-building agendas of the nineteenth century. In one of the most influential re-evaluations of those narratives, Doris Sommer has adopted Benedict Anderson's thesis that novels inspire the forging of 'imagined communities' and has argued that the authors of romance projected their nation-building ideals into the imagery of sexual union. Sommer's path-breaking *Foundational Fictions* (1991) is among an impressive corpus of recent studies (Roberto González Echevarría, Julio Ramos, Nicolas Shumway, Carlos Alonso, Josefina Ludmer) that instilled new vitality into the study of nineteenth-century Latin American literature.

All of the major European trends of this period – Romanticism, Realism and Naturalism – had a pervasive influence on Latin American writings of this 'foundational' era. While the specific manifestations of these overlapping movements were influenced by regional contingencies, individual creativity assumed a surprising variety of forms. Vivid renditions of everyday customs, local milieux, folk beliefs and oral lore were the domain of *costumbrismo* derived from Spanish literary tradition and catalyzed by the readers' predilection for distinctly Latin American themes. As *costumbrismo* anticipated the waning of Romanticism (1820–80) and signalled the shift towards Realism (1840–1910), it produced such unique forms as *la tradición*, best exemplified by Ricardo Palma's (1833–1919) *Tradiciones peruanas* (Peruvian Traditions, 1872–1910; 1945 partial translation, *The Knights of the Cape*), a ten-volume collection of vibrant anecdotes, humorous sketches and legends derived from Peruvian history and folklore. Hybrid terms such as 'Romantic Realism' or 'Naturalistic Realism' – both proposed by the critic Fernando Alegría – are sometimes used to describe the peculiarities of some of the most significant works of the nineteenth century, among them Esteban Echeverría's (1805–51) haunting short story *El matadero* (written *c*.1838 and published posthumously in 1871; tr. 1959 'The Slaughter House'), which depicts in sordid detail and with didactic excess the torture of a heroic sympathizer of the Unitarist Party by the followers of the Federalist dictator Juan Manuel Rosas (1835–52). There is a considerable ideological overlap between Echeverría's political critique and the novel *Amalia* (1851–55; tr. 1919) by his fellow Argentine José Mármol (1818–71). Stylistically, however, the immensely popular *Amalia* is the prototypical Romantic novel that highlights the heroic intrigue and the melodramatic tragedy of young lovers under the Rosas tyranny.

Rosas's oppressive regime marked the entire generation of intellectuals and created a long-lasting polarization within Argentinean society. Among the most notable writers who tried not only to debunk the Federalist regime but also to seek a path out of political turmoil was Domingo Faustino Sarmiento (1811–86), best remembered for his highly influential masterpiece *Facundo* (1845; tr. 1960 *Life in the Argentine Republic in the Days of the Tyrants, or Civilization and Barbarism*). This eclectic text – a combination of essay, novel and biography – projected the clash between the colonizing centre and the colonized periphery onto the coordinates of civilization and barbarism (see Chapter 4): the modernizing power of the city (law, culture, reason) versus the uncivilized inhabitants of the rural *pampas* (anarchy, nature, irrationality). Among later works that contributed in meaningful ways to the reworking of Sarmiento's binary, *Doña Bárbara* (1929; tr. 1931) – a highly popular novel by the Venezuelan writer and statesman Rómulo Gallegos (1884–1969) – embodied the barbarism associated with nature in a female protagonist who had to be subjected to the 'civilizing' process of taming. Finally, the figure of Facundo – as an authoritarian military chief, *caudillo* – was echoed throughout the twentieth century by most esteemed novelists who dealt with the theme of dictatorship in a variety of daunting novels: from Asturias's surreal *El Señor Presidente* (1946; tr. 1963 *The President*) to Augusto Roa Bastos's (Paraguay, 1917–) hallucinatory *Yo el Supremo* (1974; tr. 1986, *I the Supreme*), Alejo Carpentier's (Cuba, 1904–80) arcane *El recurso del método* (1974; tr. 1976 *Reasons of State*) and Gabriel García Márquez's (Colombia, 1928–) highly complex *El otoño del patriarca* (1975; tr. 1976 *The Autumn of the Patriarch*) and demythifying *El general en su laberinto* (1989; tr. 1990 *The General in his Labyrinth*).

In addition to providing a forceful denunciation of Rosas's dictatorship and a forward-looking reflection about the identity of Argentina, *Facundo* conveyed, on the one hand, a contempt for the savage and unruly *gauchos*, the nomadic inhabitants of the *pampas*, and, on the other, a fascination with their independent spirit and their unique skills. With all its ambivalence, *Facundo* became a catalyst for the development of a vast body of *gauchesca* literature, derived from the oral tradition of *payadas* (ballads). The figure of the *gaucho* was further moulded into the elite projects that sought to transform him from a marginalized renegade into a member of an orderly nation. The *gaucho*'s literary metamorphosis into a symbolic embodiment of national identity culminated in the immensely popular epic poem *El gaucho Martín Fierro* (1872–79; tr. 1948) by José Hernández (1834–86). Seven years after the publication of the first part, known as *La ida* (The Departure), *La vuelta de Martín Fierro* appeared, denouncing the suffering and economic marginalization of the *gaucho*. As with Sarmiento's civilization and barbarism, the *gaucho* theme continued to resonate in Argentinean literature and it acquired mythical overtones in *Don Segundo Sombra* (1926; tr. 1935), by Ricardo Güiraldes (1886–1927), attesting to the continuing vitality of the *gaucho*'s legacy. Recent critical re-readings of gauchesque literature attuned to gender issues and post-colonial approaches have shed new light on many of these canonical texts (Alonso, Ludmer, Rotker, Shumway).

Like *El matadero*, *Amalia*, *Facundo* and *Martín Fierro*, much of the literature of the nineteenth century was firmly rooted in the belief that writing can be an effective vehicle for fostering projects of political reform and denouncing social injustice. Since the question of slavery occupied centre stage in the slave-based, sugar-producing economies of Cuba and Brazil, both countries witnessed the rise of abolitionist literature. In Brazil, Castro Alves (1847–71) earned the distinction of 'poet of the slaves' for his abolitionist poems collected posthumously in *Os escravos* (The Slaves, 1883). In Cuba, a host of writers denounced the horrors of slavery in a variety of forms: from the romantic novel *Sab* (1841; tr. 1993) by Gertrudis Gómez de Avellaneda (1814–73) – one of the few women writers to have gained acclaim in the male-dominated literary circles of her time – to the monumental *Cecilia Valdés o la Loma de Angel* (1882; tr. 1935) by Cirilo Villaverde (1812–94), whose political engagement forced him into prolonged exile. *Cecilia Valdés* exemplified the dilemmas of Cuban nationalists whose visions of *cubanidad* assumed a gradual whitening of the population through miscegenation and integration. For an average Cuban, Villaverde's mulatto heroine continues to be an immensely popular figure embodying the nation's mixed ethnic heritage.

Few authors of colour attained recognition in nineteenth-century Latin America. Unlike the USA, where there is a substantial body of slave narratives, *Autobiografía de un esclavo* (written 1839, Spanish edition 1937; tr. 1840 *The Autobiography of a Slave*) by Juan Francisco Manzano (Cuba, 1797–1854) is the only known slave account to come out of Latin America. Manzano's testimonial authority had to do with his position as a victim and witness to the slave's predicament, but his account was manipulated to fit better the anti-abolitionist rhetoric of white intellectuals such as Domingo Delmonte (1804–53). Manzano's free mulatto contemporary, Gabriel de la Concepción Valdés (1809–44), known as Plácido, is remembered as an accomplished romantic poet, whose 1843 poem 'El hijo de la maldición' (Son of damnation) denounced both slavery and colonial rule. Plácido was executed by the Spanish for allegedly participating in a slave uprising (the Escalera Conspiracy, 1844). José Piedra's recent re-reading of discourses produced by enslaved Africans and their descendants highlights the different strategies employed by these authors to accept, superficially, European values, while in reality mocking and challenging the oppressive code of the masters.

Women were also among those marginalized by the literary establishment of nineteenth-century Latin America. Nonetheless, a handful of women writers gained professional recognition and readership. In addition to Gómez de Avellaneda and Matto de Turner, Juana Manuela Gorriti (Argentina, 1818–92) and Soledad Acosta de Samper (Colombia, 1833–1913) were successful as authors of short stories, travel accounts, novels and essays, and could be seen as transitional figures anticipating the development of gender-specific writing. However, many women authors have remained unacknowledged until recent reassessments of the literary canon by such critics as Francine Massiello, Jean Franco, Susana Rotker and Adriana Méndez Rodenas, among others.

As Romanticism and *costumbrismo* slowly yielded to Realism, the theme of national identity remained at the very heart of the narrative, albeit under a new guise. The positivist cult of pragmatism became pervasive among the intellectual elites, most notably among the Mexican *científicos* associated with the dictator Porfirio Díaz. In literature, in the face of the turbulent socio-economic transformations, Realism privileged a firm sense of social commitment and an uncompromising pursuit of 'true-to-life' representation. This attitude was accompanied by a keen awareness of rapid historical change, as evidenced by Alberto Blest Gana's (1830–1920) *Martín Rivas* (1862; tr. 1918) and *La gran aldea* (1884) by Lucio V. López (1848–94), which unravel the impact of modernization on Chile and Argentina, respectively. The novel was also a medium of choice for the proponents of Naturalism, who sought to infuse their aesthetic practice with the impression of scientific objectivity in their merciless portrayal of the most abject facets of humankind. Novels such as *Santa* (1903; tr. 1999) by the Mexican Federico Gamboa (1864–1939), *Sin rumbo* (Aimless, 1885) by the Argentinean Eugenio Cambaceres (1843–89), and *O Mulato* (1881) by Aluisio Azevedo (Brazil, 1857–1913) unravel the Darwinian forces of heredity and social milieu and denounce the most extreme abuses of power, whereas the stories of *Sub terra* (1904) by Baldomero Lillo (Chile, 1867–1923) are reminiscent of French Naturalist Emile Zola's *Germinal* (1885) because of their poignant criticism of the squalid working conditions in Chilean coal mines. The heightened sense of social reality also served as a catalyst for Euclides da Cunha's (1866–1909) novel *Os Sertões* (1902; tr. 1944 *Rebellion in the Backlands*), a pioneering portrayal of the marginalized inhabitants of the Brazilian interior. In a similar vein, socio-political awareness was transposed into the realist drama, with *Barranca abajo* (1905; tr. 1973) by the Uruguayan Florencio Sánchez (1875–1910) becoming the first significant achievement of Spanish American theatre.

Around the turn of the century most diverse trends converged in the prolific and original work of Joaquim Maria Machado de Assis (Brazil, 1839–1908). His most accomplished novels *Memórias póstumas de Brás Cubas* (1881; tr. 1952 *Epitaph of a Small Winner*) and *Dom Casmurro* (1899; tr. 1953) – self-defined as 'the most oblique and dissembling' – endeavoured to grasp the complex fabric of Brazilian society, including facets of power, gender politics and ethnicity. Machado de Assis's impetus towards unrestrained satire, introspection and exploration of the text's own making produced an unsettling image of human experience, consonant with the turmoil and anguish of modernity. His innovative standing among his contemporaries was also due to his ability to reinvigorate literary forms by parodying the basic principles of Realism and Naturalism. By breaking the confines of traditional narrative, Machado de Assis paved the way for the flourishing of Brazilian experimental Regionalist narrative in the 1930s by such authors as Graciliano Ramos

(1892–1953) and Erico Veríssimo (1905–75) and fostered the awareness of vertiginous socio-economic changes so crucial to the development of Brazilian *Modernismo* (1922–45).

In the 1880s, Realism and Naturalism gradually lost hold to *Modernismo*, a powerful new movement that challenged positivist materialism and became the first in a series of continuing confrontations of Latin America with modernity (Jrade 1998: ix). By the time it yielded to avant-garde tendencies in the early 1920s, *Modernismo* had earned an extraordinary and lasting place in Spanish American literary history and had a wide-reaching impact on the most innovative writers of the twentieth century. *Modernista* literary vision was shaped by the dramatic socio-economic and political changes on the Latin American scene that included the disappearance of the old aristocracy, the growth of industrial capital and cosmopolitan centres, the commodification of art, spectacular urbanization, increase in travel and the diffusion of new ideas through flourishing literary journals (Jrade 1998).

Modernismo was born under the spiritual leadership of Rubén Darío (Nicaragua, 1867–1916), whose extensive production of poetry and narrative exemplifies the extraordinary richness of the movement, from the advocacy of beauty and musicality in *Azul* (Blue, 1888) and *Prosas profanas y otros poemas* (1896; tr. 1922 *Prosas profanas and Other Poems*) to the unravelling of socio-political awareness and Latin American identity in *Cantos de vida y esperanza* (Songs of Life and Hope, 1905). While Darío recognized the power of literary legacy and drew upon Spanish, French and classical traditions, ultimately the unique appeal of *Modernismo* had to do with striking experimentation with syntax, metre and poetic imagery. Darío and his followers were equally vocal about their ideals and their dislikes. Their anti-bourgeois attitude was predicated on their search for spirituality and enduring artistic beauty. French Parnassian and Symbolist poets (Gautier, Leconte de Lisle, Baudelaire, Verlaine, Mallarmé) provided the *modernistas* with models of elegance, cosmopolitan refinement and sensuality, while Romanticism nourished their spiritual pursuit of the exotic, the mythical and the esoteric. All these influences notwithstanding, the shape of the new aesthetic resided in the originality, vision and talent of individual writers, who considered poetry as a literary medium best suited to create rather than reproduce reality. In their well-orchestrated, gracefully crafted and intricate poems – but also in a sizeable body of novels, chronicles, travel accounts, essays and short stories – the *modernistas* sought to encompass their desire for striking stylistic innovation with their faith in the power of poetic language.

Despite their extraordinary individual talents and inimitable personalities, the *modernistas* shared many of the same values and aesthetic principles. For some of them, however, socio-political involvement took a backseat to their own existential anguish and fascination with 'art for art's sake'. The resulting emphasis on extravagant or decadent imagery, escapism and bohemian lifestyle was most ostensibly present in the writings of Julián del Casal (Cuba,

1863–93) and José Asunción Silva (Colombia, 1865–96). On the other end of the spectrum, an unswerving political engagement distinguished the life and the work of José Martí (Cuba, 1853–95), whose highly popular *Versos sencillos* (1891) challenged the assumption of incompatibility between political passion and poetic harmony. In Brazil, a parallel movement of Parnassianism was consolidated in the prolific writings of Olavo Bilac (1865–1918).

Alongside poetry, the essay became another preferred medium of *Modernismo*. As a form it was particularly well suited to express a heightened sense of awareness of Latin American identity. The encroaching power of the United States generated concerns among Latin American intellectuals, especially in conjunction with the semi-colonial status of Puerto Rico, the provisions of the Platt Amendment of 1901 (which restricted Cuban sovereignty), and the creation of Panama (1903) in the aftermath of US intervention. Even though critics have not always associated *Modernismo* with socio-political concerns, recent studies have underscored their relevance for many of the *modernista* writers. Among the few masterful essays that exemplify both the formal refinement of the period and the obsession with Latin American identity, *Ariel* (1900; tr. 1988) – a highly polemical work by José Enrique Rodó (Uruguay, 1871–1917) – replays Sarmiento's dichotomy of civilization versus barbarism through a confrontation between two Shakespearean characters: Ariel, as a symbol of spirituality and beauty, and Caliban, as a vulgar barbarian wearing a mask of pragmatism and materialism. *Ariel* was interpreted as an allegory of cultural differences between the utilitarian USA and the spiritually oriented Latin American nations. Decades later, Rodó's text inspired yet another controversial proposal by the Cuban poet and essayist Roberto Fernández Retamar (1930–). In his *Calibán* (1971; tr. 1989 *Caliban and Other Essays*) it was precisely Caliban/cannibal who stands as a metaphor of Latin American subaltern identity, a powerful symbol of the inverted relationship between the colonial centre and the colonized periphery. Significantly, Fernández Retamar's concept continued the line of another highly influential *modernista* essay, José Martí's *Nuestra América* (1891), a powerful and visionary project that sought to build Latin American identity around the harmonious notions of *mestizaje* (miscegenation) and cultural syncretism.

Later *modernistas*, like Enrique González Martínez (México 1871–1952) and Leopoldo Lugones (Argentina, 1874–1938), can be credited with bringing the movement onto the threshold of the avant-garde. Together with a significant group of women poets, they form a transitional cluster of authors difficult to classify. It is significant to mention, however, that it was precisely in the wake of *Modernismo* that Latin American women achieved a firm standing as a distinct group seeking to express gender-specific consciousness and transgress, in a variety of ways, the literary moulds of their time. A diverse gallery of names associated with this important shift includes the poets

Alfonsina Storni (Argentina, 1892–1938), Juana de Ibarbouru (Uruguay 1895–1979) and Delmira Agustini (Uruguay, 1886–1914). Most notably, Agustini's *El libro blanco* (The White Book, 1907) and *Cantos de la mañana* (Songs of Morning, 1910) embody the rebellion against the patriarchal establishment by means of a provocative rewriting of romantic and *modernista* imagery. For example, her poems 'El cisne' (The Swan) and 'El nocturno' (Nocturne) transform the emblems of *Modernismo* by infusing them with startling references to female eroticism. Even though the insistence on novelty and unconventional imagery was not a hallmark of Gabriela Mistral's (Chile 1889–1957) poetry, her ability to bring into artistic harmony her lifelong identification with the plight of common people and her own spiritual anxieties gained her the devotion of the readers and the respect of critics world-wide. The first Latin American author to be honoured with the Nobel Prize for Literature (1945) and thus far the only woman from Latin America to have achieved this distinction, Mistral is most remembered as the author of several major volumes of evocative poetry, *Sonetos de la muerte* (1915), *Desolación* (1922) and *Tala* (1938).

The profound social and political changes brought by the Mexican Revolution (1910–17) became the powerful catalyst for a distinct wave of socially committed writings throughout Latin America. In Mexico itself the unsparing criticism of the horrors of war and of the corruption of revolutionary values produced the so-called Narrative of the Revolution, inaugurated by Mariano Azuela's (1873–1952) *Los de abajo* (1915; tr. 1963 *The Underdogs*) and continued, among others, by Martín Luis Guzmán (1887–1977) in *El águila y la serpiente* (1928; tr. 1930 *The Eagle and the Serpent*) and Nellie Campobello (1900–86) in *Cartucho* (1931; tr. 1988 *Cartucho and My Mother's Hands*). Writers throughout Latin America used a variety of styles to grapple with the most urgent issues of each region. While the Andean countries contributed to this socially oriented vein with an extensive production of *indigenista* texts, in Colombia José Eustasio Rivera's (1889–1928) *La vorágine* (1924, tr. 1935 *The Vortex*) struck a sympathetic chord in the readers by presenting a harrowing picture of the exploitation of rubber-gatherers in the Amazon. The Uruguayan Horacio Quiroga (1878–1937) also used literature as a tool for denouncing social injustice (*Los desterrados*, 1926; tr. 1987 *The Exiles and Other Stories*). However, he is most notably recognized for his masterfully crafted tales of fantasy and psychological horror compiled in *La gallina degollada y otros cuentos* (1925; tr. 1976 *The Decapitated Chicken and Other Stories*).

The regionalist trends in poetry coalesced into *Negrismo* – seen as the Hispanic counterpart of the French-Antillean *Négritude* – which flourished in Cuba, Puerto Rico and the Dominican Republic in the 1920s and 1930s and was based on the affirmation of African-based traditions. Discussions of *negrista* poetry often revolve around listings of such characteristics as onomatopoeic phrasings, mythological references, Africanized vocabulary, imitation of drumbeat rhythms and the intermixing of the Spanish lyrical legacy with popular patterns of speech (Matibag 1996: 93). Cuban poet Nicolás Guillén (1902–89) is unquestionably the most prominent figure associated with the movement. In his landmark books *Motivos de son* (1930), *Sóngoro cosongo* (1931), *West Indies Ltd* (1934) and *Cantos para soldados y sones para turistas* (1937) Guillén created a unique blend of musicality, Spanish lyrical patterns and an anti-imperialist agenda, which was artistically and ideologically effective in heightening the awareness of the African heritage, and of the intersecting issues of class and race. In the years following the Cuban Revolution (1959), the internationally recognized poet Nancy Morejón (1944–) enriched Guillén's lyrical legacy with gender-conscious overtones. Her unique contribution to the reappraisal of *negrista* aesthetics and ideology is epitomized by her well-known poem 'Mujer negra' (Black Woman) from the collection *Parajes de una época* (Places of an Age, 1979). In Brazil, Jorge Amado's (1912–2001) sustained exploration of the African cultures of the Bahian region resulted in a steady flow of commercially successful novels, ranging from the realistic *Jubiabá* (1935; tr. 1984) to the magical *Gabriela, cravo e canela* (1958; tr. 1962 *Gabriela, Clove and Cinnamon*) and the satirical *Dona Flor e seus dois maridos* (1966; tr. 1969 *Dona Flor and Her Two Husbands*). His *Tenda dos milagres* (1969; tr. 1971 *Tent of Miracles*) deals with the problem of race relations against the backdrop of the Brazilian syncretic religion, Candomblé.

In the 1920s and 1930s numerous writers of considerable merit (Azuela, Gallegos, Icaza, Quiroga, Ramos, Rivera) followed the regionalist imperative to reaffirm local specificity by drawing upon rural landscapes and autochthonous themes. At the same time, an equally prominent group of authors furnished a different vision of Latin America, which was urban and torn by the dramatic contradictions of modernity. Writers as diverse as the Argentineans Roberto Arlt (1900–42) and Eduardo Mallea (1903–82), the Uruguayan Juan Carlos Onetti (1909–94) and the Chilean Eduardo Barrios (1884–1963) succeeded in lending their unique style to the shared themes of existential anguish, solitude and the alienation of urban-dwellers. A defiant disregard for patriarchal values distinguished the experimental novels of the Venezuelan Teresa de la Parra (1889–36) – *Ifigenia* (1924; tr. 1994) and *Memorias de la Mamá Blanca* (1929; tr. 1992 *Mama Blanca's Memoirs*) – whereas María Luisa Bombal's (Chile, 1910–80) hallucinatory narratives *La última niebla* (1935; tr. 1947 *The House of Mist*) and *La amortajada* (1938; tr. 1948 *The Shrouded Woman*) exemplified a remarkable synergy of fantasy, reality, myth and memory. Bombal's texts mark a separate achievement of the avant-garde period in the representation of female subjectivity while prefiguring the ambiguous and non-linear novels of the Boom and offering a prelude to what would later become known as Magical Realism. Beginning in the 1940s, the exploration of female subjectivity was enriched by the exquisite prose of a brilliant Brazilian stylist, Clarice Lispector (1920–77). Lispector weaved together unsettling introspection, subtle metaphysical reflection and formal innovation in narratives of striking originality, of which the later ones became particularly influential (*A maça no escuro*, 1961; tr. 1967 *Apple in the Dark*; *A hora da estrela*, 1977; tr. 1986 *The Hour of the Star*).

The conflicting impulses of autochthonous nationalism versus cosmopolitanism are best exemplified by the Brazilian avant-garde movement called *Modernismo* launched in 1922 in São Paulo, during the event known as *Semana de arte moderna* (The Modern Art Week). The movement (not to be confused with Spanish American *Modernismo* or the Anglo-American term Modernism) emphasized the rejection of Parnassian and Symbolist rhetoric, while focusing on everyday speech patterns and social and existential concerns. At its height, it evolved around the provocative metaphor of cannibalization first introduced in 1928 by Oswald de Andrade (1890–1954) in his iconoclastic 'Manifesto Antropofágico' (The Cannibalist Manifesto). Andrade broached the question of Latin American cultural autonomy by stressing the incorporation, inversion and transformation of European elements in Brazilian culture, echoing the cannibalistic practices of the Tupinamba Indians. Another leader of the *Modernismo* movement, Mario de Andrade (1893–1945), articulated his quest for Brazilian identity in *Macunaíma* (1928; tr. 1984), a carnivalesque story of a mythical trickster.

The diverse avant-garde movement of the 1920s and 1930s – of which Brazilian *Modernismo* was a distinct, but not the only manifestation – was a *tour de force* artistic response to the vertiginous experience of modernity. It developed against the backdrop of rapid socio-economic growth, dramatic developments in Europe (the First World War, the Spanish Civil War) and upheavals at home (the Mexican Revolution and its aftermath), and, at least in part, under the impact of Oswald Spengler's (1880–1936) *The Decline of the West* (1918–22). The avant-garde represented the cosmopolitan and urban discernible also in Spanish American *Modernismo*, but it defined itself in terms of audacious formal experimentation and was unequivocal in its rejection of *modernista* conventions. While multiple ties existed between various avant-garde strands, the movement is not easily reducible to a list of common characteristics. Nonetheless, the 'isms' that proliferated throughout the continent shared some common features, such as a poignant sense of existential anguish, a defiant assertion of art's autonomy, an all-encompassing critique of tradition, an emphasis on the magical dimension of artistic creativity (*creacionismo*), a distrust of hegemonic discourse and a virtuoso level of technical experimentation.

An impressive number of influential cultural journals such as the Cuban *Revista de Avance* (1927–30) and later *Orígenes* (1944–56), the Peruvian *Amauta* (1926–30), the Argentinean *Sur* (1931–70) and the Brazilian *Revista de Antropofagia* (1928) provided a creative platform for writers, artists and critics while facilitating cross-fertilization between the movements and serving as a laboratory for the experimental prose of the 1960s. The *vanguardista* iconoclastic desire to break with tradition and literary norms was truly unprecedented in its boldness, as expressed in numerous manifestos and programmatic articles, such as Vicente Huidobro's (Chile, 1895–1948) 'El creacionismo' (1925) or Andrade's 'Manifesto' (1928). But it was probably the intriguing and highly experimental poetry of Huidobro's *Altazor* (1931) and César Vallejo's *Trilce* (1922) that encapsulated the most radical attempts to deconstruct the language and then recompose it by means of free verse, creative use of typography, multiplicity of points of view, obsessive wordplay, unconnected images and most unusual neologisms.

Whereas Huidobro's and Vallejo's experiments often pushed the limits of intelligibility, their contemporary Pablo Neruda (Chile, 1904–73) became the most cherished poet of the Hispanic world and gained unparalleled international popularity thanks to his talent for combining the most daring aesthetic experiments with a wide range of themes of great resonance for ordinary readers. Neruda's immensely successful and prodigious literary production earned him world-wide recognition long before he was awarded the Nobel Prize for Literature (1971). Neruda ingratiated himself to readers with *Veinte poemas de amor y una canción desesperada* (1924; tr. 1969 *Twenty Love Poems and a Song of Despair*) and with his graceful homage to such seemingly unpoetic objects as spoons, onions and socks in *Odas elementales* (1954; tr. 1961 *The Elementary Odes*). Critics, on the other hand, celebrated his dazzling experiments with the avant-garde in *Residencia en la tierra* (1933; tr. 1946 *Residence on Earth and Other Poems*) and debated the ideological and poetic values of his epic *Canto General* (1950). Finally, Neruda's autobiographical *Memorial de la Isla Negra* (1964; tr. 1981 *Isla Negra: A Notebook*) offered a monumental compendium of his diverse styles and themes, including the recurring presence of Chilean landscapes and the interweaving of politics and art.

The prodigious quantity of Latin American poetic production in the second half of the twentieth century makes any attempt at synthesis extremely difficult. While Neruda's best-selling status and far-reaching influence were difficult to emulate, the distinct poetic voice of the Mexican Octavio Paz (1914–98) also received great acclaim for opening new avenues in post-vanguardist poetry and was later honoured with the Nobel Prize (1990) 'for impassioned writing with wide horizons, characterized by sensuous intelligence and humanistic integrity'. Of fundamental importance was Paz's daring blend of avant-garde experiments with metaphysical reflection and explorations of Mexican identity (*Piedra de sol*, 1957; tr. 1969 *The Sun Stone*). Among dozens of Latin American poets whose literary innovations – from whimsical and fanciful, to politically impassioned – made lasting contributions to the early-twentieth-century poetry, the following deserve special recognition: the Argentinean Oliverio Girondo (1891–1967), the Mexicans Xavier Villaurrutia (1903–50) and José Gorostiza (1901–73), the Cuban José Lezama Lima (1910–76) and the Nicaraguan Pablo Antonio Cuadra

(1912–85). In the last three decades of the twentieth century – which brought a stunning development of prose fiction – few Latin American poets inspired the same sense of awe as the novelists of the Boom. Nonetheless, the names of the Nicaraguans Ernesto Cardenal (Nicaragua, 1925–) and Gioconda Belli (1948–), the Chilean Nicanor Parra (Chile, 1914–), the Argentinean Alejandra Pizarnik (Argentina, 1936–72) and two Peruvians, Carlos Germán Belli (1927–) and Antonio Cisneros (1942–), invariably come to mind whenever we consider the bewildering artistry of individual talent and the reinvigorating role of poetry within the framework of national literatures.

The great variety of forms, topics and ideological positions characteristic of the vast body of contemporary Latin American poetry underlies the development of the twentieth-century essay as well and should be considered as part of the relentless quest for capturing Latin American and national identity. The paradigm of identity defines some of the most influential and self-reflexive essays of the century, including José Vasconcelos's (Mexico, 1882–1959) highly controversial *La raza cósmica* (1925), Fernando Ortiz's *Contrapunteo cubano de tabaco y azúcar* (1940), Ezequiel Martínez Estrada's (Argentina, 1895–1964) *Radiografía de la pampa* (X-Ray of the Pampa, 1933), Octavio Paz's, *El laberinto de la soledad* (1950; tr. 1961 *The Labyrinth of Solitude*) and *Postada* (1970; tr. 1972 *The Other Mexico: Critique of the Pyramid*), Sebastián Salazar Bondy's (Peru, 1924–64) *Lima la horrible* (Horrible Lima, 1964), Lezama Lima's *La expresión americana* (American Expression, 1957), Antonio Benítez Rojo's *La isla que se repite* (1989, tr. 1995 *The Repeating Island*) and José L. González's (Puerto Rico, 1926–) *País de cuatro pisos* (1980; tr. 1993 *The Four-Storied Country and Other Essays*).

While Latin American drama of the twentieth century has not been able to rival the continuing growth of poetry, the consolidation of the essay and the international recognition of narrative, in the 1960s and 1970s the development of theories of collective theatre by Enrique Buenaventura (Colombia, 1925–) and of the 'theatre of the oppressed' by Augusto Boal (Brazil, 1931–) reinvigorated this area of Latin American creativity and led to the heightening of political awareness and to the flourishing of experimental theatre. Earlier works by established playwrights such as Rodolfo Usigli (1905–79) and Emilio Carballido (1925–) in Mexico, Egon Wolff (1926–) in Chile and Joracy Camargo (1898–1967) in Brazil were followed by those of Osvaldo Dragún (1929–99) and Griselda Gambaro (1928–) in Argentina, Virgilio Piñera (1912–79) and José Triana (1933–) in Cuba, and Sabina Berman (1952–) in Mexico. Far from being dwarfed by the international projection of the novel, Latin American theatre continues to resound with current themes – from post-dictatorial legacies to globalization – by combining the strands of formal innovation and political engagement.

The remarkable trajectory of Latin American prose in the second half of the twentieth century and the emergence of what would come to be known as the Boom of the Latin American novel of the 1960s were directly indebted to the genius of Jorge Luis Borges (Argentina, 1899–1986), indisputably the most influential Latin American writer. Borges – erudite, unabashedly ironic, playful and ingenious – remains a key point of reference for any discussion of topics ranging from postmodernity and metafiction to the fantastic and detective narratives. Few texts can rival the virtuoso art of *Ficciones* (1944; tr. 1965 *Fictions*), a collection of metaphysical, deliberately elusive narratives that highlight the ambiguous, irrational and mysterious aspects of reality by means of labyrinthine structure and conceptual complexity.

It is important to remember, however, that the impulse for literary experimentation came simultaneously from different directions and no single author or text marks a watershed moment between the traditional and the new novel. While Juan Rulfo's (Mexico, 1918–86) phantasmagoric evocation of the tragic plight of the Mexican peasant in *El llano en llamas* (1953; tr. 1967 *The Burning Plain and Other Stories*) and in the novel *Pedro Páramo* (1955; tr. 1959) has little to do with Borges's erudite inquisitions, Rulfo's attempt to alter the paradigm of realist representation was equally daring in its amalgamation of myth, reality and imagination. Among the narratives that heralded the rise of an experimental aesthetics during the 1940s and 1950s the following represent a limited yet significant sampling of self-reflexive stances, achronological plots and fragmented structures: *Al filo del agua* (1946; tr. 1963 *The Edge of the Storm*) by Agustín Yáñez (Mexico, 1904–80), *El Señor Presidente* (1946) by Asturias, *La invención de Morel* (1940; tr. 1964 *The Invention of Morel*) by Adolfo Bioy Casares (Argentina, 1914–99) and *La región más transparente* (1958; tr. 1960 *Where the Air is Clear*) by Carlos Fuentes (Mexico, 1928–). Despite the diversity of forms, all of these texts undermine the straightforward Realism of the Regionalist novels and bear the stamp of the artistic achievements of the avant-garde (surrealist imagery, technical complexity, perspectivism, stream of consciousness, innovative use of speech patterns, exploration of irrationality) while engaging in an ambitious exploration of national and regional identities.

However, it was not until the 1960s that Latin America appeared at the forefront of the international literary stage. A vast body of narrative – mostly novels – published in the wake of the 1959 Cuban Revolution was truly astonishing, not only for its prodigious quantity, but, first and foremost, for its unprecedented aesthetic merit. Both aspects of this type of 'new novel' were further enhanced by the publishing industry world-wide and by the spectacular rise of academic criticism. This unique and fortuitous conjuncture – a powerful political catalyst, an unusual concentration of creative talent, and skilful marketing – led to the phenomenon often referred to as the Boom (1960–75).

One of the most salient characteristics of the Boom was the ubiquity of metafictional texts exploring the mechanisms of their own making, from *Rayuela* (1963; tr. 1966 *Hopscotch*) by Julio Cortázar (Argentina, 1914–84) – a novel whose 155 chapters could be read in varying sequences – to the bewildering wordplay of Guillermo Cabrera Infante's (Cuba, 1929–) *Tres tristes tigres* (1965; tr. 1971 *Three Trapped Tigers*). Shifts in narrative perspective, overlapping identities, temporal disjunctions and conflicting versions of a story became a signature style of the leading Boom novels: Fuentes's *La muerte de Artemio Cruz* (1962; tr. 1964 *The Death of Artemio Cruz*), Mario Vargas Llosa's (Peru, 1936–) *La casa verde* (1964; tr. 1968 *The Green House*) and *Conversación en la Catedral* (1969; tr. 1975 *Conversation in the Cathedral*), and José Donoso's (Chile, 1924–96) *El obsceno pájaro de la noche* (1970; tr. 1973 *The Obscene Bird of Night*).

The most successful novels of the Boom were also deeply immersed in regional issues, but in ways that involved responding to the demands of the Anglo-European market. 'Translating' the exotic uniqueness of Latin American culture – often associated with the idiosyncratic blend of transculturated myth, magic and irrational excess – became a style in its own right, known as Magical Realism. First coined by the German art critic Franz Roh, the original term became transposed and intertwined with the concept of Latin American 'marvellous' reality, proposed in Carpentier's novel, *El reino de este mundo* (1949; tr. 1957 *The Kingdom of this World*). According to Carpentier, in modern Europe the 'marvellous' has to be artificially created, whereas in Latin America it is an integral part of everyday reality because of the hybridity that remains at the core of its culture. The critics were eager to affix the label to a wide range of texts engaged in an exploration of myth and irrationality, from Carpentier's *Los pasos perdidos* (1953; tr. 1956 *The Lost Steps*) to Fuentes's novella *Aura* (1962; tr. 1965), Elena Garro's (Mexico, 1920–95) *Los recuerdos del porvenir* (1963; tr. 1969 *Recollections of Things to Come*) and Manuel Scorza's (Peru, 1928–83) cycle of five neo-indigenist novels (1970–79). The novel that carried Magical Realism, and the Boom, to the highest level of aesthetic achievement without losing its popular appeal was *Cien años de soledad* (1967; tr. 1970 *One Hundred Years of Solitude*) by García Márquez, the Nobel Prize winner of 1982. Inextricably linked to the art of storytelling, on the one hand, and to the literary traditions of the West, on the other, *Cien años de soledad* is a work of striking originality. Fanciful and humorous, radically experimental but readable and engaging, it established parameters for a fruitful combination of politics and aesthetics and a wide-ranging, muralist portrayal of Latin American 'archetypical' reality. In Brazil, the pinnacle of Magical Realism was reached a decade earlier, by João Guimarães Rosa's (1908–67) *Grande sertão veredas* (1956; tr. 1963 *The Devil to Pay in the Backlands*), which encompassed multiple perspectives and a neo-baroque exuberance of style to offer an unusual rendition of local legends and myths.

While numerous narratives written in the Magical Realist vein went unnoticed in the long shadow cast by García Márquez's masterpiece, Isabel Allende's (Chile, 1942–) best-selling novel *La casa de los espíritus* (1982; tr. 1985 *The House of the Spirits*) was successful in foregrounding its own brand of Magical Realism, defined by a unique mixture of fantasy, myth, romance and feminist parody of patriarchal models. According to some critics, *La casa de los espíritus* also exhibits the fundamental characteristics that help separate the aesthetics of the Boom from the following promotion of writers, associated, for the lack of a better term, with the so-called Post-Boom (1975–). Various critics' efforts (see Shaw 1993, 1995; Swanson 1995; Williams 1997) to differentiate between the Boom and the Post-Boom, and in an added complication, between the latter and the vast terrain of postmodernism, resulted in the following list of features based on the works of authors as divergent from one another as Allende, Antonio Skármeta (Chile, 1941–), Manuel Puig (Argentina, 1932–90), Luisa Valenzuela (Argentina, 1938–), Gustavo Sainz (Mexico, 1940–), Reinaldo Arenas (Cuba, 1943–90), Severo Sarduy (Cuba, 1937–93), Cristina Peri Rossi (Uruguay, 1941–), Luis Rafael Sánchez (Puerto Rico, 1936–) and Rosario Ferré (Puerto Rico, 1942–): renewed confidence in the power of language; consistent use of humour, satire and parody; highlighting of pop, youth and mass culture (film, music) in an effort to attract broader readership; and the triumphant recognition of formerly marginalized viewpoints, especially those of women, gays and lesbians.

While many of the writers established by the Boom – Fuentes, García Márquez, Vargas Llosa – continued to write prolifically throughout the 1980s and 1990s, they, too, moved away from hermetic narratives based on exacerbated stylistic innovation (epitomized by Fuentes's monumental *Terra Nostra* (1975; tr. 1977)) towards such 'user-friendly' texts as *Crónica de una muerte anunciada* (1981; tr. 1982 *Chronicle of Death Foretold*) and *El amor en los tiempos del cólera* (1985; tr. 1988 *Love in the Time of Cholera*) by García Márquez, *La tía Julia y el escribidor* (1977; tr. 1982 *Aunt Julia and the Scriptwriter*) by Vargas Llosa, and *Gringo Viejo* (1985; tr. 1985 *The Old Gringo*) by Fuentes. The writing scene of the Post-Boom included also, according to Seymour Menton (1993), the unusual rise of the New Historical Novel represented by an impressive array of books particularly keen on reconfiguring the colonial period and the independence movements through fictional projections of historical figures, such as Carpentier's *El arpa y la sombra* (1979; tr. 1990 *The Harp and the Shadow*), Abel Posse's (Argentina, 1936–) *Los perros del paraíso* (1983; tr. 1989 *The Dogs of Paradise*) and Fuentes's *La campaña* (1990; tr. 1991 *The Campaign*).

Many of these historical novels depicted the cycle of repression, terror and protest as endemic to Latin America, often using the past as an allegory of the present. In the 1970s, the escalation of terror by the authoritarian regimes of El Salvador, Guatemala, Chile, Uruguay and Argentina had broad repercussions for writers and intellectuals, who were often forced into exile and, in many cases, imprisoned, tortured or 'disappeared'. The collective experience of torture, suppression and exile was reflected in a variety of innovative and aesthetically accomplished works, including Valenzuela's powerful short stories from *Cambio de armas* (1982; tr. 1985 *Other Weapons*) and Ricardo Piglia's novel *Respiración artificial* (1980; tr. 1994 *Artificial Respiration*), a compelling denunciation of Argentina's violent present disguised as a postmodern meditation on metahistory and metafiction. Diamela Eltit's (Chile, 1949–) performance-based novel *Lumpérica* (1983), and *El padre mío* (1989), which emerged out of the resistance movement to the Pinochet regime, challenged readers by eroding any remaining standards of literary representation.

With the dominant focus on the violent reality at hand, it was, however, the non-fictional genre of *testimonio* that became the most important outlet for redressing socio-political grievances. In the 1980s and 1990s *testimonio* was critically recognized as a unique narrative form representing the creative vitality of Latin American culture and its power to express the defiance of subordinate groups and to recover historically muted voices. As a form of life-writing that attempts to 'interface' several disciplines (literature, ethnology, historiography) with a progressive political agenda, *testimonio* does not fit comfortably within the contours of any single disciplinary model. Nonetheless, the paradigm of rebellion that underlies *testimonio*, combined with the moral responsibility of the intellectual, inspires multiple associations with confession, autobiography, ethnography and New Journalism, on the one hand, and the Latin American tradition of giving voice to the marginalized and defying hegemonic forms of expression, on the other. In order to define *testimonio* as a distinct form of non-fictional writing, it is helpful to limit it to the narratives that recover the unspoken experience of the oppressed by means of a 'solidarity pact' forged between intellectuals and the common people in the process of transcription and editing of an eyewitness account by a professional writer or journalist (see Gugelberger 1996; Sklodowska 1991).

Even though *testimonio* is fraught with tensions related to mediation, editorial interventions and cross-cultural (mis)understandings, in its heyday (1960–85) it produced a veritable treasure trove of texts of great artistic merit: from Carolina Maria de Jesus's (Brazil, 1914–77) *Quarto de despejo* (1960; tr. 1963 *Child of the Dark*) and the enormously successful *Biografía de un cimarrón* (1966; tr. 1968 *Biography of a Runaway Slave*) by Miguel Barnet (Cuba, 1941–) to *Hasta no verte Jesús mío* (1969; tr. 1987 *Until We Meet Again*) by the Mexican Elena Poniatowska (1933–) and the internationally acclaimed *Me llamo Rigoberta Menchú y así me nació la conciencia* (1983; tr. 1984 *I Rigoberta Menchú, an Indian Woman in Guatemala*) by Rigoberta Menchú (Guatemala, 1959–). This impassioned account – edited by Venezuelan anthropologist Elisabeth Burgos-Debray – told by a Maya Quiché woman activist whose family and village had been destroyed by the political violence in Guatemala, brought Rigoberta Menchú the Nobel Peace Prize in 1992. However, more recently, in the highly publicized book *Rigoberta Menchú and the Story of all Poor Guatemalans* (1998), American anthropologist David Stoll revealed a number of inconsistencies and fabrications in Menchú's *testimonio*, trigerring a widespread debate about truth and lies, political commitment and the creation of political myths. Menchú – the icon of indigenous resistance and testimonial authenticity – became a target of vitriolic attacks.

Even though *testimonio* has been canonized as a super-genre of sorts that has changed for good the paradigm of subaltern (under)representation in Latin America, its significance in the wake of the twentieth century also has to do with the fact that it self-critically embodies one of the most debated issues of the postmodern/post-colonial era: the constitution of the subject and the configuration of representation within the context of globalization, multiculturalism and hybridity.

SELECTED FURTHER READING

Alonso, C. 1990: *The Spanish American Regional Novel: Modernity and Autochthony*. Cambridge: Cambridge University Press.

Arias, A. 2001: *The Rigoberta Menchú Controversy*. Minneapolis: University of Minnesota Press.

Armstrong, P. 1999: *Third World Literary Fortunes: Brazilian Literature and its International Reception*. Lewisburg, PA: Bucknell University Press.

Beverley, J. and Oviedo, J. (eds) 1994: *The Postmodernism Debate in Latin America*. Durham, NC: Duke University Press.

Brooksbank Jones, A. and Davies, C. 1996: *Latin American Women's Writing: Feminist Readings in Theory and Crisis*. New York: Clarendon Press.

Bush, A. 2002: *The Routes of Modernity: Spanish American Poetry from the Early Eighteenth to the Mid-Nineteenth Century*. Lewisburg: Bucknell University Press.

Emery, A. F. 1996: *The Anthropological Imagination in Latin American Literature*. Columbia and London: University of Missouri Press.

Franco, J. 1999: *Critical Passions: Selected Essays*. Durham, NC: Duke University Press.

González Echevarría, R. 1990: *Myth and Archive*. Cambridge: Cambridge University Press.

González Echevarría, R. and Pupo-Walker, E. (eds) 1996: *The Cambridge History of Latin American Literature*, 3 vols. Cambridge: Cambridge University Press.

Gugelberger, G. 1996: *The Real Thing: Testimonial Discourses and Latin America*. Durham, NC, and London: Duke University Press.

Jackson, R. L. 1976: *The Black Image in Latin American Literature*. Albuquerque: University of New Mexico Press.

Jrade, C. L. 1998: *Modernismo, Modernity, and the Development of Spanish American Literature*. Austin: Texas University Press.

Ludmer, J. 1988: *El género gauchesco: Un tratado sobre la patria*. Buenos Aires: Editorial Sudamericana.

Luis, W. 1984: *Voices from Under: Black Narrative in Latin America and the Caribbean*. Westport, CT: Greenwood Press.

Martin, G. 1984: Boom, yes. 'New' novel no: further reflections on the optical illusions of the 1960s in Latin America. *Bulletin of Latin American Research* 3, 2, 53–63.

Masiello, F. 1992: *Between Civilization and Barbarism: Women, Nation, and Literary Culture in Modern Argentina*. Lincoln: University of Nebraska Press.

Matibag, E. 1996: *Afro-Cuban Religious Experience: Cultural Reflections in Narrative*. Gainesville: University Press of Florida.

Menton, S. 1993: *Latin American New Historical Novel*. Austin: University of Texas Press.

Meyer, D. (ed.) 1995: *Reinterpreting the Spanish American Essay: Women Writers of the 19th and 20th Centuries*. Austin: University of Texas Press.

Parkinson Zamora, L. 1997: *The Usable Past: The Imagination of History in Recent Fiction of the Americas*. Cambridge: Cambridge University Press.

Parkinson Zamora, L. and Faris, W. B. (eds) 1995: *Magical Realism: Theory, History, Community*. Durham, NC: Duke University Press.

Piedra, J. 1997: From monkey tales to Cuban songs: on signification. In M. Fernández Olmos and L. Paravisini-Gebert (eds), *Sacred Possessions: Voodou, Obeah, and the Caribbean*. New Brunswick, NJ: Rutgers University Press, 122–50.

Pratt, M. L. 1992: *Imperial Eyes: Travel Writing and Transculturation*. London: Routledge.

Ramos, J. 2001: *Divergent Modernities: Culture and Politics in Nineteenth Century Latin America*. Durham and London: Duke University Press.

Rowe, W. 2000: *Poets of Contemporary Latin America: History and the Inner Life*. Oxford: Oxford University Press.

Schwarz, R. 1992: *Misplaced Ideas: Essays on Brazilian Culture*. London: Verso.

Shaw, D. 1993: On the new novel in Spanish America. *New Novel Review* 1, 1, 59–73.

Shaw, D. 1995: The post-Boom in Spanish American fiction. *Studies in Twentieth Century Literature* 19, 1, 12–27.

Shumway, N. 1991: *The Invention of Argentina*. Berkeley: University of California Press.

Sklodowska, E. 1991: *Testimonio hispanoamericano: historia, teoría, poética*. New York: Peter Lang.

Smith, P. J. 1992: *Representing the Other: Race, Text and Gender in Spanish and Spanish American Narrative*. Oxford: Clarendon Press.

Sommer, D. 1991: *Foundational Fictions: The National Romances of Latin America*. Berkeley: University of California Press.

Spitta, S. 1995: *Between Two Waters: Narratives of Transculturation in Latin America*. Houston, TX: Rice University Press.

Stabb, M. S. 1967: *In Quest of Identity: Patterns in the Spanish American Essay of Ideas*. Chapel Hill: University of North Carolina Press.

Swanson, P. 1995: *The New Novel in Latin America: Politics and Popular Culture after the Boom*. Manchester and New York: Manchester University Press.

Versenyi, A. 1993: *Theatre in Latin America: Religion, Politics and Culture from Cortés to the 1980s*. New York and Cambridge: Cambridge University Press.

Williams, R. L. 1997: *The Postmodern Novel in Latin America: Politics, Culture and the Crisis of Truth*. Basingstoke: Macmillan.

Zavala, I. M. 1992: *Colonialism and Culture: Hispanic Modernism and the Social Imaginary*. Bloomington and Indianapolis: Indiana University Press.

6

Approaches to Latin American literature

Brian Gollnick

Contemporary Latin American literary studies can be dated to a November evening in 1940, when Pedro Henríquez Ureña (Dominican Republic, 1884–1946) gave his first lecture as the Norton Distinguished Visiting Professor at Harvard University. The book he prepared from these lectures, *Literary Currents in Hispanic America* (1945), is the best early academic history of Latin American letters. Continental in scope, analytical in approach, and written in a language which remains elegant and accessible, *Literary Currents* combines the breadth of its author's continental perspective with the depth of his historical knowledge. Henríquez Ureña's work was not a solitary achievement, however, but the consolidation of an intellectual generation, including Alfonso Reyes (Mexico, 1889–1959) and Mariano Picón Salas (Venezuela, 1901–65), which largely defined Latin America's cultural heritage during the first half of the twentieth century. Perhaps more than his contemporaries, Henríquez Ureña put into practice the nationalist agenda of José Martí (Cuba, 1853–95) and José Enrique Rodó (Uruguay, 1872–1917). Rodó's essay *Ariel* (1900) defines Latin America as a spiritual culture whose aesthetic values must be guarded against Anglo-American materialism, while Martí's *Our America* (1891) pleads for Latin American intellectuals to embrace popular culture and galvanize their societies against US imperialism. Crucially, both assign literature a privileged role in understanding Latin American society (Ramos 2001: 251–67).

Literary Currents extends this privileging of literature into a systematic cultural history which can be described as a form of humanist nationalism: nationalism in the sense of defining the particularity of Latin American culture *vis-à-vis* Europe and the USA; humanist in the sense of understanding Latin America's cultural tradition as a progressive history of self-expression. Henríquez Ureña was consistently optimisitic about the role of literature in this history: as Latin America moved towards autonomy and integration, he saw its literature as an increasingly perceptive reflection of society. Significantly, Henríquez Ureña measured this progress through the institutionalization of culture. More than great writers or aesthetic movements, *Literary Currents* documents the consolidation of cultural institutions which Henríquez Ureña hoped would unify the region's citizens: newspapers, libraries, museums, and especially schools. Henríquez Ureña never relinquished his faith in these institutions or in the importance of literature and literacy as guarantors of cultural autonomy and civil rights. Unfortunately, the need to defend those rights has only grown since Henríquez Ureña's death. Latin American literary theory, however, has come to question his belief in education and literature as the best tools for doing so.

In the first half of the twentieth century, Latin American literature was dominated by the region's poets, many of whom were active participants in the international avant-garde. Latin American narrative would not attain a similar international profile until the second half of the twentieth century, when a series of experimental novelists achieved recognition outside the region. This shift culminated in the 1960s with the 'Boom' of the Latin American novel, and the popularity of authors like Gabriel García Márquez (Colombia), Carlos Fuentes (Mexico), Julio Cortázar (Argentina, 1914–84) and Mario Vargas Llosa (Peru) quickly eclipsed the poets' legacy. The popularity of the Boom novelists coincided with an influx of critical tools. Some were imported, principally from the Paris of the late 1950s and early 1960s, where Sartrean existentialism had given way to the structuralism and post-structuralism of Lévi-Strauss, Barthes, Foucault and Derrida. One example is Cuban novelist and critic Severo Sarduy (1937–92), who lived in Paris for three decades and was directly involved in the development of post-structuralism. Both structuralism and post-structuralism reject a direct or mimetic relationship of language to the world, either in a material sense of accurately representing reality or in a Platonic sense of expressing ultimate truth. Sarduy elaborated this rejection of the mimetic function of language into a Latin American model of the baroque. The ongoing influence of post-structuralism can be felt most powerfully, however, through Cuban-American critic Roberto González Echevarría.

González Echevarría's most influential study, *Myth and Archive* (1990), theorizes Latin American narrative from the sixteenth century to the present. His theory centres on the mediating function of three forms of social discourse: law, in the colonial period; science (as expressed in travel writing) from independence to the 1920s; and anthropology, from the 1920s until the late twentieth century. For each period, González Echevarría traces how Latin American narrative strives not to give a direct reflection of social life, but to appropriate the truth-value associated with these other forms of knowledge. Latin American narrative then emerges as a doubly-mimetic expression: it represents society, but only indirectly, by mimicking the discourses which have defined authoritative knowledge. As fiction, however, narrative itself makes no claims to truth, and its ability to mimic other forms of discourse serves to reveal the fictional nature of their authority. Finally, Latin American narrative's engagement with these other discourses is understood to be encoded in the literary tradition itself, particularly in 'archival novels': works written in the mid to late twentieth century whose self-reflexive nature glosses the function of the law, science or anthropology in Latin American narrative. By problematizing the direct relationship between literature and society, González Echeverría's framework undermines the centre of humanist criticism. In *Myth and Archive*, literary history can no longer be traced as the expression of a collective subject – 'the cultural spirit of Latin America'. Instead, literature glosses its own development.

The elegance and scope of González Echevarría's theory are impressive. Yet, while he historicizes the discourses mediating Latin American narrative, he does not similarly locate the changing function of narrative itself. Narrative's doubly-mimetic critique seems to operate in the same manner in every historical period. This flattening out of history exemplifies post-structuralism's distance from the referential function of language: *Myth and Archive* understands texts primarily in relationship to other texts, and the social critique which forms the centre even of many 'archival fictions' becomes marginalized. Clear examples include the appropriation of indigenous lands in Miguel Angel Asturias's *Men of Maize* (Guatemala, 1949) or the massacre of banana workers in García Márquez's *One Hundred Years of Solitude* (1967). Finally, with language separated from its referential function, writing becomes personified as a historical actor. González Echevarría traces a critical function operated by the narrative form itself, which replaces both social history and authors as the subject of literary history. Ultimately, this means that narrative's critical function operates without concrete agents, and therefore without objectives or meaningful consequences.

The other major movement in criticism during the 1960s took its inspiration not from abroad, but from within Latin American sociology, particularly from dependency theory. Dependency theory developed in the 1950s, when Latin American scholars began to theorize the subordination of their regional economies to the global market. Dependency theorists understood the economic success of the USA and Europe as resulting from their dominance over peripheral regions: overdevelopment in some regions caused underdevelopment in others. Breaking this cycle meant altering the periphery's dependence on the global economy through a realignment of political and economic power. In keeping with its Marxian roots, dependency theory was thus a revolutionary paradigm which advocated radical social change. For many years, the Cuban Revolution offered hope that such change was possible, and dependency theory enjoyed wide currency in the late 1960s and 1970s. For economic history, dependency theory sought to understand the specific circumstances of Latin America within the world system. Literary scholars sought to understand Latin American literature within the social sphere defined by that economic history. In particular, dependency theory generated renewed interest in the moments and techniques by which Latin American literature had expressed its independence from the metropolis. Alejandro

Losada (Argentina, 1936–85) elaborated the most systematic effort in this direction. Losada replaced national frameworks with regional divisions defined by their social structures and engagement with the global economy. He then considered the possibilities of each regional literature breaking with metropolitan models. The synthetic power of his work is considerable and Losada establishes broadly insightful comparisons. However, his judgements about particular authors, works or movements are not always convincing when these are seen in their specific contexts.

Even before Losada, the eminent Brazilian critic Antônio Cândido authored a more successful reading of Latin American literature through dependency theory. In 'Literature and underdevelopment' (1969), Cândido identified three broad periods in Latin American literature based on awareness of the region's relationship to the world economy: the 'ideology of the new country' (the late nineteenth and early twentieth centuries), the 'pre-consciousness of underdevelopment' (the early twentieth century to the 1940s), and the 'consciousness of underdevelopment' (the 1950s and 1960s). The 'ideology of the new country' understood the natural wealth of Latin America as promising strong nations, while the 'pre-consciousness of underdevelopment' inverted this formula and took the overwhelming presence of the region's environment to symbolize the weakness of its institutions. Finally, the 'consciousness of underdevelopment' criticized the region's relationship to the global economy through an original aesthetic project that Cândido called 'meta-regionalism', defined in part by the Boom authors. 'Literature and underdevelopment' continues to offer a powerful alternative to periodizations based on imported nomenclatures, such as 'Romanticism' and 'Naturalism', most of which could be said not fully to address the adaptation of these aesthetics in Latin America. However, the widest impact of dependency theory in literary criticism has been through Uruguayan critic Angel Rama (1926–83).

An eclectic and innovative thinker, Rama's work is difficult to exemplify through a single text. His two most influential studies, *Transculturación narrativa en América Latina* (1982) and *La ciudad letrada* (The Lettered City, 1984), synthesize Latin America's literary history through complementary genealogies of cultural power. *Transculturación* draws on Fernando Ortiz (Cuba, 1881–69), a Cuban intellectual who replaced the unidirectional term 'acculturation' with the term 'transculturation' in order to describe the complex process by which the slave trade and agricultural production in the Caribbean combined African and Hispanic cultures, even influencing European society. Rama drew on Ortiz to revindicate the regionalist novel, a body of work dating from the early 1900s to the 1950s. Among regionalists, Rama privileges a group he identifies as 'transculturators': those whose work engages with experimental narrative techniques from the international avant-garde and forms of orality drawn from traditional rural cultures. In these writers Rama finds a measure of cultural specificity asserted against the homogenizing effects of modernization.

Ultimately, Rama posits transcultural narratives as a model for a nationalism capable of integrating the heterogeneous elements characteristic of many Latin American countries. In assigning literature the capacity to express an alternate national project, *Transculturación narrativa* follows the humanist vision of literature expressing a collective social subject. However, Rama approaches this heritage through a global concept of modernization influenced by dependency theory. In keeping with the bi-polar model of dependency theory, Rama depicts economic and social modernization as forces which move unilaterally from the centre of the global system towards the periphery. Peripheral intellectuals may preserve a measure of their own identity, but Rama does not see peripheral societies contributing to modernization itself. A break from this uni-directional conception of the centre–periphery relationship had already been announced in Ortiz's work, but a similar perspective would not emerge in Latin American literary studies until Anglophone post-colonial theory had influenced the field.

Just as most Anglophone post-colonial theory departs from Edward Said's *Orientalism* (1978), most efforts to develop a similar project for Latin America depart from *The Lettered City* (1996), Rama's posthumously published analysis of Latin America's intellectual class. Taking the elitist nature of education in the region as its starting point, *The Lettered City* questions the humanist tradition. Far from being the progressive force of integration and stability which Henríquez Ureña had imagined, Rama sees literacy as a crucial form of privilege and domination. However, education, with literacy and literature as its key expressions, has not simply functioned as the servant of power. Instead, Rama suggests that the dominant classes in Latin America have needed men of letters, writers, lawyers, historians and the like to spread their message to the people. In the light of that mutual need, the educated elite – the *letrados* – developed as a semi-autonomous guild which mediated between the elites and the general population. At the top of this guild, Rama identifies intellectuals with an explicit awareness of education as a mechanism of exclusion. These cultural directors constitute 'the lettered city': the ideologues charged with ensuring the continued interdependence of education and privilege. A large portion of *The Lettered City* traces this sector through its origins in colonial Latin America. However, Rama demonstrates that the lettered city's hold was difficult to overcome, even for radical or revolutionary intellectuals. In contrast to the optimism of *Transculturación narrativa*, *The Lettered City* thus explores how the relationship between literacy and power remained largely unchanged until the 1960s, when the mass media introduced broadcast forms of communication capable of mediating between the elites and the masses without recourse to the written word.

Two misconceptions are easily drawn from *The Lettered City*. The first rejects Rama's theory as one in which power is exercised with little space for dissent. The second accepts Rama's theory but understands it as announcing the dawn of the mass media as the main site of cultural struggle. Both misconceptions fail to locate the historical experience informing Rama's book.

If any society in Latin America should have fulfilled Henríquez Ureña's vision of education as the building block of democracy, it was Uruguay. Rama's rise to become one of the most prominent cultural figures of his day owes much to the Uruguayan public education system, the most advanced in Latin America during the 1940s and 1950s. However, the Uruguayan military coup in 1973–74, only months after a coup in Chile and ten years after a coup in Brazil, forced Rama into exile. The coup also demonstrated that even the most educated population in Latin America was not a bulwark against authoritarianism. If Rama's interest is in culture's collusion with power rather than resistance, it is because *The Lettered City* emerges from the enormous challenge presented by South American military governments in the 1970s.

Rama was not, however, prepared to abandon the possibility that intellectuals and literature might promote change. Instead Rama criticizes radical intellectuals from the early twentieth century for their 'inability to imagine forms of democratization less dependent on the state' as the primary agent of reform. He also attacks their 'failure to reflect on the capacity of institutionalized power to reproduce itself in ever more rigid and authoritarian forms' (Rama 1996: 104–5). Implicitly, correcting these failures would require realigning intellectuals away from institutionalized, vertical forms of power rooted in the state and towards more diffuse, horizontal forms of power rooted in civil society. Here one can sense the long-standing influence of Antonio Gramsci, whose reflections on the importance of intellectuals and culture in forming cross-class alliances marked a major renovation in twentieth-century Marxism. Rama's implicit appeal that intellectuals learn to work from civil society rather than from the institutional power of the state generates a utopian moment in the otherwise pessimistic history of *The Lettered City*: the symbiosis between elites and *letrados* can be broken only when the latter cease to identify the state and its institutional structures as the objective of struggle and as the agents of social change. This hope to realign the political function of intellectuals may have seemed dim in the early 1980s, when civil society was largely shut down in many areas of Latin America, but that hope is not absent from *The Lettered City*. By pointing to this need for intellectuals to engage with social movements as participants rather than as self-appointed vanguards of change, Rama does not reject the humanist dream of literature as a collective expression. Instead, he rejects the privilege which Martí, Rodó, and even Henríquez Ureña assigned to elite literary aesthetics as a form of knowledge uniquely suited to express societal norms and aspirations. In this sense, *The Lettered City* develops a broader framework for understanding the importance of transcultural writers who engage with popular culture outside the lettered city. As presented in *Transculturación narrativa*, these writers allow for imagining a more inclusive form of national culture. Read in conjunction with *The Lettered City*, their work allows for something more important: imagining new functions for intellectuals within the nation.

Despite the closely related nature of Rama's two most influential works,

The Lettered City has frequently been read as a repudiation of *Transculturación narrativa*. In this sense, *The Lettered City* has provided a Latin American genealogy of knowledge and power similar to the relationship Said traces in *Orientalism*. Said studies metropolitan intellectuals in their depictions of colonized regions and Rama studies intellectuals in colonized societies, but both demonstrate the closeness of intellectuals to political power. Said and Rama thus suggest that intellectuals (including creative writers) wield real influence over social policy. As Neil Larsen has recently argued, a corollary conclusion has often been that revealing the intellectual's relationship to power constitutes a form of post-colonial criticism (Larsen 2001: 3–31). The work of John Beverley is perhaps the most influential example of this reading of Rama.

Engaging with historians working on colonial India, Beverley has spearheaded efforts to study the role of the popular classes – or subaltern groups – in the Latin American literary sphere. Beverley initiates this project by reading *The Lettered City* as a repudiation of Latin American literature's closeness to political power. For Beverley, the most urgent object of analysis is then 'the complicity of the academy itself – *our* complicity – in producing and reproducing the elite/subaltern relation' (Beverley 1999: 10). *The Lettered City* is thus taken to mean that the question posed in *Transculturación narrativa* – how can elites engage more effectively with marginalized or subaltern cultures? – is impossible without first undertaking a critique of intellectual institutions. This critique not only precedes engagement with subaltern knowledge; in some ways, Beverley sees it as precluding such an engagement: bringing subaltern knowledge into literary expression subsumes subalterns into the very institutions which have defined subaltern cultures as inferior. Beverley's approach to subaltern studies follows Rama in questioning the humanist belief in literature as a privileged vehicle for expressing the collective consciousness. However, by excluding the possibilities that elite intellectuals might apprehend subaltern knowledge in a non-repressive manner, Beverley denies the possibility of an alternative alignment between intellectuals and civil society. The utopian moment implicit even in *The Lettered City* thus dissipates into a Manichean divide between elite and subaltern cultures.

Argentinean scholar Walter Mignolo's efforts to engage Latin American literature with debates on post-colonialism are perhaps closer to Rama's original critique. Throughout the 1980s, Mignolo became one of the principal figures in renovating the field of colonial Latin American literary studies, and his book on this topic, *The Darker Side of the Renaissance* (1995), frames a broad project for approaching non-textual forms of indigenous cultural expression and for theorizing their exclusion from literary histories. Unlike Beverley, Mignolo defends the theoretical validity of intersecting literature and subaltern cultures. By analysing non-traditional objects of study – pictographs, maps, non-alphabetic forms of writing, textiles, and so forth – Mignolo's work is closer to Rama's project of using popular knowledge to de-centre elite authority. Mignolo's interest in these non-traditional objects of study has produced a number of innovative vocabularies. Unfortunately, meta-theoretical concerns often overdetermine these vocabularies. For example, the frameworks in *The Darker Side of the Renaissance*, including 'pluritopic hermeneutics' and 'post-Occidentalism', are most convincing as interventions in the theory of European colonialism. This dynamic has only sharpened in *Local Histories, Global Designs* (2000), where Mignolo develops the concept of 'border gnosis' for communicating between elite and subaltern knowledge on a transnational scale.

Alternative models for understanding Latin American literature in relation to previously excluded forms of cultural and textual production have emerged most strongly from other innovators in the field of colonial literature. Through her collaborations with the prominent anthropologist John Murra, US scholar Rolena Adorno (1986) has located the early seventeenth-century Spanish-Quechua bilingual writings of Felipe Guaman Poma de Ayala in a densely contextualized framework which emphasizes the contestatory position of native writing in colonial Peru. In a similar vein, Swiss critic Martin Lienhard expanded his initial work on twentieth-century Peruvian narrative into a cross-cultural and historical project on Latin America's indigenous writing. His study, *La voz y su huella* (The Voice and Its Trace, 1991), synthesizes the interactions between the dominant literatures of Latin America and their depictions of indigenous peoples, on the one hand, and the counter-tradition of indigenous peoples' own writings, on the other. Like Mignolo, Adorno and Lienhard engage literature with forms of knowledge traditionally excluded from high culture. However, their approach works from the ground up, beginning with detailed counter-histories preserved in fragmentary and little-understood texts. By recuperating these texts and reconstructing the traditions from which they emerge, Adorno and Lienhard add a dimension of specificity to the contestatory engagement between oral and written culture. The complexity of the social subjects and textual production revealed by this work makes it impossible to assimilate the literature of the colonial period into a synthetic understanding of national history. Perhaps most importantly, Adorno and Lienhard also demonstrate that despite the close association of education and power traced by Rama, subaltern groups in Latin America also possess a long tradition of appropriating the written word into cultures of resistance.

Because they are inflected across ethnic and class division, studies of sexuality and gender have offered the most decisive examples of non-traditional intellectuals working to subvert the 'lettered city' from within. The social history of feminism in many regions of Latin America emerges in tandem or even ahead of such movements in the USA or Europe. Alongside the efforts of those movements to claim rights in the public sphere, women intellectuals have made decisive contributions to the arts and literature in Latin America. Electa Arenal and Stacey Schlau's study *Untold Sisters* (1989) established a programmatic framework for recuperating and valorizing the writings of nuns during the colonial period. The texts which Arenal and Schlau study have opened an important door onto the history of women intellectuals. These investigations reveal the challenges faced by women writers who had to defy and affirm the norms of colonial society to attain some degree of self-representation in patriarchal cultural spheres.

Given the barrier of education, women's literature in modern Latin America has, until recent decades, largely been restricted to the upper classes. Important women intellectuals, including Teresa de la Parra (Venezuela, 1889–1936), María Luisa Bombal (Chile, 1910–80), Elena Garro (Mexico, 1920–98), Rosario Castellanos (Mexico, 1925–74) and Clarice Lispector (Brazil, 1925–77), have used access to education to create literary works and essays critical of the limitations placed on women. Recuperation of work like theirs constitutes a major project within feminist criticism. Significant efforts have been made to recover and revindicate the production of women writers in the nineteenth century, once considered the darkest period for Latin American women intellectuals. Francine Masiello's (1992) research on Argentina offers one prominent example. Such work has not, however, simply been a project of recuperation. Like Adorno and Lienhard's studies of indigenous writing, work on women writers represents a sustained application of archival research guided by the theoretical project of displacing the masculine normative subject which has grounded nationalist and humanist literary histories. Within those established histories, the work of women writers has alternately been marginalized because of its rejection of patriarchal values or subsumed into a masculine canon which ignored its challenge to gender norms. Recovering and restoring the tradition of women's writing means re-thinking the constitution of the literary canon and the collective values it espouses and sustains. To date, perhaps the most influential effort to re-think the literary canon from a feminist perspective has been Doris Sommer's analysis of nineteenth- and early-twentieth-century narrative. In *Foundational Fictions* (1991), Sommer approaches the established canon of the Latin American novel during the period of national formation and exposes how melodrama and the family romance establish an imaginary project of social unity based on patriarchal norms. In these plots, gender dynamics – usually the allegorical marriage of characters from disparate social groups – mask the unresolved heterogeneity of Latin American society. Sommer thus demonstrates the centrality of gender analysis to the constitution of the literary sphere.

Given the political nature of this work, re-articulations of the literary canon in the light of gender have most often been associated with the emergence of women as social agents. This trend was never more visible than in the 1970s and 1980s, the darkest years of military dictatorships in South America and civil wars in Central America. Women's organizations in Argentina, Uruguay and Chile became a critical focal point of criticism against military governments. In Central America, women in guerrilla organizations, particularly in the successful Sandinista revolution in Nicaragua, brought gender issues to a new prominence, including the work of women writers.

Perhaps more than any other critic, the English scholar Jean Franco has articulated a broadly based feminist analysis of Latin American literature informed by this contemporary social history. Long considered among the foremost scholars of Latin American literature, Franco's work is as broad-ranging, influential, and difficult to synthesize as Rama's. Her early works include a study of intellectuals in Latin America and a history of Latin American literature (1967, 1969). Beginning in the 1970s, Franco's synthetic knowledge of Latin American literature and its relationship to political history allowed her to produce important reappraisals of the Boom authors and to trace changes in the position of literature in the regional and international market-place. In the 1980s, she published a series of powerful essays denouncing the systematic torture and brutalization of women by military governments in South America. In these articles, Franco demonstrated that even in the extreme deformations produced by authoritarian regimes, gender dynamics inflect the public sphere and the possibilities of resistance. In 1989, Franco published *Plotting Women*, a highly influential study of women's writing in Mexico. Other critics have updated the specific analyses Franco offers of Mexican women writers, but *Plotting Women* remains a highly influential study because of the example it offers of how a national literary canon can be re-evaluated from the perspective of gendered exclusions. However, Franco's most enduring contribution to the development of a Latin American feminist criticism has been her persistence in arguing that women's subordination in partriachal societies does not by itself situate them as effective representatives for other oppressed groups. Franco has always insisted on the need to link feminist analyses to criticism of other forms of privilege and domination, including ethnicity, social class and sexual identity.

As with women, there have always been important gay and lesbian intellectuals in Latin America, including Teresa de la Parra, José Lezama Lima (Cuba, 1910–76), Lydia Cabrera (Cuba, 1899–1991), Salvador Novo (Mexico, 1904–74) and Xavier Villaurrutia (Mexico, 1903–50). It is only in recent decades, however, that their work has been studied in relationship to their sexuality. The explicit thematization of sexual identity in high-profile authors like Manuel Puig (Argentina, 1932–90), Reinaldo Arenas (Cuba, 1943–90) and Cristina Peri Rossi (Uruguay), as well as in popular works of documentary fiction, such as Luis Zapata's *El vampiro de la Colonia Roma* (Mexico, 1979), contributed to interest in gay writing. As with feminism, however, the emergence of sexuality studies has responded largely to gay and lesbian political organization and the efforts of gay and lesbian intellectuals to produce cultural histories which include sexual identity. Prominent examples can be found in the work of Mexican critics Carlos Monsiváis (1997) and José Joaquín Blanco (1991), or the Argentinian poet and essayist Néstor Perlongher (1997). Finally, the vitality of sexuality studies also emerges from an awareness among feminists that definitions of masculinity and femininity necessarily intersect with definitions of heterosexuality and homosexuality. In many ways, sexuality studies thus extends the feminist project of questioning the bases from which traditional literary histories constructed a male, essentially European, and heterosexual writer as the protagonist of culture.

José Quiroga's *Tropics of Desire* (2000) is among the most insightful interventions into the field of Latin American literature from the perspective of sexuality. *Tropics of Desire* examines several prominent intellectuals, including Villaurrutia, Lezama Lima, Cabrera, and Cuban millionaire editor José Rodríguez Feo. All of these writers were able to live their homosexuality with surprising openness during the first decades of the twentieth century. Quiroga, however, insists that these writers did not construct themselves only through sexuality. His project in *Tropics of Desire* is thus not to create a counter-canon of great gay and lesbian authors. Instead, Quiroga sees the semi-acknowledged homosexuality of figures like Villaurrutia and Lezama Lima in terms of a deep ambiguity which undermines all fixed identities. In this sense, *Tropics of Desire* works not to elaborate a theory of gay Latin American literature, but to interrogate the possibilities of defining culture through the categories of sexuality. Sexuality, a crucial aspect of modern understandings of human identity, should not be taken as a stable category for defining social subjects. This effort to undermine established forms of identity formation places *Tropics of Desire* among the most sophisticated attempts to articulate a Latin American literary project within the field of queer theory, which sees the evasive definition of sexuality as a model for subverting essentialisms and resisting all forms of exclusion and domination. However, what kind of cultural politics can be generated from the complex intersection of race, gender, class and sexuality is unclear, particularly as Latin America moves into an era increasingly dominated by the global mass media.

The relationship of literature to commercial and popular cultures has defined the field of cultural studies in the US and European academies, but these issues have long been of concern to Latin American scholars as well. Inherent to Rama's long periodization of the lettered city was its demise in the early 1960s, not through a radical democratization of culture, but through the broadcast media. Television in particular has generated a powerful cultural sphere which does not rely on the written word to create normative social identities. Much earlier, Cândido's reflections on 'Literature and underdevelopment' emerged from a similar awareness that the mass media stood poised to displace the centrality of literature and traditional understandings of a literary education as crucial to the definition of cultural citizenship. Rama and Cândido both saw the mass media as too controlled by commercial interests to permit any kind of critical distance, and early engagements between the mass media and literary criticism in Latin America largely reflected this perspective. Ariel Dorfman's and Armand Mattelart's classic study of cultural imperialism and Disney cartoons, *How to Read Donald Duck* (1971), offers one of the most popular examples. Throughout the period of military governments in the 1960s and the 1970s, tight censorship and the consolidation of powerful media monopolies similarly cautioned against seeing the mass media as a site of contestation. However, even in the 1960s, writers like Puig in Argentina, Luis Rafael Sánchez in Puerto Rico and José Agustín in Mexico began to produce innovative literary works that incorporated techniques from the movies and popular music. These writers focused on how media products are incorporated into systems of meaning that have little or nothing to do with the intended messages. Latin American literature itself thus came to question a monolithic image of the mass media's influence, and literary critics were quick to follow.

Jesús Martín Barbero (1993) was a pioneer in elaborating a sociology of the mass media specific to Latin America, and his work has been influential on literary critics. However, Argentinean scholar Néstor García Canclini has achieved perhaps the highest international profile in this area. Educated in literary studies, García Canclini left Argentina following the 1976 coup and has since worked as a cultural anthropologist in Mexico. His studies of popular culture and the media focus on the sociology of art (its financing, display and circulation) and on the ethnography of the urban experience (1993, 1995, 2001). In particular, García Canclini's redefinition of 'hybridity' (1995) as related not simply to the composition of cultural products, but also to their circulation and interpretation, has proven highly mobile as a tool for engaging with postmodernism and cultural studies. In moving towards the anthropology of daily life, García Canclini focuses on the consumption of the mass media (2001), a significant part of contemporary identity formation. However, the diffuse nature of these processes makes constructing a concrete social movement around consumption a project as utopian as Rama's dream of realigning intellectual authority.

An alternative account of literature's engagement with popular culture can be found in *Memory and Modernity* (1991), by William Rowe and Vivian Schelling, two leading scholars in the United Kingdom. A global assessment of the relationship between the mass media, folk art, and literature, *Memory and Modernity* outlines a broad project for understanding how popular culture and high art have combined in Latin America to form contestatory counter-histories. Rowe and Schelling highlight the disjunctions between both the mass media and literature as dominant forms of expression which differ from popular culture but also use and influence it. To date, *Memory and Modernity* remains the most successful programmatic statement of a cultural studies approach to Latin American literature. However, its scope prevents the authors from developing the kind of detailed case studies demanded by the local and ephemeral nature of popular culture. Such specificity has most effectively been achieved by scholars deeply rooted in a particular context, as demonstrated by the prominent Mexican critic Carlos Monsiváis.

Monsiváis began his career as a cultural journalist in Mexico City in the 1950s, and he has never abandoned the eclectic focus and immediacy of journalism. Over the years, Monsiváis has developed a vast knowledge on a variety of subjects, including Mexican cinema, Mexican politics, Latin American popular music, urban growth, and the relationship of all these to Mexican literature. Above all, Monsiváis is the semi-official chronicler of daily life in Mexico City, one of the world's most populated urban centres. This position at the centre of the global periphery has provided Monsiváis with a privileged perspective on Latin America in the second half of the twentieth century. For many years, however, his work was little known outside of Mexico, in part because the rootedness of his essays in Mexican cultural history disguised the depth of his engagement with theories of popular culture. By the 1980s, however, he had become widely respected in the Spanish-speaking world and the appearance of a collection of his essays in English (1997) has positioned Monsiváis as perhaps the most important interlocutor for academics interested in the relationship between literature and popular culture in Latin America. Neither cynical about the mass media nor reductive about its subversive potential, Monsiváis's essays on romantic ballads (*boleros*), Mexican movies, soccer fans, and a host of other phenomena strike a remarkable balance between the criticism and celebration of popular culture. Moreover, Monsiváis is an unusually successful example of an intellectual who has made his career outside the Latin American institutions of academic authority which have defined the lettered city. More than any other contemporary literary critic, Monsiváis demonstrates that the realignment of intellectuals away from state-centred, vertical forms of power is a rare but genuine possibility. As free-market reforms and economic globalization diminish the ideological centrality of the state in Latin American culture, the kind of non-traditional intellectual authority Monsiváis has built is likely to become more appealing, especially to critics working outside Latin America. To what extent the global institutions of academic authority will succeed in adapting his work to their own ends and to what extent his work will influence the agenda of those institutions will doubtless serve as a powerful test-case for the future of Latin American literary studies.

REFERENCES AND SELECTED FURTHER READING

Adorno, R. 1986: *Guaman Poma: Writing and Resistance in Colonial Peru.* Austin: University of Texas Press.

Arenal, E. and Schlau, S. 1989: *Untold Sisters: Hispanic Nuns in Their Own Works.* Albuquerque, NM: University of New Mexico Press.

Barbero, J. M. 1993: *Communication, Culture and Hegemony: From the Media to Mediations.* London: Sage Publications.

Beverley, J. 1999: *Subalternity and Representation.* Durham, NC: Duke Univeristy Press.

Blanco, J. J. 1981: *Función de medianoche.* Mexico City: Ediciones Era.

Cândido, A. 1995: Literature and underdevelopment. In *On Literature and*

Society, trans. and ed. Howard Becker. Princeton, NJ: Princeton University Press, 119–41

Dorfman, A. and Mattelart, A. 1984: *How to Read Donald Duck: Imperialist Ideology in the Disney Comic*. New York: International General.

Franco, J. 1967: *The Modern Culture of Latin America: Society and the Artist*. London: Pall Mall Press.

Franco, J. 1969: *An Introduction to Spanish American Literature*. London: Cambridge University Press.

Franco, J. 1989: *Plotting Women*. New York: Columbia University Press.

Franco, J. 1999: *Critical Passions: Selected Essays*. Durham, NC: Duke University Press.

García Canclini, N. 1993: *Transforming Modernity: Popular Culture in Mexico*. Austin: University of Texas Press.

García Canclini, N. 1995: *Hybrid Cultures: Strategies for Entering and Leaving Modernity*. Minneapolis: University of Minnesota Press.

García Canclini, N. 2001: *Consumers and Citizens: Globalizations and Multicultural Conflicts*. Minneapolis: University of Minnesota Press.

González Echevarría, R. 1991: *Myth and Archive: A Theory of Latin American Narrative*. London: Cambridge University Press.

Henríquez Ureña, P. 1945: *Literary Currents in Hispanic America*. Cambridge, MA: Harvard University Press.

Larsen, N. 2001: *Determinations*. London: Verso.

Lienhard, M. 1991: *La voz y su huella*. Hanover, NH: Ediciones del Norte.

Losada, A. 1983: Articulación, periodización y diferenciación de los procesos literarios en América Latina. *Revista de Crítica Literaria Latinoamericana* 17, 7–37.

Martí, J. 1977: *Our America*. New York: Monthly Review Press.

Masiello, F. 1992: *Between Civilization and Barbarism: Women, Nation, and Literary Culture in Modern Argentina*. Lincoln: University of Nebraska Press.

Mignolo, W. 1995: *The Darker Side of the Renaissance*. Ann Arbor: University of Michigan Press.

Mignolo, W. 2000: *Local Histories, Global Designs*. Princeton, NJ: Princeton University Press.

Monsiváis, C. 1997: *Mexican Postcards*. London: Verso.

Ortiz, F. 1995: *Cuban Counterpoint: Tobacco and Sugar*. Durham, NC: Duke University Press.

Perlongher, N. 1997. *Prosa plebeya, ensayos 1980–1992*. Buenos Aires: Colihue.

Picón Salas, M. 1962: *A Cultural History of Spanish America: From the Conquest to the Independence*. Berkeley: University of California Press.

Quiroga, J. 2000. *Tropics of Desire*. New York: New York University Press.

Rama, A. 1982: *Transculturación narrativa en América Latina*. Mexico City: Siglo Veintiuno.

Rama, A. 1996: *The Lettered City*. Durham, NC: Duke University Press.
Ramos, J. 2001: *Divergent Modernities*. Durham, NC: Duke University Press.
Rodó, J. E. 1967: *Ariel*. London: Cambridge University Press.
Rowe, W. and Schelling, V. 1991: *Memory and Modernity*. London: Verso.
Said, E. 1978: *Orientalism*. New York: Vintage.
Sommer, D. 1991: *Foundational Fictions: The National Romances in Latin America*. Berkeley: University of California Press.

7

Latino US literature
William Luis

Latino literature is one of the fastest growing fields within Latin American and US literatures, and is helping to redefine how we approach these literatures and cultures. Written in English about the Hispanic and Latino experiences in the USA, Latino literature underscores literary and cultural issues that go beyond the confines of any particular national or geographic space. A study of Latino literature allows Latin American and US scholars to expand the boundaries of their own disciplines, venture into those of others, and develop an ongoing conversation with what used to be considered distinct fields of study. To this end, scholars of Latin American literature incorporate works written in English into their research and curricula. Similarly, scholars of US literature include works written in English about Hispanics and Latinos as inherent characteristics of an ever-expanding US culture.

Many US citizens use the terms Hispanic and Latino interchangeably. While the terms Hispanic and Latino have specific Spanish meanings (Hispanic refers to Spain, and Latino to the Roman Latin), the usage corresponds more closely to their US referents. The terms allow us to understand two different experiences of people of Hispanic descent. I propose the following distinctions: Hispanics are those who are born or raised and educated in their native country, which they leave for political or economic reasons to reside in the USA. Latinos are those who are born or raised and educated in the USA, and have been subjected to the demands of US society and culture. Hispanics have closer ties to the language and culture of their country of origin; Latinos recognize their parents' ancestry, but they feel closer to US culture. Hispanic writers tend to write in Spanish; Latino writers tend to write in English, and they contribute to a Latino literature. While I propose a definition for Hispanic and Latino, I also recognize that a Hispanic can identify himself as a Latino and vice versa. The term Latino has also acquired racial, political, cultural and economic overtones. Chicanos, Puerto Ricans, Cubans and Dominicans comprise the largest Latino groups.

As a group, Latinos contribute to the ever-expanding notion of who is an American. Latino literature has come to the attention of US and world readers, not only because of the quality of the works, but also because of the dramatic increase in the Latino population. Statisticians agree that by the year 2025, one of every four Americans will be of Hispanic descent. Significantly, Latinos have become a considerable political, economic and social force, and have influenced all aspects of US culture. They have also become a powerful literary readership.

The presence of Hispanics in the USA is directly associated with US expansionism. The USA acquired Florida from Spain in 1821, a territory whose population included Cubans and Spaniards. The USA looked westward to become a nation with two oceans. After the Mexican-American War, and as a result of the Guadalupe–Hidalgo Treaty of 1848, the USA seized large portions of Mexican territory, land that later became the states of Texas, California, New Mexico, Colorado and Arizona. Literally overnight, more than 100,000 Mexicans became foreigners in their own land. The Spanish-Cuban-American War of 1898 continued US influence in the Caribbean. The USA acquired the colony of Puerto Rico, and with the Platt Amendment controlled the political and economic life of Cuba. In the early part of the twentieth century, from 1916 to 1924, US forces occupied the Dominican Republic, an act that would be repeated some forty years later.

Migration patterns of the twentieth century reveal the displacement of large numbers of Hispanics to the USA. Puerto Ricans arrived after the Foraker Law of 1900, which made Puerto Rico a US territory, and the Jones Act of 1917, which granted them US citizenship. Their numbers increased with Operation Bootstrap, in the late 1940s and early 1950s, an economic incentive programme to attract US companies to develop the island, and make Puerto Rico a showcase of the Caribbean. But Operation Bootstrap adversely affected the Puerto Rican economy and produced an internal migration, from the countryside to San Juan, and an external one, from the capital city to New York. Cubans left their island as a consequence of the Castro government of 1959. They abandoned the island in four waves: from 1959 to 1961, from 1965 to 1972, in 1980 as a result of the Mariel Boatlift, and from 1989 to 1994, as *balseros*. Cubans continue to leave the island by subscribing to a lottery system, and by risking their lives to cross the dangerous Florida straits. Dominicans left their country, first as political exiles under Rafael Leonidas Trujillo's dictatorship, and second as immigrants, after the US marine invasion of the Dominican Republic in 1965. In the 1970s and 1980s they became a noticeable presence mainly in Puerto Rico and New York. Mexicans travelled north in large numbers during the early part of the twentieth century. However, culturally speaking, Mexicans do not recognize a geographic border that divides Mexico from the USA. They crossed the border in large numbers at the turn of the century and continue to travel back and forth, with the same persistence as their forefathers many centuries before.

Latinos share many similar characteristics. Their ancestors have a similar Spanish colonial history, Spanish language, Catholic religion, and culture. In the USA they also undergo a common post-colonial experience. In spite of these and other commonalities, each of these groups is different and unique, marked by the time of migration or exile, geographic location of residence, race, gender, level of education, economic status, and their degree of acceptance by US society.

While there is a general belief that all Latinos are alike, their differences are as important as their similarities. In addition, there is growing tension among the various groups. This is particularly evident between Mexicans and Puerto Ricans or people of Caribbean descent. Eduardo Portes, writing for the *Wall Street Journal*, captured the anxiety felt by New York's newest Mexican community and their more established Puerto Rican and Dominican neighbours.[1] In search of employment, many Mexicans have journeyed as far as New York, where *Rancheras* songs are widespread and competing with more established musical compositions, such as salsa, merengue and *bachata*. At the Our Lady of Mercy in the north-west Bronx, the conflict has gained religious significance between the Mexican La Virgen de Guadalupe, the Puerto Rican Virgin of Providence, and the Dominican Our Lady of Altagracia. However, this type of tension is not new and is evident when groups of the same or different linguistic and cultural perspectives attempt to create their own space with little regard to the culture of the existing community. It was evident when Cubans moved to Puerto Rico, and now as Dominicans continue to populate the same island.

Just as there are differences among Chicanos, Dominicans, Cubans, and Puerto Ricans living in the USA, there are also distinctions within the groups. For example, there are differences among Chicanos living in the states and regions that define the South-west. There are also differences among Chicanos residing in urban and rural areas, and among those who arrived in the early twentieth century and those who crossed later in the century. There are differences between Puerto Ricans who migrated in the first quarter of the twentieth century and those who left as a result of Operation Bootstrap. There are dissimilarities between Cubans who sought exile shortly after Castro came to power and those who left through the port of Mariel, between those who reside in Miami and those who live in New York City. There are also differences between Dominicans who left as political exiles under Trujillo and those emigrants who abandoned the country after the US invasion.

Latinos write about their lives in the USA, relying on their experiences as a source of inspiration for creating fiction. In some ways they establish a close connection between their narrative voice and that of their protagonists, for one is a recreation of the other. Latinos have a vested interest in keeping their parents' past alive within the context of US society, and for this reason their works can be read with at least two referents in mind.

Latinos' writing makes an emphatic statement about the lives of Latinos in the USA, as they undergo a search for a space that defines them, and they can call their own. The transition from their parents' culture to that of their place of residence has impacted Latinas and Latinos in varying manners. The most notable change is evident in the work of Latinas. Whereas Latinos tend to denounce their treatment in US culture and society, Latinas respond in a similar manner but from a woman's perspective that takes into account aspects of US society and in particular the impact the Women's Movement has had on their lives and works. It is not my intention to do a feminist reading of Latino works, but the role of women in US society cannot be underestimated, and serves as the writer's conscious or unconscious guiding force. These writers juxtapose the male-dominant Hispanic tradition to a male-oriented US culture, but in which the woman's discourse helps to establish a space from which to question that tradition and influence the organizational structures of relationships and thought processes. However, for Latinas, the feminist perspective that emerges from the white Women's Movement is not applied categorically, but is modified to meet the Latina experience and history, as suggested by Clenora Hudson-Weems (1993) when studying the works of women of African descent. Gender affects the transitions from a Hispanic culture of origin to that of the USA, which is transformed into another origin, and this changeover influences the writer's quest for identity.[2]

MEXICAN AMERICAN (CHICANO)

Chicano literature emerged during a particular political event, the United Farm Workers' strike in California in the 1960s. The leader of the movement, César Chavez, protested against the deplorable working and living conditions the owners imposed on their workers and attempted to organize farm workers. At one of the 1965 Grape Strikes, in Delano, California, Luis Valdés performed *Las dos caras del patroncito*, thus giving coherence to a Chicano literature. The play highlights the tense relationship between owners and workers, and even between scab workers and the Patron, who clearly opposes the unionization of his workers. He refuses to understand the position of his workers until he decides to switch places with one of them. Blind to the impact of his own actions, the Patron wants the worker to experience the difficulties of the owner's life: 'You got it good! Now look at me, they say I'm greedy, that I'm rich. Well, let me tell you boy, I got problems. No free housing for me, Pancho. I gotta pay for what I got. You see that car? How much you think a Lincoln Continental like that costs? Cash! $12,000. Ever write out a check for $12,000, boy?' (Hernández Gutiérrez and Foster 1997: 286). The Patron goes on to express the anguish of writing out cheques to pay for the car, his LBJ-style ranch, and his wife's needs.

When the owner and worker change places, and the worker puts on the mask worn by the owner, each one assumes the other's character. The worker, who had nothing, enjoys his new-found role and wealth; he becomes the exploiter. The Patron understands the misery he caused his workers and why they strike. However, without the mask, the Patron looks like a Mexican, thus suggesting that the land originally belonged to Mexicans and that with the mask, a symbol of oppression, the Patron became the enemy. This is clearly the case, since Charlie, the Patron's armed guard, only responds to the symbolic mask, and does not recognize the Patron's voice or mannerisms.

The Chicano movement obtained direction with Rodolfo 'Corky' González's *I am Joaquín*. In this epic poem of foundation, González recreates history from a Latino-Chicano perspective to justify a moment in the present. The poem offers an interpretation of events that has not been articulated by the dominant society. On the contrary, it has been suppressed, but uncovered through poetry.

The poem can be read according to the stanzas indicated by the space dividing them. But, more appropriately, it can be organized according to the refrain 'I am Joaquín', taken from the poem's title. Joaquín is a reference to a generic Hispanic name, but more appropriately recalls Joaquín Murrieta, a nineteenth-century folk hero who rebelled against US authority in the Southwest. The poem has a circular or cyclical structure: it starts out in contemporary society, transports the reader to an earlier time, and concludes in the present. At the outset of the poem, *gringo* society confuses, manipulates and destroys the speaker. The same situation occurred with his forefathers, who were confronted with choosing between economic or spiritual and cultural survival. They made the correct decision and now it is time for the speaker to decide his own future. However, his decision may not be as automatic as the one made by his forefathers, since he is forced to consider the economic benefits of *gringo* society or the spiritual rewards of his culture. In search of clarity, the speaker uncovers and reconstructs the historical past.

Joaquín reconstructs history. Origin is not associated with the history of the original thirteen colonies, or with Columbus's Encounter. Rather it is found in Aztec civilization, present before the arrival of the Spaniards:

> I am Cuauhtemoc
> Proud and Noble
>   Leader of men,
> King of an empire.
>   (Hernández Gutiérrez and Foster 1997: 208)

The speaker is Cuauhtemoc, but his 'I' is not singular but multiple. Just as he represents Cuauhtemoc, he is also the Maya Prince, and Nezahulcoytl, the Great Leader of the Chichimecas. However, the speaker is also their enemy: 'I am the sword and flame of Cortez/the despot' (208). The speaker embodies both sides of the Encounter. He is the victor and vanquished. The speaker seizes the opportunity to voice a proud history of Amerindians that Europeans had silenced.

The poetic voice is born of conflict between the Spaniards and the Aztecs. Out of this tense union emerge Spaniards, Indians and *mestizos*, who, according to the teachings of the Christian Church, are all God's children. Regardless of the subtext, they are also engaged in a battle for freedom. In the nineteenth century, the struggle is against Spanish colonialism. The speaker is a descendant of fighters: Hidalgo, who fought for Mexican independence in 1810, and after his death, Morelos, Matamoros and Guerrero, leading to Mexican independence in 1821. However, the historical transition for independence did not bring the intended results, and the fight continued. During this period, he became Don Benito Juárez, who fought, between 1863 and 1867, against Maximiliano's attempt to make Mexico a French colony.

Part II highlights the twentieth century, as the history of struggle continues with liberators like Pancho Villa, and Emiliano Zapata, who supported the peasants against dictator Porfirio Díaz. From this perspective, the speaker is also the mountain Indians: the Yaqui/Tarahumara/Chaula/Zapotec/Mestizo, an identity that does not exclude the Español. The speaker is the victim and victor, he has killed and he has been killed, the despot Díaz and Huerta, and the democratic Madero. His identity is not limited to male representation, but also includes women. Though he is Juan Diego, to whom the Virgin of Guadalupe appeared, he is also she, and her Aztec equivalent Tonatzin. The struggle takes place in Mexico and the USA, and is directed against this country's government. Joaquín is, above all, Joaquín Murrieta and Alfrego Baca, and the Espinoza brothers, in their fight for justice against US exploitation. In the present he is the *campesinos*, as well as the fat political coyote. The speaker is inferior like the Indian, and as a *mestizo* he must overcome his new designation. His lower status leads him to reject his father and mother, and assimilate into North American society. He is both a traitor and a saviour (of his brother).

In Part III Joaquín is a sacrificial being. He has bled throughout history, beginning with the sacrificial altars of the Aztecs, and continuing with the blood shed by slaves and masters, *campesinos* and *hacendados*, and all those who have spilled their blood defending Mexican dignity. In the present he bleeds in the *barrios*, prisons and wars, in Normandy, Korea and Viet Nam. The bleeding is physical and cultural. Joaquín's culture has been condemned by the Court of Justice, and has been raped by the US government and citizens, as the Treaty of Guadalupe–Hidalgo suggests. Mexicans became foreigners in their own land. Outsiders claimed mines on Mexican lands, but also 'Our Art/Our literature/Our music, they ignored' (218). The revolution is physical and cultural: 'The art of our great señores/Diego Rivera/Siqueiros/Orozco is but/another act of revolution'. The music of *Mariachi* and *Corridos* convey the souls and passions of a people. The speaker is also the woman, who represents the *Llorona*, because of the historical pain she feels for her dead sons, who died 'on battlefield, or on the barbwire/of social strife' (219).

Part IV contains a significant change. Whereas before there was a space separating the stanzas organized by 'I am Joaquín', there is unity of meaning and purpose as the next two are integrated into the previous one. Joaquín realizes that he is a fighter and he knows that he has to struggle for his future, his children and his culture. His fight is historical, dating to the reconquest of

Spain. He has also survived slavery, and contemporary society's exploitation. Music of pride and jubilation announces the most recent struggle. He is 'La Raza!/Mejicano!/Español!/Latino!/Hispano! Chicano!/or whatever I call myself' (221). Though one's name or identity is important, all have been isolated by mainstream society, and the cause of one is the cause of the others.

Part V describes a Joaquín who has found himself and the physical and spiritual strength to make him invincible. He is a new warrior, which brings together the Aztec Prince and the Christian Christ. Chicanos embody these two extremes, but with them they will be victorious. If contemporary society at the outset of the poem confused Joaquín, in the historical reconstruction the confusion is expressed by the coming together of very different traditions, represented by Aztec and Spanish, Mexican and North American cultures. However, the construction of his history has given Joaquín an insight into his past and present. With the unity of the stanzas, the confusion becomes strength, as Joaquín's purpose and struggle are now clear to him:

> I SHALL ENDURE!
> I Will Endure! (222)

Joaquín's self-awareness is also conveyed in the insistent affirmation of 'I am Joaquín', which appears five times, thus dividing the poem into five parts, the number of states that define the South-west.

While the Chicano movement expressed the history of a people who have fought throughout the centuries for their freedom, it would be a mistake to group all Chicano writing under a single rubric. Chicano writing is as diverse as the urban and rural geographic areas and the different states and regions in which Chicanos live. Moreover, there are Chicanos who do not share the discrimination and isolation addressed in González's poem or in Valdés's play. In *Hunger of Memory* (1981), Richard Rodríguez is not drawn to an Aztec past or to a present of struggle for rights and justice. On the contrary, Rodríguez has argued against affirmative action and bilingual education. But Chicanas highlight the most notable change in Chicano literature, as they define a position that emerges from the Chicano movement and takes it to a totally different level of identity and self-awareness.[3]

Gloria Anzaldúa's *Borderland/La Frontera* (1987) best represents the Chicana feminist writings of discovery and self-awareness. Just as *I am Joaquín* is a poem of coming to terms with who you are, in *Borderland/La Frontera* Anzaldúa accepts who she is and finds meaning and strength in being different: a Chicana lesbian of colour. In an article entitled 'To(o) Queer the Writer-Loca, escritora y chicana', Anzaldúa considers the term lesbian to be white and middle-class, which represents the English-only dominant culture. When lesbians name her, they bring Anzaldúa into the dominant culture, but not as an equal. They do so by erasing her colour and her class. Anzaldúa prefers the non-gender connotation of queer, which allows her to politicize the term as anti-imperialistic and anti-racist. In *Borderland/La Frontera* Anzaldúa proposes a new *mestiza* consciousness, that is, a new way of approaching knowledge. If Western thought looks at society as a binary opposition, Anzaldúa embraces it, considers a synthesis between the two, and moves to a third space.

Borderland/La Frontera points to the physical and metaphorical borders that exist between Mexico and the USA, and a borderland, a 'vague and undetermined place created by the emotional residue of an unnatural boundary. It is in a constant state of transition' (1987: 3). At the outset of *Borderland/La Frontera*, Anzaldúa defines the space to which she refers in her title with specific and broader implications:

> The actual physical borderland that I'm dealing with in this book is the Texas–US Southwest/Mexican border. The psychological borderlands, the sexual borderlands and the spiritual borderlands are not particular to the Southwest. In fact, the Borderlands are physically present whenever two or more cultures are physically present, wherever two or more cultures edge each other, where people of different races occupy the same territory, where under, lower, middle and upper classes touch, where the space between two individuals shrinks with intimacy. (Preface, n.p.)

The border is physical, between Mexico and the states of California, Arizona, New Mexico and Texas, separating the north from the south, affluence from poverty, life from death, English from Spanish, opportunity from despair, history from myth. Anzaldúa describes it as a 'steel curtain' and a 'Tortilla Curtain' (2), giving it a Spanish and English cultural identity. However, the idea of a curtain is a direct reference to the 'Iron Curtain' which separated the East from the West, communism from democracy. Contrary to the Cold War between the former Soviet Union and the USA, in which the so-called curtain, like the Berlin Wall, kept people in, this other curtain was erected to keep undesirables out. But the same space is also a borderland, where distinctions come together and lose their traditional meanings. It is the place of poetry and prose, Spanish and English, history and myth, Mexicans and Americans, Latinos and Americans, man and woman, woman and woman, body and mind, the first and second part of the book, autobiography and fiction. *Borderland/La Frontera* is a hybrid text, where differences reside.

The border is real. There is a physical fence which separates one country from the other, but it is not impenetrable, as Anzaldúa and the Mexican children playing soccer cross at will. The idea of crossing is important, for it implies crossing the border, languages, gender, history and myth, and anything else that represents singularity. But for her and others, there is a physical border, but there is no real or recognized border, because historically the land belonged to Mexicans, who continue to move back and forth as their forefathers did many centuries before.

Anzaldúa is a 'border woman'. She is Mexico and the USA, poetry and narrative, Spanish and English, and she and her work embody the two. She is the border and the land on both sides of the border, which also divides her. The opened wound refers to the suffering that the border imposes but it is also a female space, the border (*la frontera*), and alludes to the female sex, as the border *par excellence*. Referring to the 1,950-mile-long border, which is also an open wound, Anzaldúa writes:

> running down the length of my body,
> Staking fence rods in my flesh
> splits me splits me
> *me raja me raja*. (2)

In sexual terms, the vagina is the open wound that bleeds, more likely than not from force rather than from consensual sex. The border is expressed in English, but also in Spanish, and at times in Spanglish. The origin of Latinos can be traced to an open bleeding womb, of suffering and pain.

If González reconstructed a history with which he could identify, Anzaldúa undergoes a similar journey. However, she does so not to uncover a pre-Columbian history based on male rulers, but on women's power and strength. For her history begins in the south-western part of the USA, an area where archeological sites date from 20,000 to 35,000 BC. Around 1000 BC the descendants of the Cochise people travelled to Mexico. Anzaldúa continues her recounting of what could be considered a male-dominated Western history, when Cortez arrives on the continent in the sixteenth century, and Spaniards raped the Indians and formed a new *mestizo* race. History continues to the nineteenth century, when Anglos moved south into the northern part of Mexico, which later became Texas. This was followed by the Mexican-American War, resulting in the Treaty of Guadalupe–Hidalgo, of 2 February 1848.

In 'Movimientos de rebeldía y las culturas que traicionan', Anzaldúa engages in a journey of self-discovery and reveals her narrative 'I'. In so doing, she recalls her childhood and her past, her strength and rebelliousness. This attitude allows her to recognize that men hold the power, they make the rules and the laws, and women are expected to be passive and submit to the will of men. If in traditional society women were expected to marry, become nuns, or prostitutes, Anzaldúa points to a different direction that leads her to become self-autonomous. Not following the norm and creating an independent direction is associated with being queer: 'But I, like other queer people, am two in one body, both male and female. I am the embodiment of the *hieros gamos*: the coming together of opposite qualities within' (19).

Anzaldúa's 'queer' is not just a lesbian, but a lesbian of colour. Cherríe Moraga's 'La Güera' shows that lesbians are also oppressors and are not aware of how they treat other women of colour (see Hernández Gutiérrez and Foster 1997: 66–74). The oppression, without a doubt, is also present in the Catholic and Mexican traditions.

Like González's *I am Joaquín*, Anzaldúa reconstructs the history of

Chicanos, which dates to the Aztec and Mayan civilizations, but from a different perspective. Anzaldúa uses her new-found identity, entrenched in the history of Indian women of resistance, to question Chicano culture and La Raza, not as an outsider, but from within. Though Anzaldúa shows solidarity with Chicanos in their struggles against Anglos, she is also critical of her own people and culture. Unlike other Chicanas, and perhaps like Moraga, who grew up white, Anzaldúa has always been immersed in her culture, and knows it from within: 'I abhor some of my culture's ways, how it cripples its women, como burras, our strengths used against us, lowly burras bearing humility with dignity. The ability to serve, claim the males, is our highest virtue. I abhor how my culture makes macho caricatures of its men' (1987: 21).

Anzaldúa's inquiry into her own culture, and her affirmation of a new sexual identity, allow her to reinterpret history. She questions male myths about Malinali Tenepat, or Malintzin, as the betrayer, the prostitute, and does not reject her, but finds meaning in her existence. She underscores the importance of Coatlicue, the Serpent Skirt, the creator goddess, mother of the celestial deities. Coatlicue becomes Tonantsi, of the Totonacs; Tonantsi, the good mother, of the Nahuas; and, during the Conquest, Tonantsi, the Virgin of Guadalupe, the protector of Mexicans and Chicanos, the single most worshipped figure, on both sides of the border.

Prior to the formation of an Aztec militaristic state, Coatlicue was both male and female. However, the Aztec ruler Itzcoalt, who rewrote the mythology to justify his aggression on neighbouring tribes, changed her characteristics. This change initiated the period of the War of Flowers, in which enemies were sacrificed to the deities. Anzaldúa uncovers an early history and sets the record straight, when she affirms the important role women played in the Toltec and Aztec societies.

> Women possessed property, and were curers as well as priestesses. According to the codices, women in former times had the supreme power in Tula, and in the beginning of the Aztec dynasty, the royal blood ran through the female line. A council of elders of the Calpul headed by a supreme leader, or tlactlo, called the father and mother of the people, governed the tribe. The supreme leader's vice-emperor occupied the position of 'Snake Woman' or Cichacoatl, a goddess. (33)

If men hail an Aztec past, which included blaming Malinali for betraying the Aztec people, Anzaldúa recognizes that it was the Aztecs who altered the harmonious relationship that existed, and made their enemies turn against them.

Anzaldúa identifies with Coatlicue, who becomes a part of her. 'She represents: a duality in life, a synthesis of duality, and a third perspective – something more than a mere duality or a synthesis of duality' (46). In her search for Coatlicue, Anzaldúa descends into the underworld, and undergoes a spiritual death and rebirth to who she is. She becomes other, she gains knowledge, and achieves an enlightened state. Everything seems to be clearer for her. She finally gives into Coatlicue, to her inner self. Now she is able to see: 'I see oposición e insurrección. I see the crack growing on the rock. I see the fine frenzy building. I see the heat of anger or rebellion or hope split open that rock, releasing la Coatlicue' (51).

Anzaldúa's new consciousness means accepting her as a multiple being: in language, writing and gender. She assumes a third space of tolerance, contradictions and ambiguities. She proposes a new epistemology that does away with dualities and oppositions and offers a collective consciousness.

PUERTO RICAN AMERICAN[4]

Like Chicano literature, Puerto Rican American literature came into being during the turbulent 1960s. The Young Lords Party, and their defence of the Puerto Rican community against discriminatory practices, set the tone for a poetic expression that recounted the lives of Puerto Ricans in New York. The Young Lords also struggled with issues of equality relevant to the women who joined the organization. While some believed that the struggle against US society was the primary concern, others insisted that Puerto Rican liberation could not ignore that of others, including women. Regardless of the issues, both men and women expressed themselves in a manner that reflected their conditions. Though the literature emerges from the *barrios*, it was also influenced by the Last Poets (Felipe Luciano, Gyland Kain and David Nelson) and the Beat poets living in the same city. Nuyorican (that is, New York-based Puerto Rican American) poetry and literature can be characterized by a conversational tone that emphasizes the violence and hostility of US society, and the need for Puerto Ricans to accept and preserve their identity.

Pedro Pietri's 'Puerto Rican Obituary' (1971) best exemplifies an aspect of Nuyorican literature, in which identity is the main concern. Pietri's poem, which first appeared in *Palante*, of the Young Lords Party, describes the results of the migratory process, those who left Puerto Rico, abandoned a sense of self, and embraced the American Dream. In spite of their hard work, Puerto Ricans have been excluded from the rewards afforded to other immigrant groups, even though Puerto Ricans are citizens of the USA. Juan, Miguel, Milagros, Olga and Manuel's work did not produce riches, but their own physical and spiritual death:

> Here lies Juan
> Here lies Miguel
> Here lies Milagros
> Here lies Olga
> Here lies Manuel
> Who died yesterday today
> And will die again tomorrow

> Always broke
> Always owing
> Never knowing
> That they are beautiful people
> Never knowing
> The geography of their complexion.
>   (1971: 16)

The poem makes no distinction between men and women; as Puerto Ricans they are equally mistreated. However, the poem has a religious and cultural subtext. It makes reference to Sister Lopez's Spiritualist sessions, and insists upon the religious symbolism of the number three, represented by repetitions of words like Kill, Kill, Kill, and Spics, Spics, Spics, and Miguel, Milagros, and Manuel, the three names that begin with the letter 'M'. But just as there is death, there is also resurrection, which takes place at the end of the poem, with an acceptance of who they are. Pietri alludes to a nostalgic past associated with Puerto Rico. Though the journey back may be physical, it is also spiritual, in search of one's own identity. This self-discovery also has a linguistic referent as Spanish is introduced at the end of the poem as part of the poetic language.

If González's *I am Joaquín* provides a voice and a certain (albeit male) history for Chicanos, Tato Laviera's *Jesús Papote* (1981) is an epic poem that does the same for Nuyoricans. If González looks to history in order to understand the past from the present, Laviera relies on cultural and religious symbolism, and his poem is a parody of the birth and death of Christ. Jesús Papote is a Christ figure. The poem reconstructs the sacred birth of Our Lord, from a foetus conceived on Easter Sunday to his birth on Christmas Eve. However, Laviera also inverts Jesus's sacred figure. His Jesús Papote has been denied an identity. His mother is a prostitute addicted to heroine, has multiple lovers, and does not know who impregnated her.

Laviera assumes the voice of the foetus in the womb and takes the reader on a nine-month journey of self-discovery that culminates in Jesús Papote's birth. He is conceived in April, Easter Sunday, and his mother has multiple partners. His mother discovers she is pregnant in May, and attempts to abort the foetus. She commits herself to treatment to detoxify her body, and succeeds in breaking the habit through cold turkey. In July she returns to Puerto Rico, a symbol of origin and paradise. Life is peaceful and the foetus begs her not to leave the island and return to New York:

> Mamita don't go back give birth in island nativeness
> tropical greetings nurturing don't go back don't
> go back. (1981: 17)

Puerto Rico has been closed to Puerto Ricans from New York. Like Adam and Eve who have been ejected from Paradise, the foetus and his mother cannot remain in Puerto Rico and must return to New York, where they and other

Puerto Ricans are destined to make their home. Time accelerates and there is an occurrence associated with each of the months remaining in the last third of the year. In September mother and foetus return to New York where they struggle. In October the mother enrols in a drug programme and both mother and foetus fight the heroin addiction. In November the dominant theme is death. The grandmother's prayers are not answered, and the mother barely survives. In December the nine-month cycle is completed and mother and son endured the arduous journey. Jesús Papote is ready to be delivered.

Both mother and son are survivors. However, it is not the mother but the foetus who has provided the incentive to live; he has given his mother the strength to overcome insurmountable odds. As a conscious individual with a sense of purpose, the foetus wants to live. He does not want to die. He even assumes the active role in the birth process and instructs his mother to fight the urge to sleep, and push and not to give up. He is a fighter and fights from the very beginning, before birth and while in the womb, and will continue to struggle for the rest of his life.

Like the Holy Saviour, Laviera's Jesús Papote has been born to be a teacher and leader. Upon his birth, the foetus develops and recognizes his own voice and identity. His first words are pronounced in Spanish and English, in the first person plural: 'We, nosotros'. Jesús Papote is the voice of the Puerto Rican and Latino people, and of all the people who live in the ghetto, whether they speak one language or the other. In unison with Puerto Rican culture, upon birth Jesús Papote asks for his blessing, a Puerto Rican but also universal blessing. He asks permission 'of all the faiths of all beliefs', 'of this land', 'of the elders', 'of english', 'of his community', and 'of god' (20). Their acceptance will confer upon him the legitimacy he needs to undergo and complete his mission. Laviera's speaker is also a redeemer and a saviour. He has come into the world to save his mother and other Puerto Ricans and Latinos. The mother draws from the son's strength. She gets up, breaks the umbilical cord, and joins the celebration of the birth of Christ and her own son. Others will also find strength in his character. The ringing of the bells is a festivity of Christmas in the pagan and religious sense of the word. They are the bells of Santa Claus but also of the church, where Jesús Papote is present for everyone to see.

Jesús Papote represents the past, present and future, not only because Hispanics will be the largest minority in the twenty-first century, but because they are multiethnic, multiracial and bilingual, a synthesis or blending of the different cultures in the USA. If Jesus was the teacher of his people and was crucified at the age of thirty-three, Jesús Papote was crucified before he was born; his crucifixion began in the womb. He is the messiah for which Puerto Ricans have been waiting. He is not some mythical figure that only those indoctrinated into religion could understand in the abstract; he is born of the same conditions many living in the ghetto experience and understand. Jesús Papote speaks from his condition to theirs. It is important to emphasize that the struggle for survival does not originate at birth or after adolescence, but at the moment of conception; those living in poverty and in drug-infested neighbourhoods have been marked and condemned before they are born. Jesús Papote is a survivor who gives strength to his mother and to all who need help in overcoming the great odds against them. And like Jesús Papote, the poet has an obligation to develop a voice for his people. For Laviera and his character, it is not an art one develops casually; rather it is an obligation he has to his people and community – his mission is to save the Latino community.

Not all Latinos of Puerto Rican descent live in New York, nor do they write in a Nuyorican style. While there are Latinas who are concerned about the Puerto Rican struggle in the metropolis, others recall a different experience, away from violence, and closer to a childhood experience associated, in some respects, with a past innocence. In *Silent Dancing: A Partial Remembrance of a Puerto Rican Childhood* (1990), Judith Ortiz Cofer, a Puerto Rican from Georgia, revisits her past and attempts to reconcile the past of her childhood in Puerto Rico and New Jersey with the present time of writing. While a memoir is a way of understanding the past from the present, *Silent Dancing* provides insight into the world of Puerto Ricans, dominated by Mamá, the narrator's grandmother. Mamá represents Puerto Rican culture as origin, and provides life-long lessons about the evil intentions of men, and instructs women in their relationships with them. Mamá is a living example of what must be done. When her husband added a room to the house to accommodate a possible addition to the family, Mamá moved Papá into the room and obtained her freedom. Mamá's example and advice allowed for the articulation of a female discourse and space.

Early in life, the protagonist accepted a clear distinction between good and evil as defined by Hispanic culture, but from a female perspective. These polar opposites are conveyed in the stories of María Sabida and María La Loca. Calling on the common Spanish name of María, which also invokes that of the Virgin Mary, Sabida, whose name suggests *sabiduría*, wisdom, uses her knowledge to stay one step ahead of men. According to Mamá's story, men are robbers and thieves who have fallen from grace. María uses the traditional space of the kitchen, and food, to tame her husband, and rid him of his aggressive macho characteristics. In contrast to María Sabida, María la Loca is less fortunate. The once young and beautiful María, now fat and ugly, made the unfortunate mistake of giving into love; she fell in love with the rich Rogelio Méndez – his name did not matter for it constantly changed – who 'made a fool out of her and ruined her life' (1990: 18). María returned from her honeymoon a changed and aged woman.

More telling is the story of 'Marina', a protected young girl who gathered by the Río Rojo, a space reserved for maidens. Kiki, the mayor's fourteen-year-old daughter, and the fifteen-year-old Marina become inseparable friends. As the story unfolds, the protagonist and readers learn that one day both of the friends disappeared unexpectedly. In addition we are told that the sickly Marina was born a boy, a secret closely guarded by the mother and the midwife. Many years later the protagonist's mother is reminded of the story when she sees Marino and his lovely granddaughter, and conjectures that a relationship with a sensitive man, who understands the woman's space, will lead to a long and happy life. All of the grandmother's stories became life-long lessons for both mother and daughter.

The grandmother's stories found correspondence in the USA, as Ortiz Cofer met Providencia, a 'bad' woman with many lovers and babies from different fathers, and Vida, a young Chilean who lived with the Ortiz family as she prepared to marry, but who was asked to leave because she was encroaching on the mother's territory. This part of Ortiz Cofer's life is best narrated in 'Silent Dance', which gives title to the 'Remembrance of a Puerto Rican Childhood'. The story, located in the physical centre of the book, is based on a five-minute home movie made one New Year's Eve when Mr Ortiz, a sailor in the US Navy, was on leave. The Technicolor silent film has become part of the protagonist's recollections and dreams. The film, which shows everyone dancing without music and alone, also tends to blur the differences otherwise made evident by sound. In this sense, a relationship is established between Ortiz Cofer's mother, her cousin, and the bride-to-be, who sit together and wear the same red dress. The film is also accompanied by commentaries in the present that shed light on the past. Ortiz Cofer's abandoned great-uncle's common-law wife, present at the party, now clarifies that the cousin in the picture was pregnant from an American boyfriend, had an abortion, and was sent to live with her mother, where 'the men in Puerto Rico know how to put a saddle on a woman like her' (97). The Novia, we are told, if she does not marry quickly, like the cousin, will be corrupted by the city. The reader is left to wonder if the mother, who also wears a red dress, will have a similar fate.

'Silent Dancing', as both title of the book and story, refers to the home movie, but also to a metaphorical dance. It refers to the movie of the past, but also as the protagonist envisions it. It is the dance of the family secrets, as well as the silence of the father's move from Puerto Rican heritage to North American culture. Similarly, it is the author's dance between one culture and the other, which she dances regardless of the tune played. The silent dance can also point to the protagonist, as she grows and matures without the presence of her father, and the silence of her and her mother's memory about him.

The stories in *Silent Dancing* serve to educate the protagonist in life's ways, but also to make her independent from those she loves. Men and women are opposites, and so are the mother and father, who represent fire and ice, Italy and Spain, light-skinned and olive, assimilation and nationalism, freedom and prison, respectively. Ortiz Cofer's initial memory of her father is negative. In the chapter 'The Black Virgin' she writes: 'My first memory is of Father's homecoming party and the gift he brought me from San Juan – a pink iron crib like an ornate bird cage – and the sense of abandonment I felt for the first time in my short life as all eyes turned to the handsome stranger in uniform and away from me in my frilly new dress and patent leather shoes, trapped inside my pink iron crib, screaming my head off for Mami, Tía, Mamá Nanda, anybody . . . to come lift me out of my prison' (46).

Ortiz Cofer also desires to be independent of her mother's memory, Mamá's successor, and tell her own stories. The first memory of the father described in 'The Black Virgin', in the first half of *Silent Dancing*, is repeated in 'The Last Word', the final story. Reviewing a photo album, the recollections of mother and daughter differ when interpreting the father's return after his daughter's second birthday. The mother recalls happiness and the inseparability of father and daughter. The daughter remembers abandonment; she escapes from the crib and accidentally falls into a fire roasting a pig. The mother, who disagrees and challenges her daughter's recollection, shows her other pictures, with toys and a huge ornate cake. When pressed, the mother insists that the child had dragged her father's foreign language dictionary onto the fire. And the fire Ortiz Cofer felt was from the spanking she received. The chapter ends with the laughter of reconciliation, but with mother and daughter each asserting her point of view: '"*Es la pura verdad*", she says. "Nothing but the truth." "But that is not how I remember it"' (165).

Indeed Ortiz Cofer has the last word on this matter, for her recollection is the only one that matters. 'Lessons of the Past' brings the collection to a close. In this poem about her father's return, poetry expresses what is so difficult and painful to narrate: Ortiz Cofer insists on an interpretation distinct from that of her mother's. The mother, who seeks reconciliation between father and daughter, also cherishes the memories reawakened by a picture of her husband in uniform. More than anything, she rationalizes her marriage to an absent husband. Ortiz Cofer challenges this vision, and becomes independent of her mother. Her desire to burn the foreign language dictionary is a way of striking out against her father, who preferred to express himself in English. Her interpretation is sustained by a photograph, which she reproduces on the book's cover, showing her in a fancy dress and short hair. However, Ortiz Cofer tells the reader that she is not happy, 'my eyes enormous – about to overflow with fear' (167). The fire may explain why her hair had to be trimmed.

The poem is a rejection of the father but also of the mother's recollection. Ortiz Cofer's poem also refers to her mother lamenting the father's absence, not when away on duty, but when at home he disappeared and returned drunk late at night.

> But then things changed,
> and some nights he didn't come home. I remember
> hearing her cry in the kitchen. I sat on the rocking chair
> waiting for my cocoa, learning how to count, *uno, dos, tres,*
> *cuatro, cinco*, on my toes. So that when he came in,
> smelling strong and sweet as sugarcane syrup,
> I could surprise my *Papasito* –
> who liked his girls smart, who didn't like crybabies –
> with a new lesson, learned well. (167)

Within the context of the memoirs, Ortiz Cofer blames the mother for neglecting to learn Mamá's lesson of how to deal with men. This observation returns us to the women wearing red in 'Silent Dancing', for her mother was not very different from the other women sitting on the couch. Ortiz Cofer reveals another side of her father, one that her mother kept hidden, and becomes independent of the mother's memories. At the end of the book, Ortiz Cofer shows that, unlike her mother, the child has learned her lesson well, as the last line of the poem indicates. The author takes on the role of Mamá, as she creates and modifies past stories, for her own daughter, to whom she dedicates 'Lessons of the Past', and other women to follow.

CUBAN AMERICAN

Cuban American identity is influenced by the different waves of Cuban exiles, and the place of residence in the USA. Generally speaking, those who were born or raised in Miami tend to be more conservative in their political views towards Cuba; those who live in cities with other large Latino populations share a broader experience closer to those of other ethnic and racial groups. While Cuban American literature does not emerge from the same socio-economic and racial forces that acted upon Chicanos and Nuyoricans, the Areito group showed that the Miami exile experience was not monolithic (see Luis 1997: 149–52, 156–7). The sons and daughters of exiles, members of Areito gathered in New York, challenged their parents' memory, and wanted to experience the Cuban reality from their own perspective. As a group they published *Contra viento y marea* (1978), about their exile experiences in the USA. Though not a member of Areito, Cristina Garcia's *Dreaming in Cuban* (1992) and *The Agüero Sisters* (1997) place the Cuban family trauma within a larger context that also includes the Cuban Revolution. Pilar's family is forced to leave the island, and as a child of the 1960s growing up in New York she questions her parents' values, identifies with her Cuban revolutionary grandmother, and returns to the island. However, the protagonist must experience the Revolution from her own point of view, as her decision to help her cousin flee from the island shows. In addition, the novel goes beyond the revolutionary period and places the family trauma within a broader pre-revolutionary context of the grandmother's lost love.

The Agüero Sisters underscores the idea that Cuban problems did not start with the Revolution, and can be traced to an earlier time. Though the Agüero sisters have been marked by the political situation that has divided the Cuban nation (Reina lives in Cuba and Constancia lives in the USA), the family problems started before, when Reinaldo Agüero travelled from Spain to Cuba, and married Soledad, a women ten years his senior, who has an illegitimate daughter Olivia. This betrayal will also be repeated with Ignacio and Blanca, who has an extramarital affair with a mulatto, Reina's natural father.

There is a close relationship between Ignacio and Cuban history. Ignacio Agüero was born on 4 October 1904, two years into the birth of the country and the presidency of Estrada Palma, and the same year in which the national Congress was elected. Ignacio is an important barometer of Cuba's infant stage, as well as the years to come.

> No sooner had she settled back on her matrimonial bed than Mamá spotted the shadow on the far wall. Straight ahead, standing guard between the open shutters of the bedroom window was a siguapa stygian owl. My mother did not know its official name then, only that it was a bird of ill omen, earless and black and unmistakable. It was doubly bad luck to see one during the day, since they were known to fly about late at night, stealing people's souls and striking them deaf. (1997: 29)

The owl alarmed Soledad, who grabbed an etched glass lamp and threw it at the owl, and it precipitated her labour. Soledad delivered a nine-pound baby boy. The owl watched the birthing of Ignacio, and remained still, waiting for the placenta to emerge, snatching it with its beak up from the floor, and flying out the window:

> Later, my mother learned that the bird had flown low over the President's parade with her placenta, scattering the crowd and raining birthing blood. Even President Palma, trembling with fear, crossed himself twice before jumping headlong into a flowering angel's-trumpet bush, his crisp linen suit spattered with Mamá's blood. (29)

The Congressional elections proved to be a farce. Both the Republicans and the National Liberals attempted to win by *el copo*, which prevented the minority from any representation. By the time Ignacio had celebrated his first birthday, the ageing and incompetent Estrada Palma, with the help of some 150,000 fraudulent votes, was re-elected without opposition to the presidency on 1 December 1905 (Thomas 1971: 473–4).

Ignacio's birth is indeed tied to the nation's destiny. In some ways his life represents the country's outcome or future. Ignacio was born on 4 October, the day of Saint Francis of Assisi, who in Cuban Santería is known as Orula or Orúnmila. If Ignacio's birth is associated with tragedy, Orula's life begins in a similar manner. Orula, the son of Yemmu and Obatalá, at birth was taken away by his father and buried up to his waist next to a Ceiba tree. After his older son, Ogún, betrayed him by committing incest with his mother, Obatalá had vowed to kill all of his sons. Eleguá, the god of the road, witnessed the burial, and told Yemmu. She begged Eleguá to feed her son, who was also protected by the Iroko tree. Yemmu had another son, a charming black boy by the name of Changó, whom Obatalá liked and did not harm. Obatalá's daughter, Dadá, raised him. From conversations with his father, Changó learned to hate Ogún. He found out that Orula was still alive, and with permission from his father, Changó saved him; he grabbed Orula by the shoulders and unearthed him. Not knowing how he would make a living, Changó, owner of oracles, took a branch from the tree, made an oracle board, and gave it and the gift of divination to Orula, to help others. From that moment, Orula became the god of divination (Castellanos and Castellanos 1992: 38–9). With his actions, Ignacio will foretell the future of his country.

In Spanish, the bird of ill omen is called 'un pájaro de mal *agüero*'. Whether Ignacio is the origin of the bad omen that besets his family, the country and the president, there is little doubt that from its infancy, the country will be struck with the same outcome which clouded the family of *The Sisters of Ill Omen*, as a retranslation of the novel's title suggests.

The Agüero Sisters is at the crossroads of Cuban history, culture, religion and literature. Just as the Agüero family is plagued by tragedy, the Platt Amendment, the Machado dictatorship, and the most recent stage of the Cuban Revolution handicapped the Cuban nation. Both family and island-nation will experience similar tragedies.

The beginning and end of the novel reveal how Ignacio murdered his wife, narrated first in third person, then in first person, in search of an origin of the discursive event. The murder may be associated with Blanca's betrayal. However, there is another explanation associated with Ignacio's profession as an ornithologist. Blanca and Ignacio routinely travelled to the Zapata Swamp to collect rare birds. The novel describes Blanca as a changing person, and like his birds, Ignacio kills her in order to preserve her, before she becomes unrecognizable to him. His desire to capture rare birds is a way of preserving them before they become extinct, thereby losing what makes them special. Like the birds, Blanca is an exceptional specimen. The narration describes her as being unusually beautiful; and her actions, including her betrayal, made her even more attractive to Ignacio. According to this interpretation, when Ignacio raised his gun to shoot the bee hummingbird, he moved the shotgun and focused on a more rare and soon-to-be-extinct individual, his wife. The narration makes allusions to her as an extinct bird. In 'The World's Smallest Frog', which describes Ignacio and Blanca's meeting, Ignacio is struck by her delicate beauty and compares her to a bird: 'Blanca was slight, as delicately boned as certain birds, and she had a cascade of blue-black hair that fell past her shoulders' (183). In the chapter 'Owls of Orient', which explains Blanca's return to Ignacio, and highlights her transformation, Ignacio states 'Blanquita was dying like the rarest of birds' (266). And when Blanca throws Ignacio a party, the scene is described as a forewarning of what would take place later in the Zapata Swamp:

> On the night of the party, Blanca transformed herself into a dazzling bird. She wore a filmy pink bodice, a long swirling skirt, and a diadem of artificial jewels. Reinita was outfitted in a dragonfly costume that Blanca had sewn together from crepe de chine scarves. And I, rather too sensibly, dressed up as if for one of my expeditions, complete with rubber boots, a flashlight, and my fine-mesh net. (267)

If we were to superimpose this event on what follows in the swamp, Ignacio's shift from the bee hummingbird to Blanca is a way of metaphorically preserving his wife and saving his stepdaughter.

The last chapter of the novel confirms my interpretation, that Blanca was an exceptional individual. And like his birds, Ignacio also wanted to preserve her. The novel ends with a letter Ignacio writes, in which he describes the death of his wife. He recapitulates: 'I do not recall taking aim, only the fierce recklessness of my desire, the press of the twelve-gauge shotgun against my shoulder, the invitation from the bird itself. I moved my sight from the hummingbird to Blanca, as if pulled by a necessity of nature' (299). The closing words of the novel suggest that Ignacio performed a habitual act when spotting a rare bird. The grammatical construction establishes an equivalency between the hummingbird and Blanca. They both have equal value. And as with his cataloguing of rare birds, Ignacio needed to preserve his wife, before she and her surroundings continued to change. Not having the cameras and recording devices used by younger naturalists, during Ignacio's days: 'One simply had to kill a creature to fully understand it' (150).

If Ignacio tries to understand and perhaps recover the Cuban past metonymically, Reina does the same thing, but twice removed. She has inherited her stepfather's collection of specimens, books and other artefacts, which she believes provide insight into an uncertain past. Reina surrounds herself with them, and makes an effort to reconstruct what her life was or would have been with her mother and stepfather. However, she does not know her exact origin; she met her biological father once, but knows nothing about him or her parents' relationship.

In spite of the political events that separate and define Reina and Constancia's lives, both women are tied to the past. The past exists in the present and the present in the past. The past is defined as the past of the family, and the sisters' attempt to come to terms with their parents' relationship. As I have mentioned, Blanca disappeared and returned to Ignacio with an illegitimate pregnancy. Years later, Ignacio shoots his wife. And Ignacio also commits suicide. These events, without a doubt, have led to each of the sisters' trauma. But all the children live with their parents' past. Ignacio is tied to the life of a Spanish father, who travelled to Cuba, and married Soledad, a woman ten years his senior, who had an illegitimate daughter, Olivia, who died. Constancia's son, Silvestre, also lives with his past. And just as his grandfather, Ignacio, killed his grandmother for betraying him, Silvestre does the same with his father.

All the children have been denied a parent. Soledad suffers a heart attack while Ignacio works in the Zapata Swamp; Blanca's mother was trampled by a stampede of pigs; Ignacio shoots Reina and Constancia's mother, and later commits suicide; Reina never gets to know her biological father; Dulce's father drowns; Silvestre murders his father; and Heberto, Constancia's husband and Isabel's father, is killed as he and other exiles invade the island. If we continue to read the past as a manifestation of the present, the following question arises:

will the children of the Revolution turn their backs on the same government that has supported its youths?

Garcia stays close to cultural history and seems to refrain from imposing a contemporary or anachronic interpretation of the present on to the Cuban past. However, her protagonists are women, and in some cases strong women, who engage in non-monogamous relationships. This is the case with Soledad's unfaithfulness to Ignacio's father, Blanca's betrayal of Ignacio, Reina's sexual equality with men, and Dulce's promiscuous behaviour.

Garcia's description of Blanca's love affair with a mulatto inverts Cirilo Villaverde's *Cecilia Valdés* (1882), Cuba's national novel. If the Cuban master writer described the white Cándido Gamboa, who has extramarital relations with Cecilia's mulatto mother, the Latina writer narrates the relationship between Blanca (whose name describes her skin colour) and an unknown mulatto. The white male exploitation of a *mulata*, in the nineteenth century, is avenged by a mulatto's relationship with a white woman, in the twentieth. However, there is another interpretation that we cannot overlook, one based on the Women's Movement in the United States: the liberated white woman who defies the pressure of her culture and society and chooses a mulatto or black for her lover.

Gustavo Pérez Firmat's *Next Year in Cuba: A Cubano's Coming-of-Age in America* (2000) approaches the fragmentation of the Cuban family from a different perspective from the one discussed in Garcia's *The Agüero Sisters*. In this memoir, Pérez Firmat comes closer to the Miami exile experience than Garcia and attributes the Cuban family problem to Fidel Castro's dictatorship. Prior to the Cuban Revolution, Pérez Firmat and his family lived in a paradise of sorts. His father owned a store, with more than one million dollars in inventory. When Castro came to power the family fled the island; unlike other refugees, they were able to take many of their possessions.

Pérez Firmat's recollections follow more closely the Cuban exile discourse, hence the popular saying 'Next Year in Cuba', which many Cubans believed. As can be expected, Pérez Firmat's account is clouded by nostalgia. Like many exiles, his family expected to return to the island after Castro's defeat, and resume their lives as if time had not been altered. And like them, the narration is obsessed with the Cuban past, but also with the past of his childhood Miami enclave. The character experiences a double exile. The first takes place when he leaves Cuba for Miami, which he later accepts as his home. The second exile occurs when he leaves Miami for Michigan, and then for North Carolina.

A son of a well-to-do businessman, Pérez Firmat is taken away from his home at the tender age of eleven. Though Pérez Firmat cannot and will not return to Cuba, the voyage is not to the reality of the situation they had to abandon, but to that of their past memory and personal recollections. The protagonist states: 'Although my memories of Cuba may seem firm and clear, in fact I remember very little' (32). The past is not necessarily a recreation of what was, but what should have been. The past is remembered in accordance with the present life of the character and it gives meaning to him. The past is never what appears to be but always what is imagined, and this may be one of the reasons why the character does not want to return to Cuba, or listen to his brother's visit to the island, home and store.

While Pérez Firmat is careful to provide the reader with glimpses of his mother and father, and the rest of the Pérez Firmat family, he inadvertently shows that not every Cuban in his household thinks like him, and he thus does away with the myth that Miami is a homogeneous community. This is especially the case with his siblings, who are also Cuban Americans. He describes them in the following manner: 'My brother Pepe pretends to be a socialist. Mari pretends to be a banker. Carlos pretends to sell dope. I pretend to be a professor' (178). Even as Gustavo holds passionately onto his parents' past, this is not the case with the others. José is a leftist, who lived in Guatemala, and supported the Sandinista government. Carlos, to whom Gustavo dedicates an entire chapter, is a hustler willing to steal his older brother's identity, or anything else for that matter, to make ends meet. If the other children were allowed their own individual voice, would they not claim that their experiences are also a part of Cuban Americans?

Though the character never returns to Cuba, the analogous Miami exile provides an understanding of the relationship between the past and present. After many years of absence, he revisits his parents' house in Coral Gables, where he was reared. 'Retracing my steps thirty years later, I'm struck by how close my old haunts really are' (55). Though the physical geography may not change, the perspective of a child must be different from that of an adult, even if he is the same person at two different stages of his life. If this were the case, what would happen to his memories of Cuba? The past can never be the same; and as a function of time, it is always changing and evolving. This is evident when he realizes that Miami has undergone its own transformation. As other waves of Cubans arrived in Miami, the first group moved outside of Little Havana, to Coral Gables or South Miami, then to Kendall or Perrine. In recent years, other Hispanic groups have sought the same refuge enjoyed by Cubans. Miami has been transformed into a lively Latino community.

Next Year in Cuba also reconstructs his life in Miami, thus providing a glimpse of how Cubans live in a city that is considered to be another Havana. Pérez Firmat offers us a vision of how Cubans attempt to transpose and reproduce their culture in Miami, as they continue to celebrate the traditional holidays, and eat the same types of food enjoyed on the island. Continuing the traditions, in particular the celebration of Noche Buena, became a way of holding on to Cuba and the past. But he is also aware that the island he knows is undergoing its own transformation. He recognizes that Miami is like Havana, but with more abundance. Pérez Firmat's acceptance of Miami is an intermediary step to his move into mainstream society, as illustrated later by his position first at Duke and presently at Columbia University. In fact the book attempts to portray life on both sides of the 'hyphen'.[5]

When Pérez Firmat says 'I love Cuba with the involuntary, unshakable love that one feels for a parent', he is not referring to the Cuba of the present, but the Cuba prior to the events of 1959, that is, the Cuba of his childhood, the fatherland of his memories. He intends to preserve the past, so that as time changes him, his memories will always be the same. Pérez Firmat exhibits a fear of letting go of the past, as he moves from becoming an exile to becoming an immigrant, from marrying and divorcing his first wife Rosa, a Cuban American, to marrying Mary Ann, a divorced woman with two grown children. Similar to Ricky Ricardo's marriage to Lucy, or Cesar Castillos's desire for Vana Vane, in Oscar Hijuelos's *The Mambo Kings Play Songs of Love* (1989), Pérez Firmat's marriage to Mary Ann is a way of finally moving from one side of the hyphen to the other, grasping and obtaining the American Dream.

As with any memoir, the narration is not a chronological reconstruction of events, but an imposition of the present onto the past. The protagonist has already changed and his transformations are present from the initial moment of writing. From this perspective, Pérez Firmat's memoir is structured around his acceptance as a member of the 1.5-generation (a term borrowed from Rubén Rumbaut to refer to Cuban children born in Cuba but educated in the United States). This idea is evident at the outset of the work, as the boy who stays in Cuba sees the boy departing on the ship headed for America, and vice versa, thus highlighting both sides of the Cuban and American experience, that is, both sides of the hyphen. This is also evident as Noche Buena, a Cuban celebration, is juxtaposed to Christmas lunch; and Rosa, his Cuban or Cuban American wife, is juxtaposed to Mary Ann, his American spouse.

Pérez Firmat's marriage to Mary Ann speaks loudly about his own transformation from a declared 'macho'. Men from a macho culture generally tend to marry women with little experience, and virgins are more coveted. The idea of marrying a woman for who she is, regardless of background or previous experience, comes closer to an equality associated with US culture. That the author falls in love with a divorced woman with grown children is even more striking. Let us remember that his father and uncle gave him sound Cuban advice when he threatened to leave Rosa and marry Mary Ann:

> The problem with me, my father began, is that I had been a faithful husband for too long, and therefore was suffering from a bad case of *atraso*, the Cuban word for long-term or protracted horniness (the literal meaning of the word is 'backwardness'). According to his old-country mores, it was one thing to have a fling – everybody had them – but it was very different to leave your wife for another woman. Cuban men sometimes cheat on their wives, Pedro said, but we do not abandon them. (214–15)

Equally telling is Pérez Firmat's use of the memoir, the most intimate form, to express his past, which Cuban or Hispanic culture does not favour. Though the Picaresque genre gave origin to the modern Spanish and Spanish American novels, the memoir is not a preferred form of art.

A close study of Pérez Firmat's US family provides insight into his integration into mainstream society. The information is contained in the form of a family portrait. The book reproduces four pictures: three of his childhood, displayed on the book's cover and repeated in the body; and one as an adult, taken after his second marriage, embedded in the text. In this photograph, located in the chapter appropriately entitled 'Discovering America', Pérez Firmat brings together his two families, comprising his children from his first marriage, and his stepchildren from his second marriage. If we were to study the composition of the photograph, Mary Ann and Gustavo appear to divide the picture in two. Pérez Firmat's children stand next to him, and Mary Ann's children alongside her, and consequently farthest from Pérez Firmat. Each couple had a son and daughter, and they are placed in the same position as the parents, that is, the males are to the right of the females, or the females are to the left of the males. Interestingly, of the six subjects only Pérez Firmat and his daughter are looking at the camera. The other subjects appear to have other concerns. In Mary Ann's family, she is looking at Chris, thus giving him her full attention; her daughter, Jen, is standing politely with her hands crossed in front of her, looking down (perhaps polite and civil, as the author describes her demeanour when her mother and father divorced). In Pérez Firmat's family, like Chris, his son David is also looking down, and the father's arm over his shoulder reproduces the same calming effect that Mary Ann's look has on her son. Pérez Firmat's daughter, Miriam, is facing the camera and seems to be looking into it, but may in fact be glancing to the side of the camera, with the same picaresque smile seen on her father's face, and with the same strength and independence known to her grandmother Constantina. Of the six people in the picture, Pérez Firmat is the only one posing for the family portrait, whereas everyone else is concerned with his or her own issues. The family members are standing next to each other, but they are not together nor are they spiritually in harmony with one another. While Pérez Firmat wishes to read his and Mary Ann's situation as a 1990s' version of the *I Love Lucy* show, what would this other picture, the one depicted in the photograph, really say about this family?

Pérez Firmat is caught between the Cuban and the American divide. In Chapter 11, appropriately entitled 'Earth to Papi, Earth to Papi', Pérez Firmat provides a glimpse of his children. While the men are expected to follow the men and the women the women, we get a sense of how Cuban Pérez Firmat wants to make them and how North American they really are. In fact, he claims that his children have helped him in his transition to become an American. In a similar manner, in one of the shortest sections of the book, he explores the lives of his wife's children, proudly stating that the mother left the father for the narrator. He boasts that he 'broke up their happy home (which wasn't all that happy)' (261). If he broke up a happy home that was not happy, what did he do to his own? And how happy was it? While Rosa is present in the book, Mary Ann's husband, the other male rival, is conspicuously absent.

Pérez Firmat claims that Mary Ann's children will be influenced by his Cubanness.

If we were to read this description with the picture mentioned above, Pérez Firmat's American family is more discordant than harmonious. Jen is prepared to accept her status in the family; Chris needs to be consoled; David is restless and, like Chris, needs further reassurance. Miriam, on the other hand, seems to be sure of herself, and is drawn to her father, who has the same smile seen on his face.

It is puzzling to me why Pérez Firmat chose to include this picture of his American family. Would it not have made sense to take a second picture, one that would represent an apparent harmony not present in the one included in the book and render my interpretation meaningless? If that were the case, the reader would never have seen the first one, and only the second one would assure the reader of the amicable transition from the Cuban side of the hyphen to the American side. However, it is possible that there were two or more pictures, and Pérez Firmat chose the one he did because he wanted to be candid and show the complexity the process entails. There is still another interpretation. This one suggests that the discord was such that he was not able to get the children to regroup, that the members of his family would not pose for a second picture. David and Chris's movements away from the family reinforce the latter interpretation.

DOMINICAN AMERICAN

By the time Dominicans arrived in large numbers in New York, during the 1970s and 1980s, a Latino culture and literature were already in place, which helped these new immigrants with their quest for identity in the USA. Dominican writers can be classified into two groups: those who left as exiles during the Trujillo dictatorship and those who left as immigrants after his death. Of the Dominican American writers, Julia Álvarez is, without a doubt, the best representative of an emergent group of writers. Her works attempt to reconcile her adult North American experiences and her childhood Dominican past. *In the Time of the Butterflies* (1994) narrates the tragic lives of the Mirabal sisters, which precipitated the fall of Trujillo, and exposed this dark part of Dominican history to US readers. The novel is also a personal account of the author's life, since the events were taking place during her childhood in the Dominican Republic. The writing process is a way of revisiting and exploring a period that formed an integral part of the author's life. Moreover, there were four Mirabal sisters, Patria, Dedé, Minerva and María Teresa, the same number of girls as in Álvarez's *How the Garcia Girls Lost Their Accents* (1991): Yolanda, Sandi, Fifi and Carla. Their father was also involved in conspiring against the Trujillo dictatorship (see Luis 1997: 266–77).

Like *In the Time of the Butterflies*, *In the Name of Salomé* (2000) narrates an important moment in Dominican history, but also in that of the USA. By reproducing the life of the Dominican Republic's national poet, Salomé Ureña, Álvarez traces historical transitions, from the nineteenth to the twentieth centuries, events that include the country's second independence movement from Haiti in 1844, and Baez's 1861 attempt to revert the country to a Spanish colony. In the twentieth century, the US occupation of the Dominican Republic, from 1916 to 1924, and the Cuban revolutionary period stand out.

Certainly, there is a relationship between the Dominican Republic and the USA, because the US intervened in the country's internal affairs not only in the early part of the century, but also some forty years later, when Lyndon Johnson ordered the marines to invade the country and stop the popular but Communist Juan Bosch from rightfully claiming the presidency of his country. There is another connection established by exiles and members of the Henríquez Ureña family to the USA. Pedro and his sister Camila studied at the University of Minnesota. Moreover, Pedro was invited to deliver the prestigious Norton Lecture at Harvard and Camila held a teaching position at Vassar College.

Álvarez's interest in promoting women's issues allows her to alter past events. While there is no question of Salomé Ureña's literary merits, her son, Pedro Henríquez Ureña, was an internationally recognized literary figure. As poet and scholar, he was a familiar name in Spanish America, and in the USA (see Chapter 6). Also, Salomé's husband, Francisco Henríquez, was president of the Dominican Republic. From a US cultural perspective, the men are relegated to a secondary role and the novel focuses on the male-dominant Hispanic culture that subjugates women. This is clearly evident with Francisco, who has fallen in love with the National Poet and not the woman that Salomé was. More telling is his medical education in Paris, where he established and later abandoned his second family. And when Salomé is ill, and close to her death, Francisco is more concerned with his relationship with his wife's helper, whom he will later marry. After Salomé's death, he commissions portraits that depict her not as the dark-skinned person she was, but the lighter Salomé he wanted her to be.

The novel's structure allows characters and readers to undergo a search for the origin of Camila's and Salomé's female or feminist discourse. The voices of both mother and daughter alternate, but do so by unfolding in different directions. The novel starts out with Salomé's life as a youngster, poised to become her country's National Poet, and develops into her present adult life. Camilia's story is reversed. It begins in the present in the USA and continues to the past of her Cuban experiences, and finally to her childhood and birth. Each represents a diachronic line, heading in opposite directions. That of Camila follows more closely the narration of Álvarez's first novel, *How the García Girls Lost Their Accents*, as the narrator travels back in time, from her present in the USA to her childhood in the Dominican Republic, in search of an understanding of the past that will give meaning to her present. In *In the Name of Salomé*, the last chapter brings together both mother and daughter, in the same time and space, highlighting important aspects of each of their lives. This last chapter, which is both an end and a beginning, is the chronological beginning of Camila's life. We learn that the sickly Salomé knew of her imminent condition, and began to raise her daughter while still *in utero*. The reader surmises that the lessons learned pertain to Salomé's experiences with men in general and her husband in particular. This understanding of Camila and Salomé's lives help to explain the attraction Camila had for Marion; Pedro had found them kissing, and later warns his family of this dangerous relationship.

Camila and Marion are attracted to each other, and the relationship develops within the context of the USA, where same-gender attraction is more readily acceptable than in the Dominican Republic. Camila is only associated with two men. One is the Cuban Domingo, commissioned to sculpt a bust of her father. Camila's first heterosexual relationship is limited to a one-time affair. More importantly, she is drawn to his dark complexion, which resembles that of her mother. The other is Scott, one of President Roosevelt's assistants. Her challenge is to influence him so that the US government will support her father's return to the Dominican Republic. In contrast, Camila's relationship with Marion is stable and long-lasting.

There is also a personal relationship between Camila and Julia Álvarez, and the life of one recalls that of the other. Both are Dominican women who became poets and scholars. While on the faculty of Vassar College, Camila was invited to lecture at Middlebury College, where Álvarez held a teaching appointment, before she gave up her tenure to become a full-time writer.[6] Neither Camila nor Álvarez ever had children. In fact, Camila articulates Álvarez's own feelings, that her students are her children.

Julia Álvarez represents the exile, who arrives in the USA. However, she experiences a rude awakening. In spite of her privileged status back home, where she grew up with maids and guards, in the USA she is treated without regard to her status. But Álvarez's life represents one side of the Dominican experience in the USA. Junot Díaz represents the other end of the Dominican economic and social spectrum. His is the story of an immigrant who arrived in the USA after Trujillo's assassination and the US invasion of the Dominican Republic. As a male from modest means, his life resembles that of Puerto Ricans and other dark-skinned Latinos, who identify with African American culture as a means of counteracting the Anglo cultural oppression of their experiences.

Díaz's *Drown* (1996) is a collection of independent short stories with a unified theme, which takes the reader and the protagonist back and forth from the Dominican Republic to the USA. Male violence is ever present in both places of birth and residence, and evident in the protagonist's own life. It is defined in historical, political, social, cultural and spiritual terms. Chronologically, violence begins with Trujillo's dictatorship. This is evident when referring to the protagonist's father: 'His generation had, after all, been weaned on the sartorial lunacy of the Jefe, who had owned just under ten thousand ties on the eve of his assassination' (170) and includes the US invasion of the Dominican Republic, in which Papi wore a Guardia uniform (70) and Mami has a scar 'from the rocket attack she'd survived in 1965' (71), transferred to the aggression the children feel because of the absent father. Violence is physical, from one child to another, from men to women, but it is also emotional and spiritual, caused by betrayals, drugs, economic necessities and migration. In effect, violence breeds violence. Though the stories are separate, they can also be read together with a coherent and unified theme. Together, the stories propose multiple searches of temporal and spatial origins.

'Ysrael', the opening story, contains the essence of the collection. Ysrael is a country boy who wears a mask to hide facial disfigurations caused by a pig attack. The protagonist Yunior and his older brother, who are sent to the countryside to live with relatives, conspire to unmask Ysrael. The countryside as origin, prior to the edification of cities and where Yunior and his brother are friends, already is contaminated by original sin. After hitting him with a bottle, Rafa removes Ysrael's mask: 'His left ear was a nub and you could see the thick veined slab of his tongue through a hole in his cheek. He has no lips' (18–19).

Ysrael represents origin, not only because he lives in the countryside, but also because his name recalls the biblical Israelites in search of the Promised Land. Ysrael will be travelling north to undergo reconstructive surgery. But Ysrael also alludes to the narrator, and is his metaphoric representation. There are common characteristics between the two boys. Each boy's father lives in the USA, and each waits to be reunited with him. Also, Díaz's peculiar way of spelling Ysrael corresponds to the spelling of the protagonist's name Yunior, both written with a 'y'. Ysrael has no face, that is, no identity, and waits to have his face or identity reconstructed. Yunior, who has been abandoned by his father, is also in search of his own identity, which is complicated by his residence in the USA. 'No Face' continues Ysrael's story, as the boy prepares for his trip north to have an operation. Father Lou teaches him English so that he can travel to Canada for his operation. The Dominican Republic is Dante's Hell and north represents hope and ascension into Paradise.

If 'Ysrael' symbolizes the origin of the search, then the last story, 'Negocios', is its conclusion. However, 'Negocios' is also a beginning insofar as it is the chronological beginning of the collection; the protagonist's father, Ramón, leaves before Yunior is four years old (by contrast, in 'Ysrael', Yunior is nine and his brother is twelve). 'Negocios' narrates the father's departure for the USA, his hard work as an immigrant, and his dream of sending for his family. But somewhere along the journey, in some ways similar to Álvarez's character Francisco, the father is sidetracked and has a second family. This may not be a total surprise to the reader since Ramón had another lover while living with his family and before departing for the USA.

Of particular interest is the story's construction: 'Negocios' is a collage, composed of pictures ('no photos exist of his mustache days but it is easily imagined', 169), different interpretations ('There are two stories about what happened next, one from Papi, one from Mami', 174), letters written by the father ('In the first letter, he folded four twenty-dollar bills', 177), letters written by the mother ('Mami's letters would be read and folded and tucked into his well-used bags', 181), and finally the protagonist's meeting with Nilda, his father's second wife. Ramón's actions are clear: he abandons his Dominican family and has a new family with Nilda, with whom he returns to the island, and this part of the story coincides with Rafa's excitement and his father's aborted visit. After having three children with Nilda, he abandons his second family in favour of the first. The narrator uncovers his father's life when absent from the family, and how he abandoned Nilda – the accident at the job and subsequent demotion, and her increasing weight were related reasons. The story alludes to a double sadness: Nilda's second abandonment and the protagonist's mother's forgiveness of the father. However, the stories do have a positive outcome, which speaks to the migration process of Dominicans. It is not found in the order in which the stories appear, but in their chronological arrangement. Chronologically the stories can be reordered, thus producing different interpretations to narrated events.

As we have seen, in 'Negocios', the protagonist is four years old when his father worked in the USA. In 'Aguantando', 'Ysrael' and 'No Face', the protagonist is still in the Dominican Republic. In 'Fiesta', 'How to Date a Browngirl, Blackgirl, Whitegirl, or Halfie', 'Drown', 'Aurora', 'Boyfriend' and 'Edison', the protagonist lives in the USA. If in 'Aurora' and 'Drown' Yunior deals in drugs, in 'Boyfriend' he has an apartment. However, in 'Edison', which also describes a different generation of Dominican immigrant, the protagonist has a job, and appears to be headed in an upward and mobile direction.

The readings of the stories in the order suggested by Díaz and in the chronological way I have proposed allow us to understand the search which the protagonist undergoes, to find out not only about his father's life while the family lived in the Dominican Republic, but also about the protagonist's own identity. Violence is present in Dominican society, passed down from father to son, and is also manifested as a cultural marker and affects the protagonist's relationship with women. In 'How to Date a Browngirl, Blackgirl, Whitegirl, or Halfie', narrated in the second person, the protagonist's subconscious tells him what to do, therefore providing strategies of how to approach different women from different racial and economic backgrounds. White girls are sexually aggressive, and local girls, who have to live in the neighbourhood, are the most difficult to romance. But chronologically speaking, we see a development and growth on the part of the protagonist, associated with maturity, but also with his residence in the USA. 'How to Date a Browngirl, Blackgirl, Whitegirl, or Halfie' is followed by 'Aurora', which narrates the protagonist's girlfriend who is on drugs, and 'Drown', which describes a homosexual relationship with a close friend, a topic we had seen with Álvarez's Marion and Camila. In 'Boyfriend' he is the understanding neighbour who helps the lover overcome her boyfriend's rejection. Finally, in 'Edison' the protagonist has a steady job and helps his future girlfriend, a recent Dominican immigrant, escape her live-in job as a servant. If the biblical Genesis underscores Adam and Eve's ejection from Paradise, Yunior, and his embodiment in Ysrael, allude to a reverse structure, one that begins in Hades and ends in Paradise the USA, and his coming to terms with US cultural values.

In search of their identities, Latina and Latino writers attempt to reconcile their US experience with the past of their parents' Hispanic culture. Though bound by the historical forces that led their parents to reside in a particular state, region or city of the USA, liberal aspects of the adopted culture provide them with a certain distance from which to challenge many of the traditional characteristics of Hispanic culture. Those same forces that mark Latinas and Latinos as different prevent them from divorcing themselves totally from their ancestral past. Paradoxically, they cannot separate themselves totally from the dominant culture that surrounds them. Within that culture, a certain interpretation of the Women's Movement plays a significant role, if only to present a model from which to reflect upon. It influences Latinas in an obvious way that speaks to their situation as women, which they address in their works. It also impacts Latinos in a related manner, forcing them to question aspects of male-dominant values, and consider others that underscore a more equitable relationship between and among the sexes.

NOTES

1   If Puerto Ricans were once the dominant Spanish-speaking group, their numbers have reduced in recent times. Portes (2001) points out that in the 1990s the number of Mexicans increased from 55,698 to 186,872, Dominicans from 332,713 to 406,806 and Puerto Ricans shrank from 861,122 to 789,172.

2   In this chapter, I propose to study works I have selected at random of Latinas and Latinos of Dominican, Cuban, Puerto Rican and Chicano descent. While I am conscious that Chicano literature comprises the largest number of Latino writers and works, each group has come to the attention of readers within and outside of the USA. Therefore, in this study I have elected to give approximately the same space to each of the four groups.

3   Laura Elisa Pérez writes that in 1969, at the Denver Chicana/o assembly of youth, where 'El Plan Espiritual de Aztlán' was read, the Chicana caucus declared that Chicanas do not want to be liberated. However, in 1971 Francisca Flores proposed that Chicana self-determination is not negotiable, and Elizabeth Olivárez indicated that the Chicana struggle would be different from that of their Anglo counterparts. However, there were others who challenged those heterosexual and patriarchal ideas of family and sisterhood. See 'El desorden, Nationalism, and Chicana/o Aesthetics' in Kaplan et al. (1999).

4　I use the term Puerto Rican American, not to be redundant, but to differentiate between those Puerto Ricans who live on the mainland and those who live in the island.

5　This idea is developed in Pérez Firmat's *Life on the Hyphen* (1994).

6　See *Something to Declare* (1998).

REFERENCES AND SELECTED FURTHER READING

Álvarez, J. 1998: *Something to Declare*. Chapel Hill, NC: Algonquin Books of Chapel Hill.

Álvarez, J. 2000: *In the Name of Salomé*. Chapel Hill, NC: Algonquin Books of Chapel Hill.

Álvarez Borland, I. 1998: *Cuban-American Literature of Exile: From Person to Persona*. Charlottesville, VA: University Press of Virginia.

Anzaldúa, G. 1987: *Borderland/La Frontera: The New Mestiza*. San Francisco: Aunt Lute Books.

Anzaldúa, G. 1991: To(o) queer the writer-loca, escritora y chicana. In B. Warland (ed.), *Writing by Dykes, Queers and Lesbians*. Vancouver: Press Gang.

Areito Group 1978: *Contra viento y marea*. Havana: Casa de las Américas.

Barradas, E. 1998: *Partes de un todo: Ensayos y notas sobre literatura puertorriqueña en los Estados Unidos*. San Juan, PR: Editorial de la Universidad de Puerto Rico.

Castellanos, J. and Castellanos, I. 1992: *Cultura afrocubana 3: Las religiones y las lenguas*. Miami: Ediciones Universal.

Díaz, J. 1996: *Drown*. New York: Riverhead Books.

Garcia, C. 1997: *The Agüero Sisters*. New York: Alfred A. Knopf.

Hernández Gutiérrez, M. de J. and Foster, D. W. (eds) 1997: *Literatura Chicana 1965–1995: An Anthology in Spanish, English, and Caló*. New York: Garland Publishing, Inc.

Hudson-Weems, C. 1993: *Africana Womanism: Reclaiming Ourselves*. Troy, MI: Bedford Publishers.

Kaplan, C., Alarcon, N. and Moallem, M. (eds) 1999: *Between Woman and Nation: Nationalisms, Transnational Feminisms, and the State*. Durham, NC: Duke University Press.

Laviera, T. 1981: *Jesús Papote*. In *Enclave*. Houston, TX: Arte Público Press.

Leal, L. and Martínez Rodríguez, M. M. 1996: Chicano literature. In R. G. Echevarría and E. Pupo-Walker (eds), *Cambridge History of Latin American Literature*, Vol. 2. Cambridge: Cambridge University Press.

Luis, W. 1997: *Dance Between Two Cultures: Latino Caribbean Literature Written in the United States*. Nashville, TN: Vanderbilt University Press.

Ortiz Cofer, J. 1990: *Silent Dancing: A Partial Remembrance of a Puerto Rican Childhood*. Houston, TX: Arte Público Press.

Pérez-Firmat, G. 1994: *Life on the Hyphen: The Cuban American Way*. Austin: University of Texas Press.

Pérez-Firmat, G. 2000: *Next Year in Cuba: A Cubano's Coming-of-Age in America*. Houston, TX: Scrivenery Press.

Pietri, P. 1971: Puerto Rican obituary. In *Palante: Young Lords Party*. New York: McGraw-Hill.

Portes, E. 2001: Mass migration: at a Bronx church, new Latinos meet old, and tension ensues. *Wall Street Journal*, 7 August, A1, A6.

Rodriguez, R. 1981: *Hunger of Memory: The Education of Richard Rodriguez*. Boston, MA: D. R. Godine.

Thomas, H. 1971: *Cuba: The Pursuit of Freedom*. New York: Harper & Row.

8

Latin American visual cultures

Andrea Noble

VISUAL CULTURE

At the beginning of the twenty-first century it has become a commonplace to state that everyday human experience is more visually oriented than ever before. Image-centred forms dominate the way in which we interact with and comprehend the world that surrounds us: from the icons on a computer screen; through advertising billboards that we pass on our way from A to B, the Internet, television and cinema; to modern technologies, such as medical imaging. All are examples of image forms that have extended the purview of vision beyond that which could be seen before. What is more, in an age in which globalization is calling into question established national boundaries and the allegiances that they foster, images now circulate transnationally in ways that were barely imaginable only ten years ago. Indeed, the Latin American cultural critic Néstor García Canclini argues: 'Where globalization can be seen at its most effective is in the audiovisual world: music, cinema, television and information technology are all being reorganized from within a few companies in order to be disseminated across the whole planet' (Donde se ve más efectiva la globalización es en el mundo audiovisual: música, cine, televisión e informática están siendo reordenados, desde unas pocas empresas, para ser difundidos a todo el planeta) (1999: 15).

The alleged new visuality of contemporary culture, in which the metaphor for the world-as-text has been replaced by an understanding of the world-as-picture, has given rise to a new field of study: visual culture.[1] Nicholas Mirzoeff, a critic who has mapped out some of the key issues and themes of visual culture, argues convincingly that 'The gap between the wealth of visual experience in postmodern culture and the ability to analyze that observation marks both the opportunity and the need for visual culture as a field of study' (1999: 3). Taking as their object a wealth of visually encoded artefacts – film, television, photography, painting, digital imaging, etc. – scholars working in this field are not simply concerned with the analysis of visual images as they circulate in their conventional contexts such as the art gallery, the cinema, etc. They are also, importantly, interested in the relationship between the visual and everyday experience: the ways in which we encounter visual images as we go about our daily activities to the extent that our everyday experience can be said to be increasingly mediated by the visual image. In this way, the image, in its multiple forms, is understood not as a mere reflection of the context in which it is embedded, but rather is actively involved in the production of meanings and values within that context. The study of visual culture therefore places an emphasis both on the formal elements that make up the image and the crucial role of its reception in the form of the viewer's engagement with the image: an engagement that is in no way uniform or static. As subjects whose identity is determined by questions of gender, class, race, sexuality, and historical and geographical location, viewers interact with images in ways that are determined by their socio-cultural contexts. The meanings that are associated with a given image, or sequence of images, come about in this dynamic interplay between viewer and image, making of the latter 'a place where meanings are created and contested' (Mirzoeff 1999: 6).

Visual products circulate today with unprecedented fluidity and are therefore consumed by a more diverse viewing public than ever before. Popular Mexican soap operas, for example, are as avidly watched by viewers in Russia as in their original context of production. It would be wrong to assume, however, that such fluid circulation is suddenly free from the power structures that have traditionally governed the flow of goods and knowledges since the advent of Western colonization in the fifteenth century. Within globalized structures of power, Latin America is still more likely to be a receiver of cultural goods than it is to be a transmitter. Indeed, García Canclini puts this equation in stark numerical terms when he notes that 9 per cent of the world's population live in the European Union, which exports 37.5 per cent of the cultural goods in circulation. By contrast, 7 per cent of the world's population live in Latin America, and yet the subcontinent exports a mere 0.8 per cent of cultural goods (1999: 24). The asymmetrical balance of power as applied to the sphere of artistic endeavour is conveyed with striking simplicity by Uruguayan artist Joaquín Torres García in *Upside-Down Map* (1943, Torres García family collection, Montevideo). By inverting the map of South America, Torres García lays bare the way in which certain locations and geographies of art have been privileged as the arbiters of value and meaning over others. *Upside-Down Map* forces the viewer to perform a kind of mental somersault. Our initial response to this image is to reinvert the map, to put it back 'the right way up'. In provoking such a response, Torres García not only exposes the constructed nature of maps and mapping and the hierarchies of value to which they give rise. His inverted map also demonstrates how the visual image cannot be separated from the sets of viewers who give them meaning: meaning which is always anchored within a given socio-political context. *Upside-Down Map* is furthermore an example of a strategy frequently deployed in Latin

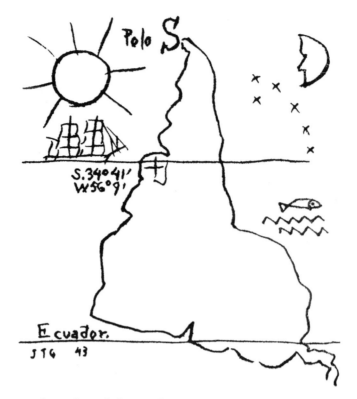

El norte es el sur (North is South/Upside-Down Map) **by Joaquín Torres García**. Reproduced courtesy of Cecilia de Torres, Ltd., New York

American visual culture to subvert and thereby convert (into something different) the dominant discourses that are the legacy of colonization and would posit the subcontinent as culturally inferior.

In fact, as a new field of study, perhaps one of the biggest challenges that faces visual culture is precisely its strategic potential to break with dominant, Eurocentric paradigms that have characterized art history, film and media studies and other disciplines that deal with the visual. Such paradigms emerged in the fifteenth century with the rise of colonial expansion, seeing Europe (and, latterly, European-modelled nations such as the USA) as superior to the rest of the world. Despite the end of colonialism, Eurocentric discourses continue to influence the way in which the world is conceptualized. Indeed, mindful of this power dynamic, Mirzoeff suggests that 'At present, it must be recognized that visual culture remains a discourse of the West about the West ... In short, the success or failure of visual culture may well depend on its ability to think transculturally, oriented to the future, rather than take the rear-mirror anthropological approach to culture as tradition' (1998: 10). In the case of Latin American visual culture, the success or failure will depend on the possibility of offering an account of what is historically and culturally specific about visual culture in the region. How, then, might we go about this?

COLONIAL IMAGE WARS

Perhaps the first step towards offering an account of the historical and cultural specificity of visual culture in Latin America involves casting our gaze back to the central role of the visual in the very processes of conquest and colonization. These processes, as Ella Shohat and Robert Stam argue, are intricately linked to the current cultural moment. Globalization, according to these critics, 'usually evokes a recent phenomenon involving complex realignments of social forces engendering an overpowering wave of international political, cultural, and economic interdependency' (2000: 384). It is, moreover, a process that elicits radically different responses that alternate from a celebration of the world-wide availability of cultural goods and information, to objections to the homogenizing tendencies that such availability may entail and that, for some, pose a threat to local diversity. Whether we read contemporary globalization as an ultimately benign or malign force, however, Shohat and Stam usefully remind us that:

> What is often forgotten is that 'globalization' is not a new phenomenon; it forms part of the much longer history of colonialism going at least as far back as 1492. Columbus, in this sense, performed the founding gesture of globalization. Although colonization *per se* pre-dated European colonialism, what was new in European colonialism was its planetary reach, its affiliation with global institutional power, and its imperative mode, its attempted submission of the world to a single 'universal' regime of truth and power. (2000: 384)

If the contemporary global moment has become associated with a new turn to the visual, it is tied to an earlier cultural event, namely Western expansion, the legacy of which we are living with today. It should perhaps not surprise us then that Columbus's 'discovery' of America and its aftermath similarly gave rise to strikingly image-centred colonial cultures. In other words, by taking the long view, it is possible to bring into focus the powerful historical role that visual culture played in the formation of cultural identities in Latin America.

In a wonderful book that has recently been translated into English, the ethno-historian Serge Gruzinski explores the role of the visual image in the conquest and colonization of the 'New World' by the Spanish. In *Images at War: Mexico from Columbus to Blade Runner (1492–2019)* (2001), Gruzinski suggests that on one level the conquest and colonization of Latin America can be understood in peculiarly visual terms as a kind of war of images.[2] As cultures with radically different conceptions of the world came into violent contact with one another, the visual image came to occupy a central position in that encounter. Just as in today's globalized world, in which images facilitate communication across linguistic boundaries, they fulfilled a similar role in the colonial encounter between the Spanish and the myriad ethnic groups. In fact, Gruzinski's analysis of the role of the visual image in the conquest and colonization is fascinating on many levels, not least in his exploration of the way in which the indigenous peoples and the Spanish had very different conceptions of what constituted a religious image. For instance, where the European colonizers perceived idols, indigenous peoples saw sacred religious objects. The process of colonization therefore involved an encounter between fundamentally different gazes – the indigenous and the Spanish – and different systems of visual representation. The clash between two different visual traditions initially led to the mass destruction of 'idols' by the Spanish. In their colonizing zeal, the latter attempted to cancel out the pre-existing visual traditions and start afresh, saturating the visual domain of the 'New World' with a specifically Catholic iconography (for example, images of the Virgin and Christ) and way of visualizing the world.

From this very brief account of what is a richly complex exploration of the role of the visual in colonial relations in Latin America, there are a number of factors that are worth underlining. First, it is plain to see that colonial looking relations are shot through with questions of power. In the struggle to impose their own world-view on the indigenous peoples through Western iconographic traditions, the Europeans encountered resistance and often the results achieved were uneven. Indeed, colonial image wars provide a graphic definition of Mirzoeff's notion that the image is 'a place where meanings are created and contested' (Mirzoeff 1999: 6). Given the complexity and diversity of the indigenous cultures, the struggle by the colonizers to impose a European frame of reference on the pre-exising visual cultures of the 'New World' was inevitably incomplete. What emerged from the process was instead an essentially syncretic cultural imaginary, that is to say, a way of seeing and imagining one's place in the world that fused elements from both systems of representation. Second, colonial image wars were very much part of everyday experience, a sphere that was radically transformed in the wake of the first waves of iconoclasm, during which the Spanish set out to destroy what, in their eyes, were indigenous idols (as opposed to their own Christian icons). In this process of transformation, visual culture was crucial in shaping the way people saw and experienced the world, themselves and others in the (new) world. And third, although the war of images that was unleashed in the colonial period was to a large degree centred on religious iconography, Gruzinski's study nevertheless has repercussions for an understanding of visual culture produced in the more secular modern period. This is because his study establishes a historical context in which to explore the power relations that underpin visual images that circulate in post-colonial Latin America and that play a fundamental role in the formation of cultural identities in the region. Indeed, Gruzinski makes the connection between contemporary visual culture and the colonial war of images explicit in the playful subtitle to his book: 'from Columbus to *Blade Runner*'.

CINEMATIC IMAGE WARS

By invoking Ridley Scott's futuristic film *Blade Runner* (1982), Gruzinski makes a direct link between colonial and post-colonial image cultures. More specifically, he is pointing towards the way in which in the twentieth and twenty-first centuries the global war of images has continued in the moving image and particularly the Hollywood domination of global cinema.

Since its rise to prominence during the First World War, Hollywood has held sway in film circuits not only in Latin America, but also in the vast majority of global cinema markets, with important implications for the development of so-called 'world' cinema(s). As Ana López forcefully argues: 'One way or another, all nations aspiring to produce a "national" cinema have always had to deal with Hollywood's presence or, sometimes, its absence' (López 2000: 418). Dealing with Hollywood is not simply a question of facing up to its dominance of the circuits of film distribution and exhibition. It is also about acknowledging how the combination of continuity editing, narrative causality and the construction of time–space coherence that characterizes Hollywood's mode of film-making has had a profound influence on the kinds of narrative expectations held by audiences and the related viewing positions that these create.[3] Furthermore, despite the fact that Hollywood is clearly linked to a precise geographical and cultural location, rarely are the values that a Hollywood film embodies considered to be linked to the national context of the film's production. Instead, these values, on the whole, pass as 'universal'. What effect, then, has Hollywood had on the development of the film industry in Latin America and how have the region's film-makers faced up to the powerful presence of their northernmost neighbour in what we might term, following Gruzinski, the cinematic war of images?

A cursory glance at some of the literature on Latin American cinema will turn up a series of watchwords that seem to characterize the development of the industry across the region: 'in crisis', 'discontinuous', 'uneven', 'in decline'. These are words that stand in opposition to the brief flourishing of 'golden ages' in key national cinemas. What is more, owing to the economic implications involved in film-making, those industries whose output has approached anything nearing regular and steady production have tended to concentrate in a cluster of countries in the region, namely Argentina, Brazil, Cuba and Mexico.[4] Hollywood's hegemonic hold over cinema in Latin America in terms of its saturation of local markets with its own product, and also control over the raw materials of film production, has not, however, been met without resistance: a resistance that was at its most energetic in the second half of the twentieth century.

The aftermath of the 1959 Cuban Revolution – an event that defined the radical political and cultural climate of the time – saw the production of films and the publication of a series of 'manifestos' by film-makers and critics that together constitute what is known as 'New Latin American Cinema'. Headed primarily by film-makers based in Argentina, Brazil and Cuba, those involved in the New Latin American Cinema conceived of film as a form of oppositional practice, with the aim of denouncing underdevelopment and economic dependence. At the same time, as a movement that was simultaneously nationalist and internationalist in its outlook, New Latin American Cinema was based on the concept of film as a medium that could transform social practice through its radical appeal to its audience.

A selection of the manifestos produced as part of the movement has recently been re-published in the useful two-volume *New Latin American Cinema*, edited by Michael T. Martin (1997). These impassioned tracts offer us a flavour of the highly politicized cultural moment out of which films made in the movement emerged. Originally published in 1969, in 'Towards a third cinema', Argentines Fernando Solanas and Octavio Getino denounce the 'expansion of U.S. imperialism and the film model that is imposed: Hollywood movies' (Martin 1997: 41). Instead, they advocate a revolutionary cinema, defining it as 'not fundamentally one which illustrates, documents, or passively establishes a situation: *rather, it attempts to intervene in the situation as an element providing thrust or rectification. To put it another way, it provides discovery through transformation*' (1997: 47). In fact, 'Towards a third cinema' was put together after the making of Solanas's landmark film *La hora de los hornos* (The Hour of the Furnaces, 1968), a four-hour epic that condemns Argentina's neo-colonial status and exhorts the spectator to become involved in political activism. In what we might imagine, given the film's marathon duration, were welcome breaks in the film, at the end of Part II of *La hora de los hornos*, a voiceover addresses the spectator directly: 'Now the film is pausing, it opens up to you for you to continue it. Now you have the floor.'[5]

Authored by a leading exponent of Brazil's *Cinema Novo*, Glauber Rocha's 'An aesthetic of hunger' (1965) recognizes hunger – in both a literal and metaphorical sense – as a key component of the Brazilian situation: a hunger which, for the Brazilian, 'is a national shame. He does not eat, but he is ashamed to say so; and yet, he does not know where this hunger comes from. We know – since we made these sad, ugly films, these screaming, desperate films where reason does not always prevail – that this hunger will not be cured by moderate governmental reforms and that the cloak of technicolor cannot hide, but only aggravates, its tumors' (Martin 1997: 60). The 'sad', 'ugly' films to which Rocha refers were made at the time of the 1964 military coup and ensuing dictatorship. This period marked a growth in the nation's cinematic output and saw the establishment of influential directors such as Rocha himself, Nelson Pereira dos Santos, Carlos Diegues and Joaquim Pedro de Andrade. In what Ismail Xavier terms 'allegories of underdevelopment', films of this period – such as Rocha's

Terra em Transe (Land in Anguish, 1967) and Nelson Pereira dos Santos's *Fome de Amor* (Hunger for Love, 1968) – make of Brazil's underdeveloped status, its lack of advanced technical resources, an expressive force to question and critique a political system that perpetuates social inequities.

Finally, at the epicentre of radical politics in the region, the Cuban Revolution effectively brought to life a cinematic culture on an island with a surprisingly large number of cinema-goers, but with little in the way of national film production. Indeed, the revolutionary leaders were quick to harness the potential of film to their project, with the formation of ICAIC (Instituto Cubano de Artes e Industria Cinematográficos) in March 1959. Here again, we find film-maker Julio García Espinosa, some ten years later, denouncing what he terms the 'perfect cinema' of Hollywood and Europe as reactionary. In 'For an imperfect cinema' (1969) he argues instead for an alternative ('imperfect') cinema that draws on popular art forms, makes the struggles and problems of ordinary people its subject matter, and encourages the active participation of its audience. As in other cinemas across Latin America of the time, debates around the relationship between culture and society figure prominently in Cuba and Cuban cinema. These are crystallized in films such as Tomás Gutiérrez Alea's *Memorias del subdesarrollo* (Memories of Underdevelopment, 1968) and Sara Gómez's *De cierta manera* (One Way or Another, 1974), which mingle fiction and documentary to reflect upon social upheaval in the aftermath of the Revolution.

New Latin American Cinema emerged out of the specific historical and social conditions that defined both the national contexts of its films and film-makers and also the continent-wide political movements of the period. It represents a move to question cinematic paradigms – particularly those inherited from Hollywood and European cinemas – and to question the function of film and how it might be put into the service of social transformation. As such, New Latin American Cinema understands film as a radical medium engaged in the struggle against the neo-colonizing forces at work in Hollywood's saturation of Latin American film markets. In short, the visual domain in the form of cinematic technology represents a site of ideological struggle and conflict. Film-makers of the movement stress the 'imperfection' of the film-making conditions in which they operate in the form of limited resources. In their films they manifest 'imperfection' and in so doing make of it a strategy to confront and challenge 'perfect cinema' and its values. And at the heart of this cinematic war of images we find the spectator. Via his/her engagement with the (in filmic terms) imperfectly presented events as they unfold on the screen, this spectator is urged to abandon the kind of passive viewing positions purportedly encouraged by Hollywood-style narrative techniques and instead to adopt a critical, socially aware stance. These factors were ultimately some of the key characteristics of the 'newness' of the New Latin American Cinema. Another was the fact that practitioners involved in the movement attempted to effect a radical break not only with Hollywood, but also with a cinema that was in some ways considered equally ideologically suspect, the so-called 'old' cinemas of Latin America. Or, to put it another way, the newness of New Latin American Cinema was also predicated, in part at least, on its not being 'old'.

Indeed, until recently the 'old' cinemas of Latin America – produced in the 1930s, 1940s and 1950s – have languished in critical neglect. Condemned as derivative of Hollywood models, over-reliant on the sentimentalities of melodrama and beholden to the interests of the ruling classes, for many years critics wrote off films made in this period as third-rate and what we might today call 'politically incorrect'. In so doing, however, such critics were dismissing a form of cinema that had a genuine appeal to a mass audience. What is more, as Ana López states, they 'did not take into account that this was the first indigenous cinema to dent the Hollywood industry's pervasive presence in Latin America; the first to consistently circulate Latin American images, voices, songs and history; the first to capture and sustain the interest of multinational audiences throughout the continent for several decades' (1993: 148).

The critical neglect that the old cinemas of Latin America suffered has now, however, been rectified. Thanks, in part, to a re-evaluation in film studies of melodrama as a filmic mode, to a critique of the elitist assumptions that underpin the rejection of mass cultural forms, and also to the work of scholars such as López, the old cinemas are currently enjoying renewed interest. So, there may be no doubt that the majority of the films produced in the period were imitative in one form or another of Hollywood models. Nevertheless, it is now widely acknowledged that the translation and transformation of such models from one cultural context to another are much more complex than the notion of a straightforward act of cultural imposition will allow.

The first half of the twentieth century was a time of intense cultural activity and change in many Latin American republics, and particularly in the three centres that dominated film production of the period, Argentina, Brazil and Mexico. Cultural activity took the form of heightened nationalism as Latin American nation-states sought to consolidate a homogenous national identity in what were effectively complex, multiethnic societies. Given the fundamentally capitalist thrust of these nation-states, cultural nationalism went hand in hand with the move towards cultural modernity. Across the region everyday life underwent rapid and radical change as segments of the population experienced the inevitable shifts in mores and values that occur in societies going though the vertiginous (and in all cases) incomplete transition from tradition to modernity, from Catholic to secular, from rural to urban, from agricultural to industrial. As an example of a complex new technology, and as an urban-based form that reached a mass audience, the cinema itself was a quintessential symbol of cultural modernity. The moving image was, moreover, a vital tool in the consolidation of a single national identity: film was a perfect vehicle through which to play out at a fictional level the conflicts and struggles encountered by characters experiencing the disorienting effects of the processes of modernization that gained momentum alongside nationalist discourses.

In considering the role of cinema in the processes of cultural modernity it is helpful to consider a key film text from the Mexican cinema, a cinema that in the early 1940s experienced a brief 'golden age'. During this period, film production rose exponentially, a specifically Mexican star system developed (including actors such as Dolores del Río, María Félix, Pedro Armendáriz and Pedro Infante) and key film genres were established. Amongst the latter, melodrama was central. The film in question is the family melodrama *Una familia de tantas* (Alejandro Galindo, 1948) and is particularly lucid in its thematization of the conflicts brought about as a result of processes of modernization.

Set almost entirely inside the stiflingly claustrophobic confines of the Cataño family home, *Una familia de tantas* centres on the relationship between middle daughter Maru (Martha Roth) and vacuum-cleaner salesman Roberto del Hierro (David Silva). The latter manages to infiltrate the family home, a bastion of traditional values (associated in the film with the ex-dictator Porfirio Díaz) presided over by the violently patriarchal figure Don Rodrigo del Cataño (Fernando Soler). In the course of his courtship with Maru, Roberto convinces Don Cataño to purchase two prime modern commodities (a vacuum cleaner and a refrigerator), before whisking Cataño's daughter off against her father's will to what the film sets up as a more democratic and modern marriage. That the film can be read at a national level as a metaphor for Mexico's transition from the feudal, authoritarian values of traditional society to a more enlightened, modern society with its values implicitly modelled on those of the USA (the name of the company for which Roberto works is significantly The Bright O' Home Corporation) is signalled clearly. The Cataño family is 'one of many' (*Una familia de tantas*). And in the opening sequence the camera pans from right to left across a panoramic cityscape into the Cataño home through Maru's bedroom window, thereby establishing a connection between the urban setting as macrocosm and the family's status as a microcosm within it.

In the film's mediation of the implicitly progressive values associated with modernization, it is important to emphasize the way in which *Una familia de tantas* engages its audience through the processes of identification that are inherent in the act of cinematic spectatorship. In very bald terms, the film invites its audience to reject the old-fashioned patriarchy embodied by Don Cataño and his comically feckless eldest son Héctor (Felipe de Alba), and to identify with Maru, admire her defiance of her father and approve of her marriage to the thoroughly modern Roberto. In so doing, it is effectively inviting an engagement with cultural modernity as a progressive force for change.

Una familia de tantas is just one film of many made during the period and across the cinemas in question that plays out the familial – and by extension national – conflicts associated with societies in a state of flux. In so doing, it undoubtedly buys into an important and popular genre in the Hollywood cinema: family melodrama. However, in the process of cultural importation, the 'foreign' model is nationalized and thereby transformed for consumption by a local audience steeped in the traditions not only of Hollywood but also, importantly, local popular culture. Indeed, across the cinemas of Latin America, the presence of the local is perhaps nowhere more keenly felt than in the proliferation of film genres that incorporate music and dance numbers. Argentine cinema's most buoyant moment was arguably dominated by tango-led productions starring Carlos Gardel in the 1930s; in Brazil the musical comedy or *chancada* was immensely popular in the period; in Mexico the *cabaretera* or brothel melodrama became a key national genre of the country's old cinema.

When reconsidering Latin America's cinemas of the 1930s, 1940s and 1950s, it is therefore important to remember that as a popular form of mass entertainment, the old cinemas developed a language and style that reflected the local within the framework of the more international idiom of cinema as it was developing in Hollywood. As such, film played an important role in nation formation in that it activated common codes that invited the audience to recognize and to imagine themselves as members of a given community. Furthermore, as in the earlier period of colonial identity formation, the visual (now the audio-visual) became a key site for mediating the dramatic changes that were permeating everyday life.

STILL IMAGES AND CULTURAL IDENTITY

The moving image was but one mode of visual representation engaged in the negotiation of cultural identity and mediating the transition to modernity in the twentieth century. The still image in its multiple forms has also been constitutive of national collectivities in the region. In fact, in Mexico, in the aftermath of the 1910–20 Revolution, in the first instance it was not film, but rather painting that assumed this mediating role. Indeed, in a statement that has echoes of the New Latin American Cinema some forty years later, a key cultural architect of Mexican cultural nationalism, José Vasconcelos (1882–1959), argued in the 1920s that the cinema was 'a typically US cultural product impossible to develop as a national form' (López 2000: 425). Vasconcelos may have given the cinema short shrift; he was, however, a major advocate of the still image and more particularly monumental muralism which, via his role as Minister for Education, he promoted as a revolutionary national art form.

For all that it was lacking in clearly definable ideological goals, the 1910 Revolution was a decisive event that defined the course of Mexican history and had reverberations across the whole of Latin America where it was hailed as the subcontinent's first major social revolution. The Revolution swept aside the dictatorship of Porfirio Díaz, removed many of the landowning elite, and, in its nationalist rhetoric at least, made way for new figures within national culture: the indigenous peasant and the worker. After the initial violent struggle – during which, out of a population of some 15 million, 1.5 million perished –

the Revolution entered a phase of institutionalization during which the highly factionalized dispute was effectively reinvented as a coherent and socially cohesive myth of national origin. In a largely illiterate society, fractured by ethnic and regional divisions, visual culture came to play a central role in this process of reinvention not only of the Revolution itself, but also of Mexico's history.

The Mexican muralist movement was dominated by three artists, the so-called 'tres grandes', Diego Rivera (1886–1957), José Clemente Orozco (1898–1974) and David Alfaro Siquieros (1883–1949). Throughout the colonial and extending into the post-independence period, visual culture in Mexico (and indeed elsewhere in Latin America) had been dominated by European artistic traditions, which in the eyes of the proponents of revolutionary art were seen as elitist. Creating huge images on the walls of public buildings, the muralists instituted a monumental form of art about the (Mexican) people, for the people. Art moved out of the private, elitist European-style art institutions and into the public, egalitarian spheres of national buildings. In this way art, which was held to have explicitly didactic powers, was to become part of the everyday environment. Rivera in particular became interested in revisioning Mexican history in his murals, looking to the past, to pre-Columbian culture in his search for the authentic, quintessentially Mexican roots of the contemporary nation.

In *The Great City of Tenochtitlán* (1945), part of the cycle of murals initiated in 1929 in the National Palace at the heart of Mexico City, Rivera depicts an idealized view of the Aztec capital. The viewer is presented with a harmonious market scene in which the busy people that fill the mural are engaged in commerce based on a system of bartering. The panoramic, open, bird's-eye view of the city, coupled with the light blues and whites that preponderate in the composition, add to the harmonious feeling that the mural creates. This contrasts sharply with *The Disembarkation in Veracruz* (1951), also at the National Palace, which is a damning indictment of the violence and cruelty of the Spanish conquerors of Mexico. The mural's representation of the pale, sickly, green-tinged Spaniards reminds the viewer of the deadly epidemics that wiped out the millions of Indians with no immunity to the diseases that the Europeans harboured. The enslaved Indians have been made to destroy the natural environment, their small anonymous figures reminding us that, with the arrival of the Spaniards, they were to become effaced from history until, in theory at least, the Revolution. In the left-hand corner the mural draws a visual parallel between a cross, symbolizing the evangelical designs of the colonizers, and the diminutive figures of Indians who have been strung by their feet from the remaining trees and whose forms echo that of the cross.

In this brief snapshot of just two murals from Rivera's vast *œuvre*, we can begin to grasp some of the conflicts and paradoxes that underpin muralism, particularly as it was practised by Rivera. On the one hand, Rivera's work stands as a strategic corrective. Its glorification of the pre-Columbian past served to restore a sense of value and worth to Mexico's indigenous heritage which for so long had been denigrated and marginalized in favour of more 'sophisticated' models of European origin. On the other hand, however, as a visual strategy it also raises a series of problems. Rivera's revisions of the past are arguably too black-and-white and lacking in nuance and complexity. His idealization of indigenous culture was, moreover, deeply ambivalent and chimed with contemporary *Indigenista* discourses. In the aftermath of the Revolution, the *Indigenista* movement sought to reinstate Mexico's indigenous communities into the heart of national life. In the final analysis, however, what it really involved was co-opting the picturesque, folkloric elements of indigenous cultures and incorporating them as myths and symbols within the powerfully centralizing and homogenizing nationalist discourses.[6] This is perhaps where the ultimate paradox of Rivera's muralism lies. For all that muralism claimed to be an egalitarian form of art about the people, for the people, its didactic intentions were arguably directed more at the elite sectors of society who had, so to speak, 'to learn to love' the indigenous past, or at least a pristine, sanitized version of it.

For a more nuanced vision of the complexities of Mexican identity in the post-revolutionary period we need to read the monumentality of muralism in tandem with the diminutive work of Rivera's wife, Frida Kahlo. Since an important 1982 exhibition at the Whitechapel Gallery in London that re-presented Kahlo's paintings alongside the photographs of Italian-American photographer Tina Modotti, curated by British critics Laura Mulvey and Peter Wollen, there has been an upsurge of interest in Kahlo. After a period of critical neglect, the Whitechapel exhibition relaunched Kahlo, re-packaging her in the light of feminist interventions into art history. Such interventions sought to make good the erasures of women artists from the texts of art history and at the same time to critique the masculinist bias of traditional work in the field. In fact the Whitechapel exhibition – with its emphasis on the blurring of the boundaries between the personal and the political and on the body as cultural artefact in Kahlo's work – was to set the tone for much critical work on Kahlo in the 1980s and 1990s. This work reads her intensely personal and dramatic self-portraits as embodying a feminist aesthetics. And to be sure, Kahlo's imagery pushes back the boundaries of what can be legitimately represented in the visual domain: from bloody miscarriages to scenes of domestic violence. There can be no denying the powerful and shocking impact of images such as *A Few Small Nips* (1935, Collection of Dolores Olmedo, Mexico City), which depicts a naked woman who lies prone on a bed, her body covered in vicious, bloody slashes, besides which stands a man, knife in hand. The image's wooden frame, like the woman's body, is splashed with red paint/blood, thereby preventing the viewer from distancing him/herself from the violent scene contained within the frame.

However, the tendency to read Kahlo and her work as iconically feminist has at times obscured the way in which her images offer a more complex vision of issues of identity than that found in the work of Rivera. The latter's work tends to be rather reductive and binaristic in its visual narration of the nation which 'was being crafted as a "true" essence, with either the Indian or the mestizo standing in as the "authentic" Self in contrast to a "false" Other, the Spanish, European and colonial past' (Volk 2000: 171). By contrast, in paintings such as *Self-Portrait on the Border between Mexico and the United States* (1932, Collection of Mrs Manuel Reyero, New York), *The Two Fridas* (1939, Museo de Arte Moderno, Mexico City) and *My Nurse and I* (1937, Collection of Dolores Olmedo, Mexico City), Kahlo thematizes the complexity of Mexican identity, emphasizing its multiplicity, exclusions and conflicts.[7] In so doing, she faces up to the colonial past and, rather than rejecting, incorporates the 'false' others demonized by Rivera as an integral part of contemporary Mexican (and Latin American) identity.

Facing up to the legacy of colonialism within visual culture also involves confronting the powerful presence of European artistic traditions in the form of the 'Old Masters'. As Oriana Baddeley and Valerie Fraser suggest in their invaluable book *Drawing the Line*:

> Another feature of the traditional academic training with far-reaching consequences for Latin American art is that of copying from the Old Masters. It is axiomatic that art cannot be reproduced in the same way as can music or literature, so for aspiring young artists in countries where the public collections contain little or nothing apart from their own colonial and nineteenth century past the impact of a trip to Europe can be immeasurable, and the art of copying whilst on such a visit of special value. (1989: 43)

It is, however, one thing for a European artist to copy from the 'Old Masters'. It is quite another for a Latin American artist to do so. This is because copying from European images was one of the ways in which the indigenous subject was re-educated simultaneously into Christianity and the Western traditions of representation and visualizing the world that Gruzinski outlines in his study on colonial image wars.

Parodic copying has therefore, unsurprisingly, become a strategy deployed by Latin American artists in a decolonizing gesture similar to that displayed by Torres García's inverted map. Arguably the best known of the 'copyists' is the Colombian Fernando Botero, famous for his inflated, *faux naif* figures, and who, in a number of his most reproduced images, turns explicitly to his European intertexts. Thus *The Presidential Family* (1967, Museum of Modern Art, New York) is based on Spanish artist's Goya's *Family of Charles IV* (1800, Museo el Prado, Madrid), which is itself a parodic version of another Spanish 'master', Velázquez's classic painting, *Las Meninas* (1656, Museo el Prado, Madrid). The pomposity and vacuity of the inflated 'first family' in Botero's image are sent up via its reference to Goya's version of his equally vacuous royal subjects. So too in Botero's image is the artist, who has included himself in the painting, standing at his easel in a visual echo of both Goya and Velázquez, in the left-hand corner of the frame. The parodic inflation of the artist, and by extension the institution of art, turns on the way in which in Velázquez's original the artist garnered elevated status for himself via his association within the frame with the Spanish royal family. Such status is clearly short-circuited in Botero's 'copy', in that far from prestige, the presidential first family by association can only bestow ridicule on the artist.

Velázquez and the institution of art are also central to our understanding of *Self-Portrait in Velázquez Costume* (1986, Galerie Beyeler, Basel). At the centre stands the artist who has donned a costume reminiscent of that worn by his Spanish, seventeenth-century counterpart in *Las Meninas*. Botero is clearly about to paint a female nude, a theme that has come to connote art itself within the Western tradition of art. The robust female figure that stands before the artist, however, has her back turned to the viewer, signalling that this painting is not a conventional nude as such, but rather a painting about art and its institutions. That Botero is dressed in a Velázquez costume serves to remind us that the category of artist that is enacted in the frame is one that is acquired within the cultural institutions of art. Furthermore, the costume also indicates that artistic genius – a status that Velázquez achieved – is not something that one is born with, but rather is itself a cultural artefact. Therefore if Latin American artists have struggled to achieve status in a European-dominated art world (or to put it in Torres García's terms, if Latin America has conventionally been situated at the bottom of map), this is not due to some form of 'natural' inferiority. Rather, it is the result of the processes of cultural colonialism that have produced such a position. Therefore, in such overtly self-referential paintings as *The Presidential Family* and *Self-Portrait in Velázquez Costume*, Botero is able to reflect on and critique art as an institution: an institution that through the legacy of colonialism has condemned Latin America to the status of a second-rate, pale copy to Europe's (and the North's) status as originator of value and meaning.

THE FUTURE OF LATIN AMERICAN VISUAL CULTURES

The foregoing discussion has, by necessity, offered the briefest and most fleeting of glimpses at a very limited selection of the wealth and variety that are the visual cultures of Latin America. The emergence of visual culture as a field of study that flourishes across a range of disciplinary contexts without being confined and thereby circumscribed by any one does, however, open up a new kind of space for considering questions of vision and visuality in Latin America. In this space it becomes possible to put new visual objects onto the critical map that have previously been occluded from view. At the same time, as an exciting new development, visual culture provides an opportunity to scrutinize and critique the Eurocentrism of disciplines such as art history and film and media studies. In their most conservative and conventional forms, these disciplines have been blind to the cultures that exist beyond their limited field of vision. But perhaps more than this, the ongoing and dynamic development of the study of Latin American visual cultures represents an invitation: to explore the historical and cultural specificities of the 'image at war' in an area in which the colonial encounter brought into contact two very different ways of visualizing the world.

NOTES

1 Martin Jay (1994) provides a helpful definition of the slippery distinction between vision and visuality where the former is used to describe the physiological process of seeing and the latter understands the practice of vision as inevitably embedded within and therefore shaped by culture and history.

2 Although the focus of Gruzinski's book is Mexico, as comments in the introduction make clear, the broader ramifications of the study have implications for an understanding of the image in Latin America more generally.

3 Continuity editing, narrative causality and the construction of time–space coherence are all elements that characterize conventional Hollywood cinema and which together serve to make the telling of a story through filmed images seem transparently 'natural', akin to 'real life'. They are, of course, simply conventions. See Vasey (1997) for more on Hollywood's conventions and attitudes towards its overseas markets.

4 This is not to claim that other Latin American countries are not involved in film-making – they are, but not on the same scale as the countries mentioned above. Owing to the constraints of space, this chapter can only touch upon the more established industries.

5 Quoted in King (1990: 87).

6 See Knight (1990) for an excellent discussion of the complexity and problems associated with *Indigenismo*.

7 See Volk (2000) for an excellent discussion of Kahlo's representation of the nation.

REFERENCES AND SELECTED FURTHER READING

Ades, D. 1989: *Art in Latin America: The Modern Era*. New Haven, CT: Yale University Press.

Baddeley, O. and Fraser, V. 1989: *Drawing the Line: Art and Cultural Identity in Contemporary Latin America*. London: Verso.

Barnitz, J. 2001: *Twentieth-Century Art of Latin America*. Austin: University of Texas Press.

Benjamin, T. 2000: *La Revolución: Mexico's Great Revolution as Memory, Myth, and History*. Austin: University of Texas Press.

Burton, J. (ed.) 1986: *Cinema and Social Change in Latin America: Conversations with Filmmakers*. Austin: University of Texas Press.

Craven, D. 2002: *Art and Revolution in Latin America, 1910–1990*. New Haven, CT: Yale University Press.

Folgarait, L. 1998: *Mural Painting and Social Revolution in Mexico, 1920–1940*. Cambridge: Cambridge University Press.

Fox, C. F. 1999: *The Fence and the River: Culture and Politics at the US–Mexico Border*. Minneapolis, London: University of Minnesota Press.

Franco, J. 1970: *The Modern Culture of Latin America: Society and the Artist*. London: Harmondsworth.

Franco, J. 1989: *Plotting Women: Gender and Representation in Mexico*. London: Verso.

García Canclini, N. 1999: *La globalización imaginada*. Buenos Aires: Paidós.

Goldman, S. M. 1994: *Dimensions of the Americas: Art and Social Change in Latin America and the United States*. Chicago: University of Chicago Press.

Gruzinski, S. 2001: *Images at War: Mexico from Columbus to Blade Runner (1492–2019)*. Durham, NC: Duke University Press.

Hershfield, J. 1996: *Mexican Cinema, Mexican Woman, 1940–1950*. Tucson: University of Arizona Press.

Hershfield, J. and Maciel, D. R. (eds) 1999: *Mexico's Cinema: A Century of Film and Filmmakers*. Wilmington, DE: SR Books.

Jay, M. 1994: *Downcast Eyes: The Denigration of Vision in Twentieth-Century French Thought*. Berkeley and Los Angeles: University of California Press.

Johnson, R. and Stam, R. (eds) 1982: *Brazilian Cinema*. New Jersey: Associated University Press.

Joseph, G. M., Rubenstein, A. and Zolov, E. (eds) 2001: *Fragments of a Golden Age: The Politics of Culture in Mexico Since 1940*. Durham, NC: Duke University Press.

King, J. 1990: *Magical Reels: A History of Cinema in Latin America*. London: Verso.

King, J., López, A. M. and Alvarado, M. (eds) 1993: *Mediating Two Worlds: Cinematic Encounters in the Americas*. London: British Film Institute.

King, J. and Torrents, N. (eds) 1987: *The Garden of Forking Paths: Argentine Cinema*. London: British Film Institute.

Knight, A. 1990: Racism, revolution, and indigenismo: Mexico, 1910–1940. In R. Graham (ed.), *The Idea of Race in Latin America, 1870–1940*. Austin: University of Texas Press, 71–113.

Lindauer, M. A. 1999: *Devouring Frida: The Art History and Popular Culture of Frida Kahlo*. Hanover and London: Wesleyan University Press.

López, A. M. 1993: Tears and desire: women and melodrama in the 'old' Mexican cinema. In John King, Ana M. López and Manuel Alvarado (eds), *Mediating Two Worlds: Cinematic Encounters in the Americas*. London: British Film Institute.

López, A. M. 2000: Facing up to Hollywood. In C. Gledhill and C. Williams (eds), *Reinventing Film Studies*. London: Arnold, 419–52.

Martin, M. T. (ed.) 1997: *New Latin American Cinema: Volume One: Theory,*

Practices and Transcontinental Articulations. Volume Two: Studies of National Cinemas. Detroit: Wayne State University Press.

Mirzoeff, N. 1998: *The Visual Culture Reader*. London: Routledge.

Mirzoeff, N. 1999: *An Introduction to Visual Culture*. London: Routledge.

Mora, C. J. 1982: *Mexican Cinema: Reflections of a Society*. Berkeley, Los Angeles and London: University of California Press.

Mosquera, G. (ed.) 1995: *Beyond the Fantastic: Contemporary Art Criticism from Latin America*. London: inIVA.

Newman Helms, C. 1986: *Diego Rivera: A Retrospective*. New York: Norton.

Noriega, C. A. 2000: *Visible Nations: Latin American Cinema and Video*. Minneapolis and London: University of Minnesota Press.

Paranaguá, P. A. 1995: *Mexican Cinema*. London: British Film Institute.

Pick, Z. M. (ed.) 1993: *The New Latin American Cinema: A Continental Project*. Austin: University of Texas Press.

Pilcher, J. M. 2001: *Cantinflas and the Chaos of Mexican Modernity*. Wilmington, DE: Scholarly Resources.

Rochfort, D. 1987: *The Murals of Diego Rivera*. London: Journeyman.

Rowe, W. and Schelling, V. 1991: *Memory and Modernity: Popular Culture in Latin America*. London: Verso.

Scott, J. F. 1999: *Latin American Art: Ancient to Modern*. Gainseville: University of Florida Press.

Shohat, E. and Stam, R. 1994: *Unthinking Eurocentrism: Multiculturalism and the Media*. London: Routledge.

Shohat, E. and Stam, R. 2000: Film theory and spectatorship in the age of the 'posts'. In C. Gledhill and C. Williams (eds), *Reinventing Film Studies*. London: Arnold, 381–401.

Spies, W. 1986: *Fernando Botero*. New York: Prestel.

Stevens, D. F. 1997: *Based on a True Story: Latin American History at the Movies*. Wilimington, DE: SR Books.

Sullivan, E. 1986: *Fernando Botero: Drawings and Watercolours*. New York: Rizzoli.

Traba, M. 1994: *Art of Latin America 1900–1980*. Baltimore: Johns Hopkins University Press.

Vasey, R. 1997: *The World According to Hollywood, 1918–1939*. Exeter: University of Exeter Press.

Volk, S. S., 2000: Frida Kahlo remaps the nation. *Social Identities* 6, 165–88.

Xavier, I. 1997: *Allegories of Underdevelopment: Aesthetics and Politics in Modern Brazilian Cinema*. Minneapolis: University of Minnesota Press.

9

Popular culture in Latin America

Silvia Bermúdez

It seems only fitting to begin a discussion of popular culture in Latin America by referring to one specific manifestation of such a form: tango and its current popularity in many locations of what we now have come to know as our global village. The elaborate choreography of the Argentinean dance born in the 1880s among the popular classes of the emergent Argentine nation provides us with a few, if slippery, characteristics most commonly associated with what we have come to understand as popular culture: manifestations that are both a product and a process in which, as in the tango, we cannot separate the dancers from the dance. Moreover, in taking our cue from tango, we need to understand these manifestations as ones which appear to serve the interests of groups occupying subordinate positions in relation to the dominant society. But, since popular culture at the dawn of the twenty-first century is most frequently bound up with the technology of mass culture brought on by industrialization, we must first address the issue of modernity in Latin America in order to explore better the distinct manifestations of popular culture.

While modernity is a complex and multidimensional process that followed different trajectories (Therborn 1995; Wagner 1994; Larrain 2000), we understand modern societies to be those consolidated in Western Europe during the Enlightenment period and based on the ideas of progress, reason, the sovereignty of secular nation-states, and the explosion of scientific technology. The growth of cities, and rapid social change coupled with massive migration from rural areas, set in motion the emergence of new social classes that, through the mass media and the new technologies of communication, came into contact with each other. Therefore, mobility and social change became experiences associated with the emergence of modernity. It is within these parameters that Latin America has been described by Spivak as the 'first born of modernity' (1985), while Beatriz Sarlo ironically names it a 'peripheral modernity' (1988). For García Canclini, an examination of Latin America's trajectory towards modernity brings to the forefront the role played by popular culture, and modernity thus needs to be considered as the site of the hybridization of cultural forms (1989).

In the case of Latin America's specific trajectory towards modernity, we must take into account its historical articulation, first as the colonized 'other' of Western Europe and later, in the post-independence period, as nation-states situated on the outskirts of modernity and of the capitalist system. Due to this uneven development, what we have in Latin America is a heterogeneous kaleidoscope where pre-modern and modern modes of production, as well as ways of life and of understanding or knowledge, coexist simultaneously. Alejo Carpentier's novel *Los pasos perdidos* (The Lost Steps, 1953) best summarizes this kaleidoscopic nature when a lawyer addresses a comment by the unnamed narrator by stating: 'Piense que nosotros, por tradición, estamos acostumbrados a ver convivir Rousseau con el Santo Oficio, y los pendones al emblema de la Virgen con *El capital*' (You must remember that we are accustomed to living with Rousseau and the Inquisition, with the Immaculate Conception and *Das Kapital*) (1978: 174). Under the influence of a neo-liberal ideology, economic and political modernization continued in the period of late modernity, which according to Jorge Larrain became consolidated in Latin America only in the 1990s (2000: 166). And, while the postmodern phenomenon associated with late modernity 'comes to rearrange the relationship between modernity and traditions' (Martín Barbero 1995: 226), heterogeneity and fragmentation continue to be one of Latin America's long-standing characteristics.

To be more precise, Latin America's heterogeneity and uneven development are crucial to understanding the striking cultural differences that can work against the idea of a unitary nation within a single country. For a start, the cultural practices traditionally carried out by and for the peasantry (such as *artesanías*, religious rituals, folk music and dance) tend to be situated within pre-modern and pre-capitalist cultures. It is evident that these practices cannot be separated now from the mass media nor from the culture industry connected with tourism, since both have altered the way these supposedly pre-modern and pre-capitalist cultural manifestations are produced, circulated and interpreted. Popular culture in Latin America has indeed many faces, and all of them need to be considered in the processes of state-formation. This is so because popular consciousness of national identity is usually mediated by practices such as music, dance, soccer and religious rituals, just to mention the performative forms with which this chapter is concerned. This process can be seen, for example, in the birth of the Argentinean tango and the Dominican merengue, since both dances overcame the racial and class prejudices of their countries' elite to become symbols of national identity. And while both are believed to articulate the key concerns of their respective national cultures, they are also identified as manifestations of Latin American popular music as a whole.

Let us examine the historical evolution of these musical and dance forms (which emerged around the same period in the 1880s, but in two geographically distinct areas: the Caribbean and the Southern Cone) as democratic expressions that, as Robin D. Moore puts it, 'serve as a means of real and symbolic empowerment for those who would otherwise have no voice' (1997: 4). While merengue emerged in 1884 in the midst of the independence battles against the Haitian occupation of the Dominican Republic (1822–44), tango was born in the outskirts of the turbulently expanding city of Buenos Aires. Linked to African roots with a mixture of Italian and Spanish influences, the tango emerged from this cross-cultural musical crossroads as the favoured dance of the social underclass of Buenos Aires, initially danced in bars, cafés, prostitution houses, and *milongas* – the dance salon or event where one dances tango. Thus, while the tango was born with a distinct urban identity, merengue emerged first as a rural folk dance accepted only as a ballroom dance in the 1920s.

Merengue's rural identity can still be found under the name of *perico ripiao*. Nowadays the *perico ripiao* is considered the prototypic manifestation representing a dance form of the Dominican peasantry. The name derives from the brothel 'El Perico Ripiao' situated in the city of Santiago de los Caballeros where in the beginning of the twentieth century merengue was first danced amid the popular social classes that frequented the place. It is not surprising, then, that the popular term '*ripiar*' and its reflexive form '*ripiarse*' have became synonymous with having a ball in the Caribbean and the expression can be heard likewise in Puerto Rico, Cuba and the Dominican Republic. Eventually, merengue's syncopated and rapid rhythm took hold of the Dominican population so much that it became a central vehicle through which to narrate national aspirations, with the help of none other than the dictator Rafael Trujillo, who incorporated merengue into his electoral campaigns in the 1930s. During Trujillo's lengthy dictatorship, merengue was transmitted via radio and television broadcasts and promoted as a symbol of national expression. In underpinning the established order, this popular musical form lost some of its original transgressive stance, most notably, as Jorge Duany points out, in the compositions of Luis Alberti (1994: 73).

Moving on from its origins and coming into contact with different social realities and historical periods, merengue went on to acquire other configurations, such as in the music of Johnny Ventura, and even becoming a trendy dance and musical form at the hands of singer/songwriter and producer Juan Luis Guerra and his 4.40 Group. Guerra's international success during the 1980s and up to the late 1990s have made him a contemporary Latin American icon. Hence, along with Cuban Celia Cruz, Brazilian Caetano Veloso, and Panamanian Rubén Blades, among others, Guerra is aware of his role as 'cultural mediator' (Franco 1996: 267). Thus, it is not surprising that Guerra understands his music as representing popular sentiments and is concerned with using his popularity with a sense of responsibility towards 'the people' or popular classes, as revealed in the compositions of his acclaimed

1989 album *Ojalá que llueva café* (Let's Hope It Rains Coffee). It is in this context that the lyrics 'buscando visa de cemento y cal,/Y en el asfalto ¿quién me va a encontrar?' (Searching for a visa of cement and limestone,/And on the asphalt, who will find me?), from his song *Visa para un sueño* (Visa for a Dream), address the issues of immigration within the globalization of markets. The song bears witness to the devastating effects of border-crossing and transnational movements. By exposing how the flow of goods from the so-called First World to Latin America is hailed and promoted while the movements of people to the 'dream land' are brutally prevented and not evaluated in an equitable context, Guerra restores to the merengue some of its oppositional character. But we must remember also that, as Philip Swanson pithily puts it in his analysis of the Latin American new novel, '[t]he problem really is one of playing politics with the popular' (1995: 11): thus we must be careful not to idealize completely the contestatory nature of Guerra's merengue.

In the case of tango, it emerged in the midst of the bustling urban landscape of Buenos Aires in the late 1880s, with its mixture of recently arrived immigrants and indigenous natives, and shares with the merengue the same ambience of prostitution. To give an idea of the importance of immigrants in terms of population growth in the new metropolis of Buenos Aires, one can note, for example, that in 1887, out of a population of 664,000 inhabitants, 53 per cent were immigrants (Assunção 1984: 49–50). But the privileged sons of the wealthiest Argentinean families also played a role in the diffusion of tango, since, after having learned the stylized steps of its choreography in the brothels euphemistically called *academias de baile*, they took them to Europe where tango swept the continent during the 1920s: Paris fell in love with the erotic/exotic aspects of the dance as tango reigned supreme in the entertainment venues frequented by the rich. But Europe's love affair with tango is far from over, and its current popularity in the United Kingdom, for example, is attested by the fact that classes are offered through the web on sites such as www.totaltango.com, where Londoners are invited to learn to tango.

Tango, perceived as the popular musical form that embodies the desires, needs, hopes and aspirations of the Argentine nation, has been recognized in literature through the work of Manuel Puig, most notably in his *Boquitas pintadas* (Heartbreak Tango, 1969), where popular music in the form of tangos and boleros provide some of the sources and models for the narrative. The title is a reference to Carlos Gardel (1883–1935), the mythical tango singer and perhaps the first embodiment of the 'Latin lover'. The words 'boquitas pintadas' are taken from the lyrics of the song 'Rubias de Nueva York' (Blondes of New York). The song was performed by Gardel in the film *El Tango en Broadway* (1934) while in contract with Paramount. And while the song is not a tango but a fox-trot, the title of the film does foreground the involvement of the mass media in the diffusion of tango and the manufacturing of its ultimate appeal, as well as indicating its belonging to 'modern' culture as emblematized by the film industry and the Broadway musicals of the 1930s. It was between the 1920s and the 1940s that tango, according to William Rowe and Vivian Schelling, became popular because it 'reached a mass audience through the culture industry, retained some oppositional character, and became a populist form' (1991: 36).

While the wealth of popular dances that characterize Latin America from one end of the continent to the other cannot be fully covered here, there are two other manifestations of popular dance that are closely identified, musically speaking, with Latin America: bolero and salsa. Bolero's relevance in the cultural imaginary of Latin America can be seen in the fact that by the 1930s it rivalled the tango. The bolero developed in Cuba during the ten-year Independence War against Spain in the 1880s (Zavala 1991). The first known bolero, entitled *Tristeza* (Sadness), was composed by Pepe Sánchez in 1883. Bolero was born and nurtured in Cuba, but Mexico and Puerto Rico took it to its highest performative levels in the first three decades of the twentieth century, and it is currently considered to be a musical and dance form that crosses national boundaries. Love and desire are the main concerns of the bolero's lyrics, voicing a new sentimental archaeology that shifted the emphasis away from merengue and tango's opposition to the social order towards, instead, the realm of personal emotion. Agustín Lara's *Solamente una vez* (Only Once), Alvaro Carillo's *Sabor a mí* (Taste of Me) as performed by Rafael Hernández, and Armando Manzaneros's *Esta tarde vi llover* (This Afternoon I Saw it Rain) have become essential components in the sentimental education of Latin American lovers. Indeed, bolero's cultural relevance in Latin America's imaginary was not lost to Mexican megastar Luis Miguel when he decided to record his *Romances* album in 1997: it includes timeless bolero classics such as *Bésame mucho* (Kiss me a Lot) and *El reloj* (The Clock), and the album ended up selling two million copies in Argentina and Mexico alone. Boleros occupy the space of Latin America's cultural imaginary in such a manner that several authors have paid homage to the mood of nostalgia and desire that nurture its lyrics, the already mentioned *Boquitas pintadas* by Puig being a case in point. More recently, Mayra Montero's *La última noche que pasé contigo* (The Last Night I Spent with You) (1999) – structured in eight sections each headed by the titles of well-known boleros – and Silvia Molina's *El amor que me juraste* (The Love You Swore to Me) (1999) rely on boleros' lyrics to present their stories.

In the same manner, salsa, a catch-all term that encompasses Afro-Caribbean styles of various derivations and origins, is also considered a Latin American cultural product, and perhaps the one that most extensively crosses national boundaries in that it is also particularly associated with the Latinos residing in the USA. Some consider 1971 to mark the birth of a musical commotion that also gave birth to a new marketing strategy to sell records. That is the year when the legendary group Fania All Stars played at a New York nightclub called the Cheetah. However, it is important to remember that while New York created the term, it did not create the dance. The origins of salsa are to be found in Cuba's *son*, which later began to mix with the rumbas of African origin, while similar syncretisms occurred in varying degrees in other countries such as the Dominican Republic, Puerto Rico and Colombia, to name but a few. When bands from these countries travelled to New York, more syncretism occurred along with the promotion and commercialization of this kind of music. It is not surprising then that Rowe and Schelling find in the history of salsa the perfect narration of how Latin American popular culture moved from 'local pre-capitalist forms to late-twentieth-century international ones' (1991: 101) – international, indeed, if we think of the 'Queen of Salsa', Celia Cruz, and her transnational popularity and media star power, unparalleled in a musical world that has seen stellar *salseros* such as Willie Colón, Tito Puente and Rubén Blades, among the many excellent musicians that contribute to the genre.

The most recent Latin American contribution to mass-mediated popular music is the so-called *rock en español*. It emerged both as a sign of modernity and as a vital instrument of cultural and political resistance in nations such as Argentina, Chile and Mexico. According to Pablo Vila, Argentina witnessed, between 1976 and 1983, the development of a phenomenon of cultural resistance that came to be known as *rock nacional* and ended up challenging the ideology of the right-wing military dictatorship (1992: 209). In the late 1970s and the early 1980s, Argentinean youth found a space in which to scream and rebel: in the lyrics and performances of the now legendary Charly García and Fito Páez. Later on, and after Argentina returned to democratically elected governments, groups such as Soda Stéreo and Los Fabulosos Cadillac have become 'a wedge against traditional social values and a vehicle for self-expression' (Zolov 1999: 102). Even recognized by the North American record industry, Los Fabulosos Cadillac won a Grammy in 1998 in the so-called Latin Rock/Alternative category for their album *Fabulosos Calaveras*.

Mexico's Maldita Vecindad enjoy similar popularity and international name recognition in the USA and Western Europe. Maldita Vecindad emerged in 1985, the same year Mexico was hit by a devastating earthquake while in the midst of one of the worst economic crises of its contemporary history. Since their first album, *Maldita Vecindad y los hijos del quinto patio*, the group has criticized the Mexican government's corrupt culture and has voiced the plight of those who risk their lives to migrate to the USA as *mojados* (the term, wetbacks, makes reference to the crossing of the Rio Grande). For its part, Colombia's Aterciopelados has also been catapulted to international stardom and stands out as one of the most recognized bands of *rock en español* because of Andrea Echeverri, a powerful female lead singer-songwriter and a charismatic presence in the male-dominated rock scene. The group took the scene by storm in 1995 with their second album *El Dorado* and songs such as 'Bolero Falaz' where the bolero tradition is parodied. Their sound is a fusion of rock with a mixture of Latin American musical traditions such as *cumbia* and *rancheras*, amongst others. Their third and fourth albums, *Pipa de la Paz* (1997) and *Caribe atómico* (1998), both received Grammy nominations. Their latest release, *Gozo Poderoso* (2001), signals both a return to the band's folk-rock roots as well as a glimpse of their future as a tropical pop-rock band. A discussion of *rock en español* would not be complete without also mentioning the names of *rockeras* Alejandra Guzmán and singer-songwriter Ely Guerra, both from Mexico. While Guzmán helped to bring a rock sound into Mexican popular music in the late 1980s, Guerra is considered 'a heroine of Mexico's rich alternative music scene for the twenty-first-century' (Gurza 2002: F1). And one other female trail-blazer is Shakira: while well-known in Latin America and Spain since the mid-1990s for her records *Pies descalzos* and *¿Dónde están los ladrones?*, the Colombian-born singer-songwriter launched her debut English-language album *Laundry Service* in 2001 to phenomenal success.

As has been suggested, Latin American music often has its origins in African rhythms and dance related to religious ceremonies and customs. For example, the origins of salsa are to be found in Cuba's *son*, which is connected to the practice of *santería*. But religion itself has also undergone popular transformations in Latin America. This can be seen most obviously in the use of specifically hybridized versions of Catholicism mixed with African and indigenous American rites and beliefs. In fact, the capacity for resistance and innovation generally associated with popular culture comes to the fore in the creative ways in which people have developed forms of religiousness that do not have a formal place in official religion. That is why, Cristián Parker argues, popular religion 'can be better understood as a counterculture to the "modernity" mentality propagated by the dominant culture of globalized capitalism' (1996: 111). It is in this sense that popular religion is articulated as an affirmation of life that glorifies feelings, pathos, the festive and the carnivalesque. The festive lies at the heart of the religious festivals and collective celebrations that fill the rural and urban calendars of Latin America. The festive nature of these celebrations is expressed in the iconic images and practices of devotion that pay homage to *santos patronos de ciudades* or patron saints, the pilgrimages that in the cities take on revitalizing aspects, and the magical religious rituals of the Afro-American cults.

Brazilian *candomblé* comes immediately to mind when thinking of Afro-American religious manifestations, and it is perhaps the most studied popular religious phenomenon in Latin America, along with Cuban and Puerto Rican *santería*. In contrast with Christian articulations of the role played by the body, *candomblé* considers the body to be the vehicle by which the divine manifests itself. Hence, we find the rituals of possession by which one of the *orixás* – which make up the pantheon of African divinities – becomes embodied in the believer. The exaggerated movements, and even hysteria, associated with the trances and possessions – for which *candomblé* is constantly chastised and reproached by the official religion and dominant culture – need to be understood within a faith system that believes in heightening emotions and in alternative manners of exteriorization that are opposed to the formalized and rationalistic manners of bourgeois society and official culture. This oppositional stance is not only relevant for an understanding of *candomblé* in particular, but for Afro-American cults in general as religious manifestations that offer the disinherited a symbolic space in which to recover the cultural memory of their African past. In this sense, Afro-American cults sustain a solidarity that aims to protect blacks and mulattos from the devastation of urbanization and play a vital role in the maintenance of a popular memory by preventing social amnesia.

This vital function is also at the core of *santería*, the syncretic religious system integral to Cuba's cultural legacy, Puerto Rican cultural practices and present as distinct manifestations throughout the Caribbean (e.g. Haitian Voodou). Born as a powerful survival strategy to manipulate and resist the oppressive values and dehumanizing codes of slavery, Cuban *santería* is also known as *La Regla de Ocha*. It is a complex religious system derived from Yoruba beliefs and rituals, in which Yoruba divinities known as *orichas* and their corresponding Catholic saints (*santos*) are worshipped. In fact, a key element for the practitioners of *santería* is the worship of the *santos* 'through veneration, feeding, and the ritual observance of all consecrated dates of the liturgy' (Barnet 1997: 83). The belief that the *santos* manifest themselves by taking possession of a person's body is also at the core of the practice. Thus, possession plays, as Miguel Barnet explains, not only have a social and representational function but also a religious one since they entail the will to represent an archetype, the determination to assume an identity that connects the possessed to the native culture (86).

Another use of popular religion in Latin America is best exemplified in the tradition of the *milagritos*. These are copper or brass miniature representations of mostly body parts – legs, arms and hearts – that are either pinned to the clothes of statues of Christ, the Virgin, or any of the many Catholic saints approached for a miracle or favour. The *milagritos* can also be placed on the altars or adjacent walls where any of the religious images are located and they synecdochally expose the favour granted or where the healing is needed. Thus, the visual display of *milagritos*, photographs, and mostly hand-written notes narrating the requests and the favours granted become part of the religious imagery of the Catholic Church in an appropriation manoeuvre that fends off the dominant discourse and resists complete absorption. The relevance of such a practice is made evident by Latina writer Sandra Cisneros, who, according to Ellen McCracken, offers 'a form of collective *testimonio*' in her 'Little Miracles, Kept Promises' from *Woman Hollering Creek and Other Stories* (1999: 19). The notion of a collective *testimonio* appears to capture the role played by popular religion in contemporary Latin America, since the ritualistic display of *milagritos* is a 'symbolical survival strategy' that allows people the ability to construct a favourable sacred universe in the midst of all kinds of threats and uncertainties (Parker 1996: 75).

Similar, if not quite equal devotion to that found in religious fervour can be noted in the passion with which Latin America has made *fútbol* (football, or soccer) an integral part of its popular culture, to such a degree that a so-called 'Latin American' style of play has been equated with pure poetry and magic as opposed to a European style considered efficient and systematic. Known as the 'passion of the people', *fútbol* arrived in South America when the British came in the late 1890s to build railroads, telegraph lines, and invest in mining and banking. South Americans adopted, adapted, and refashioned the sport by transforming it from the elite recreation it was upon its arrival into a popular spectacle. It gradually became the sport of other Latin American countries and now, together with *telenovelas*, takes up most of the television screening time, with televised matches covering all kinds of different leagues shown throughout the week but with Sundays reserved as the main day dedicated to the specific cultivation of this ritual.

In soccer, violence is transposed from the physical realm to a symbolic one because of the rules that govern the game; but soccer nonetheless remains, to the core, a performative act dependent on the physicality of the body. As a particularly privileged space of the popular culture industry, soccer is 'the biggest staging of the expressive possibilities of corporeal behaviours' (Alarbaces and Rodriguez 1996: 67). The problem is that these expressive possibilities have also been used politically by the state. One such example is how the 1970 victory of the Brazilian team in the World Cup was used by the military government to legitimate its vision of modernity and development for Brazil. Thus, the victory became articulated as follows: if Brazil had won the Cup and was therefore the nation *par excellence* at soccer, then it must be equal or superior to the nations spawning the European teams it had defeated.

Such vocabulary prompts us to consider how soccer has come to stand in for other traditional male-centred conflicts such as war. Due to a set of interweaving identifications and the fact that soccer matches offer a particular occasion for the theatricalization of social relations, warlike values are expressed via antagonisms that go from the local to the regional, and ultimately the national in events such as the World Cup. The analogy between war and soccer also rests on the fact that the game is played in an alternation between defence and attack that requires the planning and studying of strategy before every match. By means of a mimetic participation, the supporters become the expressive choruses of these symbolic wars by their emblematic accessories – all kinds of paraphernalia in their clubs'/nations' colours – and their slogans, drums and fanfares.

Interestingly enough, the mere recognition of a discourse of virility and masculinity fails to evaluate the homosocial space within which soccer is played while in the midst of often homophobic societies. This particular connection is poignantly made in Vargas Llosa's novella *Los cachorros* (The Cubs, 1967) by its signalling how heterosexual masculinity and virility are constructed among a young group of upper-class *limeños* through activities such as playing soccer and having girlfriends. Interestingly enough, the relevance of soccer as a bastion of male identity is situated in stark contrast with what the story presents as the central character's 'descent' into homosexuality: the loss of his penis during a dog's brutal attack, thus losing the actual and symbolic signifier that supposedly identifies him as a man.

The passion for consuming soccer as spectacle in Latin America is only rivalled by *telenovelas* or soap operas. Framed within the specific features of the mass medium (television) that gives them their name, *telenovelas* are considered the Latin American cultural product *par excellence* (Mazzioti 1996: 167). They are the quintessential television genre and the most-watched since people see up to three or four *telenovelas* per day. Moreover, they bring together in front of the television sets audiences from all walks of life, transcending cultural, social and gender boundaries. And while *telenovelas* have been considered a popular manifestation reserved mainly for women, at present the viewing public is wide and diverse. In fact, in the majority of households the viewing public is no longer only housewives: instead the family unit as a whole – father, son/s and daughter/s – is emerging as the mediator of reception. This gender factor does have a historical explanation, however, since *telenovelas* were first shown as part of the afternoon programming aimed at women, as is the case of the first *telenovela*, *El derecho de nacer* (The Right to be Born), shown both in Brazil and Mexico as the televised version of the famous radio serial transmitted in 1948 in Cuba.

The massive appeal of *telenovelas* has translated itself into huge economic benefits for the networks producing these cultural products. Thus, they are of great economic importance to an industry increasingly global and globalized. To garner an idea of this economic impact, we only need to consider that Brazilian network Rede Globo has exported its own telenovelas to some 130 countries since the 1970s (Marques de Melo 1988). More recently in the year 2001, more than 80 million people in Latin America and the USA tuned in to see Colombia's *Betty La Fea*, whose premise was the 'Ugly Ducking' story framed within a skin-deep feminist discourse. And while, for cultural critics such as Marques de Melo, the way to understand the genre's popularity is to study its production processes, we cannot underestimate the fact that at the core of *telenovelas'* popularity is their adherence to the recipe for success derived from the long tradition of serialized melodrama.

The basic format is the narration of a love story intertwined with a social plot and usually a rags-to-riches story where characters experience social mobility. The classic example can be found in the unchallenged success of the Peruvian *Simplemente María* (1965). The story follows the trials and tribulations of a provincial young woman who comes to the city, Lima, in search of a better life but is seduced and abandoned by the son of the wealthy family where she is working as a maid. The plot has been used by other *telenovelas* within Latin America, and thus twenty years later in 1986 it was used again in the Venezuelan production *Cristal*, where the labour issues present in *Simplemente María* between employers and employees were constructed within the framework of corporate power struggles. *Telenovelas*, then, have also evolved in relation to the ever-changing social and cultural realities so as to contribute to a perceived sense of Latin American integration, in which the television soaps are seen as offering social instruction, cultural models or comprehensive portrayals of a mixed society. In fact, Jesús Martín Barbero argues that they are a new development in the process of 'Latin American sentimental integration' in the same manner that tango and bolero were before them (1995: 283). Thus, we have come full circle in our discussion of those cultural manifestations more closely associated with the performative.

In emphasizing in this chapter how Latin America is particularly marked by its popular cultures, I have tried not to idealize the power of popular culture, since at the dawn of the third millennium the globalization of the mass media and the implementation of neo-liberal policies have closed down the once-public spaces dominated by the popular. However, the study of Latin American popular culture allows us to identify or at least glimpse the gaps in the system by calling attention to cultural activities and forms that question the power of hegemonic discourses and practices. It is precisely within a 'double movement of containment and resistance' that Stuart Hall (1981: 228) situates the inherent ambivalence of popular cultural forms and where we are to find, according to him, what is 'essential to the definition of popular culture' (234). And what is it that is essential? It is the incessant tension that keeps popular culture in an antagonistic relation to dominant culture. It is from within this tension that popular culture in Latin America produces serious challenges to hegemonic forces.

REFERENCES AND SELECTED FURTHER READING

Alabarces, P. and Rodríguez, M. G. 1996: *Cuestión de pelotas: Fútbol, deporte, sociedad, cultura*. Buenos Aires: Atuel.

Assunção, F. O. 1984: *El tango y sus circunstancias (1880–1920)*. Buenos Aires: Librería El Ateneo.

Barnet, M. 1997: La regla de ocha: the religious system of santería. In M. Fernandez Olmos and L. Paravisini-Gebert (eds), *Sacred Possesions: Voodou, Santería, Obeah, and the Caribbean*. New Brunswick, NJ: Rutgers University Press, 79–100.

Carpentier, A. 1978. Los pasos perdidos. In *Obras completas de Alejo Carpentier*, Vol. II. México: Siglo Ventiuno Editores.

Duany, J. 1994: Ethnicity, identity, and music: an anthropological analysis of the Dominican merengue. In G. H. Behague (ed.), *Music and Black Ethnicity: The Caribbean and South America*. Florida: North–South Center Press, 65–90.

Franco, J. 1996: Globalization and the crisis of the popular. In T. Salman (ed.), *The Legacy of the Disinherited: Popular Culture in Latin America: Modernity, Globalization, Hybridity and Authenticity*. Amsterdam: CEDLA, 263–76.

García Canclini, N. 1989: *Culturas Híbridas. Estrategias para entrar y salir de la modernidad*. Mexico: Grijalbo.

Gurza, A. 2002: For her, the fight is far from over. *Los Angeles Times*, 17 March.

Hall, S. 1981. Notes on deconstructing 'the popular' In R. Samuel (ed.), *People's History and Socialist Theory*. London: Routledge, 228–39.

Larrain, J. 2000: *Identity and Modernity in Latin America*. Cambridge: Polity Press.

McCracken, E. 1999: *New Latina Narrative: The Feminine Space of Postmodern Ethnicity*. Tucson: University of Arizona Press.

Marques de Melo, J. 1988: *As telenovelas da Globo: produção e exportação*. São Paulo: Summus.

Martín Barbero, J. 1995: Memory and form in the Latin American soap opera. In R. C. Allen (ed.), *To Be Continued . . .: Soap Operas Around the World*. London and New York: Routledge, 276–84.

Mason, T. 1995: *Passion of the People? Football in South America*. London and New York: Verso.

Mazzioti, N. 1996: *La industria de la telenovela: La producción de ficción en América Latina*. Buenos Aires, Barcelona and México: Paidós.

Moore, R. D. 1997: *Nationalizing Blackness: Afrocubanismo and the Artistic Revolution in Havana, 1920–1940*. Pittsburgh, PA: University of Pittsburgh Press.

Parker, C. 1996: *Popular Religion and Modernization in Latin America: A Different Logic*. New York: Orbis Books.

Rowe, W. and Schelling, V. 1991: *Memory and Modernity: Popular Culture in Latin America*. London: Verso.

Sarlo, B. 1988: *Una modernidad periférica: Buenos Aires, 1920–1930*. Buenos Aires: Nueva Visión.

Spivak, G. 1985: The Rani of Simur. In. F. Barker *et al.* (eds), *Europe and Its Others: Proceedings of the Essex Conference on the Sociology of Literature July 1984*. Colchester: University of Essex Press, 128–51

Swanson, P. 1995: *The New Novel in Latin America: Politics and Popular Culture after the Boom*. Manchester and New York: Manchester University Press.

Therborn, G. 1995: *European Modernity and Beyond: The Trajectory of European Societies, 1945–2000*. London and Thousand Oaks, CA: Sage Publications.

Vila, P. 1992: *Rock nacional* and dictatorship in Argentina. In R. Garofalo (ed.), *Rockin' the Boat: Mass Music and Mass Movements*. Boston: South End Press, 209–29.

Wagner, P. 1994: *A Sociology of Modernity: Liberty and Discipline*. London and New York: Routledge.

Zavala, I. M. 1991: *El bolero: historia de un amor*. Madrid: Alianza Editorial.

Zolov, E. 1999: *Refried Elvis: The Rise of the Mexican Counter Culture*. Berkeley: University of California Press.

10

Race in Latin America

Peter Wade

THE MEANING OF 'RACE'

Race is a word that seems to have an obvious meaning. It is often taken to refer to differences between 'blacks', 'whites', 'Asians' and other such categories. In fact, race is difficult to define. It has been recognized for some time that there are no biologically defined entities called races. Within the human species, there is variation of genotype (the genetic complement of an individual) and phenotype (the person's outward appearance), but this variation cannot be divided up into separate 'races'. The history of the human race has been of migration and intermixture and anyway we all share the vast majority of our genes. Race does not exist biologically, but it does exist as an idea – often with very potent social consequences. As an idea, it has different forms, but a common thread is that humans are divided up into categories of people who generally look different and may act differently from each other; there is an underlying notion that such differences are heritable, both physically and culturally. This idea of race came into existence in the fifteenth century, when the term appears in various European languages (Banton 1987). The idea developed especially in the context of European domination of Africa and the New World, and some argue that the idea of race fully emerged with the enslavement of Africans by Europeans. From this time and especially in the nineteenth and early twentieth centuries, race was assumed to have some real foundation in human nature. It was only in the course of the twentieth century that this assumption was proved false (Smedley 1993). This is what makes race difficult to define now: for if race does refer to the *idea* of differences between such categories as 'black', 'white' and 'Indian', then the question remains of what these differences are supposed to consist of. There may be many differences between 'blacks' and 'whites' in the USA, the UK or Brazil – in terms, for example, of cultural behaviour and average income and educational levels. But the causes of these differences are social. And these categories will also be very similar in many ways. So 'race' becomes a way of referring to a set of supposed differences, linked vaguely to perceptions of physical appearance and/or assumptions about ancestry, without ever defining what these differences are or why they exist. Such ideas about race may nevertheless help motivate such behaviour as candidate selection in the job market, murder, voting, and choice of friends and sexual partners.

In Latin America, the term race generally refers to supposed differences between 'blacks' (descendants of African slaves), 'Indians' and 'whites' (descendants of Europeans, broadly defined). The indeterminacy around the idea of race is compounded in this context by the importance of ideas about the biological and cultural mixture of 'races' (Sp. *mestizaje*). Thus, for example, the term *la raza* may occur in the phrase *la raza negra* (the black race) and may be used alone to refer to a national people, evoking the image of a homogeneously mixed nation, as in the 12 October celebration of El Día de la Raza which commemorates the day Columbus landed in the Americas and began the creation of a new 'race'.

THE COLONIAL BACKGROUND

Spanish and Portuguese colonists first exploited existing indigenous people for labour. Slavery was initially used for this purpose, but the enslavement of indigenous people was soon prohibited, as they were deemed to be vassals of the crown. Informal enslavement of indigenous people did continue in some regions, especially Brazil. In areas where a large, settled and politically organized indigenous population existed, such as central Mexico or the central Andes, the colonists were able to fulfil many of their labour demands, despite the decimation of the native population by disease and mistreatment. In other areas, the native labour force was inadequate and an alternative was sought. The enslavement of Africans was already practised in the Old World and it became a common form of labour in the new colonies.

Africans were imported to all the Spanish and Portuguese colonies – and to the colonies of the northern European powers in North America and the Caribbean – and initially quite large numbers went to Peru and Mexico, which are not well known for their black populations today. The main destinations for African slaves included Brazil (principally the north-east), Cuba (especially in the nineteenth century) and New Granada (today's Colombia, Panama, Ecuador and Venezuela). From early on, some slaves were freed by their masters or, more usually, were able to buy their own freedom with money saved from working on their days off. These freed blacks were an important element of the workforce in many countries.

Mixture between Africans, Europeans and indigenous people was common all over the Americas (except where the native population had been exterminated, as in much of the Caribbean), but the frequency of such mixing and, more importantly, its social consequences varied enormously. In North America, the trend was for such mixing to remain covert and the children that resulted from it were not, in the long term, accorded a distinct status from that of the subordinate partner, usually a black woman. In many of the Caribbean colonies of the northern European powers, such as Jamaica and Haiti, where whites were a tiny percentage and slaves a huge majority, mixture was frequent and the mixed-race 'mulatto' offspring were recognized as socially intermediate between white and black. In Latin America, mixture was also very frequent – including mixture of indigenous peoples with whites and blacks – and again mixed people were socially intermediate (Mörner 1967). This gave rise to a socially stratified pyramid with Europeans at the apex, black slaves and *indios* (indigenous people) at the bottom, and an ambiguous and contestable set of intermediate categories in the middle in which ancestry, appearance (including dress), occupation and wealth all influenced social standing.

The three polar categories of black, white and indigenous did not have clear boundaries, but many people were easily placed within them. *Indios* paid tribute in goods and/or labour and lived in indigenous communities. Slaves also had a definite social status, although they might be black, *mulato* (white–black mixed race) or even *zambo* (indigenous–black mixed race). Black people had a less institutionalized status than *indios*, but still existed as a significant social category. As such they, along with indigenous people and *mestizos*, suffered racial discrimination which tended to confine them to certain occupations and residential areas.

Resistance to this colonial oppression and discrimination was common and took varied forms. Indigenous people rebelled violently in many cases, and also fought for the well-being of their communities even under colonial rule (Stern 1987). Black slaves, especially those born in Africa, instigated rebellions and also constantly became *cimarrones* (fugitive slaves) who sometimes formed rebel communities called *palenques* or *quilombos* (Price 1996). In Haiti, blacks and mulattos joined forces to overthrow their French masters, establishing a free black republic that struck fear into the hearts of white elites all over the Americas. Indigenous and African religious practices were subject to persecution, but they persisted in secret and/or adapted to Catholic practices without losing some of their original meanings (Harding 2000). In many urban areas, slaves and free blacks were allowed to form associations in which they could play music, sing and dance. These mutual aid associations were important contexts for the persistence of African religions and music and for the development of new hybrid forms (Howard 1998).

THE INDEPENDENT NATIONS

Independence from Spain and Portugal, achieved for most areas by the 1830s, also heralded the abolition of slavery, which occurred by 1854 everywhere in Latin America except for Puerto Rico (1873), Cuba (1886) and Brazil (1888). Slave imports from Africa continued into the 1860s in the latter two areas, giving black cultures there perhaps the most evident African component in Latin America.

Ideologies of European liberalism had a profound impact on intellectual elites in the region and it was thought inappropriate to recognize different categories of citizen, such as *indio*. Consequently, the specific legal status of indigenous communities – e.g. as landholding collectives – was attacked. However, such communities were not effectively undermined in many areas and their official position was even later reinstated in countries such as Peru which recognized the indigenous community as a legal entity in 1920.

In the late nineteenth and early twentieth centuries, the question of race greatly occupied Latin American elites (Graham 1990). In Europe and North America, race had become a major concept in the intellectual armoury and many medics and naturalists argued for the existence of separate human races, hierarchically ranked with whites at the top. The eugenics movement of the time allied social reformers, doctors and scientists in an attempt to control sexual reproduction with a view to improving the 'racial' quality of national populations.

Latin American intellectuals were worried that not only did many of their nations have significant black and indigenous populations, but often the majority of the nation's people were mixed, and hybrids were, according to current racial theory, degenerate, weak and even infertile. Stepan (1991) argues that many intellectuals promoted ideas of 'constructive miscegenation', arguing that mixture was not degenerative, that it was an important means of integration of black and indigenous minorities and that the nation's 'racial' qualities could be improved through education and hygiene.

The notion of *mestizaje* was thus enshrined in some countries as the basis of national identity: Mexico, Colombia, Brazil and Venezuela were good examples of this. Places such as Argentina, where black and indigenous minorities were small and fast disappearing or being wiped out, had less recourse to notions of mixedness and instead emphasized their relative whiteness, which was being reinforced by large numbers of European immigrants. Even countries which emphasized their mestizoness preferred to focus on the whiter end of their racial spectrums and also encouraged European immigration in the hopes of 'whitening' their nations. Meanwhile, countries which had large indigenous populations also developed ideologies of *indigenismo* which glorified the indigenous past and held up indigenous people as a symbol of nationhood. Such ideas generally existed alongside ideologies of *mestizaje*, so that indigenous people were seen as backward populations in need of integration into the *mestizo* nation.

Meanwhile, ideologies of black and indigenous affirmation and autonomy were not swamped by such notions of mixture, although such self-determination was generally not separatist in character and entailed fighting for a place *within* the nation. In Peru, indigenous leaders promoted literacy campaigns in the 1920s which contradicted the prevailing idea that a literate person could not be an *indio* (De la Cadena 2000: ch. 2). In early twentieth-century Guatemala, K'iche' leaders struggled to maintain a place for indigenous people within a modernizing nation that saw them as obstinate resistors of progress (Grandin 2000). In south-western Colombia, the Paéz leader, Manuel Quintín Lame, headed a resistance movement in the early twentieth century which was based on recuperating land for indigenous people (and which gave its name to a 1980s' guerrilla movement in the same area). Black Brazilian intellectuals ran various lively newspapers in the 1930s and formed the Frente Negra Brasileira (Andrews 1991). In Cuba, black associations lobbied for an improvement in the situation of the black working class and black leaders formed the Partido Independiente de Color in 1908 (Helg 1995; Howard 1998). Meanwhile, in the Francophone Caribbean and France, black pride ideologies of *négritude* were being promoted by intellectuals such as the Martinican Aimé Césaire.

IDEAS OF RACE IN THE TWENTIETH CENTURY AND AFTER

Ideas about race in the first half of the twentieth century tended to take a number of forms. Some intellectuals studied their nation's black populations, worrying about the problems posed for national progress by the existence of these supposedly 'primitive' people. Others celebrated the mixed nature of their nations and valued African and indigenous inputs, even if actual blacks and indigenous peoples were seen as disappearing into a tolerant, integrated, mixed society which was a 'racial democracy' in comparison to the USA where racial segregation ruled supreme and white mobs routinely lynched black men. Brazilian Gilberto Freyre is a good example of this trend (see Graham 1990). In Colombia, one could find examples of both tendencies (Wade 1993: 14–16). At the same time, black and indigenous leaders were struggling for land, jobs, education and social equality. In this struggle, they might highlight race in drawing attention to racial inequality (as did the Colombian rebel indigenous leader Manuel Quintín Lame in the 1930s when he wrote about 'the defence of my race' (Lame 1971)) or they might seek a truly raceless society in which racial identity played no role in defining life chances (as did some Afro-Cuban leaders).

In the wake of the Second World War, academic studies of race began to take a different turn, less constrained by nationalist ideals. In the 1950s, there was a concerted effort, sponsored initially by UNESCO, to study Brazil's so-called racial democracy in an attempt to explore multiracial societies where racism and racial conflict were reputedly not a problem. This endeavour came in the wake of Nazi racism and the destabilizing impact of the Second World War on race relations in the USA, including the desegregation of the armed forces in 1948 and the strengthening of the civil rights movement. Meanwhile, decolonization movements had gained impetus in Africa where native populations sought to throw off the European colonial yoke. In short, the issue of race had a high profile on the international political agenda.

The studies in Brazil were carried out by French, US and Brazilian scholars and they concluded not only that Brazil was a society in which racial inequality was evident – after all slavery had only been abolished there in 1888 – but also that racism still existed. The fondly held notion of a Brazilian racial democracy was challenged. Yet overall an important divide was retained between the USA and Brazil. Some analysts saw race as an idea on the decline in Brazil, fading as a market-based capitalist society developed. Others saw race as frankly peripheral. Due to mixture, racial categories were not clearly identifiable and this made US-style segregation impossible: it was not clear *who* was to be segregated. It was noted that, in Brazil, a person's racial identity was defined by ancestry, appearance, dress, behaviour, class status – in a word, as much by culture as by biology. In contrast, in the USA, racial identity was defined primarily by biological ancestry. Brazil came out as a society in which class was more important than race in defining people's lives (see Wade 1997: chs 3, 4; Winant 1992).

In Peru, too, race was not seen as the most appropriate category to understand national society. De la Cadena (2000) argues that, as early as the 1920s, intellectuals had abandoned the idea of race as it was being purveyed in contemporary discussions world-wide about different 'races' and relative ranking. Instead they focused on what we would now call culture, but what they referred to as spirit or soul: this was what defined different sorts of people, not biology. Yet she also shows that spirit or soul was thought of as innate in people, as moulded by the environment and hence malleable in principle, but also rather permanently ingrained in a given population. In effect, a silent, 'culturalist' racism continued which saw indigenous people as basically inferior. Attitudes to the indigenous and mixed-race population were, however, varied and complex. Indigenous people were seen by elites as basically inferior – uneducated and primitive – but some forms of *indigenismo* glorified them and recommended the maintenance of their racial and moral purity, keeping them safe from degenerative processes of mixture. *Mestizos* were often seen as corrupt, immoral and threatening. On the other hand, other currents of *indigenista* thought saw the *cholo* (the culturally and/or biologically mixed person) as a glorious, valiant figure – and the *chola* as a sexy, available woman. Meanwhile, working-class *mestizos* themselves did not necessarily see themselves as non-indigenous. Instead they were successful indigenous people who, through their hard work, had gained respect.

There is no doubt that ideas about race in Latin America are different from those in the USA and perhaps other areas of the world such as Europe and South Africa. The social recognition of mixture leads to some indeterminacy about racial identity, which then tends not to be a primary way of thinking about oneself in relation to others. Race rarely takes on the political significance it does in the USA or South Africa where racially identified voting patterns exist. Yet the contrast is easily overdrawn and this happens at different levels.

First, the idea that race is 'biological' in the USA and 'cultural' in Latin America is overly simple. It has been widely documented that race as a general concept tended to become culturalized in the late twentieth century. Public reference to race as a biological entity faded as the scientific basis for such a reference was dismantled, and it became politically incorrect to even talk about race at all (with terms such as ethnicity taking over). Instead reference is made to 'cultural' differences. However, as in the Peruvian case, such talk of cultural differences becomes fundamentalist and essentialist: culture is seen as a fundamental, essential, ingrained aspect of a person or group and thus stands in for racial difference (Stolcke 1995). In that sense, a divide between Latin America and the USA is made less clear: in the USA too references to race have become culturalized. More generally, culture and biology are not in themselves easily opposed as modes of discourse, despite an apparently clear distinction in Western thought between 'nature' and 'nurture'. When people talk about the differences between 'Indians' and 'mestizos' or 'blacks' and 'whites', whether in Latin America, the USA or Europe, they may refer to such ideas as blood, ancestry, physical appearance (which is itself a mixture of biological and cultural processes), culture, environment and upbringing. In all three regions, a mixture of elements is invoked to explain supposed differences and the mixture is not easily separated into the cultural and the biological. This argument does not imply that Latin American ideas about race are simply the same as those in the USA; it does imply that the difference does not lie in some straightforward distinction between culturalist and biological ideas of race.

Second, the difference between the USA and Latin America has been steadily eroded by changes in the social scene in both regions and by associated changes in academic approaches to understanding race. Studies of race in Latin America have increasingly emphasized the significance of this category. Studies in Brazil indicate that racial identity does have an important impact on life chances. Lovell (1994) shows that average income difference between white men and black men is partly due to variations in education and qualifications (which may themselves be due to patterns of racial discrimination outside the immediate job market), but that 24 per cent of the difference is due to processes of discrimination within the job market. Importantly, Lovell also brings gender into the analysis – a significant change in analysing race which began in the 1980s when it became clearer that racism affected men and women differently – and shows that the equivalent figure was 51 per cent when comparing white men with black women. Some scholars have also contended that, statistically, Brazilian mixed-race people (who identify as *pardo*, brown, in the censuses) are little different from blacks (*preto* in the censuses) when compared to whites (*branco*). *Pardos* may be slightly better off in some respects, but it makes sense to class them economically with blacks, thus suggesting a bi-racial divide in Brazilian society and making it seem more like the USA (Silva 1985). Such a statistical manoeuvre, however, does not eliminate the fact that on average *pardos* are better off than blacks and thus do form an intermediate category; nor does it address the fact that, in Brazil, people do recognize and attribute important social differences to intermediate racial categories.

These Brazilian studies analytically separate race, class (and gender) to assess their different impacts on life chances. A different approach is taken by Streicker (1995), who looks at how working-class black people in Cartagena, Colombia, think about race. Consistent with many earlier studies, he finds that race is not a common way of talking about and identifying people. Most people in the neighbourhood are varying shades of black and brown and they assert that they are all equal and that racism is not a problem. However, Streicker argues that ideas about race form a moral discourse of good and bad, proper and improper, high and low status. Notions of class status, racial identity and gender behaviour intertwine and evoke each other. To be *negro* is also to be low status and to be a father/husband who neglects his obligations or a loose woman and poor wife/mother. Equally, to impute sexual looseness to a woman evokes images of blackness and low class status. All told, blackness is seen as inferior and is associated with immorality. Its apparently subdued presence in people's lives is due in part to the fact that it is evoked in other ways.

Other studies in Colombia and in the neighbouring north-western Pacific coastal region of Ecuador also demonstrated that racism existed and that racial identities were important in local contexts. Whitten (1986) describes a process of 'black disenfranchisement' in the town of San Lorenzo in north-western Ecuador. This Pacific coastal region, a humid, underdeveloped littoral which stretches through Colombia all the way to southern Panama, is numerically dominated by black people taken there as slaves to mine gold and who now subsist on agriculture, fishing, gold mining and logging. Starting in the 1960s, there was an influx of *mestizos* from the highland interior into San Lorenzo, some of whom had enough capital to buy out local successful blacks. *Mestizos* also began to monopolize the role of broker and trader (e.g. in trade of shellfish); they had better contacts in the interior of the country and better access to credit than local black entrepreneurs. Local blacks who tried to broker deals between black labourers and outsider entrepreneurs got labelled as communists: politically they were blocked and they met with the racial exclusiveness of the *mestizo* highlanders. Meanwhile, racial categories, which were already perhaps clearer than in other areas of Latin America, due to the geographical concentration of black people in the region, became even clearer, as *mestizo* highlanders lumped together all the locals – whatever their racial identity – as blacks and arrogated the term *blanco* (white) for themselves.

This basic scenario has been seen for much of the Pacific coast region of Colombia and was identified by Wade (1993) for the area just south of Colombia's border with Panama. Wade also studied migrants from the Pacific coastal region to the city of Medellín in the highland interior of Colombia and also found quite clear racial identities and patterns of racial discrimination in the job and housing markets. However, as has been observed for other areas, Wade also found generally low levels of racial segregation, some significant black upward mobility into the middle classes and quite high levels of intermarriage between blacks and non-blacks. That is, alongside racism, there were also important processes of mixture.

Racism is also directed against indigenous people, although there has been a tendency to avoid calling it racism, at least in its modern form, due in part to the idea that the concept of ethnicity is more applicable to indigenous people than that of race (see Wade 1997: 37–8). Recently, the term racism has been used more frequently to describe the situation (De la Cadena 2000; Grandin 2000; Warren 1998).

Weismantel (2001) does see 'race' as a useful analytic category for the Andes. She notes the apparent contradiction that many have observed between the fact that people in the Andes insist that race is a physical reality, different from class and from what is generally termed ethnicity (i.e. a purely 'cultural' phenomenon not based on ideas about bodies), and the fact that people routinely talked about neighbours who had changed their race. Some scholars have resolved this by arguing that 'ethnicity' is indeed what is at issue: in their definition, race connotes something permanent, physical and indelible; therefore what exists in the Andes cannot be termed race, but must be the cultural phenomenon of ethnicity. Weismantel, however, contends that, in the Andes, race exists, but in a more malleable form. It is rooted in bodily similarities, but such similarities are created by the way the body develops over time in a given social environment, rather than by genetic codes. In the Andes, race can be part of the body and yet also be changeable because race accumulates in the body over time; it is the embodied product of history. For example, while indigenous identity is indicated by a host of interacting social markers – appearance, language, place of residence, occupation – one particular marker is going barefoot. A *mestizo* will never go barefoot and anyone who does is very liable to be called an Indian (Orlove 1998). Those who habitually walk barefoot develop a foot that is physically quite different from those who normally wear shoes: it is a foot that is splayed, gnarled and with a thick and horny sole. Thus one of the indicators of indigenous identity actually becomes a physical part of the body. Weismantel also argues that the definition of the physical self is expanded to include clothing and adornment and contends that Andean people do not necessarily separate artifice and nature when seeing the human body. Thus, for example, the white body is not just a body with a white skin, it is also an accumulation of things that white people typically have.

A further factor that has raised the profile of issues around race in Latin America has been the impact of black and indigenous social movements, fighting against racism and for recognition and cultural and material rights.[1] As mentioned above, black and indigenous resistance is a very long-standing phenomenon, but from about the 1960s such movements began to multiply and to focus in a more self-conscious way on questions of identity as an end in itself. They also became more transnational: 'indigenous rights' became an issue connecting Canadian Inuit, Brazilian Kayapo and Australian Aborigines. 'Black rights' linked black people in the USA, Colombia and South Africa; indeed the US civil rights and Black Power movements were an inspiration to many Latin American black movements. Increased educational levels in Latin America and growing national and global communications were instrumental in this. The resurgence of these social movements was also influenced by the continuing penetration of marginal areas where black and indigenous minorities lived by destructive capitalist business and by the often economically stressful impact of neo-liberal structural adjustment programmes in the 1980s.

For these social movements, questions of racial identity and racism are not always the central concern. Rights to land may be of more immediate importance and, especially for indigenous organizations, local ethnic identities may take precedence over a more national and transnational identity of *indígena*. But the movements still insistently raise the issue of what kind of nations Latin American countries should be in terms of the role of racial and ethnic identities in them.

Warren analyses the Maya movement for cultural resurgence that arose in Guatemala in the late 1980s, in the wake of a military campaign of terror that targeted indigenous people (Warren 1998). The movement asserts the solidarity of all Maya peoples, against the racist Ladino state (*ladino* is the local term for *mestizo*) and focuses on issues of language, education, religion and the need for environmentally sustainable development. Its leaders avoid being called political activists and have not formed a political party; many important activists in the rural communities are religious leaders. The movement does not have a programme of armed resistance as did the Zapatistas in neighbouring Chiapas, Mexico. Like many of these movements, the Mayanists are not a single organization but a complex network: they draw their strength from many roots, from Mayan university students in debate with left-wing colleagues, to indigenous intellectuals in rural communities engaged in development planning and especially in the Catholic Action catechist movement; they work in multiple activities, including education and research; and they have different ideological orientations in terms of, for example, the importance attached to tradition. The movement's results include the emergence of a new class of indigenous professionals who retain their identity as Mayans, when in previous times they might have been tempted to 'pass' as Ladinos; the creation of a network of private Maya schools; and forcing an Accord on Identity and the Rights of Indigenous Peoples (1995) into the peace accords that ended the counter-insurgency war. The movement has also had a diffuse but important impact on Guatemalan society, altering the way questions of nationhood and citizenship are debated.

As with many similar movements, there remain difficult issues in the Maya movement. There is a tendency towards an essentialist view in which all Maya are seen as basically the same, unified by a Maya culture that has remained unchanged at its core since pre-colonial times, and opposed to an equally homogenous category of Ladinos who oppress them. There may be a tendency towards ethnocentrism or even 'reverse racism' in which Maya are seen as superior to Ladinos. The gender, class and religious differences among Mayas may sometimes be submerged by assertions of pan-Mayan solidarity. Anthropologists who study the movement tend to be opposed to essentialism and instead see ethnic and racial identities and cultures as complex historical constructs which, far from being fundamental and ingrained, change over time. Yet they also sympathize with the struggle for indigenous self-determination which may use essentialist ideas. This tension is not easily resolved, but anthropologists and Maya activists can fruitfully exchange perspectives on the matter rather than remaining on separate levels of communication. The Maya movement cannot be reduced to essentialism, but is a complex mix of ideas about cultural continuities and new elements of identity that often emerge and take meaning in the process of resistance.

The black movement in Brazil is similarly complex (Andrews 1991; Burdick 1998; Hanchard 1999; Winant 1992). The 1960s' Black Soul movement was based on US black culture and fashion. Rather than engaging directly in political debate, it evoked more challenging meanings for blackness. Later, more coherent organizations were formed, including the Movimento Negro Unificado (1978), but this was in the context of hundreds of Afro-Brazilian groupings including cultural and carnival groups, *capoeira* schools (teaching a form of African-derived dance-cum-martial art), theatre and dance companies, groups of black artists and writers, and individual black politicians running for office. This heterogeneity can be seen as a debilitating fragmentation and it certainly makes coherent political organization difficult. But it can also be a strength, as it makes questions of race and nation ubiquitous.

As in the Maya movement, religion also plays a fundamental role. Afro-Brazilian religions, particularly *candomblé*, blossomed in Brazil from the nineteenth century. In the city of Salvador, the centres devoted to these religions increased from about 100 in 1940 to over 2,000 in the 1990s. Not all of them have an overt agenda of identity politics, but they can add to the overall profile of blackness in the nation. The Catholic Church was also important in the emergence of the black movement by training black seminarians in the theology of liberation. At a more popular level, the Church gives room to the worship of 'slave saints' such as Anastácia, a semi-mythical black slave forced to wear a face-mask by her master for refusing to have sex with him but who ultimately forgave him his cruelty (Burdick 1998). Although the Church refused her canonization, she is widely worshipped in Brazil by blacks and non-blacks alike, both in churches and in centres for *umbanda* (a popular religion, combining Afro-Brazilian, spiritist and Catholic practices). Black movement activists are ambivalent about her: she is a figure of submission and forgiveness, in contrast to Zumbi, the hero of the black movement, who was a famous slave rebel leader. Yet Burdick argues that among working-class Afro-Brazilian women, Anastácia can be a channel for raising consciousness about blackness and racial inequality – although as a symbol of resistance to male oppression she does not always meet with approval from male black activists. As the saint is also popular with non-blacks, Burdick finds that she acts as a medium for them to question their own attitudes to black people. The figure of Anastácia sums up some of the complexity of the Brazilian racial situation: a black woman who accepts her lot and forgives her oppressors resonates in different ways for many people. An ideal image for those who believe Brazil is basically a racial democracy, anathema to many (male) black activists who value self-assertion and defiance, she can also be an important affirmation of moral value for working-class black women.

In several countries there has been an official recognition of multi-culturalism. In Colombia in 1991 constitutional reform redefined the nation as pluriethnic. Special legislation exists not just for indigenous peoples, but also – unusual in Latin American – for black communities. Law 70 of 1993 allows land title claims by rural black communities in the Pacific coastal region and contains a number of measures designed to protect black people's rights and cultural presence (Arocha 1998; Grueso *et al.* 1998; Wade 1995). The Law was partly the fruit of black mobilization (itself spurred significantly by the Catholic Church), but black organizations burgeoned quickly after the Law was passed. Some of these were formed to make specific land claims, others to raise the profile of blackness more generally, engaging in a wide variety of activities, especially music and dance, from folkloric material, to US hip-hop, Caribbean-influenced styles such as ragamuffin and West African highlife. Legal reform has opened many opportunities and gives the question of race in the nation an unprecedented profile. But for black communities at least, Law 70 also constrains, focusing principally on one region of the country and privileging the question of rural landholding above other concerns such as urban poverty and police harassment.

CONCLUSION

Race in Latin America has particular features. It has been argued that, with the increasing significance of racial identities and social movements emphasizing race and ethnicity, Latin American countries look more like the USA (see Winant 1999 on Brazil). The notion of Latin American racial democracy is just a myth. Yet others have argued that, although Latin American racial orders have changed markedly, they are still particular. They involve exclusion, but also inclusion in ways that make the idea of racial democracy not *just* a myth but also something that resonates with aspects of daily experience in which mixture and tolerance also exist (Burdick 1998; Ferreira da Silva 1998; Fry

2000; Wade 1993). This does not excuse Latin American forms of racism. It does recognize the complexities involved which make this racism difficult to address and combat.

NOTE

1 For a brief account of these and some further references, see Wade (1997: ch. 6). See also *NACLA Report on the Americas* 15, 4, 1992, on 'The black Americas' and 29, 5, 1996, on 'Gaining ground: the indigenous movement in Latin America'; Whitten and Torres (1998), Warren (1998).

REFERENCES AND SELECTED FURTHER READING

Andrews, G. R. 1991: *Blacks and Whites in São Paulo, Brazil, 1888–1988*. Madison: University of Wisconsin Press.

Arocha, J. 1998: Inclusion of Afro-Colombians: an unreachable goal? *Latin American Perspectives* 25, 3, 70–89.

Banton, M. 1987: *Racial Theories*. Cambridge: Cambridge University Press.

Burdick, J. 1998: *Blessed Anastácia: Women, Race, and Popular Christianity in Brazil*. London: Routledge.

De la Cadena, M. 2000: *Indigenous Mestizos: The Politics of Race and Culture in Cuzco, 1919–1991*. Durham, NC: Duke University Press.

Ferreira da Silva, D. 1998: Facts of blackness: Brazil is not (quite) the United States . . . and racial politics in Brazil? *Social Identities* 4, 2, 201–34.

Fontaine, P-M. (ed.) 1985: *Race, Class and Power in Brazil*. Los Angeles: Center of Afro-American Studies, University of California.

Fry, P. 2000: Politics, nationality, and the meanings of 'race' in Brazil. *Daedalus* 129, 2, 83–118.

Graham, R. (ed.) 1990: *The Idea of Race in Latin America, 1870–1940*. Austin: University of Texas Press.

Grandin, G. 2000: *The Blood of Guatemala: A History of Race and Nation*. Durham, NC: Duke University Press.

Grueso, L., Rosero, C. and Escobar, A. 1998: The process of black community organizing in the southern Pacific coast of Colombia. In S. Alvarez, E. Dagnino and A. Escobar (eds), *Cultures of Politics, Politics of Cultures: Re-visioning Latin American Social Movements*. Boulder, CO: Westview Press, 196–219.

Hale, C. R. (ed.) 1996: Mestizaje. Special issue of *Journal of Latin American Anthropology* 2, 1.

Hanchard, M. 1994: *Orpheus and Power: The Movimento Negro of Rio de Janeiro and São Paulo, Brazil, 1945–1988*. Princeton, NJ: Princeton University Press.

Hanchard, M. (ed.) 1999: *Racial Politics in Contemporary Brazil*. Durham, NC: Duke University Press.

Harding, R. E. 2000: *A Refuge in Thunder: Candomblé and Alternative Spaces of Blackness*. Bloomington: Indiana University Press.

Helg, A. 1995: *Our Rightful Share: The Afro-Cuban Struggle for Equality, 1886–1912*. Chapel Hill: University of North Carolina Press.

Howard, P. A. 1998: *Changing History: Afro-Cuban Cabildos and Societies of Color in the Nineteenth Century*. Baton Rouge: Louisiana State University Press.

Lame, M. Q. 1971: *En Defensa de Mi Raza*. With an introduction and notes by Gonzalo Castillo Cárdenas. Bogotá: Rosca de Investigación y Acción Social.

Lovell, P. 1994: Race, gender and development in Brazil. *Latin American Research Review* 29, 3, 7–35.

Mörner, M. 1967: *Race Mixture in the History of Latin America*. Boston: Little Brown.

Orlove, B. 1998: 'Dirty Indians', radical *indígenas*, and the political economy of social difference in modern Ecuador. *Bulletin of Latin American Research* 17, 2, 185–206.

Price, R. (ed.) 1996: *Maroon Societies: Rebel Slave Communities in the Americas*, 3rd edn. Baltimore: Johns Hopkins University Press.

Safa, H. (ed.) 1998: Race and national identity in the Americas. Special issue of *Latin American Perspectives* 25, 3.

Silva, N. do Valle 1985: Updating the cost of not being white in Brazil. In P-M. Fontaine (ed.), *Race, Class and Power in Brazil*. Los Angeles: Center of Afro-American Studies, University of California, 42–55.

Smedley, A. 1993: *Race in North America: Origin and Evolution of a Worldview*. Boulder, CO, and Oxford: Westview Press.

Stepan, N. 1991: *'The Hour of Eugenics': Race, Gender and Nation in Latin America*. Ithaca, NY: Cornell University Press.

Stern, S. J. (ed.) 1987: *Resistance, Rebellion and Consciousness in the Andean Peasant World, 18th to 20th Centuries*. Madison: University of Wisconsin Press.

Stolcke, V. 1995: Talking culture: new boundaries, new rhetorics of exclusion in Europe. *Current Anthropology* 36, 1, 1–23.

Streicker, J. 1995: Policing boundaries: race, class, and gender in Cartagena, Colombia. *American Ethnologist* 22, 1, 54–74.

Urban, G. and Sherzer, J. (eds) 1991: *Nation-states and Indians in Latin America*. Austin: University of Texas Press.

Wade, P. 1993: *Blackness and Race Mixture: The Dynamics of Racial Identity in Colombia*. Baltimore: Johns Hopkins University Press.

Wade, P. 1995: The cultural politics of blackness in Colombia. *American Ethnologist* 22, 2, 342–58.

Wade, P. 1997: *Race and Ethnicity in Latin America*. London: Pluto Press.

Warren, K. B. 1998: *Indigenous Movements and their Critics: Pan-Maya Activism in Guatemala*. Princeton, NJ: Princeton University Press.

Weismantel, M. 2001: *Cholas and Pishtacos: Stories of Race and Sex in the Andes*. Chicago: University of Chicago Press.

Whitten, N. E. 1986: *Black Frontiersmen: A South American Case*, 2nd edn. Prospect Heights, IL: Waveland Press.

Whitten, N. E. and Torres, A. 1998: General introduction: to forge the future in the fires of the past: an interpretive essay on racism, domination, resistance, and liberation. In N.E. Whitten and A. Torres (eds), *Blackness in Latin America and the Caribbean: Social Dynamics and Cultural Transformations*, Vol. 1. Bloomington: Indiana University Press, 3–33.

Wilson, R. 1995: *Maya Resurgence in Guatemala: Q'echi' Experiences*. Norman: University of Oklahoma Press.

Winant, H. 1992: Rethinking race in Brazil. *Journal of Latin American Studies* 24, 173–92.

Winant, H. 1999: Racial democracy and racial identity: comparing the United States and Brazil. In M. Hanchard (ed.), *Racial Politics in Contemporary Brazil*. Durham, NC: Duke University Press, 98–115.

11

Gender and sexuality in Latin America

Nikki Craske

This chapter considers some aspects of gender and sexuality in Latin America. In doing so, it seeks to explore how gender and sexuality interact and to give some historical context. It examines different expressions of female and male sexuality in the region and how certain ideas of being a 'proper man' or 'proper woman' are reproduced. To understand such issues, it is important to consider how ideas of gender and sexuality have changed, as well as how political and historical factors have shaped understandings of gender and sexual identities. Despite appearances, gender identities, and even sexuality, are not fixed. Rather they reflect a myriad of different influences which affect how an individual understands and acts upon her/his notion of gender and sexual identity. The content and meaning of such identities vary across time, geography, class, ethnicity, age and so forth: for example, being a middle-class, professional, white woman in her thirties in Buenos Aires is quite distinct from being a poor, black woman in her fifties from north-east Brazil. It is also important to remember that sexuality is not a descriptor merely for what one does, but also for how one identifies: in Latin America men who have sexual relations with men do not necessarily consider themselves gay or bisexual, as the discussion below highlights.

Social, economic and political contexts are influential whereby, like gender, '[s]exuality is not a given. It is the product of negotiation, struggle and human agency' (Weeks 2000: 129). In the Latin American case, the process of colonization had a particular impact, particularly with regard to the racialization of sexuality and gender hierarchies. Institutions including legislatures, the medical establishment and the Catholic Church have also sought to regulate and control gender constructions and sexuality both directly, by passing laws, or indirectly through 'scientific' arguments linking sexuality and deviancy, or by reinforcing notions of decency, honour and morality which constrain personal autonomy. In Latin America, notions of honour and decency hold particular sway in these hegemonic discourses and they help shape the terrain on which gender and sexuality are negotiated.

Although these identities are open to a degree of renegotiation, they are not completely fluid. Many aspects are deeply embedded and there are many structural constraints which inhibit groups or individuals from redefining their gender identity or sexuality. Certain identities are privileged over others: there are clear gender hierarchies where women are perceived to be the 'weaker sex'. Similarly, heterosexuality is prized over 'deviant' lesbian, gay and transvestite sexualities. In such situations some have power over others and, importantly, some are more able to control their own identities: in this way they have the 'power to be able' and are more empowered as individuals than those who are labelled by others. Given the hierarchies at play, I argue that heterosexual males have greater power to label others and to be able to do so is important in the maintenance of their dominant position.

Alongside the dominant, hegemonic discourses, there is also resistance. Women have long resisted the gender hierarchies imposed upon them and have struggled to become subjects of rights on the same terms as men.[1] Although not all women participate, women's organizations have been an important development of the twentieth century. Resistance to dominant conceptions of sexuality is seen in the flip side of 'decent' society where 'exotic' and freer expressions of sexuality are at play. Carnival is perhaps the most celebrated example of this and there is a vibrant transvestite subculture. Latin American women, particularly Brazilian and Caribbean women, have long been prized as 'exotic' and sensual by men, both local and foreign. It is unclear whether this challenge to decency is empowering for those concerned. Despite this, these images can offer greater scope for women and men, gay, straight, bisexual, transvestite, to find their own niche. At the same time, however, locating a niche may result in reinforcing gender stereotypes or in denigrating others' sexuality (see the discussion on transvestism below), which limits its potential as an emancipatory project. Women and men challenge their subordinate positions by playing with stereotypes, or balancing conformity and insubordination, engaging in what might be called a 'double discourse' (Shepard 2000).

To explore these issues, this chapter first briefly examines perspectives on gender and sexuality, before considering their historical context in Latin America. The bulk of the chapter discusses different aspects of male and female sexuality and how these reflect gender relations. The focus of the chapter reflects the predominance of literature on non-heterosexual relations but this also sheds light on understanding gender and heterosexuality.

PERSPECTIVES ON GENDER AND SEXUALITY

It is difficult to separate gender and sexuality given that dominant ideas of gender rest on privileging heterosexuality and reproduction – particularly for women. In Latin America this has been mediated by notions of *machismo* and, to a lesser extent, *marianismo* which still have cultural weight.[2] Although these bi-polar conceptions do not describe reality, they offer an understanding of the parameters within which people can negotiate their own gender positions. In contemporary Latin America extreme manifestations of either *machismo* or *marianismo* are no longer considered positive attributes (see, for example, Gutmann 1997: 229–30) and greater emphasis is placed on complementarity between women and men than on subordination (Schifter and Madrigal 2000: 93, 103). Yet, within this is the view that women are more vulnerable and require protection (100). Although the idea of complementarity does not necessarily imply gender hierarchies, historically there have been more constraints on women's autonomy. Furthermore, these dualisms are reflected in sexuality. Padgug (1999: 17) argues that although sexuality is central to our lives, it is hard to define. Given its complexity and ambiguities, it is always difficult to make definitive statements on sexuality and this necessarily limits the ensuing discussion. In the following sections two approaches to understanding sexuality are examined: first, the relationship between sex, reproduction and pleasure, and second, the dominant dualisms of passive/active, male/female.

Sex, pleasure and morality

Horrocks (1997) argues, convincingly, that the only way to understand contemporary views of sexuality in the West is through understanding the development of Christianity and its break with the more lascivious practices of the Romans and the more sensual attitudes of their Jewish forebears. Furthermore, in the early Christian Church there was a belief that the second coming was imminent and therefore reproduction was not necessary. The denial of sexual pleasure, whether for reproduction or not, was seen as a challenge to dominant Roman views, as well as offering freedom from earthly and material desires. By the tenth century a rather forbidding view of sex had developed within parts of the Catholic Church, and whilst this was not the only perspective, it came to dominate. Catholic teaching became regulatory and limiting even if sexual practice was not. This negative vision was imported into Latin America with colonization, although Catholicism did not take hold across the region in a uniform manner.[3] Stavans (1998: 229) argues that along with this negative view of sex, came misogyny. The treatment of sex as sinful has permeated many aspects of contemporary attitudes towards sex and encouraged notions of good and bad sex, not in terms of pleasure but in terms of morality.

The issue of morality was something that preoccupied nineteenth-century thinkers and led to judgemental views on sex, particularly for women. Dominant views at the time were contradictory. On the one hand there was an emphasis on morality and legislation (focused on prostitutes, homosexuals and venereal diseases[4]), whilst on the other there were vibrant expressions of sexuality in art and literature. Legitimate sexuality was decent, honourable and regulated (through recognized marriage)[5] and sexual enjoyment was the preserve of men. As such, decent women should not enjoy sex, so the links between 'legitimate' sex and reproduction, rather than pleasure, were reinforced (on contemporary Peru, see Nencel 1996: 61). From the late nineteenth century psychology, sexology and feminism challenged these stylized visions of sexuality.

Sexuality in the West is often viewed in a dichotomous and bi-polar fashion where biological sex is transposed onto sexuality. Although much of the discourse on this emphasizes 'natural' instincts, it is in fact highly ideological. This rather black-and-white understanding has been challenged over the last few decades but its legacy can be felt, not least in Latin America. This binary female/male perspective sees men as having male sexuality which is active and dominant whilst women have female sexuality which is passive and submissive. This stereotype has also been superimposed onto notions of ideal types such that men *should* be active and dominant and women should be passive and submissive. As such, men have natural sexual urges which cannot be contained and controlled; although they should be faithful and restrained, they cannot be held responsible if they are seduced into 'sinning' by unchaste women. In Latin America, this active male sexuality is often depicted as explosive and barely containable (Nencel 1996: 64; see also Amuchástegui Herrera 1998: 115; Barker and Lowenstein 1997: 115). Prieur (1996: 93) suggests that although Christianity is deeply ingrained in Latin American culture, it is seen as a more feminine preserve and consequently masculinity, including its sexual expression, is constructed in opposition to Christian rules (cf. Schifter and Madrigal 2000: 177 on Protestantism). As such, men's negative practices (like heavy drinking and adultery) are in fact markers for male honour and masculinity: i.e. such behaviour can indicate male strength. Thus men's transgressive sexual behaviour, particularly with other men, should be understood in this context. Yet, men who take on the 'passive' role in same-sex relationships are at risk of being feminized and losing their masculinity (see below). Despite this dominant idea of men as active and beyond control in their sexual desires, it must be remembered that this is balanced by ideas of good men as loving fathers and providers.

Female/male: passive/active

If Western conceptions of men's sexuality stress the active, women's sexuality has been dichotomized around the virgin/whore complex. In the former, women are seen as pure and non-carnal, more associated with mothering than female sexuality (this is taken to its extremes in the iconography of the Virgin Mary). In the latter women are temptresses and anything but passive. This representation fits the Eve paradigm where she tempts Adam away from good behaviour and into sin. Overt female sexuality, then, has been posited as problematic, as being sinful, to be feared and something which needs to be controlled. This is exacerbated by the nature of women's bodies, particularly in relation to sexual organs which are hidden and unknown unlike the male phallus which is overt and on show (see Stavans 1998 on the centrality of the phallus in Latin American culture; cf. Kulick 1998: 304). Furthermore, women's bodily excretions are seen as unclean and distasteful, so much so that some religions have placed menstruating women out of bounds.[6] This distaste reflects an underlying misogyny that permeates many aspects of institutionalized religion. Women have to negotiate between idealized visions of the virgin,[7] the mother and the 'scarlet woman'. Although this dichotomous view has been exaggerated in Latin America, it is also found in Northern countries. Despite the stereotyping, it indicates the parameters for sexual behaviour, where women's overt sexual engagement poses a greater risk for their status than men's, whose engagement is viewed positively.

Although this active/passive stereotype is a rather blunt tool for understanding gender and sexuality, the discussion below demonstrates how elements of it are reproduced by many different actors. It also indicates how sex and pleasure have been experienced differently for women and men and how controlling women's sexuality has been a male privilege (cf. Schifter and Madrigal 2000: 94–5).

CHALLENGING THE STEREOTYPES IN THE TWENTIETH CENTURY

Women's lives are more restricted by these gender constructions than men's in ways that go beyond expressions of sexuality. They have been constrained from earning a living, gaining an education, and having a political voice. These constraints were mediated by class and race, and there were always some who succeeded in flouting convention. One of the legacies of these limitations is that women have been perceived as uninterested in politics, which was seen as the natural preserve of men. From the late nineteenth century, women began to organize across Latin America to challenge these restrictions, in particular focusing on the right to education and the right to vote. Gaining the vote was a slow process and many women, particularly indigenous women, fell foul of literacy clauses which continued until the 1970s in some countries. Not all women were keen to have the vote, arguing that it would 'corrupt' women, whose power came from being morally superior to men and removed from the political arena (Craske 1999; Miller 1991). Nevertheless, during the course of the twentieth century, women did become equal citizens, formally at least. The struggle for the vote illustrated various elements of 'political motherhood'. It was often on the basis of characteristics inherent in mothering (care for others, selflessness) that claims for a political voice were promoted. Women's participation was seen as necessary for improving the quality of politics. Even Argentina's Eva Duarte de Perón engaged in rhetoric employing female stereotypes and became 'mother of the nation'. Despite positioning herself as Juan Perón's helpmate and inferior, she wielded considerable power (Craske 1999: 80–2). The importance of maintaining appropriate gender norms is also evident in Chaney's study of women legislators in 1960s' Chile and Peru (Chaney 1979).

Political motherhood again came to the fore in the 1970s and 1980s when social movements proliferated across the region.[8] Many women became politically active based on their understanding of mothering commitments: for some, this was an explicitly political act; others argued that they were apolitical or above politics. For yet others, using the language of mothering was strategically advantageous in the repressively authoritarian regimes which dominated the region at the time. Using 'political motherhood' politicized the private and uncovered the links between public, government actions and private consequences. It also gave women a legitimate space in which to make demands and gave rise to the language of rights and citizenship. In the past, the 'ideal' citizen reflected male characteristics, and often assumed the existence of a public–private divide where the citizen's private needs were catered for by another: in reality the citizen was a man and the carer his wife. Through social movements, women moved from making demands on governments based on needs, to claiming rights (see Molyneux and Craske 2002 for a fuller discussion). The developments in social movements ran parallel to the emergence of feminism in the region. Dominated by professional women in the urban conurbations, feminism nevertheless became an important political movement in late twentieth-century Latin America. It reinforced the struggle for an 'engendered' citizenship which was as meaningful to women as it was to men. Although feminism has been critiqued for its middle-class bias, it has been an important force in post-authoritarian regimes in ensuring that legislation and public policy are more gender-aware, and that women are less excluded from political life than previously.

Although men have not engaged in a similar movement to challenge dominant notions of masculinity, they have responded to the challenges raised by women's movements and many of the excessive elements of *machismo* are unacceptable to the majority of contemporary Latin American men, particularly younger ones (see below). Despite positive developments, some aspects of gender constructions are more resistant to change than others and men are still sensitive to being identified in ways which might compromise their notions of masculinity. This resistance is particularly evident in the relatively slow progress made by Latin American lesbians and gays in their struggles for equal rights (see below).

REGULATING SEX IN LATIN AMERICA: RACE, PROSTITUTION AND HOMOSEXUALITY

As in many other parts of the world, Latin America experienced an increase in sex regulation in the late nineteenth century and this was overlaid with racism.

It is unsurprising that the language of sex and sexuality should reflect the brutal conquest of large parts of Latin America and the colonial legacy.[9] In the early days of colonization, there was a shortage of European women, making them a prized commodity. In contrast, the vulnerability of indigenous women and the inability of their men to protect them left a legacy of hierarchies where ethnicity, gender and sexuality were intertwined to produce racialized sexualities, which have been evident in attitudes towards prostitution. As in Europe and the USA, nineteenth- and early twentieth-century Latin America experienced the rise of sex regulation. The cultural weight of the Catholic Church often led to a conflation of morality and criminality. During this period views on sex embraced a double standard both encouraging and limiting free sexual behaviour. The regulation of sexual behaviour focused on two targets: the fear of disease led to control and regulation of prostitution, while homosexuals were judged by spurious links made between criminality and 'deviant' sexuality, and these were often overlaid with race, leading to scientific racism (Lancaster 1997a: 195). With prostitution female prostitutes not their male clients were regulated. Caulfield (1997, 2000) shows that although there was toleration of prostitutes in late-nineteenth- and early twentieth-century Rio de Janeiro, there was also great concern for 'moral hygiene'. This became highly racialized with 'French' and some mulatta prostitutes being allowed greater freedom than Polish or Preta (black) women.[10] Buenos Aires also experienced a racialization of its prostitution and attempts to regulate prostitutes were not greatly successful (Guy 2000). The issue of ethnicity helped create the view of Latin American sexuality as exotic and picturesque, even a tourist attraction (Caulfield 1997: 94) and this continues today (see below). The toleration of some prostitutes reflects the passive/active stereotype where ideal middle-class wives should not enjoy sex, so men needed an outlet for their 'naturally' active sexuality. But even prostitution needed to conform to aspects of 'decency', so streetwalkers were tolerated less than members of brothels/bordellos, reflecting class positioning.

Whether homosexuality was 'imported' to the Americas by Europeans or was a 'native' characteristic was a matter of debate in early colonial Latin America (Trexler 1995). European rejection of homosexuality underpinned this debate and later regulation of homosexuality was legitimized by linking it to 'scientific' ideas of medicine and criminology. Buffington (1997) discusses the obsession of Mexican criminologists with sexuality in the late nineteenth century. Assumptions were made about the 'inevitable' homosexual past of criminals. After the Revolution, criminals were considered 'redeemable' through education and improved welfare, whilst homosexuality was biological. Consequently, criminals were at risk of 'corruption' by homosexuals (particularly 'active' ones) in prison and so were to be 'protected' from them (123). Homosexuality itself became increasingly subject to legislation and its practices outlawed, although in Latin America, as elsewhere, less attention was paid to female homosexuality. Buffington (1997: 127) suggests that this is because female criminality posed little threat and because women had little political voice. Alongside the legal approach to homosexuality there were also attempts to cast gay men as mentally ill and to offer 'cures' for the 'ill' (Green 1999: esp. ch. 3). In contemporary Latin America there are still significant legal and cultural constraints on lesbian and gay sexuality,[11] but political organizing is helping to challenge these.

The exoticization of Latin American sexuality has offered a space for public expressions of gay culture in the region, particularly through carnival. But there are disadvantages to the racialization of sexuality, which are evident at many levels. Gutmann (1996: 127) comments that foreigners and light-skinned Mexicans pick up young, dark-skinned male prostitutes in one of Mexico City's central parks.[12] Abiodun (2001) discusses the increased sexual tourism in late-twentieth-century Cuba and points to the increasingly young age of the women/girls involved. In the Cuban example in particular, officials turn a blind eye to much sexual tourism. Alongside this contemporary sexual imperialism, however, there is also a sense of nationalism in the different attitudes of Latin men towards women, where foreign women (often tourists) are seen as 'easy', unlike 'nice' local girls who will go on to be mothers and reproduce the next generation of Latin men and women.

MEN, GENDER AND SEXUALITY

From their discussions with young male Costa Ricans, Schifter and Madrigal (2000: 99) note the centrality of power to the men's identity, but the men emphasized the need to use power 'responsibly'. Power, however, does not just come through being sexually dominant (i.e. active and aggressive) but also through language: the ability to define your own sexuality and not have others label you and, maybe more importantly, having the power to define and label others, both female and male.[13]

Men and heterosexuality

Male heterosexuality has a privileged position in the lexicon of gender and sexuality, but this does not make it less complex and relations with both women and other men are complicated. First, it is important for men to be 'active'; second, and paradoxically, the construction of masculinity includes homoerotic playing in male bonding; finally, men have ambivalent and complex relationships with women. Given the importance of the active/passive duality in Latin America, being a 'man' depends on being heterosexual, since anything that might be interpreted as homosexual is construed as feminized and passive. Fear of being perceived as feminine is arguably at the heart of Hispanic male sexuality. Franco (2001) highlights the scandal when independence hero Simón Bolívar was depicted with breasts and rounded hips by the artist Juan Dávila. But this fear is contradicted by the homoerotic elements of men's interaction with one another. Gutmann (1996: 123) comments that in Mexico men are particularly keen to show off their genitalia to one another, albeit in 'culturally sanctioned times and places' (cf. Schifter and Madrigal 2000: 164). The importance of highly sexualized male 'space' is also evident in Barker and Lowenstein's (1997: 193) study of young men in Rio de Janeiro. Whilst they suggest that there is a lack of adequate sex education and what little does exist underlines and endorses heterosexual behaviour, there is a certain acceptance of homosexual engagement as part of sexual experimentation (Lancaster 1997a: 197; cf. Gutmann 1996: 129; Parker 1999: 259). Everyday language is also highly sexualized with particular emphasis on the penis (Gutmann 1996: 123). Stavans (1998: 230) suggests that there is an intense 'adoration' of the Latin phallus and gives a short summary of the terms used to describe male genitalia (see also Schifter and Madrigal 2000: 165). Archetti's (1996) work on Argentina demonstrates that engaging with sexual innuendo, much of it homoerotic and racialized, is part of establishing masculine identity. This acceptance of homoeroticism is tempered by Amuchástegui Herrera's (1998: 116) observations that fear of being labelled homosexual made young men in rural Mexico keen to engage in sexual intercourse with women to demonstrate 'proof against the threat of homosexuality': having a girlfriend becomes insurance against homosexuality.

Men's relationships with women are complicated, with the polar extremes of the veneration of the mother and the undervaluing of other women, especially casual sexual partners. For many Latin American men the romanticized notion of the mother is reinforced for many by the absence literally or emotionally of the father (although Gutmann 1996 notes that this is also changing rapidly; cf. Mirandé 1998). Men often have their first sexual experience with prostitutes or, for the more wealthy, with maids (Nencel 1996; Stavans 1998; see also Gutmann 1996: 132–3): i.e. women with whom they have little emotional engagement. Barker and Lowenstein's (1997: 184) study of Rio de Janeiro indicates that young men accept their sexual activities as natural and sex is seen as conquest rather than as a display of affection. Although they see their sexuality as difficult to control, it is not always 'according to their desires and wishes' (170). The study also demonstrated that women have an early mistrust of young males both in terms of their ability to provide (an important male characteristic) and in their use of physical beatings of women (187).

As women renegotiate their own sexuality, men are adjusting their expectations: Nencel (1996) shows how Peruvian men are more accepting of women's sexual activity, but they continue to distinguish between types of women. This reflects their views on 'marriageable' women and their separation of emotions from more casual relationships (see especially 1996: 68). Amuchástegui Herrera (1998: 118) sees similar tendencies in Mexico, but more worryingly she suggests that men not only label women, they also make them into objects of male desire rather than subjects of female sexuality. The issue of male power and control over women is again identified by Melhuus in her discussion of Mexico (1996). Women's long-running struggle for emancipation, broadly understood, is having an impact on gender relations and female and male sexuality. Active sexuality can no longer be seen as the preserve of heterosexual men.

Men and homosexuality

Understanding Latin American homosexuality is complex since the lexicon used to describe practice is not translatable directly onto the European norm. Prieur (1996) offers a variety of descriptions used in Mexico: identification as 'gay' (*joto* in Mexico) is for those who take on the 'feminine, passive' role (cf. Schifter and Madrigal 2000: 106 on Costa Rica). Bisexual men are those who appear somewhat effeminate and who engage in both active and passive roles together (so they are both feminine and masculine). The men who are 'active' in the penetration frequently identify themselves as heterosexual. Prieur points out that the men who had sexual relationships with transvestite men also had relationships with women and saw no impact on their heterosexuality, considering themselves neither gay nor bisexual. Yet Kulick (1998: 307) notes that a transvestite couple in Brazil were identified as a lesbian couple. In the Cuban case, some male prostitutes who are 'active' have devised a new label to indicate their willingness to have sex with men, but without compromising their macho identity: they call themselves *pinguero* (Hodge 2001). The continuation of this binary separation between active and passive is evident across the region[14] and sheds some light on what it means to be macho. Gutmann (1996: 128–9) notes that knowledge of alternative lifestyles has changed how people use sexual labels, even if they do not come into close contact with them. Class and education play a role in sexual identity; for example, there is some evidence to suggest that more middle-class professionals engage with a gay identity whereas more working-class men see their same-sex encounters as part of their active heterosexual identity, or at least it does not challenge their heterosexual identity much (Green 1999).

Despite the existence of vibrant gay and bisexual communities, there is still significant repression of homosexuals. Lumsden (1996) discusses the institutionalized homophobia in Cuba, where reports of harassment of gays, lesbians and transvestites is commonplace, and Green (1999: 3) cites a study which found that 'a homosexual is brutally murdered every four days, a victim of homophobia that pervades Brazilian society'. The use of homosexual labels as insults is widespread and in many countries there is still significant stigma attached to the notion of homosexuality.[15] The rise of HIV/AIDS has been an important factor in pushing Latin American authorities into recognizing the prevalence of particular practices but also the need to educate everyone about its implications. The limitations on gay sexuality are evident in the lack of space for sexual experimentation in formative years. Murray (discussed in Lancaster 1997a: 198) argues that since most young Latin Americans live at home, at least until they are married, there are practical restrictions on expressions of intimacy, which has a greater impact on young homosexuals than their heterosexual counterparts. Furthermore, there are few positive gay role models to help young people as they develop their own sexuality.

Transvestites

Transvestism is an important subculture within the Latin American homosexual scene. Understanding Latin American attitudes towards transvestites has to reflect the importance of carnival in some countries, not least Brazil (Green 1999; cf. Lancaster 1997b on Nicaragua). Transvestites glory in reproducing femininity in an exaggerated form: some consider themselves more feminine than women because they always 'dress up' and 'look after their men', unlike women who have become too masculine (Lancaster 1998: 265). Prieur (1996) and Kulick (1998) discuss how transvestites manipulate their physical appearance to emphasize the womanly: big hair, enhanced buttocks and breasts. Many transvestites work as prostitutes, although it is unclear whether their clients are looking for male or female companions. Although transvestites revel in the feminine, Kulick (1998) notes that in El Salvador, Brazil, they see lesbianism as 'fraudulent' since there is no penile penetration. An antipathetic relationship between women and transvestites appears widespread and misogyny plays a strong role in the rejection of women (Sifuentes Jáuregui 1997: 49). In positioning themselves as more authentic females than women, transvestites undermine attempts to find a common struggle for gay and lesbian rights. In their antipathy towards women, especially 'non-feminine' women, transvestites appear to blur ideas of sexuality whilst reinforcing many gender stereotypes.

Latin American male sexuality is constantly renegotiated, but some elements are more resistant to change than others. For example, there is increasing acceptance of men displaying emotions (Schifter and Madrigal 2000) but this is difficult to negotiate. Gutmann's (1996) work on Mexico shows that some traditional elements (adultery, rejection of contraceptives, fecundity) are changing, but the old and the new live side-by-side, often in contradictory ways. Understanding male sexuality in Latin America necessitates us looking beyond Eurocentric visions which rely more on sexual practice. Latin American men tend to use binary models of sexuality when talking and visioning their sexuality, but these give rise to identities distinct from the European norm. There is a strong element of power and *machismo* in expressions of Latin American male sexuality, with some continuation of the passive/active, female/male dualisms. Although men are keen to be seen as 'active' and therefore masculine, power is also invested in controlling the labels and thus in limiting other people's sexual autonomy and self-identification.

Therefore, to be able to be heterosexual whilst engaging in what in other contexts might be called homosexual activities, or to decide whether women are *de su casa* (homely or 'one of ours') or *pacharacas* (easy, usually of a lower social class), or whether other men are straight or *jotos* (gay or effeminate), often indicates greater power than that vested in simply being a straight man. But in all these cases, it is also clear that there are ongoing developments which make any definitive understanding of male sexuality impossible.

WOMEN, GENDER AND SEXUALITY

As indicated above, women have tended to be depicted either as non-sexual beings or as exoticized consumer items, and their identity is more constrained by ideas of decency than that of men. Given women's disadvantaged position in terms of gender hierarchies, their struggle to be more visible as sexual subjects has been part of the women's movement more broadly, particularly in relation to promoting reproductive rights. It is perhaps as a result of this that lesbianism has often been a more politicized identity with a greater emphasis on rights than that of their gay male counterparts. As was argued above, male sexuality is strongly linked to maintaining power; conversely, then, female sexuality has often been about challenging the dominant view of passivity. Attempts to assert female autonomy are manifested in a variety of ways, through feminism, political organization, 'transgressive' playing with different images of womanhood, to employing a double discourse to negotiate the maximum space possible.

Women and heterosexuality

The gender construction of femininity in Latin America has placed great emphasis on marriage and motherhood (Craske 1999), as women's sexuality has been marginalized and their lack of carnality emphasized. In history, women with an overt sexual identity, such as Hernán Cortés's consort La Malinche, have tended to be viewed as transgressive, and in this particular case she has become synonymous with treachery. The impact of Catholicism and the emphasis on the figure of the Virgin Mary have reinforced this negative interpretation of active female sexuality. Melhuus (1996) highlights the ambiguity between motherhood and virginity that underscores women's sexuality. Even in contemporary Latin America these legacies can be felt. Willmott (2002) shows how, when asked to identify pictures of their sexuality, women at a workshop in Chile pointed out pictures of brides or babies.[16] Barker and Lowenstein (1997: 170) also show that female sexuality is linked to motherhood and nurturing at a young age. Across the region women and girls enter marriage or consensual unions younger than their male counterparts and are more likely to identify themselves as involved in such relationships than men (Valdés and Gomáriz 1995: 54–7). This could suggest that women see being part of a relationship as important, whilst men may wish to advertise their availability. Young women are 'coached' into heterosexual unions early on and motherhood is a strong part of this feminine sexuality myth, but this is unrelated to the practice of sex. The close identification of female sexuality with mothering may reflect the difficulties in finding adequate methods for controlling their fertility. Access to good contraceptives and to safe, legal abortions is limited and frequently depends on financial resources. With the fear of unwanted pregnancy, the freedom to engage in heterosexual relationships purely for pleasure is more limited.[17] Figueroa Perea and Rivera Reyes (1993: 153–4) indicate that in Mexico education and geography play an important part in determining whether motherhood and pregnancy dominate women's view of sexual relations, with less educated and more rural women maintaining a stronger link between reproduction and sex.

Women more than men have experienced rapid change in their gender identities in recent years. Their political organization has helped 'empower' them and they are now more able to assert themselves in terms of expressing their sexuality, and in demanding equality in education and paid labour. Although female virginity has traditionally been highly valued, this is changing. As indicated above, men, particularly the younger generation, do accept that young women will engage in sexual activities, including penetration, before marriage (Gutmann 1996; Nencel 1996; cf. Rivas Zivy 1998). In Mexico both Amuchástegui Herrera (1998) and Rivas Zivy (1998) find, however, that women are still ambivalent about admitting to their sexual encounters, demonstrating the gap between reality and appearances. In particular, Rivas Zivy (1998: 150) notes that women still find it difficult to discuss sexual pleasure. This more limited view of sexuality starts early: Osterman and Keller-Cohen (1998) found that US and Brazilian teen magazines not only reinforced heterosexuality, but they did so to young girls barely in their teens and were coaching them to be 'ideal' partners who are neither too pushy and assertive (feminist) nor too timid. Furthermore, some argue (Schifter and Madrigal 2000) that more liberal attitudes place more pressure on women since they are now supposed to be perfect mothers and lovers, *and* emotionally support their partners. To this extent, the male gaze continues to define women and their sexuality and women are still 'bodies for others', although this is declining with higher educational attainment (Figueroa Perea and Rivera Reyes 1993: 147).

Although changes have occurred, it remains more difficult for women to express their sexuality freely. This is mediated by class and geography, but women are more at risk from losing their 'decent' identity than men as a result of living with men or openly having sexual relations before marriage (Amuchástegui Herrera 1998: 118; Melhuus 1996: 245; Stavans 1998: 230). Anecdotal evidence supports the view in the literature: that men go out with 'liberated' independent women but marry 'nice' girls (cf. Nencel 1996), or that even when women are 'experienced', they should not be as experienced as the men (Barker and Lowenstein 1997: 170; Schifter and Madrigal 2000: 101). Similarly there is pressure on women to look attractive and sexy for men but without being too overt. A brief stay in Buenos Aires is sufficient to illustrate the tyranny of female perfection, and statistics suggest that Argentina has one of the highest rates of anorexia in the world,[18] which again serves to control women through their self-image. It is reasonable to suggest that the sexual double standards that women have to endure in many parts of the world are also an issue in Latin America.

Women and lesbianism

In comparison with gay men, lesbians seem invisible in the region, although there are many organizations that promote lesbian rights. Despite the fact that lesbians appear to be more politically active than gay men, there is also a cultural aspect which tends to position lesbians as socially marginal and even a little crazy (Arguelles 1998; Yarbro-Bejarano 1997). Some lesbian icons, like the Chicana singer Chabela Vargas, succeed in undermining dominant notions of gender by using the traditional mythologies of the suffering and rejected woman and women's destiny to suffer, and 'queering' these to make them part of lesbian culture (Yarbro-Bejarano 1997). This can provide a space for young lesbians who might otherwise feel excluded (Arguelles 1998). It is possible that this more marginalized character makes it easier to organize politically. Thayer (1997) illustrates the difficulties of 'coming out' in Costa Rica, even within the feminist movement, despite the fact that many of their struggles are part of the broader women's movement. It is clear from Thayer's article, which compares Nicaragua with Costa Rica, that the broader social, political and economic context has an important impact on the ways in which sexuality can be expressed and thus on the development of gender and sexual identities. Although many lesbians are politically organized, as hinted above, it is not easy for lesbians to organize with gay men: as Lumsden (1996: 151) notes in Cuba, '[a]s a rule, lesbians who challenge and refuse to conform with such oppressive stereotypes [conventional feminine and *machista* norms] are no more a part of an integrated homosexual scene than they are anywhere else in Latin America'.

As societies become more plural in their acceptance of non-hegemonic sexual relationships, lesbians, gays, transvestites and transsexuals become more open about their practice and identity. In 1997 Patria Jiménez became the first 'openly gay legislator in Latin America' when she was elected to the Mexican congress for the PRD (Partido de la Revolución Democrática/Party of the Democratic Revolution).[19] Many others had already taken on such important roles but had decided to keep their sexuality out of the headlines.[20]

There is space to renegotiate gender identity and female sexuality: feminists are challenging sexism at all levels; women are educating themselves more and increasingly engaging in paid labour; working-class women are increasingly rejecting coupledom to enhance their autonomy (Schifter and Madrigal 2000: 107). Although sexual autonomy is more difficult for women to attain than for men, progress has been made: some women choose to accept some constraints of the male gaze, others transgress and succeed in gaining community support for their activities,[21] others are more confrontational but without necessarily having more autonomy.[22] The struggle for women's greater sexual freedom will continue to be linked to the overall struggle for women's emancipation, in contrast to negotiation over male sexuality. The continued limitations placed on women's right to choose in relation to their own bodies will be part of the backdrop in this endeavour.

CONCLUSION

This chapter has offered a brief overview of the interplay between gender and sexuality in contemporary Latin America and sought to place this in a conceptual and historical context. In doing so it has understood gender and sexuality as flexible constructs that can be renegotiated, yet such change is not easy. It is difficult to do justice to the complexity and diversity inherent within the subject in such a limited space. The concepts identified here are not reproduced verbatim by the actors concerned. Each person grapples with finding her/his own sense of gender identity and sexuality. This is mediated by the power vested in particular identities, which influences how open people may feel in expressing non-dominant gender or sexual identities. As such ethnicity, class, geography, age, education and so forth play an important part. For some, there is a gap between rhetoric and practice: women may not freely admit to being sexually active, or men might not acknowledge their homosexual encounters. Institutions play an important part in reinforcing certain gender and sexual hierarchies and colonization helped create a racialized legacy. The shadow of sexual tourism and the exoticization of some Latin Americans is still evident, particularly for darker-skinned women and male youths. Under current economic conditions it is difficult to see this being eroded in the near future.

Renegotiating gender relations and sexuality is also political activity. Developments within female gender identity and sexuality cannot be separated from the broader struggle for women's rights over the twentieth century, which looks set to continue in the twenty-first. Women's lives in Latin America, as elsewhere, have changed dramatically, but this has had both costs and benefits, and the rules governing their sexuality remain harsh: 'decency' continues to constrain women more than men. For men, the challenge is how to adjust to these changing conditions, which might be perceived as a potential loss of power for them. The struggle for lesbian and gay rights is less evident than the women's movement but it is there. Repression is still widespread and there are difficulties in establishing a unified struggle for gay and lesbian rights. In understanding the multiple variations of sexuality, it is important not to transpose European notions of sexual identity on to Latin American actors. The lexicon for discussing sex is highly varied, and gay, straight, lesbian and bisexual can have meanings quite distinct from Northern equivalents and they are constantly reformulated. Gender and sexuality will always be subjects of contestation where human agency and structural constraints interact.

NOTES

The author would like to thank Peter Lambert and, in particular, Andrew Davies for their comments on earlier drafts of this chapter.

1   This does not imply that women necessarily want to be the same as men.
2   *Machismo* endorses aggressive behaviour including heavy drinking and violent behaviour when protecting 'honour', stresses fecundity, and assumes a male breadwinning role. *Marianismo* is based on characteristics associated with the Virgin Mary, including the 'destiny' to suffer for children, to be self-sacrificing and to be focused on the home. The emphasis on protecting loved ones can lead to the endorsing of some kinds of political engagement.
3   It is unclear to what extent pre-Hispanic cultures' sexual teaching was compatible with Christianity. Dávalos López (1998) suggests that, in Mesoamerica, there were some coincidences, but that this varied from culture to culture. He also suggests that the Christian dualism was between body (sinful) and soul (pure), whilst the pre-Colombian Mexicans 'combated sexual transgression in order to maintain cosmic and social equilibrium', which excessive sexual activity could upset (Dávalos López 1998: 98). In the Andes it appears from ceramics that pre-Colombian cultures were much more overt in public expressions of sexuality than their Spanish conquerors (Hocquenghem 1987).
4   Frequently those legislating against prostitution were the same people who visited brothels. Legislation on venereal disease was often draconian and concerned with making prostitutes pariahs by blaming them, rather than their clients, for the spread of diseases: this was particularly the case when soldiers were rendered too ill to fight. Homosexuals were outlawed (or more particularly, homosexual acts) but lesbianism was frequently ignored on the grounds that it was against women's nature.
5   For the UK, Smith (2001) links this with increased privatization of deepening capitalism, where marriage became more regulated and reduced women's autonomy.
6   Particularly in strict interpretations of Judaism and Islam, where sexual

relations are forbidden during menstruation. See also Gutmann (1996: 122) for mythologies around menstruation in Mexico.

7   See, for example, Octavio Paz's 'The Sons of Malinche' in his *Labyrinth of Solitude* (1959).

8   There is a significant amount of literature on women's social movements: see, for example, Alvarez (1990); Fisher (1993); Jaquette (1994); Radcliffe and Westwood (1993); Stephen (1997).

9   The links between sex, gender and nationalism are ones that have been explored by feminists, and the use of rape as a tool of war illustrates the intertwined nature of these. Yuval-Davis (1997; Yuval-Davis and Anthias, 1989; Anthias and Yuval-Davis, 1989) has worked extensively on these connections; see also Wilford and Miller (1998) and, on rape in war, Meznaric (1994).

10 French was used generically to describe lighter-skinned and West European women.

11 See Chant with Craske (2003 forthcoming, box 6.1) for a survey of legislation and attitudes towards homosexuals in selected Latin American countries.

12 Although ethnicity is an important facet of contemporary sexuality, there is little literature that deals with indigenous people and sexuality. Most material looking at Maya, Nuautl or Andean sexuality tends to focus on the colonial period (Dávalos López 1998; Stavig 1995).

13 Sifuentes Jáuregui (1997) illustrates this particularly effectively in relation to José Donoso's novel *El lugar sin límites* (1966). The importance of labelling is evident is discussions of male views of male and female partners (Amuchástegui Herrera 1998; Melhuus 1996; Nencel 1996; Prieur 1996; Stavans 1998).

14 On the region see Lancaster (1997a) and Stavans (1998); on Brazil see Parker (1999); on Cuba see Hodge (2001); on Mexico see Gutmann (1996).

15 See note 9.

16 By the end of the workshop one was arguing for the 'right' to have a lover: this shows how much space there is for women in particular to reconsider and rearticulate their sexuality.

17 Parker (1999: 259) suggests that anal sex is one alternative for avoiding pregnancy employed by young heterosexual couples in Brazil.

18 Argentina ranked joint second with India in a recent twenty-nation study, with 29 per cent suffering from eating disorders (www.edeo.org/newsdetails/October19.html).

19 Ferriss, Cox News Service, 23 August 1997 (www.eco.utexas.edu/~archive/chiapas95/1997.08/msg00291.html).

20 It was rumoured that the Mexican president, Vicente Fox, overlooked an ideal ministerial candidate when naming his cabinet in 2000 on the grounds of her sexuality.

21 Gutmann (1996: 132) offers an example of a woman who has ongoing affairs although she's married; he tempers this (137) with comments that women's affairs are viewed more harshly than men's.

22 In Mexico Gloria Trevi became the region's version of the singer Madonna with her raunchy image that was overtly sexual. She became an idol for many young women and some people considered her to be a generally positive image since she expressed confident young womanhood and control. This vision was crushed when she was accused of helping her older manager to seduce young girls who were recruited as dancers for her show. When she was finally arrested in Brazil she became as much a victim as the girls and the image of being in control was shattered. The overt use of female sexuality was shown to be a high-risk strategy pushing her to the heights of fame but also to infamy. In defending herself she declared herself to be a roman and apostolic Catholic (not a member of a satanic sect). The verbiage in the reporting shows the difficulties that many still have in engaging with female sexuality.

REFERENCES AND SELECTED FURTHER READING

Abiodun, N. 2001: Havana's *Jineteras*. *NACLA: Report on the Americas* 34, 5, 24–5.

Alvarez, S. 1990: *Engendering Democracy in Brazil*. Princeton, NJ: Princeton University Press.

Amuchástegui Herrera, A. 1998: Saber o no saber sobre el sexo: los dilemas de la actividad sexual femenina para jóvenes Mexicanos. In I. Sasz and S. Lerner (eds), *Sexualidades en México: Algunas Aproximaciones desde la Perspectiva de las Ciencias Sociales*. México DF: El Colegio de México, 107–35.

Anthias, F. and Yuval-Davis, N. 1989: *Racialized Boundaries: Race, Nation, Gender, Colour and Class and the Anti-Racist Struggle*. London: Routledge.

Archetti, E. 1996: Playing styles and masculine virtues in Argentine football. In M. Melhuus and K. A. Stolen (eds), *Machos, Mistresses and Madonnas: Contesting the Power of Gender Imagery*. London: Verso, 34–55.

Arguelles, L. 1998: Crazy wisdom: memories of a Cuban queer. In A. Darder and R. D. Torres (eds), *The Latino Studies Reader: Culture, Economy and Society*. Oxford and Malden, MA: Blackwell, 206–10.

Barker, G. and Lowenstein, I. 1997: Where the boys are: attitudes related to masculinity, fatherhood and violence toward women among low-income adolescent and young adult males in Rio de Janeiro, Brazil. *Youth and Society* 29, 2, 166–96.

Buffington, R. 1997: *Los Jotos*: contested visions of homosexuality in modern Mexico. In D. Balderston and D. J. Guy (eds), *Sex and Sexuality in Latin America*. New York and London: New York University Press, 118–32.

Caulfield, S. 1997: The birth of mangue: race, nation and politics of prostitution in Rio Janeiro 1850–1942. In D. Balderston and D. J. Guy (eds), *Sex and Sexuality in Latin America*. New York and London: New York University Press, 86–100.

Caulfield, S. 2000: *In Defense of Honor: Sexual Morality, Modernity and Nation in Early Twentieth-Century Brazil*. Durham, NC, and London: Duke University Press.

Chaney, E. 1979: *Supermadre: Women in Politics in Latin America*. Austin: University of Texas Press for the Institute of Latin American Studies.

Chant, S. with Craske, N. 2003: Gender and sexuality. In S. Chant with N. Craske, *Gender in Latin America*. London: LAB/New Jersey: Rutgers University Press, 128–60.

Craske, N. 1999: *Women and Politics in Latin America*. Cambridge: Polity.

Dávalos López, E. 1998: La sexualidad en los pueblos Meso-Americanos prehispánicos: un panorama general. In I. Sasz and S. Lerner (eds), *Sexualidades en México: Algunas Aproximaciones desde la Perspectiva de las Ciencias Sociales*. México DF: El Colegio de México, 71–106.

Figueroa Perea, J. G. and Rivera Reyes, G. 1993: Algunas reflexiones sobre la representación social de la sexualidad femenina. In S. González Montes (ed.), *Mujeres y Relaciones de Género en la Antropología Latinoamericana*. México DF: El Colegio de México, 141–67.

Fisher, J. 1993: *Out of the Shadows: Women, Resistance and Politics in South America*. London: LAB Books.

Franco, J. 2001: Bodies in contention. *NACLA: Report on the Americas* 34, 5, 41–4.

Green, J. N. 1999: *Beyond Carnival: Male Homosexuality in Twentieth-Century Brazil*. Chicago: University of Chicago Press.

Gutmann, M. 1996: *The Meanings of Macho: Being a Man in Mexico City*. Berkeley: University of California Press.

Gutmann, M. 1997: The meaning of being macho: changing male identities. In Louise Lamphere, Helena Ragoné and Patricia Zavella (eds), *Situated Lives: Gender and Culture in Everyday Life*. New York and London: Routledge, 223–4.

Guy, D. J. 2000: *White Slavery and Mothers Alive and Dead: The Troubled Meetings of Sex, Gender, Public Health and Progress in Latin America*. Lincoln: University of Nebraska Press.

Hocquenghem, A. M. 1987: *Iconografía Mochica*. Lima: Pontificia Universidad Católica del Perú/Fondo Editorial.

Hodge, G. D. 2001: Colonization of the Cuban body: the growth of male sex workers' Havana. *NACLA: Report on the Americas* 34, 5, 20–8.

Horrocks, R. 1997: *An Introduction to the Study of Sexuality*. Basingstoke: Macmillan.

Jaquette, J. (ed.) 1994: *The Women's Movement in Latin America: Participation and Democracy*. Boulder, CO: Westview Press.

Kulick, D. 1998: Fe/male trouble: the unsettling places of lesbians in the self-images of Brazilian travesti prostitutes. *Sexualities* 1, 3, 299–312.

Lancaster, R. 1997a: On homosexualities in Latin America (and other places). *American Ethnologist* 24, 1, 193–202.

Lancaster, R. 1997b: Guto's performance: notes on the transvestism of everyday life. In D. Balderston and D. J. Guy (eds), *Sex and Sexuality in Latin America*. New York: New York University Press, 9–32.

Lancaster, R. 1998: Transgenderism in Latin America: some critical introductory remarks on identities and practice. *Sexualities* 1, 3, 261–74.

Lumsden, I. 1996: *Machos, Maricones and Gays: Cuba and Homosexuality*. Philadelphia, PA: Temple University Press.

Melhuus, M. 1996: Power, value and the amiguous meaning of gender. In M. Melhuus and K. A. Stolen (eds), *Machos, Mistresses and Madonnas: Contesting the Power of Gender Imagery*. London: Verso, 230–59.

Meznaric, S. 1994: Gender as an ethno-marker: rape, war and identity politics in the former Yugoslavia. In V. M. Moghadam (ed.), *Identity Politics and Women: Cultural Reassertions and Feminisms in International Perspective*. Boulder, CO: Westview Press, 76–97.

Miller, F. 1991: *Latin American Women and the Search for Social Justice*. Hanover: University Press of New England.

Mirandé, A. 1998: *Hombres y Machos: Masculinity and Latino Culture*. Boulder, CO: Westview Press.

Molyneux, M. and Craske, N. 2002: The local, the regional and the global: transforming the politics of rights. In N. Craske and M. Molyneux (eds), *Gender and the Politics of Rights and Democracy in Latin America*. Basingstoke: Palgrave, 1–31.

Murray, S. O. 1995: *Latin American Male Homosexualities*. With additional contributions by Manuel Arboleda *et al*. Albuquerque: University of New Mexico Press.

Nencel, L. 1996: *Pacharacas*, *putas* and *chicas de su casa*: labelling, femininity and men's sexual selves in Lima, Peru. In M. Melhuus and K. A. Stolen (eds), *Machos, Mistresses and Madonnas: Contesting the Power of Gender Imagery*. London: Verso, 56–83.

Osterman, A. C. and Keller-Cohen, D. 1998: 'Good girls go to heaven; bad girls. . .' learn to be good: quizzes in American and Brazilian teenage girls' magazines. *Discourse and Society* 9, 4, 531–58.

Padgug, R. A. 1999: Sexual matters: on conceptualizing sexuality in history. In R. Parker and P. Aggleton (eds), *Culture, Society and Sexuality: A Reader*. London: UCL Press, 15–28.

Parker, R. 1999: 'Within four walls': Brazilian sexual culture and HIV/AIDS. In R. Parker and P. Aggleton (eds), *Culture, Society and Sexuality: A Reader*. London: UCL Press, 253–66.

Prieur, A. 1996: Domination and desire: male homosexuality and the construction of masculinity in Mexico. In M. Melhuus and K. A. Stolen (eds), *Machos, Mistresses and Madonnas: Contesting the Power of Gender Imagery*. London: Verso, 83–107.

Radcliffe, S. and Westwood, S. (eds) 1993: *Viva: Women and Popular Protest in Latin America*. London: Routledge.

Rivas Zivy, M. 1998: Valores, creencias y significaciones de la sexualidad femenina: una reflexión indispensable para la comprensión de las prácticas sexuales. In I. Sasz and S. Lerner (eds), *Sexualidades en México: Algunas Aproximaciones desde la Perspectiva de las Ciencias Sociales*. México DF: El Colegio de México, 137–54.

Schifter, J. and Madrigal, J. 2000: *The Sexual Construction of Latino Youth: Implications for the Spread of HIV/AIDS*. New York, London and Oxford: Haworth Hispanic/Latino Press.

Shepard, B. 2000: The 'double discourse' on sexual and reproductive rights in Latin America: the chasm between public policy and private actions. *Health and Human Rights* 4, 2, 110–43.

Sifuentes Jáuregui, B. 1997: Gender without limits: transvestism and subjectivity in *El lugar sin límites*. In D. Balderston and D. J. Guy (eds), *Sex and Sexuality in Latin America*. New York and London: New York University Press, 44–61.

Smith, J. 2001: *Moralities: Sex, Money and Power in the 21st Century*. London: Penguin Press.

Stavans, I. 1998: The Latin phallus. In A. Darder and R. D. Torres (eds), *The Latino Studies Reader: Culture, Economy and Society*. Oxford and Malden, MA: Blackwell, 228–39.

Stavig, W. 1995: 'Living in offense of Our Lord': indigenous sexual values and marital life in the colonial crucible. *Hispanic American Historical Review* 75, 4, 598–622.

Stephen, L. 1997: *Women and Social Movements in Latin America*. Austin: University of Texas Press.

Thayer, M. 1997: Identity, revolution and democracy: lesbian movements in Central America. *Social Problems* 44, 3, 386–407.

Trexler, R. C. 1995: *Sex and Conquest: Gendered Violence, Political Order and the European Conquest of the Americas*. Ithaca, NY: Cornell University Press.

Valdés, T. and Gomáriz, E. 1995: *Latin American Women: Compared Figures*. Santiago de Chile: FLACSO/Madrid: Instituto de la Mujer.

Weeks, J. 2000: *Making Sexual History*. Cambridge: Polity Press.

Wilford, R. and Miller, R. L. (eds) 1998: *Women, Ethnicity and Nationalism: The Politics of Transition*. London: Routledge.

Willmott, C. 2002: Constructing citizenship in the *poblaciónes* of Santiago, Chile: the role of reproductive and sexual rights. In N. Craske and M. Molyneux (eds), *Gender and the Politics of Rights and Democracy in Latin America*. Basingstoke: Palgrave, 124–48.

Yarbro-Bejarano, Y. 1997: Crossing the border with Chabela Vargas: a chicana femme's tribute. In D. Balderston and D. J. Guy (eds), *Sex and Sexuality in Latin America*. New York and London: New York University Press, 33–43.

Yuval-Davis, N. 1997: *Gender and Nation*. London: Sage.

Yuval-Davis, N. and Anthias, F. 1989: *Woman, Nation, State*. Basingstoke: Macmillan.

12

Latin American Studies and the global system

Jon Beasley-Murray

> Clap your hands once
> And clap your hands twice
> And if it looks like this
> Then you're doing it right
> (Lou Bega, 'Mambo No. 5')

VIRAL *LATINIDAD*

In July 2001 the London *Guardian*'s front page announced the arrival of a new and particularly infectious Internet virus.[1] The virus, dubbed W32/SirCam@MM or SirCam, raided its victim's hard drive for a random file, which it then distributed to other addresses, attached to an email message taking that file's title as its subject line. Company files, student essays, poetry, recipes, holiday snaps and more were all randomly redistributed and recontextualized to produce strange new mixtures.[2] The private was made public, and even official secrets were compromised.[3] Moreover, what made the virus particularly hard to detect was the fact that it came camouflaged, spread by messages whose subject headings were always different. Unlike the famous 'Love Bug' virus (propagated via emails that announced 'I Love You!'), here computer users could not know they had received a suspect message until they read the message text. This text, however, was always more or less the same, in English or, more often, in Spanish. The virus addressed its recipients in an upbeat, friendly, and almost intimate manner: 'Hola como estas? Te mando este archivo para que me des tu punto de vista. Nos vemos pronto, gracias.' Intimate agent of hybridity and *mestizaje*: SirCam was, after all, a Latin American virus.

We could take SirCam to be both symptom and metaphor for a new relation between Latin America and the world. Traditionally, Latin America has been portrayed in the West as exotic, distant and different; indeed, for

Tzvetan Todorov, Columbus's arrival in the Americas in 1492 constituted Europe's discovery of 'the exterior Other', and continues to serve as the model for the relation between 'self' and 'other' (Todorov 1984: 50). Even for much of the twentieth century, Latin America could be envisaged as a strange, primitive territory, as 'magical' as it was real (and it was, precisely, under the rubric of 'Magical Realism' that its culture was consumed in Europe and the USA); Latin America was alluring perhaps, but irredeemably different nonetheless. These days, however, thanks in part to the technology and the globalizing forces that give us the Internet and its attendant viruses, Latin America appears to be itself viral, and hence familiar, even intimate. What we might term *latinidad* (to describe whatever properties are, at any given time, ascribed to Latin American culture) has been 'de-territorialized', crossing national and regional borders to break free from the geographical territory of Latin America itself. *Latinidad* is contagious, circulating through the most diverse of networks, cropping up in the most unexpected of places, making new connections with strange, hybrid results. Like the SirCam virus, this de-territorialized Latin America comes in many guises: *latinidad* is felt as a sense of style or spirit; it is an affect or feeling often associated with food, dress, dance, music and sexuality, but also transferable to other commodities or activities. *Latinidad* can affect anyone, anywhere. Yet, unlike other viruses, this is an infection to be welcomed. We can all be Latin Americans now, and we all *want* to be Latin Americans, too: in the words of Lou Bega's 'Mambo No. 5', 'if it looks like this, then you're doing it right'.[4]

In this chapter, I examine the infectious propagation of this Latin spirit, and then investigate its material and historical roots, to uncover a hidden history of the 'global system', that is, the networks of communication, power and exchange that constitute our world. I argue that Latin America has in fact always been viral, that it has never been confined to any specific geographical locality, but that the spread of *latinidad* has taken place for the most part underground, beneath the level of consciousness. Historically, therefore, this infectious spread of Latin spirit has been overlooked; when its symptoms have been noted, it has been regarded with some suspicion. It is only recently, with its current outbreak, that this infectious *latinidad* has been both acknowledged and (generally) welcomed. In response to these changes, Latin American Studies itself will surely change. What should emerge will be a new Latin Americanism, appropriate to its new object, but also better prepared to re-evaluate this fluid history in a new light. A new Latin Americanism may build on the most significant tendencies of the old Latin Americanism – dependency theory, which held sway in the 1960s and 1970s, and post-colonial theory, from the 1980s and 1990s – but it should also move beyond them, perhaps to become viral itself in a bid to track down and understand both the contemporary spread and the historical roots of viral *latinidad*.

LATIN SPIRIT

A number of factors contribute to the contagiousness of *latinidad*. Most obviously, the USA acts as a mediating agent, carrier of a Latin spirit that takes advantage of the promiscuous ubiquity of its host. Latin American immigration to the USA, and a high birth-rate among Latinos in the USA, are producing profound demographic changes within what is now the world's sole superpower.[5] Latinos are displacing African-Americans as the USA's largest minority group, and becoming a majority in some areas. In turn, this demographic expansion is gradually being turned into political and cultural influence: both George W. Bush and Al Gore went out of their way to court the Latino vote during the 2000 US presidential election campaign, while the growth of Spanish-language television, radio and music is prompting advertisers and corporations to address and adapt to this vibrant sector of the economy. In consequence, and as the USA thus becomes a Latin American country, Hollywood and the all-pervasive US music industry act as a conveyer belt for the spread of *latinidad* elsewhere – profiting from the (re-)export of Latin stars such as Jennifer Lopez, Jimmy Smits or Salma Hayek.

But demography is not everything. The US entertainment industry has always had its Latinos and Latinas – such as Rita Hayworth, Anthony Quinn or Raquel Welch. Yet such stars usually did not *act* Latin; indeed, often they went to some lengths (changing their names, for instance: Hayworth was born Margarita Carmen Cansino; Quinn was born Antonio Rudolfo Oaxaca Quinn) to disguise the fact of their Latin heritage and to 'pass' as Anglo-American. Such 'passing' is perhaps easier for Latinos than for other ethnic groups, in that *latinidad* is less clearly tied to race than are other ethnic identities – Hispanics are the one group counted in the US census not to be regarded as a racial group. We can thus mark a distinction between being and acting, between essence and *performance*. *Latinidad* is more a performance than it is an essential quality, more a matter of acting than of being; or rather, being (being Latin American) is determined as much by acting as it is by demography, biology or geography.[6] As Latino identity becomes more obviously unmoored from any essence, so it becomes more freely available for appropriation and recycling; it is its performative character that means that Latin American identity has come to seem transferable, that we can all be Latin Americans now.

None of this is to suggest that (for instance) *latinidad* is 'simply' an act, that everybody is in a position to take on whatever identity they choose, or that either anti-Latino discrimination or the structural inequality between Latinos and Anglos have somehow disappeared. It is still true (for instance) that Latinos in the USA are much more likely to be employed in low-wage, low-status jobs, just as Latin America as a whole remains subject to the economic, political and cultural neo-imperialism of (particularly) the USA. Moreover, it is likewise true that the very notion of *latinidad* also serves to obscure differences between and among Latino or Latin American communities, just as it suppresses differences between those who 'act' Latin. On the other hand, it would be wrong to see the spread of Latin spirit as 'simply' ideological, or simply the result of publicity campaigns dreamt up in the higher reaches of corporate capitalism. As Arlene Dávila argues, 'these processes are not properly seen as a top-down development, resulting from the commodification and appropriation of Latino culture . . .; rather, they stem from the contrary involvement of and negotiations between dominant, imposed, and self-generated interests' (Dávila 2001: 16–17). Clearly, Lou Bega or (as we will see later) Bacardi do not tell us all we need to know about Latin identity; yet they may tell us more than they intend, in that they are also symptoms of more general changes within the global system, among which may be a realignment of the relation between ideology and reality. Everything points towards a recognition of the slipperiness and availability of *latinidad*. This should not lead to uncritical celebration: on the one hand a recognition of the slipperiness inherent in *latinidad* may also be a misrecognition in that though it may be that we can all be Latin American, we should not forget that we will not all be Latin American in the same way; and on the other hand, any unsettling of fixed identities is not necessarily liberatory in that at the same time new forms of inequality open up, predicated on performativity. Still, re-examining Latin America from the perspective of its now ubiquitous, viral globalization corrects the more rigid and perhaps now unworkable perspectives that have dominated Latin American Studies.

For the slipperiness of *latinidad*, albeit more recognized and more accepted today, is not in itself necessarily new, and it has not always been welcomed. First, those who have wished to lay claim to Latin American identity have wrestled with the fact that it seems so difficult to pin it down. The entire history of Latin American intellectual self-reflection can be read as an agonized attempt to answer the question 'who are we?' and as a series of responses to an apparent failure to achieve a stable sense of identity. This failure to achieve identity, in turn, has been seen as allowing for Latin America's dependence upon external influences. It was with the aim of achieving true independence (from Europe and North America alike) that the Cuban writer José Martí claimed that 'the pressing need of Our America is to show itself as it is, one in spirit and intent, swift conquerors of a suffocating past' (Martí 1999: 119); but what if Latin America is *not* 'one in spirit and intent'? Second, the instability of Latin American identity could also appear threatening to those wishing to avoid 'catching' *latinidad*. Europeans and North Americans, for instance, have often described their experiences of travel to Latin America as disturbing their own sense of themselves: from Columbus's report that some of his crew 'got the pagan notion that we had been bewitched and still persist in the belief' (Columbus 1969: 298) to Joan Didion's account of the effect of El Salvador's 1980s' civil war on US visitors – 'each in his or her own way inexorably altered by the fact of having been in a certain place at a certain time . . . like survivors of a common natural disaster, they are equally marked by the place' (Didion 1983: 98) – we see the experience of *latinidad* unsettling otherwise fixed identities. Such unsettling experiences were often read within modernity as signs of the persistence of premodern, archaic (and savage) elements; now, however, they are increasingly welcomed as part of a postmodern disbelief in essences.

Hence if, as Benigno Trigo also shows, Latin America has continuously been diagnosed as suffering a 'general state of crisis' that has often been presented in terms of 'an acute metaphoric disease' (Trigo 2000: 1), this infection now seems to have reached epidemic proportions, and to have merged with and become itself symptom of the fact that with postmodernity all identities are fluid and both under- and over-determined (in that none of us seems to possess any one identity fully, yet we all are possessed by multiple identities). A globalized postmodernity provides the context for the spread of *latinidad*, the petri dish culture within which the virus develops and reproduces. This culture has elements that are corporate and commodifying (Taco Bell, *Buena Vista Social Club*, Bacardi) and others that are more free-wheeling, almost covert (SirCam, *zapatismo*, currency crises). Although the fragmentation and flow that globalization entails still sometimes provoke fear or opposition (as expressed, variously, by anti-capitalist protestors at Seattle or by Western governments' campaigns against 'asylum seekers'), in general we seem to have heeded Slavoj Zizek's advice to 'enjoy your symptom' (Zizek 1992). Certainly in Western Europe, *latinidad* now comes coded in terms of leisure, relaxation and entertainment. With the end not only of the Cold War, but also of the Latin American dictatorships, there has been a broad shift in the image of Latin America from an association with struggles for political liberation and high culture (say, Che Guevara and Gabriel García Márquez) to an association with sexual liberation and mass culture (Shakira and Ricky Martin). And although these associations are not necessarily novel – indeed, in part they repeat earlier images offered by, say, the 1940s' film star Carmen Miranda or the original 'king of Mambo', Dámaso Pérez Prado – they coincide with an era in which *latinidad* is more available than ever, rather than something that has to be represented to us by the cultural ambassadors of Good Neighborliness.[7] In postmodernity, the intimacy of association replaces the distance of representation.

Together, then, geo-demography, performativity, history and postmodernity constitute and propagate a new, global, Latin America – and consequently require a globalized, perhaps similarly viral, Latin Americanism. In other words, if the object of Latin American Studies has mutated, then the subject (in both senses) must likewise mutate to keep pace with it, albeit perhaps to find that traditional distinctions between subject and object can no longer be maintained.

An indication of the pressures forcing such a mutation can also be seen in the general crisis of Area Studies. Area Studies consists in the academic division of the world into relatively self-contained regional objects of specialization – East Asia Studies, African Studies, Latin American Studies, and so on. Within this framework, historians, political scientists, sociologists, cultural critics (and so on) work in more or less interdisciplinary manner, their basis for cooperation being the relatively stable institutional site from which the so-called 'developing' world's crises could be observed. Though Area Studies draws on the legacy of what Edward Said (1979) terms 'Orientalism' (to describe the relations between the study of the Middle East and the politics of European imperial projects), it is also, and especially in the case of Latin American Studies, a product of US post-Second World War geo-political (and thus neo-imperial) interests. At root, the project of Area Studies is to 'know thy (potential) enemy' (which equally entails the project of representing him *as* a potential enemy), but this project enters into crisis once it becomes more difficult to differentiate foe from friend; or rather, once globalization unhinges the machinery of representation that constructs the difference between foe and friend. For if it is now recognized that there is no absolutely external viewpoint from which to delineate the neatly compartmentalized global system that Area Studies presents, the entire academic enterprise (and with it Latin American Studies) enters into the crisis that it intended to manage; it becomes part of the problem, rather than part of the solution.

Yet beyond being simply a critique of the old Latin Americanism and its attempt to construct a transcendent, external viewpoint, any new Latin Americanism must be immanent to the new Latin America, and must thereby produce new forms of understanding and knowledge. In the course of this re-positioning, it may become clearer that the contemporary spread of Latin spirit is not simply the result of a recent if relatively rapid demographic explosion confined to one country, but is a symptom of a broader history that can tell us much about the constitution of the global system as a whole. As an entry into this new Latin Americanism, let us consider a case study of one way in which the new Latin America is interwoven with contemporary British culture.

LEARNING FROM BACARDI

Following the British Labour Party's general election victory of 1997, the UK witnessed a brief cultural efflorescence soon labelled 'Cool Britannia'. London was suddenly the place to be, British culture (from Oasis to Damien Hirst) was hitting the headlines and admired abroad, and there was a mood of optimism and confidence in Britain's place on the world stage. It was as though pent-up social energies had been released after eighteen years of more or less insular conservative Little Englandism. Though this bubble soon burst, Cool Britannia did mark a significant shift in the relation between British culture and the world. Ironically, what may seem to have been a highpoint of nationalism in fact served as beach-head for a new internationalism. For although this efflorescence seemed to be marked by all the signs of national pride (marketed as a series of brands: 'BritArt', 'BritPop' and so on), in fact it can now be seen as the point at which the British embraced the consequences of globalization. And while most recently the symptom of this embrace of globality has been first the (previously unimaginable) acceptance and then the practical canonization of a Swedish manager for the England soccer team, in fact it was *latinidad* that led the way and undid the defences of national parochialism. For from the outset, Latin America functioned as the cultural unconscious of Cool Britannia.

Nowhere was this more clearly suggested than in the advertising campaigns for Bacardi Breezers, which explicitly played with the idea of a subterranean *latinidad* underwriting British society. Breezers are a range of bottled, pre-mixed and carbonated drinks combining Bacardi rum with fruit flavours such as orange, watermelon, pineapple and peach. Breezers were introduced in the mid-1990s, and by the late 1990s were the subject of concerted cross-media advertising.[8] The television campaign consisted of a number of spots featuring young men and women in situations in which they have to present themselves to an embodiment of social hierarchy and respectability: at a job interview or on a psychoanalyst's couch; introducing a girlfriend to the parents or being shown around a flat by a landlady.[9] In each case, and in a rather sombre, grey British setting, the advertisement's protagonist faces an inquisition that then prompts what we take to be flashbacks, transposing and subverting the questions asked through vividly colourful depictions of frenzy and decadence, set in some generic Latin American location. The protagonist's task is to answer the questions posed as truthfully as possible without revealing the true (decadent and Latin) significance of the answers given. So, for example, in the 'interview' advertisement, as the interview panel comb the candidate's curriculum vitae and ask 'an interest in ornithology?', there is a rapid cut to a scene of the interviewee leaping in an outsized bird outfit through a foreign street in some crazed post-*Carnaval* dawn. A further cut then returns us to the interview scene, governed by a ticking clock measuring out the patience of its subdued candidate. Each advertisement ends with a close-up on the product and the slogan 'there's a bit of Latin spirit in everyone'.

Bacardi, then, portrays British youth, protagonists of Cool Britannia, as split subjects: frenetic party animals by night, but prepared (at least to appear) to conform by day. The point here is not so much that Bacardi is purveying a set of stereotypical images of Latin sensuality – it is, though its depictions of British restraint are equally stereotypical. The point is rather that these two stereotypes are seen as complementary: in tension but not necessarily in contradiction. The relation between Britain and Latin America is not here the relation between (familiar) self and (exotic) other; rather, it is an internal division, between different aspects of the same subject. The fact that one advertisement sets its protagonist on a psychoanalyst's couch is hardly insignificant; Bacardi purports to perform a dissection of British psychosocial structures, along almost classically Freudian lines (youthful ego, traditionalist superego, Latin id).

Latinidad, it is implied, has made its way deep into our collective psyche; literally, we have ingested a Latin spirit that is now fully under our skin. Indeed, if there is 'a bit of Latin spirit in everyone', it is to be found in that part of the psychic apparatus that psychoanalysis declares to be key to the meaning and significance of the whole. Thanks to Bacardi, we consume and internalize Latin America, and perhaps it is only such (night-to-night) internalization that motivates us to continue in our external, day-to-day lives. The Latin American unconscious both informs and motivates the British conscious and its associated rituals of social deference – although, naturally, for this corporate incarnation of postmodern *latinidad*, it never completely *upsets* it. Though the questions posed by authority always threaten to reveal the subject's unconscious desires, and so to unmask his or her social compliance as a sham, in fact social decorum is always maintained. Rationality, the profit principle, and familial cohesion are perhaps (to adopt another liquid metaphor) shaken, but not stirred. We are encouraged simultaneously to act out our Latin desires, and to repress and sublimate them.

THE SOCIAL LIFE OF THINGS

Bacardi offers us a dual reading of the place of *latinidad* within the global system – to show us that *latinidad* has always served as an integral if subordinate part of the world-wide circulation of desires and commodities. Even in its appropriation and stereotyping of Latin American culture (with the aim, in the end, of selling us a given product), its advertising can be read also as a revelation, an acknowledgement of a historic role that Bacardi, too, has ambivalently both repressed and depended upon. Emphasizing the immediate co-presence of a Latin unconscious always pressing upon consciousness, threatening to destabilize social order, these advertisements underline the complexity of Latin America's place within the global system.

Bacardi's own relation to Latin America is, after all, fairly complex, and says something about the pre-history of contemporary globalization incarnated in what Arjun Appadurai (1996) calls 'the social life of things'. Despite its claim to bottle 'Latin spirit' and the centrality of the commemoration 'Established Cuba, 1862' in its trademark bat symbol, the company has no simple national or regional affiliation. Founded by an immigrant Catalan (hence the family name was originally accented on the final syllable: Bacardí), the firm was in the 1940s and 1950s strongly associated with Cuba's pre-Revolution Batista regime and its assets were quickly confiscated after Castro's take-over, the family fleeing the island for the USA in October 1960, prompting a long-running lawsuit over the ownership of both trademark and name. Its corporate headquarters is now in the Bahamas, though it imports molasses from plantation holdings in Puerto Rico, Mexico and Brazil, and has distilleries in Puerto Rico and Mexico. It claims to have been the number one spirit brand in the USA since 1978 and, in the course of its branding, especially for the US market, deliberately distanced itself from its Cuban roots. In Puerto Rico, site of the firm's largest distillery, Bacardi advertised under the slogan 'Manos puertorriqueñas' ('Puerto Rican Hands') and sponsored the Bacardi Folk Arts Fair so as to associate the company with this premier expression of Puerto Rican cultural identity (see Dávila 1997: 232–45). In the USA itself, Bacardi went to great lengths to 'de-latinize' its identity, presenting its rum as the ideal mixer – a perfect instance of modest *mestizaje* – and in the 1960s teaming up to produce joint advertising campaigns with that quintessentially North American brand, Coca-Cola. By the end of the decade (less than ten years after leaving the island), 'the one thing the brand *didn't* stand for . . . was Cuba, with its political complications and personal resentments' (Foster 1990: 156). In the late 1980s Peter Foster could write that:

> The [Bacardi] business empire . . . has found a niche in a global, commercial culture whose symbols are most often associated with the U.S., but whose reality transcends any notion of nationality. In fact, Bacardi has become the ultimate global company. It has no holding company or head office. Its most precious asset, its name, is held in a lawyer's office in Liechtenstein. Its family shareholders live in a dozen different countries. Its image depends on national preference: quality in Mexico, mixability in the U.S.; sun, sand, and sea in Europe. (Foster 1990: 247)

Arguably, then, Bacardi's corporate structure prefigures the model followed by companies such as Nike or Benetton, which have attracted more attention in recent debates over globalization. Unnoticed, this instance of viral Latin Americanism anticipated the major economic and corporate changes of the 1990s. It was only with the new millennium that it resurfaced, visibly re-latinized.

The global significance of rum, however, long predates Bacardi's foundation: through rum, Latin America helped anchor the commercial flows of imperial modernity. Rum, distilled in New England from Caribbean molasses, was a vital component of the slave-trading circuit of colonialism. As Fernando Ortiz says, 'alcohol was always the cargo for the slaver's return trip, for with it slaves were bought, local chieftains bribed, and the African tribes corrupted and weakened' (Ortiz 1995: 25). Rum also served as (literally) an essential solution for the medical advances enabling fleets to remain at sea for the long periods that the maintenance of global maritime security demanded.[10] By the 1960s, white rum had become fashionable among the newly adventurous middle classes, and in the popular form of Bacardi and Coke offered a nice synergy between modern imperialism and postmodern cultural imperialism. More fundamentally, sugar – and both rum and coke are essentially just flavoured sugar derivatives – has always been a global trade; indeed, Sidney Mintz (1985) notes how Latin American sugar, along with the tobacco, coffee and tea with which it is closely linked, helped establish and develop both a world market abroad and a mass market at home. Ortiz argues that 'the production of sugar was always a capitalistic venture because of its great territorial and industrial scope and the size of its long-term investments' (Ortiz 1995: 56).

Sugar grown in the Spanish, Portuguese, French and British Latin American and Caribbean colonies thus led directly as well as indirectly to the growth of industrial capitalism, and hence development, in Europe.[11] At the same time, the way those colonies (later independent nations) came to be dependent upon sugar production for external markets retarded their own development: dependent upon a single crop that had to be exported at prices set on the world market, they were unable to develop an internal market or diversified industry. Moreover, sugar cane, the 'selfish plant' (Galeano 1973: 71), is notorious for the way in which it exhausts soils. No wonder, then, that the material unconscious that a study of the rum and sugar industry opens up – unconscious because all too quickly repressed by theorists of development – should provide the basis for the 1960s' dependency theory that explained Latin America's economic woes by reference to the region's historically unequal place in the global system. Dependency theory, in the words of Fernando Henrique Cardoso and Enzo Faletto, argues that because advanced economies 'require complementarity from dependent economies', this ensures that the latter 'remain dependent [in that] their capital goods production sectors are not strong enough to ensure continuous advance of the system' (1979: xxi). The North, thus, develops only in so far as it ensures the development of underdevelopment in the South; the aim of dependency theory was, in part, to demonstrate Latin America's crucial, albeit unacknowledged, driving role in the global system.

Throughout the 1960s and 1970s, dependency theory (especially as popularized by Eduardo Galeano and by André Gunder Frank) served as a powerful theoretical tool that placed Latin America (and the Third World more generally) 'on the map', both in that it was an intellectual current that originated in Latin America and in that it offered a fairly sophisticated understanding of the political and economic relations that structured the global system. Dependency theory thus provided a justification for Latin American Studies: Latin America would be the source of new ideas (not simply the arena for point of application for ideas derived elsewhere); and analyses of the world economic system would no longer be complete without an understanding of the 'unequal exchange' whereby Latin American raw materials were appropriated by European and US manufacturing industries. Perhaps against the grain of the field's foundation, Latin American Studies thereby also gained a critical edge: it was no longer so unequivocally aligned with First World interests. And as the political balance of and within the field seemed to shift (also with the 1959 Cuban Revolution and the 1970 election of Salvador Allende's socialist government in Chile), Latin American Studies began to serve for some as a politicized arena for solidarity and commitment. At the very least, it became a contested space, a context within which students and researchers in Europe and the USA became open to other influences and alternative potential models of social organization. As what was once unconscious, taken for granted in the global flow of unequal trade, became available for criticism and dispute, so a terrain of ideological struggle opened up.

A GEOGRAPHY OF DESIRE

In their focus upon ideology, politics and economics, what dependency theory and the concept of Latin America as the West's material unconscious omit, however, is the question of desire. The material unconscious of production and distribution does not in itself explain the way in which commodities have to be desired to be consumed; even sweetness, as Mintz shows, is not a natural taste. Advertising is the industry dedicated to producing desire, and if we return to the Bacardi advertisements we see that their aim is to excite, and then frustrate (and so perpetuate), desire. In the 'psychoanalyst' advertisement, the analyst's question is 'tell me the first thing that comes into your head'. This prompts a series of narrative fragments of Latin sexual adventure, but the full narratives – and the full answer to the question – are foreclosed when the woman replies 'chocolate', provoking a frustrated grunt projected onto the analyst, who expects to hear something much more revealing.

This then is Latin America as exotic and primitive other, locus of sensuality and the primitive. This is a familiar trope of colonialism and it is no accident that Latin America, the first world region to be colonized by a European state, should remain a privileged incarnation of both noble savagery and sensuous abandon. But with desire comes fear. From the moment of the first Spanish conquest, the continent has provoked an intense ambivalence – represented by Bacardi with a bottle spinning between the chalk-marked words 'love' and 'hate'. The fear is that Latin America is a locale in which even the most rational of colonial administrators could somehow take desire too far, taking leave of their senses to demonstrate some innate solidarity with the disturbingly familiar yet disturbingly strange indigenous population of (perhaps) cannibals and sorcerers. Desire leads us to become Latin, and so, shockingly, other to ourselves.

Western culture has been haunted by this ambivalent reaction to its other, from Shakespeare's *The Tempest* to Conan Doyle's *The Lost World*, Lowry's *Under the Volcano*, or Herzog's *Aguirre, Wrath of God*, to refer only to some of the most explicit thematizations of a feeling that we are both threateningly tempted and haunted by Latin spirits and monsters. Within Latin America, *The*

Tempest particularly has become a template on which intellectuals have embroidered differing conceptions of their place in the global system and their relations (or their desired relations) either to primitivism or to modernism. Hence for José Enrique Rodó's *Ariel*, modernity lies in the ethereal spirit of Shakespeare's play; while for Roberto Fernández Retamar's *Caliban*, it is the play's earthy figure of indigenous autonomy that suggests a more liberatory future. Yet within this ambivalence, and as Michael Taussig argues, the spectre is raised that modernity and development themselves are but another mode of superstition, that modernism and primitivism are 'co-determining magics, the one cradled in the hope of the future offered and simultaneously denied by the modern world, the other in the dream mythology latent in that hope, drawn on the imagined origin of things' (Taussig 1987: 282).

Post-colonial theory has taken this Western preoccupation with the apparently thin line that separates civilization from 'barbarism' as a rich seam to mine. Theorists from Frantz Fanon to Homi Bhabha have shown how developmentalist assumptions themselves, in imagining that the South can follow where the North leads, invoke the panic of mimicry and mimesis. On the one hand, the West has to define itself against the non-West; identity is constituted in the border between rational consciousness and the sensual unconscious. On the other hand, that border is constantly threatened both as the West imbibes sensuality and as non-Western societies increasingly seem to mimic and parody our own. This is an inevitably hybrid global system in which Latin America is one of the prime markers of what disrupts any confident assertions about the axis of history.

In the wake of dependency theory's disrepute (and out of the crisis of Marxism, which unravelled for Latin American Studies between Pinochet's 1973 coup in Chile and the Nicaraguan Sandinistas' 1990 electoral defeat), post-colonial theory has proved to be one of the most productive alternative critical approaches in the 1980s and 1990s. Though some disagree that the label 'post-colonial' entirely fits Latin America (certainly the history of the region's decolonization differs from that of the parts of Asia and Africa for and within which post-colonial theory was developed), even the debate as to whether Latin America might be considered post-colonial has itself helped encourage and interrogate new ways of understanding Latin America's place in the global system. The uses of post-colonial theory have generally entailed careful readings of literary and cultural texts to highlight both the historic relations of power that such texts encode and the ways in which power finds no sure footing in any text – it is always betrayed (if not completely undone) by the desires and seductions that traverse those who claim to wield it. In Latin America particularly, post-colonial critics have also responded to the ethical imperative that might variously be interpreted as the demand to listen more carefully to subaltern voices or as the demand at least to outline the historical silences that unrecoverable subaltern voices might otherwise have filled. Emblematic of this ethical drive has been the attention paid to testimonial writing – texts such as, most famously, Rigoberta Menchú's *I, Rigoberta Menchú* that are neither fully literary nor fully documentary, but that bear witness to what has escaped imperial and neo-colonial consciousness, and act as a 'return of the repressed' to ensure that the (cultural and physical) violence done to Latin America does not go unacknowledged.

A NEW LATIN AMERICANISM?

It is this notion that to understand our own modernity (and indeed premodernity or postmodernity) we need to understand its surreptitious infiltration by a Latin American unconscious that, finally, might mark any new configuration of Latin American Studies. This, however, would be a Latin Americanism divorced from Area Studies (in that precisely the notion of subdividing the world so easily into areas would be under interrogation), and decoupled from the translation model that sets Latin Americanism only the task of explaining the other to ourselves. This new Latin Americanism, by contrast, would above all emphasize the extent to which 'we' are already other, already unhinged by the viral influence of Latin America subtending and infecting our metropolitan prestige. We 'here' (in the USA and Europe) are the product of a history, and both beneficiaries and victims of a global system, that inevitably has Latin America as one of its origins and present influences.

Yet a new Latin Americanism would have to go further still. Dependency theory and post-colonial theory alike are still too mired in a modern consciousness that clings to a North–South hierarchy, however much that hierarchy emerges troubled and uncertain. Dependency theory, after all, even as it underlines the importance of peripheral, dependent economies in the generation and maintenance of development in the metropolis, also reinforces that centre–periphery distinction. Likewise, post-colonial theory's under-mining of the distinction between identity and otherness still tends to locate identity in the North and otherness in the South. It could be said that these are simply pragmatic, realistic appraisals: Europe and the West *do* have the global system's strongest economies; the non-West *has* historically been denied a sense of identity. Yet it is precisely such pragmatism that drives the *Realpolitik* of corporate capital. It is also possible to think of Latin America as our preconscious, in quite a strict historical sense. For at a number of significant moments – such as the birth of the nation-state, the rise of populism, and the unleashing of neo-liberalism – it has been the locus of real historical initiatives, and not merely a shadowy subversion of the West's claims to historical singularity.

We have seen one example of this already in the way in which the Bacardi corporation prefigured the shape of contemporary global corporations such as Nike and Benetton. More generally, one might also argue that Latin America anticipates and prefigures neo-liberalism as an economic system and set of policies. Famously, Chile under Pinochet, for instance, served as the testbed for Milton Friedman's students to implement the economic shock treatment and privatizations they had learned at the University of Chicago. It was only later that these same policies were implemented elsewhere, such as in Thatcherite Britain and the Reaganite USA. But beyond this example of Latin American priority, there is a whole history to be unearthed that might also include, for instance, Benedict Anderson's (1991) argument that the Latin American patriots of the eighteenth and nineteenth centuries were 'creole pioneers' of a nationalist ethos and political form that would only later come to prominence in Europe; or Sidney Mintz's thesis that the plantation, far from being an anomalous holdover in its putting slavery to work within a capitalist frame, was in fact the site at which the principles of modern industrialization, Fordism and factory discipline were first developed (Mintz 1985: 48).

We should, in short, consider the possibility that we have, all this time, been reading history backwards in always assigning to the West, to the metropolitan centre, the creative forces of historical progress. Marxism, post-colonialism, and indeed the old Latin Americanism *in toto* have only colluded in this misreading. It would be the project of a New Latin Americanism, whose strategy and tactics might be modelled on the viral infectiousness of (the new) Latin America, to endeavour to turn this inverted vision of the global system back to rights. And the ethico-political imperative, taken up and continued from the dissident elements of Latin American Studies, ought now to attempt to differentiate between, on the one hand, a viral *latinidad* that is one with contemporary capitalism's globalizing re-imposition of hierarchical difference, and, on the other, a viral *latinidad* that is potentially liberating, potentially one part of a coalition of forces that would construct a new global system that gives collective performance and creativity full rein.

NOTES

I would like to thank Susan Brook, Julia Hell and Richard Kirkland for their comments on earlier drafts of this chapter; the Institutes of Latin American Studies at London and Liverpool for enabling me to present versions to their seminars; and, especially, the University of Aberdeen students who participated in my course on 'Latin America in the Global System' in Spring 2000.

1   Stuart Millar, 'Now it's getting personal: the prying email virus', *The Guardian*, 24 July 2001.
2   For some of the documents that SirCam circulated, see Glenn Fleishman's list at http://glennf.com/blog/2001/07/23.html.
3   For SirCam's distribution of state secrets, see Eduard Launet, 'Les virus attaquent', *Libération*, 7 August 2001.
4   Bega (né David Loubega), a German-born singer of Ugandan and Italian

parentage whose version of the (originally instrumental) classic 'Mambo No. 5' was a world-wide hit in 1999, himself incarnates this transferability of *latinidad*. An RCA press release quotes him as saying 'I got to know the songs of the Mambo Kings without ever imagining I would become one myself' (see Bega's unofficial website at http://members.aol.com/ dharris498/loubega/bio.html).

5   The 2000 census found that over 35 million (13 per cent) of the US population were of Hispanic origin, and that their numbers were rising at a rate six times faster than the rest of the population.

6   Of course, this is not to say that other identities may not also be performative, even those that are more tied to what might appear to be the essential category of race. Indeed, arguably all identity is performative.

7   The 'Good Neighbor' policy was the attempt by the USA during and immediately following the Second World War to foment cultural and economic exchanges between the Americas (and so both to prevent Latin America from siding with the Axis, and to ensure a continued supply of vital raw materials for the US economy). Jean Franco (2002) details some of the cultural exchanges and representations of *latinidad* to US audiences that were orchestrated by, among others, Nelson Rockefeller, Coordinator of the Office of Hemispheric Affairs.

8   Perhaps the highpoint of these campaigns was Breezers' sponsorship of free public transport in London the night of New Year's Eve, 1999; they became, literally, the drink of the millennium. By 2001, the intensity of Breezers' advertising had died down, having fulfilled its function – in 2000 total UK sales had reached £69 million, more than double that of the brand's nearest competitor. For more information, see Massey's unofficial 'alcopops' website at http://owen.massey.net/alcopops/; Breezers also have their own website at http://www.bacardi-breezer.co.uk/, from which some of the television advertisements can be downloaded. As far as I am aware, Breezers have not (yet) been introduced to the USA – were they to be so, it would certainly be worth comparing their US advertising with the way in which they have been promoted in the UK.

9   More recently, Bacardi has used a cat ('Tomcat'), who goes out at night and parties extravagantly at nightclubs only to return to what we take to be a normal suburban home, as the icon of its Breezers campaign. The Tomcat campaign literalizes the earlier campaigns' image of party animals.

10 From 1795, the British Royal Navy required a daily dose of lemon juice to combat scurvy, and this was served mixed with rum, in 'the form of a pint of "grog" at noon', as John Burnett observes, 'the rum acting as a preservative as well as encouraging take-up' (Burnett 1999: 96).

11 Thus 'it was in the Caribbean that the wars between the Spanish, French, British and Dutch were fought in the battle for colonial supremacy; it was through the marketing of sugar that they developed new forms of economic behaviour and international trade' (Harrison 2001: 90–1).

REFERENCES AND SELECTED FURTHER READING

Anderson, B. 1991: *Imagined Communities: Reflections on the Origin and Spread of Nationalism*, 2nd edn. London: Verso.

Appadurai, A. (ed.) 1996: *The Social Life of Things: Commodities in Cultural Perspective*. Cambridge: Cambridge University Press.

Burnett, J. 1999: *Liquid Pleasures: A Social History of Drinks in Modern Britain*. London: Routledge.

Columbus, C. 1969: *The Four Voyages*, ed. and trans. J. M. Cohen. London: Penguin.

Dávila, A. 1997: *Sponsored Identities: Cultural Politics in Puerto Rico*. Philadelphia, PA: Temple University Press.

Dávila, A. 2001: *Latinos Inc.: The Marketing and Making of a People*. Berkeley: University of California Press.

Didion, J. 1983: *Salvador*. New York: Washington Square Press.

Fernández Retamar, R. 1989: *Caliban and Other Essays*. Minneapolis: University of Minnesota Press.

Foster, P. 1990: *Family Spirits: The Bacardi Saga, Rum, Riches, and Revolution*. Toronto: MacFarlane, Walter, and Ross.

Franco, J. 2002: *Decline and Fall of the Lettered City: Latin America in the Cold War*. Cambridge, MA: Harvard University Press.

Galeano, E. 1973: *Open Veins of Latin America: Five Centuries of the Pillage of a Continent*. New York: Monthly Review Press.

Gunder Frank, A. 1967: *Capitalism and Underdevelopment in Latin America*. New York: Monthly Review Press.

Harrison, M. 2001: *King Sugar: Jamaica, the Caribbean, and the World Sugar Economy*. London: Latin American Bureau.

Henrique Cardoso, F. and Faletto, E. 1979: *Dependency and Development in Latin America*, trans. Marjory Mattingly Urquidi. Berkeley: University of California Press.

Martí, J. 1999: Our America. In D. Shnookal and M. Muñiz (eds), *José Martí Reader: Writings on the Americas*. Melbourne: Ocean Press, 111–20.

Menchú, R. 1984: *I, Rigoberta Menchú: An Indian Woman in Guatemala*. London: Verso.

Mintz, S. 1985: *Sweetness and Power: The Place of Sugar in Modern History*. London: Penguin.

Ortiz, F. 1995: *Cuban Counterpoint: Tobacco and Sugar*, trans. H. de Onís. Durham, NC: Duke University Press.

Rodó, J. E. 1988: *Ariel*, trans. M. Sayers Peden. Austin: University of Texas Press.

Said, E. 1979: *Orientalism*. New York: Vintage.

Taussig, M. 1987: *Shamanism, Colonialism, and the Wild Man: A Study in Terror and Healing*. Chicago: University of Chicago Press.

Todorov, T. 1984: *The Conquest of America: The Question of the Other*. New York: HarperCollins.

Trigo, B. 2000: *Subjects of Crisis: Race and Gender as Disease in Latin America*. Hanover, NH: Wesleyan University Press.

Wolf, E. 1982: *Europe and the People without History*. Berkeley: University of California Press.

Zizek, S. 1992: *Enjoy Your Symptom! Jacques Lacan in Hollywood and Out*. New York: Routledge.

Glossary

What follows is a list of selected terms likely to be encountered by the student of Latin American studies. Some are specific to Latin America, others of more general relevance. Spanish or Portuguese words are given in italics.

acculturation refers to the process of a native culture's assimilation of and absorption into the dominant (in the case of Latin America, basically European) culture, usually seen as a one-way process

Amerindian refers to the indigenous peoples living in the area later known as Latin America

audiencia administrative units that operated within colonial viceroyalties

balseros Cubans who leave the island in *balsas*, i.e. makeshift rafts

Baroque originally referring to the extravagantly ornamental style of late Renaissance architecture, the term also refers to a style of highly cultivated literary writing principally from the seventeenth century

barriada shantytown

Black Legend *leyenda negra* in Spanish and a term associated with the rise of the Spanish Inquisition, it was linked to a perception of Spain (and its culture, values and institutions) as backward and oppressive

Boom the culmination of the Latin American new novel in the 1960s and its explosion onto the world literary scene

cacique a local political boss whose power base was traditionally based on landownership, often seen as a tyrant

campesino peasants, country folk or agricultural workers

candomblé an Afro-American religious cult or practice from Brazil

canon refers to the accepted great authors and works which make up the tradition of a national, continental or world literature; a notion nowadays much criticized as elitist and based on unarticulated assumptions

cartel refers to an affiliation of individuals or groups which come together to control an aspect of trade in a given area, most commonly associated today with the drugs trade, especially cocaine and especially involving Colombia

cartography the making of maps

caste refers to one's race or, more specifically, one's racial grouping

caudillo refers to a type of powerful leader or chieftain, mainly from the nineteenth century, who often came to political power on the back of heroic militaristic feats; they are usually seen as populist and dictatorial

chabolas shantytown

chicano US Mexican American

cholo a person of mixed race, usually from the Andean region; the term is frequently pejorative, but in the feminine form, *chola*, can often mean 'sexy'

cimarrón a runaway slave

colonialism the development and sustaining of European settlements and interests in distant territories such as those of the Spanish and Portuguese crowns in Latin America; more generally the term refers to the mentality or ideology behind such expansionist practices; it can also refer to the status of now independent nations who nonetheless are dependent on or unduly influenced by more powerful countries – this is sometimes referred to as neo-colonialism

commodity fetishism the idea, in Marx's theory of capitalism, that the 'use-value' of an object produced by human labour is replaced by its 'exchange-value' (linked to money), resulting in the 'alienation' of the worker; 'use-value', however, has been reassessed by some as more meaningful and flexible in the contemporary context of mass consumption

conquistador literally conqueror, the term usually refers to those Spaniards who originally invaded, subdued and began the colonization of the New World

contras refers to so-called counter-revolutionaries (*contrarevolucionarios*) who fought against the Sandinistas in Nicaragua between, roughly, 1981 and 1987, with the backing of the administration of US President Ronald Reagan

costumbrismo a type of literary writing that concerns itself with the detailed description of local colour, customs and manners; particularly popular in Spain in the eighteenth and nineteenth centuries, it became fashionable in Latin America in the nineteenth century and gave rise to a form of folkloric sketch known as the *tradición*

counter-insurgency methods and the action of containing, undermining, resisting or dismantling usually guerrilla-based insurrection or revolt

criollo creole, meaning of Spanish descent but born in the Americas; usually refers to the ruling elite of the nineteenth century

cultural studies an interdisciplinary form of inquiry based on the idea that culture is central to social and political life and with an emphasis on culture in the broadest sense and on the contexts of cultural production; it is often associated with everyday and popular rather than high literary culture, and tends to focus on areas such as race, ethnicity, gender, sexuality and subalternity, often from a leftist and highly theorized perspective

desaparecidos literally meaning the 'disappeared', the term refers to those killed by Latin American military dictatorships, particularly in the 1970s and particularly in Argentina and Chile

Dirty War refers to the so-called *guerra sucia* in Argentina in the 1970s in which state violence, torture, murder and repression were used to eliminate any perceived leftist threat; the military euphemistically referred to this programme of social and political 'cleansing' as the *proceso* or 'process'

encomienda an institution by which Spanish colonizers were assigned, through royal concession, the rights to collect tributes from natives, sell their produce and exploit their labour

Enlightenment, the a philosophical and cultural movement that came to prominence in Europe in the eighteenth century centred on the primacy of reason and emphasizing progress and equality; it had an enormous impact on the French and American Revolutions, and had an impact on the independence movements and post-independence nation-states of Latin America. The Age of Enlightenment is referred to in Spanish as *la Ilustración* or *el Siglo de las Luces*

Eurocentrism a way of perceiving the world resulting from the process by which European values have come to be imposed on the world as a whole, to the extent that European assumptions come to define all experience; in Latin America the idea is that its own history and culture have traditionally been described and understood in terms of European paradigms. The term is implicitly critical and alludes to a need for cultures such as those of Latin America to define themselves in their own terms. Eurocentrism is often extended or used loosely so as to incorporate North American conceptions of other areas of the world

FARC the Armed Revolutionary Forces of Colombia, a Communist-led guerrilla movement that emerged in the 1960s and has now developed into a potent force in the complex arena of conflict-torn Colombia

favela shanty housing in Brazil

fuero a kind of legal charter exported from Spain to the colonies that guaranteed certain rights or privileges for particular groups, especially the military and the religious

gaucho perceived as free-roaming cowboys from the Argentinean grasslands, the *gauchos* (originally the descendants of liaisons between natives and settlers) began to disappear in the nineteenth century and in the twentieth were largely subsumed into the formal economy as paid labour; still, they remain a powerful symbol of Argentine national tradition and identity

globalization initially referring to the expansion of markets in late-twentieth-century capitalism, with Western companies, products and cultures saturating even the non-Western world, the term now tends to be associated with the way capitalism has come to transcend national borders; there are many debates about whether globalization implies the dominance of Western culture or offers the possibility of new ways of formulating cultural identities based on diversity

gringo a sometimes pejorative term for a non-Spanish speaking foreigner, usually from the USA; roughly the equivalent of 'Yank' *guerrilla* a guerrilla army, usually referring to groups pursuing an irregular war often against the state

hacienda agricultural fields or large estate

hegemony tends to refer to a kind of cultural conformism, in which a social system effectively shares or is persuaded to share common values that in fact embody the ideology of the establishment or ruling class; the term refers to a more subtle form of social dominance than direct or formal control by the state

heterogeneity diversity; often used to refer to cultural diversity within society

Hispanic referring to that pertaining to Spain and its people, the term has come to be commonly used to refer to the Spanish-speaking world in general (and sometimes, more loosely, includes the Portuguese-speaking world, especially Portugal and Brazil); it is now commonly used to refer to people of Latin American origin living in North America, though often used more loosely to refer to all those in the USA of Latin American ancestry

homogeneity the opposite of heterogeneity, the term refers to things that are alike or uniform in nature; often used to refer to cultural conformity or conformism within society

humanism originally a term for a philosophical outlook that places the human being or the individual mind at the centre of experience, it is now used commonly as a shorthand for 'liberal humanism'. The term liberal humanism tends to be used negatively to refer to a kind of traditional (usually literary) criticism that was based on the assumption of a coherent individual human identity and on the primacy of accepted or universal human values; much contemporary criticism tends to see these assumptions as a mask for specific class or power-group interests and seeks instead to expose the ways in which values and beliefs are constructed in specific social and political contexts, offering either multiple viewpoints or explicitly strategic or interested viewpoints

hybridity refers to the new culture which emerges as a result of the interaction between minority or migrant groups and the established order; the term alludes to the mixed or hybrid nature of communities or societies in certain contexts and to the nature of the texts and cultural practices which express this condition, which often mix forms, genres and types of language

Iberia usually used to refer to the Spanish peninsula, in common use the term normally includes Portugal since Iberia as a concept sometimes harks back to the period when Spain and Portugal were united

iconography referring originally to the identification of the subjects of portraits, the term has now come to be used to refer to conventional images in general, and their classification and examination

imperialism the process of conquest and colonization of one nation by another; more generally, the term is now used to denote the ways in which a powerful nation exploits the resources of a weaker one and exercises effective economic or cultural control over it *indianismo* a type of literature in nineteenth-century Brazil that promoted a romantic image of national identity through the figure of the Indian

indigenismo sometimes translated as Indianism or indigenism, the term commonly refers to a trend in early twentieth-century fiction in which the condition and treatment of the native indigenous communities are described and denounced in an attempted social realist style; the authors were usually not of indigenous extraction themselves. Later, in the 1940s, a trend called *neo-indigenismo* emerged, in which a less realist style was used in an attempt to recreate or give the impression of an indigenous point of view.

indigenous native to the region; the adjective is often considered preferable to the term Indian

indio the term originally used to describe the native inhabitants of the New World and subsequently used more generally to refer to their descendants; the term has its origins in the misapprehension that Columbus had reached the Indies via a western route

insurgency insurrection or rising in revolt, often associated in Latin America with peasant or guerrilla movements in opposition to the state

ladino Central American version of *mestizo* or mixed race

latifundia latifundia also in English, the term refers to large estates of land; the term and its offshoot *latifundismo* refer to the system of landownership which developed in Latin America, creating powerful landowners and large numbers of dependent peasants

latino refers to a person of Latin American ancestry living in North America, usually implying that the person has been born or brought up in the USA

letrado lettered or learned

llanos the huge plains or flatlands of the interior of Venezuela

Llorona, la refers to the legend of a female ghost said to roam about wailing (perhaps most commonly associated with Mexico)

machismo a kind of sexist male chauvinism, sometimes manifested via the flaunting of stereotypically masculine characteristics such as virility

Magical Realism a term which has become increasingly associated with Latin American fiction since the 1960s, it traditionally refers to a style of writing in which fantastic events are depicted in a straightforward, matter-of-fact way; more recently, critics have often preferred to see Magical Realism as a means of expressing Latin American reality via local rather than Eurocentric or 'First-World' perspectives. In practice, the meanings of the term are much debated and it has come to be used extremely loosely, often referring to a style that has transcended the specifically Latin American. The term is linked historically to Alejo Carpentier's proposition in 1949 of the notion of the 'marvellous real' or *lo real maravilloso*, which suggests that Latin American reality is somehow magical or fantastic by nature because of its history, geography and indigenous belief systems

Malinche the Spanish name for a native girl who became the interpreter, helper and mistress of Hernán Cortés, the conqueror of the Aztecs; in Mexico her name and the term *malinchismo* have come to mean betrayal or selling out to foreigners. Also referred to as Malintzin

mameluco in Brazil, a term for someone of mixed white and Indian descent

maquila or maquiladora a low-cost assembly plant or sweat-shop located in Mexico, usually near the US border

marianismo the cult of the Virgin Mary

Mesoamerica a term used by archaeologists to refer to the area comprising roughly central and southern Mexico, Guatemala, El Salvador and parts of Honduras, Nicaragua and Costa Rica.

messianism refers to cults believing in the coming of a Messiah

mestizaje miscegenation, or the mixing of races; often used more loosely and often positively to refer to a national identity based on the mixture of races and cultures

mestizo of mixed race, generally of mixed Spanish or Portuguese and American Indian descent

metafiction though the term is used more broadly, it essentially refers to a type of fiction that is self-conscious about its own status as fiction and draws attention to the role of writing and reading in the construction of meanings

metahistory a more self-conscious notion of history, that sees history not as a neutral factual or scientific discourse but as a narrative process or construct underpinned by particular philosophical or ideological assumptions

Modernism an Anglo-American term used to characterize twentieth-century literature and other forms of cultural production; the essential characteristic of modernist production is a sense of radical break-with-tradition and formal innovation or experimentalism, usually seen as a response to the condition of living in the modern world

Modernismo as distinct from Modernism, *Modernismo* is either a Spanish American (or Spanish) term or a Brazilian one. Spanish American *Modernismo* is a late nineteenth- and early twentieth-century literary movement, principally associated with style-oriented escapist poetry; more recently, critics have developed our understanding of *Modernismo*, establishing clearer links between it and Romanticism before and later experimental writing in the twentieth century. Brazilian *Modernismo* is closer to the Spanish American *vanguardia*; beginning in the 1920s, it is characterized by formal and linguistic experimentation, though coupled with the desire to create a particularly Brazilian mode of writing.

Monroe Doctrine refers to a statement made by US President James Monroe in 1823, essentially asserting the sovereignty of 'the American continents' and setting out the USA's interest in maintaining the independence of its hemisphere; in practice, the Monroe Doctrine came to be seen as a way of legitimizing North American intervention in the affairs of its Latin American neighbours, a position more formalized by the Roosevelt Corollary to the Doctrine in 1904

mulato mulatto, that is of mixed black and white race

muralism in Latin America, the term is most commonly associated with the originally officially sponsored programme of commissioning painters to decorate the walls of public buildings in Mexico after the Revolution with images of national culture; the paintings of the muralists depicted major events and national heroes, but also celebrated the contribution of the common people

NAFTA North American Free Trade Agreement; the agreement, made in 1994 between the USA, Canada and Mexico, was designed to create more competition and cheaper costs, but has been criticized for failing to produce more jobs in North America and for increasing poverty and other problems in Mexico

narco-guerrilla a guerrilla movement financed by the cocaine trade and most commonly associated with Colombia

narcotraficante drug trafficker

Naturalism a strand of nineteenth-century literary Realism, based on the assumption that human beings are the products of heredity and their environment, and that seeks to describe reality with scientific accuracy

neo-baroque a term used to describe aspects of some experimental twentieth-century literary writing (especially, though by no means exclusively, from Cuba) that recreates something of the ornamental floridity associated with the seventeenth-century Baroque

neo-liberalism refers to the adoption of free-market economics in the context of globalized capitalism; though often seen as economically necessary, the claims that economic improvement would benefit the majority have not yet been realized

New World a term used to refer to the Americas after it had been grasped that the continent was unconnected to Asia, it is attributed to the Italian explorer Amerigo Vespucci

nueva narrativa a kind of complex and challenging experimental fiction that began in Spanish America in, roughly, the 1940s and 1950s and climaxed in the 1960s, associated with a reaction against traditional realism; usually referred to in English as the new novel, the phenomenon continued throughout the latter part of the twentieth century

nuyorican an adjective referring to the language and culture of Puerto Rican groups in New York City

oligarchy a form of government in which power is confined to a few individuals or families; the term is often used to refer to those whose economic power gives them an inordinate political influence

pampa the vast flat interior grasslands of Argentina

patriarchy literally meaning something like 'the rule of the father', the term refers to the idea of a society ruled by men and has been more loosely used to refer to the way of the world when understood as based on male domination

peninsular an adjective referring to things specifically Spanish, i.e. from the European Spanish peninsula

Peronism a popular movement in Argentina built around the cult of Juan Perón (and his wife Evita), which developed into a formal political party

popular culture an apparently straightforward but, in fact, much debated and uncertain term, popular culture is used most commonly to refer to mass culture (that is, widely consumed cultural products such as thrillers or soap operas) or the culture produced by ordinary people (the latter including folk culture and perhaps even youth subculture)

Positivism based on the philosphy of Auguste Comte (1798–1857), Positivism became popular amongst the elites in Latin America (especially Brazil) after independence and became associated with the idea of the advancement of human society through science and progress

post-Boom refers to a type of fiction that emerged in Latin America after and in reaction to the Boom from, roughly, the 1970s onwards; an indistinct and much-contested phenomenon, the post-Boom is usually seen to comprise fiction that is more direct, more popular in orientation and more politically engaged

post-colonialism the theoretical study of cultures shaped by colonialism and its aftermath and their (often hybrid) cultural production

postmodernism a term that is used in many loose and varied ways, it is perhaps most commonly used to describe cultural products that self-consciously play with and/or dissolve the distinction between high culture and popular culture, thus challenging the seriousness of 'difficult' modernist works. More philosphically, postmodernism has been seen as a rejection of apparently legitimized systems of knowledge (sometimes alluded to as 'grand narratives') and as an assertion of pluralism; on the other hand, it has also been seen as a manifestation of extreme individualism and the logic of a global system saturated by capitalism and technology

post-structuralism a very loose term applied to a range of theoretical approaches to culture that emphasize the unstable and multiple nature of meaning

PRI the Mexican Institutional Revolutionary Party that evolved from a governing party established after the Revolution and that dominated government until its defeat in the elections of 2000

quechua a language from the Andean region, the most commonly mentioned surviving indigenous language

queer a reappropriation by gay activists of a previously pejorative term for homosexuals, 'queer' in cultural theory refers to an approach that seeks to destabilize fixed notions of sexual identity and show how such identities are constructed or contingent

Realism a term which is used in very loose and varied ways, it most commonly refers to a style of fiction, often seen as coming to prominence in the nineteenth century, which tended to describe individual characters as part of society and seeks faithfully to document society; the noun realism, however, has come to be used popularly to validate or valorize works of fiction according to a rather subjective notion of how accurate or realistic they are

Reconquista the Christian war against the Muslims who occupied southern Spain from 711 until their final defeat in 1492

Romanticism a notoriously vague term used to describe trends in literature that are associated with the late eighteenth to mid-late nineteenth century and are seen as privileging emotion or mood over reason and expressing a fascination with the self, the imagination, creativity, spiritual striving, the human relationship with nature and rebelliousness; a related interest, of particular relevance to Latin America, is the fascination with primitivism, including the idea of the noble savage as well as myth and legend

salsa the term has now become an extremely broad one referring to Latin music and dance often operating beyond any original national or continental boundary; in popular usage, especially outside of Latin America or US Latino communities, it is often used loosely to encompass other distinct forms of music and dance such as *merengue, cumbia, samba* or even the more sentimental *bolero* among others

Sandinistas taking their name from the liberal leader Augusto Sandino assassinated in 1934, these are members of the Nicaraguan FSLN or Sandinista Front for National Liberation who overthrew the dictatorial Somoza dynasty and were in power between 1979 and 1990

santería a popular religious system or cult associated mainly with Cuba that mixes originary African beliefs and rituals with notions about Catholic saints

Sendero Luminoso a violent Peruvian guerrilla movement of Maoist inspiration that emerged in the 1980s, its leader being captured in 1992

sertão the barren lands of north-eastern Brazil

subalternity essentially referring to the condition of inferiority or subordination, the term alludes to the state of the politically uncoordinated subaltern masses (e.g. the urban poor or the peasantry) whose relationship to dominant groups has been seen to be insufficiently recorded or studied

Surrealism specifically refers to an anti-realist 1920s' French artistic movement based on anti-rationalism and the liberation of the unconscious, though the term is sometimes also used to describe similar manifestations around the world

syncretism the fusing of differing or opposite tenets or practices, especially in philosophy and religion

tango a type of music, dance and later song associated particularly with Buenos Aires from the early twentieth century onwards, now hugely commercially and culturally important and still commonly danced by ordinary people in get-togethers called *milongas*

taxonomy the categorization or classification of types and areas within a subject

telenovela a television soap opera

transculturation a more positive term than the one-way process of acculturation, transculturation refers to the complex ways in which cultures are mutually transformed through contact

universal traditionally used to refer to shared concerns or values common to all humanity, the term has been much criticized as the unthinking imposition of (usually white, male) bourgeois assumptions onto widely diverse human experience

vanguardia associated with the early twentieth century, especially the 1920s, this is the manifestation of the French and European avant-garde in Spanish America and refers to writers (especially, in this case, poets) whose work was deliberately experimental in form and reference

viceroyalty a large colonial administrative unit, designed to consolidate the power of the Spanish crown in the Indies; two main viceroyalties were created, New Spain and Peru, with Mexico City and Lima as their respective capitals

wetback a generally pejorative term for illegal immigrants entering the USA via Mexico (the term refers to the crossing of the Río Grande river)

zambo often pejorative term usually used to refer to individuals of mixed black and Amerindian origin

Zapatistas taking their name from a peasant leader in the Mexican Revolution, Emiliano Zapata, these are members of the rebel EZLN (the Zapatista National Liberation Army) led by Subcomandante Marcos and associated with the region of Chiapas; their agenda is essentially to defend the rights of the indigenous peoples and peasantry, and to resist the effects of neo-liberalism and globalization

Time chart

As an aid to orientation, below are listed selectively the dates of some key moments in Latin American history together with the dates for some selected moments of cultural significance.

1492	Columbus lands on the continental land mass now known as the Americas, thinking he has found a western route to India. Columbus's subsequent voyages to the Indies are in 1493, 1498, 1502.
1500	First Portuguese landing on the continent.
1519–20	Hernán Cortés reaches and conquers Mexico, overcoming Aztec emperors (including Montezuma and Cuauhtemoc) and taking Tenochtitlán or Mexico City (the Viceroyalty of New Spain is created in 1535).
1524	The Council of the Indies is created. The first missionaries arrive to begin the conversion of the Indians.
1530	First Portuguese colony founded.
1532–72	Francisco Pizarro begins the conquest of Peru and has the Inca leader Atahuallpa executed. Lima is founded as capital. Inca rebellions and internal conflicts between the Spanish conquistadors follow, but royal authority is restored by 1548. The remnants of the Inca state are crushed and the leader Tupac Amaru is executed.
1535	A printing press is established in Mexico (1583 in Lima).
1537–61	The Dominican friar Bartolomé de las Casas defends the rights of the Indians. In this period key debates take place involving him and influential writings are produced by him.
1538	The first Spanish American university is established, in Santo Domingo.
1542	The New Laws of the Indies are promulgated; these regulate the processes of the conquest, reform the *encomienda* system and outlaw slave raids, but provoke rebelliousness amongst Spanish settlers.
1567–1615	Felipe Guaman Poma de Ayala produces *El primer nueva Corónica y Buen Gobierno*.

1570–71	Tribunals of the Inquisition are set up in Lima and Mexico.
1595	The Spanish crown awards contracts to Portuguese slave traders, resulting in a massive rise in the numbers of slaves.
1609	'Inca' Garcilaso de la Vega produces *Comentarios reales que tratan del origen de los Yncas*.
1648	Sor Juana born (died 1695).
1750–74	Brazil's borders are agreed and the whole territory comes to be administered from Rio de Janeiro.
1754–56	Conflict with the Jesuits over their and the Guaraní Indians' resistance to Portuguese authority.
1759	Jesuits expelled from Brazil (1767 from Spanish America).
1776	Viceroyalty of Río de la Plata is created, administered from the port of Buenos Aires.
1781–1811	A series of significant Indian, Negro and republican revolts throughout the subcontinent.
1805	Battle of Trafalgar marks the end of the Spanish trade monopoly with the Indies.
1808–13	Joseph Bonaparte installed as King of Spain; this creates constitutional uncertainty in the Indies and encourages *criollo* aspirations towards autonomy.
1810	Independence struggle begins in earnest. Part of the Indies (Buenos Aires) is declared independent for the first time; independence is largely complete in most cases by 1828 (Brazil in 1822). By mid-century a pattern of nations similar to the current situation is more or less in place.
1823	Monroe Doctrine.
1823–72	Slavery is largely abolished country by country, except for Cuba and Brazil.
1829–52	Juan Manuel de Rosas takes Buenos Aires and later becomes dictator of the Argentine Federation (from 1835).
1831–89	Pedro I abdicates in Brazil and after an interregnum Pedro II becomes Emperor from 1841.
1833	Britain seizes Las Malvinas (the Falkland Islands).
1845	Domingo Faustino Sarmiento produces *Facundo*, with its famous allusion to *Civilización y barbarie*. The USA annexes Texas, marking an era of interventionism in Latin America that will escalate over the next century.
1849–61	Wars between Liberals and Conservatives in Colombia.
1862–67	French intervention in Mexico.
1868–74	Sarmiento is President of Argentina.
1886 and 1888	Slavery is abolished in Cuba and Brazil respectively.
1889	First Republic of Brazil created.
1893–96	Revolt of messianic loyalist peasants against Republic at Canudos in Brazil.

1895–1902	Cuban War of Independence, followed in 1898 by Hispano-Cuban-American War and US occupation of Cuba and Puerto Rico (the latter until 1952).
1896	Publication of *Prosas profanas* by Rubén Darío, often seen as the quintessential work of Spanish American *Modernismo*.
1899–1901	War of a Thousand Days in Colombia.
1904	Roosevelt Corollary.
1908	Juan Vicente Gómez assumes power in Venezuela and rules as a dictator until 1935. Similar strongman leaders of different sorts emerge elsewhere in the first part of the twentieth century, such as Getulio Vargas (Brazil, 1930–45), Rafael Trujillo (Dominican Republic, 1930–61), Jorge Ubico (Guatemala, 1931–44), Fulgencio Batista (Cuba, 1934–44 and 1952–59), Anastasio Somoza (Nicaragua, 1937–56), Juan Perón (Argentina, 1946–55), Alfredo Stroessner (Paraguay, 1954–89) and François Duvalier (Haiti, 1957–71).
1910–20	Mexican Revolution.
1914	Panama Canal opens.
1922	*Semana de arte moderno* in São Paulo; launches Brazilian *Modernismo*.
1923	Diego Rivera starts producing his first murals in Mexico and continues into the 1950s.
1934–40	The popular Lázaro Cárdenas is President of Mexico and nationalizes oil in 1938.
1935	Tango star Carlos Gardel dies in an air crash.
1939	Mexico's Frida Kahlo (the wife of Diego Rivera) paints *Las dos Fridas*, considered by many to be her greatest work.
1944	Publication of *Ficciones* by Jorge Luis Borges, one of the most influential works in the history of the Latin American new narrative.
1946	Publication of *El Señor Presidente* by Miguel Angel Asturias, regarded by some critics as a key moment in the birth or development of the Latin American new novel.
1948	Riots (referred to as the *bogotazo*) in Colombia following the assassination of a Liberal leader and leading to a civil war known as *la violencia* that lasts up to the 1960s (and even beyond). In Cuba *El derecho de nacer* is broadcast as a *radionovela* or radio series: this would become a model for the *telenovela*.
1952	Puerto Rico becomes a sovereign state of the USA. Eva Perón (Evita) dies at the age of only 33.
1956–59	Cuban Revolution, with Fidel Castro emerging as leader.

1961 and 1962	Invasion of the Bay of Pigs (known as the Battle of Girón in Cuba) and the Cuban Missile Crisis, both in the context of the Cold War.
1962	Publication of *La ciudad y los perros* by Mario Vargas Llosa; the novel went on to win the Spanish literary prize the *Biblioteca Breve* from the Seix Barral publishing house, something seen as a key moment in the internationalization of the Latin American novel and often seen as marking the beginning of the so-called Boom of Latin American fiction. The first Taco Bell is opened (in Downey, California) – at the time of writing there are now approximately 4,800 Taco Bell locations.
1964	A military junta rules in Brazil until 1985. Military dictatorship becomes a feature of political life in Latin America up to the 1980s, e.g. in Argentina, Chile, Uruguay, Panama (Peru has a more reformist military leadership along socialist lines from 1968–75).
1967	Publication of *Cien años de soledad* by Gabriel García Márquez. Che Guevara is killed (in Bolivia).
1968	Olympic Games in Mexico. The international focus on Mexico is exploited by the radical student movement to protest against the government; clashes between students and troops culminate in the Tlatelolco massacre which is seen by many as discrediting the PRI's revolutionary credentials.
1970	There is a split within the Barcelona publishing house Seix Barral and the Premio Biblioteca Breve is cancelled – an event sometimes seen as marking an end to the Boom of Latin American fiction.
1971	Pablo Neruda wins the Nobel Prize for Literature. The Cuban poet Heberto Padilla is arrested as a 'counter-revolutionary' – an event that divides Latin American writers and intellectuals and which is sometimes seen as also marking an end to the literary Boom.
1973–90	General Augusto Pinochet is military dictator of Chile; a bloody coup is followed by intense repression and dramatic economic reform.
1976–83	Military rule in Argentina, characterized by intense repression.
1978	Soccer World Cup in Argentina, exploited by the military junta for political purposes.
1979	*Sandinista* Revolution in Nicaragua, followed by the *Contra* war 1981–87.
1979–90	Figures show that the rate of destruction of the Brazilian

rainforest for this period is 5.4 million acres per year; by 1992 less than 200,000 indigenous people remain in the rainforest (in 1500 there were 6 to 9 million); the rainforest becomes an increasing focus of global concern, especially from the late 1970s and early 1980s onwards.

1982	Falklands War. García Márquez wins the Nobel Prize for Literature.
1985	Democracy restored in Argentina, as well as in Brazil and Uruguay. The consolidation of democracy becomes a feature of the late twentieth century.
1990	Democracy restored in Chile. In Peru, Alberto Fujimori defeats the novelist Mario Vargas Llosa in presidential elections (Fujimori's later internal coup or *autogolpe*, in which he dissolves the Congress with the support of the military, is one of the last major manifestations of authoritarianism in the twentieth century). Octavio Paz wins the Nobel Prize for Literature.
1992	Quincentenary celebrations of the 'discovery of America' prompt a widespread re-examination and rethinking of Latin America's relationship with Europe.
1993	Colombian drugs baron Pablo Escobar is killed by a police team.
1994	NAFTA is agreed. *Zapatista* revolts begin in Chiapas in Mexico.
1999	Puerto Rican Ricky Martin's first English-language single 'Livin' la vida loca' makes Number 1 in the US and UK charts (as well as in Canada, New Zealand and Ireland). In California, the population figure for non-Hispanic whites falls below 50 per cent for the first time (Hispanics are at 31 per cent of the population).
2000	PRI loses presidential elections for the first time in Mexico. Alberto Fujimori flees Peru in disgrace (Alejandro Toledo is democratically elected President the year after).
2001	A Colombian *telenovela* called *Betty la fea* is a huge success in Latin America and the USA. Argentina is plunged into massive economic crisis, which worsens in 2002.
2002	Shakira has a Number 1 hit in the UK. The Mexican film Y *tu mamá también* becomes the biggest box-office hit in the nation's history – at the time of writing, its director Alfonso Cuarón is reported to have signed to direct the third Harry Potter movie.

Index

Note: page references in *italic* refer to glossary entries